# The Complete Tradesman

*Frontispiece*  Images of London life, *c.* 1800. The print is interesting firstly because it indicates how important shops and shopping were in London society life, and secondly because it portrays in symbolic form the external appearance of a fashionable London shop, *c.* 1800, including large bow windows and a central door with a name board over it.

# The Complete Tradesman

## A Study of Retailing, 1550-1820

NANCY COX

## Ashgate

Aldershot • Burlington USA • Singapore • Sydney

Published by
Ashgate Publishing Limited
Gower House
Croft Road
Aldershot
Hants GU11 3HR
England

Ashgate Publishing Company
131 Main Street
Burlington
Vermont 05401-5506
USA

Ashgate website: http://www.ashgate.com

British Library Cataloguing in Publication Data

Cox, Nancy
  The Complete Tradesman: A Study of Retailing, 1550-1820.
  (The History of Retailing and Consumption)
  1. Retail trade—Great Britain—History—16th century.
  2. Retail trade—Great Britain—History—17th century.
  3. Retail trade—Great Britain—History—18th century.
  I. Title.
  381.1'0941'09031

Library of Congress Control Number: 00-102015

ISBN 1 85928 169 9

This book is printed on acid free paper

Printed and bound by Athenaeum Press, Ltd.,
Gateshead, Tyne & Wear.

# Contents

# The History of Retailing and Consumption
## General Editor's preface

It is increasingly recognized that retail systems and changes in the patterns of consumption play crucial roles in the development and societal structure of economies. Such recognition has led to renewed interest in the changing nature of retail distribution and the rise of consumer society from a wide range of academic disciplines. The aim of this multidisciplinary series is to provide a forum of publications that explore the history of retailing and consumption.

Gareth Shaw

*University of Exeter*

# List of figures

# List of tables

# Preface

The inspiration for *The Complete Tradesman* was twofold. The first was the concept of a prudent, well-informed and appropriately connected tradesman,[1] an idea well developed in the early modern period. Countless books of advice were written for him and about him, out of which an image of the successful or 'complete' tradesman emerged. However, two or three centuries away from him, the picture is now too fuzzy and too distant to allow a full understanding of how he operated and how he fitted into the world of trade as a whole. The aim of this study is to sharpen the image and to provide a corrective to widespread historiographical myths about early modern retailing.

The second source of inspiration was my Project at the University of Wolverhampton to create a *Dictionary of traded goods and commodities 1550-1800*. This seeks a fuller understanding of traded goods, their nature and their meaning. Just as these can not be divorced from the mechanisms by which they were bought and sold, so the retailing tradesman can not be fully depicted without an awareness of the goods found in his shop. The two projects therefore grew together and each has strengthened the other, although the publication of this study will precede that of the Dictionary by some years.

The *Dictionary* is constructed principally from several distinct sources, such as probate inventories of tradesmen, tradecards and bill heads, diaries and accounts, newspaper advertisements, industrial patents, statutes of the realm, Books of Rates, and Houghton's *Husbandry and trade improv'd*. These sources have contributed crucially to this study and have informed many of my conclusions. A further decision made by the Dictionary Project to focus principally if not exclusively on certain counties as representative was also adopted in this study. The counties are: from the North, Cumberland, Westmoreland and Lancashire, from the Midlands, Derbyshire, Staffordshire and Shropshire, and from the South, Hampshire and Sussex.

The development of the *Dictionary* and *The Complete Tradesman* in tandem has been a source of inspiration, while the members of the Dictionary Project have provided an stimulating environment in which to work, where ideas have been exchanged and support offered. I thank all my colleagues who over the years have formed part of the Dictionary Project; Angela Brown, Polly Hamilton, Pat Andrews, Jan Broadway and especially Simone Clarke. Other

---

[1] Early modern writers referred exclusively to tradesmen as male. It is in this context I use the male pronoun here.

members of the History Department, both past and present, whose help and support is much appreciated include Malcolm Wanklyn, John Benson, Margaret Ponsonby, David Hussey, Laura Ugolini, Peter Wakelin and Graeme Milne, as well as my Ph.D. students, Sylvia Watts, Diane Collins and Karin Dannehl. I also thank the University of Wolverhampton for offering me the position of Honorary Research Fellow and then providing me with all the facilities usually only available to permanent members of staff. I am aware that some honorary research fellows in other institutions are less fortunately served, and am grateful. In particular I would like to thank the several Deans and Associate Deans of Research under whose directions I have been unfailingly supported, David Crowe, Jean Gilkison, the late Ian Connell and Dee Cooke.

I am also grateful to members of the wider academic community who have at various times offered me more encouragement and inspiration than perhaps they were aware, especially Barrie Trinder, who re-introduced me to history after a long gap, Margaret Spufford, David Harley, Margaret Pelling, Mark Overton, John Styles and Claire Walsh, my co-author of chapter 3.

The many Record Offices and Libraries visited are listed in the Bibliography and I thank all their archivists, librarians and assistants who have dealt patiently with my excessive demands on their time and resources.

And finally two especial thanks; first to my publishers, Ashgate, and the general editor of the series, Gareth Shaw, who asked me to write this work and who have encouraged me throughout, and secondly to my husband, who has listened patiently to my problems, read much work in draft, and offered trenchant criticism along with endless cups of tea.

Nancy Cox
Wolverhampton, 2000

# Introduction

# 'Consumption is the sole end and purpose of all production':[1] the current debate on consumption and retailing

It is impossible to isolate the history of retailing from the study of other aspects of economic, social and cultural change and the historiography reflects which connections historians have chosen to make from time to time. When retailing first became a topic of serious study, much attention was paid to the relationship between industrialization and the development of retailing facilities, particularly with regard to the food supply of large towns.[2] A similar interest in the implications of the development of large towns is reflected in studies by historical geographers into the location of retailing outlets.[3] Other historians have focused on particular developments in retailing like the department store,[4] multiple outlets,[5] the co-operative movement,[6] and mail order.[7] In the last few years Benson and Shaw have opened up a new direction in the history of retailing, stressing the importance of comparative studies.[8]

All these topics, except possibly the last, were seen to be relevant to an industrialized and urbanized people, and as a result virtually all studies were concerned primarily if not exclusively with the nineteenth century or even the

---

[1]   Smith (1776), *Wealth of nations*, vol. II, p. 155.
[2]   For example, Fisher (1934-35), 'Development of the London food market'; Blackman (1963), 'Food supply in an industrial town'; Blackman (1967), 'Development of the retail grocery trade; Alexander (1970), *Retailing in England*; Scola (1992), *Feeding the Victorian city*.
[3]   For example, Shaw and Wild (1974), 'Retail patterns in the Victorian city'.
[4]   For example, Ferry (1960), *Development of the department store*; Adburgham (1981), *Shops and shopping*; Miller (1981), *The Bon Marché bourgeois culture*; Crossick and Jaumain (1999), *Cathedrals of consumption*.
[5]   For example, Jefferys (1954), *Retail trading*; Mathias (1967), *Retailing revolution*; Shaw (1992), 'Evolution and impact of large scale retailing'.
[6]   For example, Purvis (1992), 'Co-operative retailing'.
[7]   For example, Adburgham (1964), *Shops and shopping*, pp. xi-xii, 233; Shaw (1992), 'Evolution and impact of large-scale retailing', pp. 146-9.
[8]   Benson and Shaw (1992), *Evolution of retail systems*. For comparative studies on consumption, see Strasser, McGovern and Judt (eds) (1998), *Getting and spending*.

twentieth. Furthermore, apart from a few notable exceptions,[9] most attention has been devoted to economic and social change; until recently much less has been directed towards investigating the relationship between retailing and cultural change. The introduction of such concepts as 'Consumer revolution' and 'consumerism' initiated a shift towards the cultural implications of retailing and it is to the development of ideas of consumer revolution that we now turn.

## Consumer revolution

'Consumer revolution' is a phrase that has suffered much from over use since its relatively recent introduction. It has spawned a number of definitions and applications and, with its underlying ideas, has provided a framework upon which scholars have built conflicting theories about economic, social and cultural change. The wider the chronological span to which the phrase has become attached, the more it becomes apparent that there is no agreement on precisely what the term means. Most scholars of modern economic and social history would assert that the only true consumer revolution occurred in the late nineteenth century and the early twentieth, when the urbanization and industrialization of the country produced a working class with opportunities not available to their forebears.[10] To these historians, the consumer revolution is synonymous with mass production, mass marketing and mass consumption, and the Market is the key to that revolution. Attractive streets and gleaming shop windows encouraged avarice and day dreaming far beyond the immediate reach of many purses, while stores like Woolworths and Marks and Spencer allowed all but the destitute some share in the new world of luxury and its imitators. Defined like this it is impossible not to agree with this interpretation of the nature of consumer revolution.[11]

However, another school of thought has argued that the seeds of change were sown in the eighteenth century if not even earlier.[12] They see an increased variety of goods, some once imported as luxuries but now produced more cheaply at home, and a developing sophistication in marketing from a very

---

[9]   Davis (1966), *History of shopping*; Adburgham (1979), *Shopping in style*.

[10]  For example, Jefferys (1954), *Retail trading in Britain*; Fraser (1981), *Coming of the mass market*; Benson and Shaw (1992), *Evolution of retail systems*; Benson (1999), *Rise of the consumer society*.

[11]  For a useful summary of the development of ideas on consumption and the historiography, given very much from the viewpoint of twentieth-century historians, see the Introduction to Strasser, McGovern and Judt (eds) (1998), *Getting and spending*, pp. 1-7.

[12]  Alexander (1970), *Retailing in England during the industrial revolution*; McKendrick, Brewer and Plumb (1982), *Birth of a consumer society*; Weatherill (1988), *Consuming behaviour*.

primitive base. The evidence for the change is most easily observed, they would argue, in the home where raised standards of comfort, particularly for the middling sort of people, were matched by specialized room use, rising expenditure on the presentation of a public face to visitors and increased facilities for leisure. Just as the later period is typified by the threepenny and sixpenny stores, so this earlier age has its symbol of consumption - the new commodity of tea. Tea drinking was a new pleasure and not a replacement for other similar practices. By the beginning of the eighteenth century it was firmly associated with sugar, another commodity also new to most of the population. By the end of that century tea drinking had become not only an adjunct of polite conversation but also a popular drink providing comfort to the poor.[13] Right across the social and economic spectrum tea drinking required a range of new or modified utensils for its consumption; tea kettles, tea tables and trays, crockery like teapots, teacups and saucers, and cutlery like teaspoons and sugar tongs. Innumerable craftsmen and industrial entrepreneurs were challenged to produce these necessary commodities and a host of retailers expanded their range of goods to satisfy demand. If tea were an isolated innovation in the period it would hardly warrant the use of a term like a consumer revolution, but it was not. It was rather the most dramatic of many new goods that intruded into all levels of life; furnishings, clothing, food, medicine and leisure.

To date few have attempted seriously to push back the seeds of change to the period before the Restoration in 1660. Dorothy Davis and Joan Thirsk are notable exceptions. Davis suggests that a significant feature of the retail trade in Elizabethan London was 'the first glimpses of consumers feeling a new authority in their purses, a new confidence in the exercise of choice ... Something that we nowadays recognize as shopping had begun'.[14] Thirsk, on the other hand, sees the impetus coming, not from the consumer, but from the producer. She argues that the 'projects', so called, of the second half of the sixteenth century established several new industries in this country like the manufacture of stockings and of linen thread. These gave to some surplus cash to spend on consumer goods and to many greater choice. Quoting Gregory King, she estimates that by 1688 nearly 10s. per head was spent on apparel, that 10 million pairs of stockings, nearly five million caps and hats, and two million neckerchiefs and tuckers were bought each year in a population of five million or so.[15] These are truly remarkable figures suggesting spending on

---

[13] For a study of tea drinking narrowly focused on the so-called commodification of women, see Kowalski-Wallace (1997), *Consuming subjects*; for the alternative view that for some women the introduction of tea seems to have had a more positive effect, see for example Mui and Mui (1989), *Shops and shopkeeping*, pp. 218-19; Shammas (1990), *Pre-industrial consumer*, pp. 136-7.

[14] Davis (1966), *A history of shopping*, p. 55.

[15] Thirsk (1978), *Economic policy and projects*. The figures from Gregory King appear on p. 176.

consumer products by a large proportion of the population. Either way, which ever is right as to the cause, each saw change amounting to revolution in retailing.

It is apparent that all three schools of thought are based on observed, documented changes in the pattern of consumption on such a scale that a term like 'consumer revolution' could justifiably be applied to each. It is no less clear that it is dangerous to apply the same term without further definition to each of the three main periods reviewed, since the changes perceived either in the late sixteenth century and the early seventeenth or in the long eighteenth century were patently different from those of the late nineteenth century and the early twentieth, both in scale and nature. The debate has, nevertheless, been useful in drawing attention to changes in the early modern period which had not previously received much attention, although recently historians have moved on away from attempting to pin-point the start of the consumer revolution to address methodological or taxonomic issues or to investigate other aspects of consumerism.

De Vries raises what could be a serious problem concerning the so-called consumer revolutions of the early modern period.[16] Not only does he question the appropriateness of the term itself, but he also demonstrates apparently irreconcilable discrepancies between the evidence of increased consumption as outlined above and that of a fall in real wages over the whole period, only partly reversed by rising rates for the first half of the eighteenth century. His figures, based on data concerning the real wages of building workers over a very long period, challenge assumptions about a rise in consumption during the early modern period based on equally incontrovertible evidence of another sort.[17] De Vries suggests that these two conflicting models can be reconciled by changes he believes amount to 'an industrious revolution'. The essential features of this are threefold. First, there was a shift from production of goods intended for home consumption towards those more orientated to the market. This necessitated the substitution of bought goods and services for those produced at home. Secondly, hitherto unused labour resources were tapped in terms both of longer hours of work and of greater use of female and child labour. And thirdly, there was an increase in the intensity of work leading to a higher rate of production. The crucial consequence of these changes would have been that many households would have had some surplus cash to spend on desirable consumer goods such as sugar, tea and cotton.

---

[16] De Vries (1993), 'Between purchasing power and the world of goods'. De Vries uses data taken from Brown and Hopkins (1956), 'Seven centuries of the prices of consumables'.

[17] For example, Thirsk (1978), *Economic policy and projects*, particularly Gregory King's figures on p. 176; Shammas (1993), 'Changes in English and Anglo-American consumption'.

By suggesting ways in which apparently contradictory data may be reconciled to explain the mechanics of increased consumption, De Vries has attempted to 'establish a real dialogue among the varied parties in the history of consumption'.[18] Whether he is successful in that may be debatable, but he provides a useful model for the historian of retailing who stands somewhat on the sidelines of this debate, though having of necessity to make some sense of the conflicting evidence on purchasing power and consumption.

Styles addresses another nagging anxiety of the historian of retailing in demonstrating the dangers of using carelessly terms like consumer revolution which had been coined to meet conditions of another age. He analyses and then tears apart the use of 'mass production', 'standardization', consumer society', 'mass consumption' in terms of eighteenth-century industrial activity, warning against 'taxonomic entrepreneurship run riot'.[19] With his line of main argument, Styles moves away from the technical mechanics of manufacture,[20] to the complex relationships between what the manufacture produced and what the consumer wanted to buy. Although he illustrates his theme with examples of quite mundane goods like Yorkshire worsteds, Birmingham wares and glass bottles, other scholars have preferred to look at the luxury end of the market where the relationship between production, design, fashion and demand is more apparent.[21]

## Luxury

Luxury is seen by many historians as an essential component of the growth of consumerism. It attracted attention first because it seen to be crucial to the theories of emulation and the trickle-down effect.[22] These concepts have since been questioned and even discredited,[23] but luxury has remained a topic of interest whether it is the *objets d'art* and bespoke silver ware of the rich or the ribbons and small metal ware so attractive to the poor.

---

[18] De Vries (1993), 'Between purchasing power and the world of goods', p. 85.

[19] Styles (1993), 'Manufacturing, consumption and design', particularly p. 535.

[20] Berg (1985), *Age of manufactures*, gives a useful summary of this approach.

[21] For example, Berg and Clifford (eds) (1999), *Consumers and luxury*.

[22] Veblen (1925), *The theory of the leisure class*; McKendrick et al. (1982), *Birth of a consumer society*, Introduction and many subsequent indexed references. For a short discussion on recent work on theories of emulation, see French (2000), 'Ingenious and learned gentlemen', particularly pp. 44-6.

[23] For example, Campbell (1987), *Romantic ethic*, pp. 49-57; Weatherill (1986), 'Consumer behaviour', p. 191; Weatherill (1988), *Material culture*, pp. 25-42, 168-89. For useful summaries of the theory of emulation and the attacks on it, see Vickery (1993), 'Women and the world of goods', pp. 275-6; Hunt (1996), *Middling sort*, pp. 1-5; Bermingham (1995), 'Introduction: Consumption', pp. 9-14.

Luxury itself is also a topic on which thinkers in all ages have expended much thought,[24] but a crucial change in perception occurred in the eighteenth century. This was best articulated, though not actually introduced, by Mandeville in his *Fable of the bees*.[25] Mandeville stood on their heads ideas that had been accepted almost without question since first expressed in Classical times, when Plato had argued that once basic needs were met, any concession to the satisfaction of desire inevitably led to competition, emulation, disharmony and ultimately to the destruction of the state.[26] Mandeville, while recognizing the relationship between luxury and vice, nevertheless insisted, in the words of the subtitle of the Fable that 'Private Vices' gave 'Public Benefits'. His arguments were laid out in the much quoted opening poem, and developed in a series of 'Remarks':

> The Root of evil Avarice,
> That damn'd ill-natured baneful Vice,
> Was slave to Prodigality,
> That Noble sin; whilst Luxury
> Employ'd a Million of the Poor
> And odious Pride a Million more.
> Envy itself, and Vanity
> Were Ministers of Industry;
> Their darling Folly, Fickleness
> In Diet, Furniture and Dress,
> That strange ridic'lous Vice, was made
> The very Wheel, that turn'd the Trade.
>
> ...
>
> Thus Vice nursed Ingenuity,
> Which join'd with Time and Industry
> Had carry'd Life's Conveniences,
> It's real Pleasures, Comforts, Ease,
> To such a Height, the very Poor
> Lived better than the Rich before;[27]

Mandeville thought it folly even to attempt to distinguish needs from desires, or luxuries from necessities, decencies and conveniences, since none were immutable and all varied over time and between different sections of

---

[24] For an exposition on the history of attitudes to luxury, see Berry (1994), *Idea of luxury*.

[25] Mandeville (1714), *Fable of the bees*. The introduction by Philip Garth gives a history of this complicated and much altered text.

[26] Berry (1994), *Idea of luxury*, chapters 1-3, but particularly p. 51.

[27] Mandeville (1714), *Fable of the bees*, pp. 68-9. The poem itself, from which these lines were taken, was first published in 1705 and entitled 'The grumbling hive', but it was subsequently incorporated in the Fable.

society.[28] He argued that, however undesirable it might be for the individual's moral fibre, the pursuit of luxury provided employment for the many, encouraged inventiveness and added to the national wealth.[29]

Concerns about the dangers of luxury were not assuaged. An American writer in 1747 could still refer to luxury as making 'her appearance so engaging' with 'the show of Politeness and Generosity, that we are not aware of Danger, 'till we feel the fatal poison'.[30] A contemporary pamphleteer could write that 'Every Man has a *natural Right* to enjoy the fruit of his own Labour, both as to the *Conveniences*, and *Comforts*, as well as *Necessaries* of Life', but not apparently the luxuries.[31] Similar anxieties were expressed on this side of the Atlantic. For example, Kames in several of his 'Sketches' attacked luxury on the grounds that it led to depopulation and the destruction of industry. He even went so far as to question the merit of commerce, arguing that, while it may have appeared advantageous in the short term, it was 'hurtful ultimately by introducing luxury and voluptuousness which eradicate patriotism'.[32]

By the time of Adam Smith, the dust of moral debate had settled somewhat, and he was able to discuss the issues less provocatively. In two respects, however, he remained suspicious about luxury. First, for most ordinary people, he believed that virtue, by which he meant the avoidance of excess, was the true way to fortune, thus mirroring the views of the American pamphleteer quoted above. The corollary of this was that desire had to be controlled. Secondly he remained doubtful about the merit of luxury (though with some qualifications), considering that luxuries 'will always appear in the highest degree contemptible and trifling'.[33] Despite these reservations, Smith acknowledged, as Nicholas Barbon had done a century before,[34] that satisfying man's basic needs took up only a tiny fraction of trade, and that a far greater proportion was given to 'the amusements of those desires which cannot be satisfied, but seem to be altogether endless'. Smith defined these as 'of conveniences and ornaments of building, dress, equipage and household

---

[28] Mandeville (1714), *Fable of the bees*, Remark L, particularly pp. 136-7.

[29] For a discussion of the background to Mandeville's ideas and the reaction to them, see Berry (1994), *Idea of luxury*, chapters 5 and 6; Berg and Clifford (1999), *Consumers and luxury*, Introduction.

[30] *Boston Gazette*, 17 November 1747, quoted in Breen (1993), 'The meaning of things', p. 255.

[31] *The Good of the community impartially considered* (1754), pp. 18-19, quoted in Breen (1993), 'The meaning of things', p. 258. Breen does not name the author.

[32] Kames (1774), *Sketches*, pp. 63-4, p. 474, quoted by and discussed in Berry (1994), *Ideas of luxury*, pp. 175-6.

[33] Smith (1759), *Theory of moral sentiments*, quoted by De Marchi, 'Adam Smith's accommodation', pp. 18, 19.

[34] Barbon (1690), *Discourse of trade*, pp. 13-14; see also Berry (1994) *Ideas of luxury*, pp. 108-11.

furniture' or any other 'wants and fancies'.[35] Although he did not acknowledge it, the possibilities of satisfying these 'altogether endless' desires were boundless, constrained only by the resources of the natural world and Man's capacity to exploit them.

## The world of goods

The American newspapers reflect in a way that the British ones do not the ever-growing plethora of goods available during the eighteenth century and the increasing opportunities of choice for the consumer. In the 1720s merchants advertising in American newspapers listed only about fifteen items; by the 1790s lists of 9000 manufactured goods were not uncommon. In the 1740s just paper was listed; by the 1760s it could be as many as seventeen varieties distinguished by colour, function or quality.[36] In this country newspapers are less fruitful in this respect, since it was not a medium used greatly to help consumers directly to make choices, but rather to point them in the right way. Some British trade catalogues of the eighteenth century are comparable with the newspaper advertisements from America. For example, Nathaniel Steell of Falmouth (*c*. 1760) on a tightly packed hand bill offered well over 300 types of metal ware and small wares, many of them in variety;[37] Skill of London in 1800 through his catalogue covering four pages offered five types of salt, at least six varieties of 'Portable soup', at least nine of dried fish, and twenty sorts of cheese including a 'Good Family' one 'for Servants',[38] while Bettison's catalogue for 1794 'containing a LIST of PERFUMERY, TRINKET, AND TOY ARTICLES' spreads itself over 24 pages, including five pages of Tunbridge wares and nine of children's toys.[39]

Other sources are more informative in that they cover the whole period. The Books of Rates charged by Customs show an increase in the number of rateable goods in every reissue; in 1507 some 300 commodities, by 1558, some 1100, and by 1784 over 1800.[40] Since the books increasingly conflated some entries into single generic ones, the actual number of commodities covered by the later books was much higher. For some commodities that were a matter of some concern to the authorities, goods continued to be listed in detail giving a more accurate idea of the increase in variety. For example, for paper, only seven

---

[35]   Smith (1776), *Wealth of nations*, vol. I, pp. 150, 149.
[36]   Breen (1988), 'Baubles of Britain', p. 80.
[37]   Cornwall RO X267/3
[38]   Banks collection, 89.36* [*sic*].
[39]   Banks collection, 93.8.
[40]   Cox (1994), 'Objects of worth', p. 25.

varieties were listed in 1582, but there were 55 in 1784. Drugs give similar figures; 29 in 1582 but 360 in 1784.[41]

The Books of Rates imposed at all ports of entry a uniform vocabulary for use with imported goods, many of them new to this country. Probate inventories, tradesmen's accounts and other similar documents show that imported goods - and the terms used to describe them - were remarkably uniform over the whole country. While British manufacturers were increasingly eager to imitate foreign imports, they were not so rash as to change their names so that the same terms continued to be used. As Fuller found in the mid-seventeenth century, fustians made originally in distinctive styles in Germany and in Italy, retained 'their old names at this day, though these several sorts are made in this country'.[42] The long list of other textile terms derived from foreign words testifies that the process of adoption had been going on for a long time.[43]

The requirement of Excise performed the same office as the Books of Rates for some goods made, processed or sold in this country. Precise records had to be kept by manufacturers and or sellers of many articles like alcoholic liquors, vinegar, starch, soap and candles as well as tea, coffee and chocolate and this encouraged a uniform vocabulary over the whole country.[44]

As goods such as Sheffield cutlery, Birmingham small wares, Manchester tapes and cottons and Stoke pottery, became available nationally, a certain uniformity of mercantile vocabulary was further encouraged by the distributors. The probate inventories of mercers, haberdashers, linen drapers and grocers rarely reveal indications of regional identity in their lists of stock so that the shop goods of a mercer, say, in Cornwall were described in identical terms as those in Berkshire or Norfolk or Cumberland - or incidentally in the American colonies.[45] Although certain types of goods such as agricultural equipment and basketry retained distinctively local characteristics well beyond 1800,[46] most consumer products did not. Many textile businesses in the eighteenth century

---

[41] Books of rates are difficult of access, except for the 1582 book, Willan (1962), *Tudor book of rates*. The figures used were abstracted from the database of Rates held by the Dictionary Project at the University of Wolverhampton.

[42] Fuller (1662), *Worthies*, under Lancashire.

[43] But see Cox (1994), 'Objects of desire', particularly pp. 28-31, about assuming that terms always applied to the same article.

[44] See chapter 1 for a fuller discussion on Excise.

[45] See the shop inventory of Casper Wollenhaupt of Luneburg (1809-10) in Field (1992), 'Claiming rank'. It could easily be taken for an English retailer's inventory of the late eighteenth century. The anglicization of the colonial market is discussed in Breen (1986), 'Empire of goods', pp. 467-99.

[46] Hennell (1934), *Change on the farm*, pp. 27-8, shows that agricultural equipment like wagons and ploughs continued to exhibit local preferences into the nineteenth century so that it is 'scarcely an exaggeration to say that there is a different style of waggon to each county'. Many of the different types are illustrated in Arnold (1977), *Farm waggons and carts*.

revolved around the production of a limited but changing range of products. For example, Samuel Hill, one of the largest manufacturers in the 1730s, offered about eight basic types of cloth of different qualities and prices. These were decided upon by sending out pattern cards and samples to wholesalers, whose orders governed which lines would be produced for that season.[47]

The near universal availability of consumer goods in this country meant that objects were able to assume meanings which applied generally and not just personally, though acquisition of meaning by things is not a simple matter and the personal and the communal are closely intertwined. Vickery analyses the way Elizabeth Shackleton, a well-to-do provincial woman in the latter part of the eighteenth century, acquired, ordered and managed her possessions. Vickery suggests the 'social and personal life of things began once they had been acquired and entered the household', but it certainly did not end there. The careful record of storage, listing, breakages and recycling shows that things mattered to her, not just because the 'practice of housekeeping provided Elizabeth Shackleton with an esteemed role', but also because she could and did at times feel a personal loss at a breakage or a personal satisfaction at the cleverly contrived re-use of a sentimentally valued but worn out dress. But she was no less aware of the statements her possessions could make in the public sphere and she judged others by the statements their possessions made no less than she used hers to like effect.[48]

Where I believe Vickery is mistaken is in her suggestion that things only acquired meaning once they entered the home. If that were so, the probate listing of a retailer's shop would indeed be no more than a list of objects, with a value on each but no meaning. But this is not so. A person reading an inventory would have been able to interpret the stock in much the same way as a customer entering the shop would have done. Meaning came to shop goods through the collective experiences of individual customers and retailers, through fashion publications, newspaper advertisements, trade cards and pattern cards and countless other ways. It was because things had social and cultural meanings as well as personal ones that the rough traveller described by Breen was able to establish both his personal identity and his social status by referring to the possession of a Holland shirt, a 'neat' night cap, silver buttons and buckles and a wife that drank tea twice a day. He knew that these things 'meant' something to the person he was talking to no less than to himself. The Holland shirt and all the other objects of esteem entered the conversation as mutually understood markers of identity and status.[49]

---

[47] Styles (1993), 'Manufacturing, consumption and design', p. 532 onwards.
[48] Vickery (1993), 'Women and the world of goods', particularly pp. 282-5.
[49] Breen (1993), 'The meaning of things', pp. 249-50.

## Changes in retailing

Diversions into concepts of consumer revolution, luxury and the world of goods have led the discussion away from retailing, and it is now time to return. Just as the study of consumerism spawned the term 'consumer revolution', so there has been a tendency for changes in retailing to be viewed in revolutionary terms, although the phrase 'retailing revolution' is seldom used.[50]

There are similarities in the way that both the so-called consumer revolution and the creation of the modern retailing industry are viewed. Like the consumer revolution, the present retailing industry is frequently claimed to be the product of industrialization, which gave the benefits of mass production to whole populations. With these assumptions in mind historians of retailing have surveyed the last hundred years or so and have found what they expected to find; consumer and marketing revolutions running parallel with industrialization. The possibility of well-developed retailing systems adapted to different circumstances and different environments has generally been ignored. Because the necessary pre-conditions of shopping in the modern style were absent before industrialization, it is sometimes assumed that shopping itself must formerly have been primitive and the retailing system at best rudimentary. Only the modern shoppers, it is argued, have an attractive shopping environment that makes shopping a pleasure as well as a necessity; only the modern customers have a substantial choice of products, of price and of methods of payment; and only modern retailers can deploy the full range of marketing techniques to seduce the multitude into buying. These views have been fostered, no doubt, by the way that most historical research has been directed towards phenomena associated with large towns and therefore towards the modern period.

Even so, some recent writers on marketing present a quite surprising ignorance of the history behind present systems. For example, Lancaster and Massingham suggest that before the Industrial Revolution producers generally sold their products to a very localized market, dismissing with hardly a thought 'the rather myopic production and sales orientation of earlier times' and 'the obvious shortcomings of these less sophisticated philosophies'.[51]

Historians have been no less prone to see former marketing and shopping strategies from the viewpoint of modern history. The pioneering study of shopping by Dorothy Davis should have corrected some of these misconceptions. However, despite her perception of significant changes in

---

[50] Winstanley (1983), *Shopkeeper's world*, p. 2 asks 'Was there a retailing revolution?', a question he never really answers, though he seems to consider the retailing sector generally rather static and unadaptive with 'a leisurely rate of change' and just 'islands of change', pp. 7-9.

[51] Lancaster and Massingham (1993), *Essentials of marketing*, pp. 8, 13.

London retailing during the sixteenth century and her use of several sources to show a well-developed retailing system in the eighteenth, Davis herself appears to find difficulty in accepting the evidence. In a chapter headed 'Bright Lights and Bow-windows', (in itself a comment on the marketing expertise of the early modern period) she quotes from the diary of a foreign visitor Sophie Van la Roche. 'Behind the great glass windows absolutely everything one can think of is neatly, attractively displayed, in such abundance of choice as almost to make one greedy'.[52] The evidence here suggests a sophisticated retail outlet, with the shop window, the plentiful, attractive goods and the seductive display, all combining to generate desire. Apart from a certain naïve wonder on the part of the diarist, it could almost be the description of a shopping mall today. Yet Davis suggests that her readers might feel that it 'sounds too modern to be credible' and there is rather more than a hint that she believes that herself. Davis goes on to demonstrate that the scene la Roche described was not atypical of the West End of London, but she then marginalizes such shops by stressing how much more common was the 'draper, or mercer, or grocer of the old school, in a cramped, dark, muddled shop'. Notice here the association of 'old' with such pejorative terms as 'cramped' and 'muddled'.[53] Never once does Davis suggest that these retailers 'of the old school' might also have exploited their opportunities in an efficient and profitable way with sensible marketing strategies adapted to their own circumstances.

Outside London Davis finds no evidence of adequately stocked shops, let alone attractive shopping environments. She prefaces her analysis of the shopping habits of one gentry family, the Purefoys of Buckinghamshire, with a quotation that emphasizes the draw of the great city and the inadequate provision of most provincial towns. 'Many families who live in the neighbourhood of small town' wrote the anonymous author of her quotation, 'purchase half yearly from London many articles they want, as the cheapest and most economical means of supplying themselves'.[54] Davis accepts this statement at its face value, ignoring the fact that her author was involved in the debate about the introduction of a Shop tax and undoubtedly had an axe to grind. Davis concludes that the Purefoys did indeed use London substantially for their shopping, while dismissing with no apparent thought of inconsistency the scores of shopping letters the Purefoys sent every year, to shopkeepers, not just in town, but also in the country. [55]

Adburgham has similar problems with a body of evidence that conflicts with her pre-conceptions. She quotes a contemporary description of late eighteenth-

---

[52]  Roche (1933), *Sophie in London*, p. 87

[53]  Davis (1966), *History of shopping*, pp. 181 onwards.

[54]  Anon. (1786), Policy of the tax upon retailing considered; Davis (1966), *History of shopping*, pp. 224 onwards.

[55]  Davis (1966), *History of shopping*, pp. 224, 234.

century shop fronts that were clearly designed to attract the passers-by and to persuade them of the tastefulness and elegance of the shop and its wares, but then later implicitly dismisses such evidence by claiming that it was only 'from 1815 that new methods of retail distribution began'.[56]

Other historians appear unwilling to consider how earlier systems were adapted to the society they served, preferring rather to view them almost as a two-dimensional backcloth against which modern, 'proper' retailing emerged. Miller, in an otherwise perceptive analysis of shopping innovation in France during the latter half of the nineteenth century, suggests that before this period 'the idea that consumption could be encouraged through price or service innovations never occurred to these merchants', that there was no 'attempt made to turn buying into a pleasant or convenient experience', and that 'the idea of "shopping" was, for all practical purposes, non-existent as entry into a shop entailed an obligation to purchase'; sweeping statements that he makes no attempt to justify.[57]

Turning to McKendrick, the omissions are rather more subtle. In a study that stuns the reader with descriptions of a burgeoning, hungry population eager to buy and thousands of innovative and inventive producers eager to supply, the men in the middle are somehow allowed to remain invisible. Systems that joined the producers like Josiah Wedgwood or George Packwood directly to their customers are examined in detail, but Matthew Boulton's insistence on the importance of the 'Hawkers, pedlars and those who supply Petty shops' is not pursued, although it was they, according to Boulton, along with the shops they supplied, who did 'more towards supporting a great manufactory than all the Lords in the Nation'.[58] Indeed, perhaps in order to emphasize the changes in production and consumption that took place in the eighteenth century, McKendrick implicitly dismisses the whole retailing system in Lancashire in the late seventeenth century, when he claims that the Quaker Sarah Fell 'was 278 miles from a lemon, ... and the same even from a larding needle'.[59] He appears to be suggesting that in those unreformed days the shopping facilities of Lancashire were so inadequate that Sarah Fell was forced to shop in London. The idea that she chose to do so in these instances from several possibilities is not considered. Whereas central features of modern shopping systems are the consumer's power to choose and the retailer's power to manipulate that choice, our ancestors are assumed to have had neither the choice nor the power.

The beliefs of most historians before the 1980s are summed up in a recent article, where it is suggested that:

---

[56] Adburgham (1964), *Shops and shopping*, p. 6.
[57] Miller, M. (1981), *The Bon Marché bourgeois culture*, p. 24.
[58] Letter from Matthew Boulton to R. Chippenhall, 9 August 1764, quoted in McKendrick (1982), 'Commercialization of fashion', p. 77.
[59] McKendrick (1982), 'Commercialization of fashion', p. 89.

In pre-industrial rural society, it is usually argued, shops were few in number, highly specialised, and run by 'producer-retailers', rather than by middlemen. Moreover these shops, it is thought, catered mainly for the wealthier classes, whilst the rest of society patronised markets or itinerant traders.[60]

The publication of Willan's *The inland trade* in 1976 and several important studies since[61] should have gone some way to remove these misconceptions, though they have proved remarkably resistant to change and still need to be addressed.

## The Complete Tradesman

*The Complete Tradesman* continues the trend of recent work in early modern consumerism, so that the largely statistical approaches of such historians as Jefferys, Alexander and even Mui and Mui have in the main been avoided.[62] Questions about the availability of goods mean they can not be ignored totally (see chaper 2). For the most part this study, as its title suggests, is about the tradesmen themselves; how they designed a suitable environment to maximize sales (chapter 3), how they handled their customers (chapters 4 and 5) and how they created supportive networks among fellow tradesmen (chapter 6). This central core is sandwich between two chapters of a more general nature; chapter 1 looks at early modern attitudes to retailing and the government's response and chapter 7 at the challenge of novelty.

Within this framework, *The Complete Tradesman* pursues two main lines of enquiry. First, the retailing sector in the early modern period is investigated in order to assess how successfully it satisfied the needs of the consumer at that time and met the challenge of change. Secondly, the great divide is addressed which is so often seen to separate the early modern period from the modern, the pre-industrial or proto-industrial society from the industrial, the largely rural population from the largely urban, and the retail sector dominated by the weekly market and the travelling pedlar from the department store, multiple shops and mail order.

---

[60] Benson et al. (1999), 'Sources for the study of urban retailing', p. 167. Another summary with much the same message can be found in Benson and Shaw, *The retailing industry*, vol. II, p. 1.

[61] For example, Mui and Mui (1989), *Shops and shopkeeping*; Shammas (1990), *Pre-industrial consumer*, Chapter 8; Walsh (1999) 'Newness of the department store'.

[62] Jefferys (1954), *Retail trading*; Alexander (1970), *Retailing in England*; Mui and Mui (1989), *Shops and shopkeeping*.

The retailing sector is a large and complex subject, and it is not possible to cover the whole of it effectively in one book. This study therefore focuses on those retailers who operated from a fixed shop and who concentrated primarily on retailing. Defoe is invariably helpful in providing definitions. In the introduction to his own study of the complete English tradesman, he includes under the term 'tradesman' 'our grocers, mercers, linen and woollen drapers ... tobacconists, haberdashers ... glovers, hosiers, milliners, booksellers, stationers and all other shopkeepers, who do not actually work upon, make, or manufacture the goods they sell'. Apart from including ironmongers, and preferring the term 'retailing tradesman' to merely 'tradesman',[63] this is the definition adopted here. Excluded are Defoe's 'handicrafts', usually called producer/retailers by modern historians, market and street traders, pedlars, hawkers and chapmen, (which were ignored by Defoe), the merchants, or 'those who carry on foreign correspondence', and wholesalers under whatsoever name they chose to conduct their business.[64] Excluded also are women retailers in the sense that they have not been treated here as a distinct group with its own challenges and its own agenda. But, as will be demonstrated, no part of the network of inland trade operated in isolation so that it is impossible to ignore entirely what other types of tradesmen were doing. The boundaries were in any case blurred and labels can be deceiving. Since London was so different from the rest of the country because of its size, its complexity of manufacture, and its position as the foremost port, it deserves a book on its own and this study concentrates on the provincial tradesman.

This type of retailing tradesman, so often heretofore assumed to be an essentially modern phenomenon, already had a long history before the beginning of the early modern period. A large provincial town like Shrewsbury in the early fourteenth century already had several substantial tradesmen of the type that would later be called grocers or mercers. The Subsidy Rolls for 1309 put Robert le Espycer with spices worth 21s. and a total valuation of over £8 among the richest men of the town; 15 tradesmen selling 'silk and muslin'[65] appeared in the Roll for 1306, and they or their fellows sold as well many of

---

[63] I am very aware of the issue of gender in using the term 'tradesman'. One possible alternative would be the neutral 'shopkeeper', but that sometimes had particular connotations in the early modern period, which are discussed in chapter 2, rendering it unsuitable as a substitute. Another possibility considered was 'retailer', but that was rarely used in my sources and sometimes sits uncomfortably near quotations where other terms were used. Where this is not the case, I do use it. Most of the sources used here confine themselves to the male pronoun. Rather than indulging in the contortions necessary to twist what they say into neutral frame, I have followed their example. Unlike the authors of my sources, I do recognize that both men and women acted as retailing tradesmen, though men were more common in most parts of the retail sector.

[64] Defoe (1726), *Complete English tradesman*, pp. 7-8.

[65] The text of the Subsidy rolls has been translated into English. I am not entirely happy with the term 'Muslin' at this date.

the goods later sold by mercers. Although some probably sold from stalls in the market, some appear to have had shops.[66] We are not looking, therefore at a type of retailing tradesman who emerged in the early modern period as a response to changing society but at one who was already part of the established scene. In the next chapter we look at contemporary attitudes to retailing tradesmen and the goods they sold and at the government's response.

---

[66] Cromarty and Cromarty (1993), *Wealth of Shrewsbury*, for example, pp. 48, 51, 62, 103.

# Chapter 1

# A 'dangerous Consequence if the Trade of a Nation run into over-much Shop-keeping':[1] contemporary thoughts on the retail sector, 1550-1800

As a background to any study of retailing and distribution there must lie a proper understanding of the economic theories of the day and the way they were implemented by the authorities. It might seem, since most economic writers concern themselves with macroeconomics and the grand issues of Trade with a capital T, that the minutiae of the market town mercer or the village shopkeeper would be of little moment. To an extent this is true. But the activities of the retailing tradesman impinged themselves on the theories of trade and the wealth of nations and, albeit often indirectly, they were the object of concern for the government of the day.

Napoleon Bonaparte is famously supposed to have dismissed the British as a Nation of shopkeepers. The remark, whether or not the attribution is genuine, was intended to be the very reverse of complimentary to his former adversary. Clearly if to be a nation of shopkeepers were derogatory to Britain, then it follows that, in his eyes at least, to be a shopkeeper was not a route to social success or respectability. Nor did Napoleon stand alone in taking this approach. The assumption that shopkeepers were in some way of dubious worth was a strand of thought that ran right through the early modern period, and even found expression, though in muted form, in the works of Adam Smith, the famous advocate of free trade and the probable originator of the phrase attributed to Napoleon.[2]

The work of Adam Smith seriously challenged the thoughts of his contemporaries and even altered government policy, not just during his lifetime, but for generations. To some extent he had developed his theory in response to the economic pressures of his time, but he also synthesised a growing body of thought that had been edging towards his conclusions for well

---

[1] Anon. (1680), *Britannia Languens*, p. 302.
[2] Smith (1776), *Wealth of nations*, vol. II, p. 110.

over a century without ever quite attaining their coherence. However, the view of many Whiggish historians such as McCulloch that the work of Adam Smith was the apex of economic thought in the early modern period towards which some other thinkers feebly struggled gives an entirely wrong impression of the times.[3] From the sixteenth century onwards several economists, usually men well versed in matters of trade, were developing very different theories about what some of them chose to term the wealth of nations - a phrase that Adam Smith was to hijack so successfully that it has been associated with his name ever since. Their philosophy was the complete antithesis of his; they postulated control and regulation as opposed to free trade, and government intervention as opposed to *laissez faire*. They believed that the true wealth of the nation lay not in the volume of trade but in a favourable balance of payments that brought increased stores of bullion into the national coffers. These ideas had important implications for the retailing and distributive trades and encouraged an environment that was hostile to their development.

In the sixteenth century when these ideas were clearly articulated and rarely challenged, the economic environment was very different from that of the eighteenth. England was seen, and indeed was, a country producing a surplus of raw materials or semi-finished goods whose exports paid for the importation of desirable consumer artefacts and of a range of exotic goods from warmer climes. Under these circumstances it was deemed sound economic sense to regulate trade to redress a perceived imbalance. Even so, there are some clear similarities between these earlier economists and Adam Smith. Like him they focused their attentions on trade, by which they invariably meant foreign trade. They gave only a sideways glance at internal distribution at the wholesale level and, if they looked at the retail sector at all, it was more often than not to heap suspicion and abuse on the shopkeeper. Perhaps the most vituperative came from the mouth of the Lawyer in Thomas Wilson's *Discourse upon usury*. Retailers, he said, are 'not worthy of the name of merchants, but of hucksters, or chapmen of choyse, who retayling small wares, are not able to better their own estate but wyth falsehode, lying and perjurye'.[4]

One exposition of these theories touched directly upon retailing. It was probably written in about 1549 by John Hales, but it was not published until 1581, ostensibly by an author identifying himself only by the initials W.S.[5]

---

3    McCulloch (1856), *Select collection*, Preface. It is perhaps unfair to cite the single example of a mid-nineteenth-century historian. However, he did set out succinctly the prevailing view of his day that the Smithian approach was axiomatically correct and that any ideas of economic planning or control were axiomatically the reverse. The approach of world leaders, including our own, during the nineteen eighties and early nineties have endorsed these views.

4    Wilson (1572), *Discourse on usury*, quoted by Willan (1976), *Inland trade*, p. 50.

5    W.S. (1581), *A discourse of the common weal*. In the Introduction to the 1929 edition Lamond suggests that the author was probably John Hales, possibly William Smith. She

This work was presented in the form of a conversation between a naïve and innocent Knight of the shires and a learned Doctor who was able to explain all. Ignoring the heavy overlay of complaint about the degeneration of modern times, which is an aspect common to all such polemic writing, the author presented a solid attack on those tradesmen who did not combine retailing with manufacturing.

W.S. divided what he called artificers into three groups. The first, consisting of 'all mercers, grocers, vinteners, haberdashers, mileyners, and such', were involved primarily in selling goods imported from beyond the seas. In so doing, they were encouraging money to go out of the country and thereby did 'but exhause the treasour out of the Realme'. The second group, the 'Shomakers, tailors, carpenters, masons, tilers, bowchers, brewers, bakers, vitailers of all sortes', were neutral in that they neither brought money in nor encouraged it to flow out. The third group was the one that attracted his praise. It was this one consisting of the 'clothiars, tannars, cappers, and worsted makers', that alone 'doe bringe in anie treasour'. So far as W.S. was concerned foreign trade that brought goods in and let treasure out was wholly undesirable as were those retailers who fostered this drain on national resources by providing outlets for the goods involved. If W.S. had had his way, there would have been few if any of those tradesmen who specialised in retailing and who did not manufacture what they sold.

As the discussion between the Knight and the Doctor developed, it became clear that W.S. was not opposed to the goods as such, thus running somewhat counter to current ideas about luxury discussed in the Introduction, but he did display the typical unease of the well to do at the perceived desires of the poor to adorn themselves with the prerogatives of the rich. Unlike some religious thinkers he saw nothing wrong *per se* with such goods as 'drinkinge and lokinge glasses, paynted clothes, perfumed gloves, daggers, kniues, pinnes, pointes, aglets, buttons, and a thowsand other things of like sort'. He focused his disfavour on their importation rather than on their consumption. Thus he advocated the same policy that characterized Tudor government, particularly in the Elizabethan period, of setting up 'Projects' in this country.[6] With proper encouragement from the government he envisaged the revival of towns 'replenished with all kind of artificers; not only clothiars, ... but with cappers, glovers, paper makers, glasiers, pointers, goldsmithes, blacke smithes of all sortes, coverlet makers, nedle makers, pinners and such other ...'. As for 'mercers, and haberdashers, vinteners and grocers', W.S. could 'not se what

---

identifies the date of writing through internal evidence, pp. xi-xiv, xxv-xxix. More recently it has been accepted that it was the work of John Hales, with later annotations by William Smith. See Tawney and Power, *Tudor economic documents*, vol. III, p. 305.

[6] For an extended study of Tudor projects see Thirsk (1978), *Economic policy and projects*.

they doe in a towne, but finde a livinge to v or vj howsholdes, and in steade thereof impoverished twise as manie'.[7]

A somewhat later tract by Philip Stubbs laid out the moral and political rather than the economic objections to the 'foreigners trifling merchandizes, more plesant thann necessarie'. In this sense he was more concerned with the dangerous attractions of excessive luxury. Initially, perhaps because he was anxious to avoid offence to his patron, the Earl of Arundel, Stubbs argued that such exotic goods were appropriate only for the nobility and gentry 'to innoble, garnishe, & set forthe their byrthes, dignities, functions, and calling'. This approach was in line with most current thinking - and official policy - on the importance of maintaining distinctions of status through dress. Later his attack became more general; unlike Hales and W.S. he saw 'these two collaterell Cosins, apparel and Pride' as' the Mother and Daughter of mischiefe'. He railed against decorations like 'great and monstrous ruffes' or a feather in the cap as 'sternes of pride and ensigns of vanitie'. Although his attack was never explicitly directed against the retailing tradesmen who sold such wares, his sustained and vituperative attack added a moral dimension to the economic arguments against the value of an active retail market in anything but necessities. It was a dimension that had a continued presence for nearly a century.[8]

A development of W.S.'s economic arguments appeared early the next century set out by Thomas Mun.[9] He was a Director of the East India Company and he published his Discourse against the background of a serious depression in the cloth industry.[10] Like other economic experts of the time, he was concerned about the way bullion and specie were attracted abroad. Later he was to articulate a influential explanation of the exchange mechanism,[11] but back in the 1620s he was more concerned to defend the East Indian trade, which by its nature was unacceptable to the received wisdom of the day on the balance of payments, even if it brought huge profits to its participants. Mun confronted this dilemma quite cleverly. In place of the three types of artificer delineated by W.S., Mun divided goods into three categories; the essential, 'such as are foode, rayment, and munition for warre and trade', the desirable, such as those 'wares, fitting for health, and arts', and the unnecessary 'which serue for our pleasure, and ornament'.[12] For the purposes of his argument he had to convince his readers of the desirability of the 'moderate vse of wholesome Drugges and comfortable Spices' since most were imported by the East India Company.

---

[7]   W.S. (1581), *A discourse of the common weal*, pp. 91, 125, 129.
[8]   Stubbs (1583), *Anatomie of abuses*, vol. 1, pp. 33, 44, 51.
[9]   T.M. (1621), *Discourse of trade*.
[10]  Wilson (1965), *England's apprenticeship*, pp. 57-8.
[11]  Mun (1664), *England's treasure*.
[12]  T.M. (1621), *Discourse of trade*, p. 6.

Where he could not defend the East Indian trade on the grounds of necessity or use, and this would particularly have applied to the importation of Indian textiles, he turned from defence to attack, inveighing against imports such as 'Sugars, Wines, Oyles, Raysons, Figgs, Prunes and Currandes', not to mention the even less defensible 'Tobacco, Cloth of Gold and Silver, Lawnes, Cambricks, Gold and Silver lace, Veluets, Sattens, Taffetries, and diuers other manufactures', most of which came either from continental Europe, particularly France, or from the New World. Their importation he would have been happy to see curtailed. Like W.S. he recognized that the importation of luxuries was indefensible in general, even if he attempted to make a special case for the Indian trade.[13] His attitude to goods of luxury was rather more ambivalent than the positions taken up by W.S. or by Stubbs, but he seems to have had no particular prejudice against luxuries in themselves, only against their importation. Nevertheless his animosity towards imported luxuries was an implicit attack on the retailing tradesmen like mercers, haberdashers and grocers whose livelihood depended on just these commodities.

A feature of all these economic works is a failure to appreciate the potential of internal trade. Its possible contribution to the nation's wealth was not discussed and the mechanics of distribution were virtually ignored. The writers seem to have had relatively simplistic ideas about the ideal internal market, which found no place for the retailing tradesman and precious little for the wholesaler. Presumably these writers accepted the existence of a group who conveyed the surpluses of agriculture and industry to the ports, but the mechanisms were unspecified. Only the exporting merchant was viewed with favour so long as he brought back, not goods, but bullion.

The rather later anonymous author of *Britannia Languens* published in 1680 drew attention to a dichotomy existing in the nature of trade. Calling himself Philanglus, or lover of England, he argued that, whereas 'The National Trade doth influence the Wealth and Strength of a whole Nation', by contrast what he called private trade might 'be very beneficial to the private Trader, but of harmful, nay of very ruinous Consequence to the whole National' interest. Although home manufactures 'must advance or save the National Wealth', there were those 'home-Traders, ... whom we call Shopkeepers', who added to their own personal wealth by 'buying cheaper and selling dearer' (a complaint later echoed by Adam Smith), but they did not 'add a peny to the National Riches'. What was worse, if they dealt 'over-much in Consumptive Forreign Wares', they would assist in 'the beggary of the Nation'. Here then is a positive denial of any value to the retailing and distributive trades whose participants were perceived as concerned only with personal profit and not with the national good. It 'may truly be said', he continued, 'of one poor Manufacturer, that he

---

13  T.M. (1621), *Discourse of trade*, pp. 8-9.

adds more in a year to the Wealth of the Nation than all such Retailers and Shop-keepers in England'. He concluded that 'It must therefore be of dangerous Consequence if the Trade of a Nation run into over-much Shop-keeping ...',[14] an interesting fore runner to the more famous Napoleonic quotation.

Although in his polemic, Philanglus did concede that some shopkeepers were a necessary evil, there is no doubt that he hankered after the widely accepted model of the market by which goods were transferred directly from producer to consumer. Farmers grew crops and reared stock, and sold them directly to the consumer at the local market; while artisans manufactured wares and sold them directly to the would be user, all without the use of an unproductive intermediary. Of course the market probably never had worked entirely in this simplistic way, and it certainly did not in the early modern period, though that model may have been more prevalent in 1500 than it was in 1800. Even in 1500, setting aside the seductive charms of imported goods, some elements of the English cloth trade had a national, not to mention an international, dimension. For example, as early as 1492 middlemen in the cloth trade at Beverley, Yorkshire, were defined as 'everyone ... who attends fairs and markets, buying cloth to resell and retail in the town ...', though their freedom to sell whether wholesale or retail as so called foreigners was severely regulated.[15] London and some provincial towns were by 1500 too large to be supplied with food from the locality; and some crafts like pewtering and scythe making were already beginning to settle in particular areas so that their marketing was on a regional if not a national scale.[16] All these involved distribution networks alien to the simplistic model outlined above.[17] By 1700 such developments were establishing themselves in many economic spheres. Under these conditions there were hundreds, if not thousands, of wholesalers and retailers who bought to sell on again (a common phrase in trading circles during the eighteenth century). Whether the goods were imported from abroad or from distant parts of the realm or produced locally was of little relevance in the face of profit.

There was a spate of publications at about the same time as the *Britannia Languens* of Philanglus which agreed only in part with its findings and which took a more positive view of some sectors of the retailing trades. The anonymous author of *The trade of England revived* published in 1681

---

[14] Anon. (1680), *Britannia Languens*, pp. 289, 301-2. McCulloch suggests in his Introduction that the author might have been William Petyt, only to reject the idea, p. x.

[15] Leach (1900), *Beverley town documents*, quoted in Westerfield (1915), *Middlemen in English business*, pp. 306 and 309.

[16] See Hatcher and Barker (1974), *History of British pewter*, pp. 251-2 for references to the complexity of the pewter trade in the sixteenth century and earlier.

[17] Many of these networks for the century after the Restoration are described in Westerfield (1915), *Middlemen in English business*.

inveighed against those who 'do believe that all men promiscuously ought to have liberty to set up any trade for a livelihood, and especially the shopkeeping trade, and that a restraint hereof doth impeach ingenuity.' On the contrary, he suggested, 'the bane almost of all trades' had been 'the too great number of shopkeepers in this Kingdom.' Apart from an attack on the Quakers, which was a common theme of the time, he pinpointed as the root of the problem the ease with which unskilled men could enter the trade. He believed that 'in every country village where is (it may be) not above ten houses, there is a shopkeeper, and one that never served any apprenticeship to any shopkeeping trade whatsoever ...'. This was an evil in itself, threatening the health of the cities and market towns which were the proper centres of trade, but it was compounded by the fact that these petty shopkeepers did not pay 'one farthing of any tax at all, either parochial or national.' He had two further complaints. Firstly he expressed his dislike of the practice much grown of late years of proffering commodities to the buyer both by wholesale and retail, 'which hath much impaired all trades, because there is a vast difference between *What will you give*? and *What shall I give*? Secondly he delivered a vitriolic attack on middlemen, whom he called hawkers, who travelled round selling wholesale, thus injuring 'the wholesale trade in all the cities and market towns in England, but especially in the City of London ...'. [18]

His solution was twofold: first that established tradesmen in each town should do all they could to make distinct each trade such as 'a woollen draper, a linen draper, a mercer ... a milliner ... the semester ... the upholsterer, the ironmonger, the bookseller, the apothecary, the grocer, and the chandler ...'. Secondly, when trades were once distinguished, all who wished to join a particular trade should be obliged to submit to apprenticeship and to seek admission to the Company of the appropriate trade. If any shopkeeper should then wish to change his trade for another branch of shopkeeping. he was to leave his Company and 'within a certain time, that may be thought convenient ... to take his freedom of that company as the trade is of he intends to set up ...'. As a regulatory system it was not only reactionary, finding its inspiration in the medieval guilds, but it was also far beyond the means of the local governments of his day to enforce. But however impractical, it was as a proposal hostile to much of the retail sector even if it might have afforded a cosy protection to some of those established tradesmen in cities and market towns. [19]

His concerns were echoed almost word for word by 'H.N. Merchant in the City of London' who published in 1684 a small handbook for the guidance of incomers to the trade. Like his immediate predecessors he started by addressing 'the Bane of all Trades ... the too great number of shop-keepers in this

---

18 Anon. (1681), *The trade of England revived*, pp. 390-93.
19 Anon. (1681), *The trade of England revived*, pp. 394-401.

kingdom',[20] though he did not tar the whole group with the same brush as Philanglus had done. Instead, he set out a scheme not dissimilar to the one in the *Trade of England revived* to tackle the proliferation of undesirable retailing tradesmen who were threatening to undermine what he perceived as the respectable end of the internal market. Gone were the railings of W.S. against the 'mercers, and haberdashers, vinteners and grocers' who were here acknowledged as the acceptable face of retailing. At least they contributed something to the common wheal; they payed taxes and rents, took local offices, kept 'good Houses, relieved the poor at their door, and bought meat for which they payed in ready money'. Their status and probity, he felt, was already established and protected to some extent by entry through apprenticeship. He suggested that this requirement should be extended to all retailers, who should be permitted to set up trade only in the towns where they could be controlled by local trade associations. This would eliminate the travelling salesmen who carried their shops on their backs and got up to goodness knows what mischief out of the public eye. It would discourage the entry into the business both of those who saw the shopkeeping trade as 'an easie life' and of the Quakers, who undermined one of the principles of decent and fair-trading by insisting on a fixed price.[21] His arguments were more cogently laid out than those in the *Trade of England revived* and represent an early recognition on economic grounds of the value of retailing and distributing, even if the corollary was a murky lower end of the trade which must be regulated and controlled, if possible to extinction.

The full title of his booklet is revealing. It runs 'The Compleat Tradesman or the exact Daily Companion Instructing him thoroughly in all things absolutely Necessary to be known by all those who would thrive in the World and in the whole Art and Mystery of TRADE and TRAFFICK, and will be of Constant USE for all MERCHANTS, WHOLE-SALEMEN, SHOP-KEEPERS, RETAILERS, YOUNG TRADESMEN, COUNTREY CHAP-MEN, INDUSTRIOUS YEOMEN, TRADERS in Petty Villages, And all FARMERS, AND Others that goe to Countrey FAIRS and MARKETS, and for all men whatsoever, that be in any TRADE, or have any considerable Dealings in the WORLD'.[22] In this one title we can see something of the complexity of the seventeenth-century internal market and how far removed it was from the models some economic writers of the day liked to believe represented reality.

H.N. recognized a hierarchy of trade, from the merchants trading overseas, through the wholesalers down to the retailers. These he differentiated into no less than five categories from the fixed shop retailers (by implication in towns) to the 'traders in Petty Villages' and the travelling chapmen. Although the book

---

[20] H.N. (1684), *Compleat tradesman*, p. 17.
[21] H.N. (1684), *Compleat tradesman*, pp. 17-26.
[22] H.N. (1684), *Compleat tradesman*, title page.

is in part polemic, much of it is a serious attempt to provide the multifarious elements of internal trade with the knowledge needed to operate effectively.

Although writing just prior to H.N. Merchant of London, the anonymous 'real and hearty Lover of his King and Countrey' who published *England's great happiness* in 1677 developed further ideas about the potential value of internal trade. In a closely argued tract written in the form of a conversation between himself and one called Complaint, he started by looking at trade in its broadest sense, defending even the trade with France, the common bogy man of so many economic writers. To him the key to national wealth was trade, not the balance of trade as it was so often interpreted. For him it mattered not whether the goods traded were the epitome of useless luxury such as 'Apes and Peacocks' or the more mundane and essential Norwegian deals. Take away our supernecessary trades', he argued, 'and we shall have no more than Tankard-Bearers, and Plowmen; and our City of London will in a short time be like an Irish Hut ...'. Asked by Complaint, what he would do against the 'multitude of Trades-men?' his answer was unequivocal; encourage more and by competition increase the total wealth. 'Do not some of our Trades-men spend one or two hundred pounds a year, whose parents never saw forty Shillings together of their own in their lives? Doth it not make the Capons and the Custards go off at a good rate? Doth it not mightily encrease his Majesties revenue, by Customs, Excise, and Chimney-Money? Doth it not make a tax light, by having many Shoulders to bear the burden?' He thus extended to all the riffraff in trade the benefits accorded by H.N. only to the established retailing tradesman of the town. Among the signs of wealth he hoped to see in his own time he included 'six times the Traders and most of their Shops and Ware-houses better furnisht than in the last Age' with 'many of our poor Cotagers children ... turn'd Merchants and substantial Traders'.[23]

Once into the eighteenth century the arguments in favour of internal trade as a contributor to the national wealth became somewhat more prominent. Daniel Defoe was a prolific writer on trading matters. His propensity to indulge in imaginative flights of fancy and his naturally satirical and journalistic style of writing make it difficult at times to separate fact from fiction in his work. Nevertheless, his pronouncements deserve serious attention. His perception was acute, and even his fictions could not have been accepted at the time if they had not been based on a reality recognizable to his readers. His *Complete English Tradesman* first published in 1726 seems to have been intended as a serious work of advice to young men setting up in the retail trade. In this he was producing another book in the same genre as H.N.'s *Compleat tradesman* half a century before, though he took the argument forward to a marked

---

[23] Anon. (1677), *England's great happiness*, p. 271. The work is sometimes attributed to John Houghton.

degree.[24] It is significant that he chose to entitle one of his concluding chapters 'Of the inland trade of England, its magnitude, and the great advantage it is to the nation in general'. His language verges on the ecstatic. This inland trade is, he averred, 'the wonder of all the world of trade' and by 'this prodigy of trade, all the vast importation from our own colonies is circulated and dispersed to the remotest corner of the island, whereby consumption is become so great ...'.[25] He draws attention to the 'multitudes of people employed, cattle maintained, with wagons and carts ... , barges and boats ... , ships and barks ... , and all for circulating these manufactures from one place to another, for the consumption of them among the people. So that, in short, the circulation of the goods is a business not equal, indeed, but bearing a very great proportion to the trade itself.' The final link in the chain from producer or importer through to the consumer was the retailer, so that 'in every town, great or little, we find shopkeepers, wholesale or retail, who are concerned in this circulation, and hand forward the goods to the last consumer'. The chain stretched from London to the 'great towns' and from thence to the 'smaller markets' and even to the 'meanest villages'. At times he loses control of his hyperbole as with 'every body here trades with every body' so that it is impossible to calculate the number of shopkeepers - 'we may as well count the stars'.[26]

For all its exaggerations, Defoe's analysis introduced two significant concepts; firstly that a flourishing and efficient internal market encouraged consumption and secondly (though this was not made so explicit) that consumption contributed to the nation's wealth. However, Defoe clearly felt it necessary to educate his readers in the mechanics of internal trade if he were to persuade them of its merit. No modern writer on the economy would feel it necessary to explain, for example, how the various common furnishings in the ordinary household each comes from a different part of the country and how each may pass through several hands before it reaches the final retailing tradesman. Today such manufacturing and trading complexity is common knowledge. Defoe, on the other hand, apparently deemed it necessary to spell it out over more than two pages. The inclusion of this section suggests that the mechanics of the distributive and retailing sector were little understood, and had to be explained to readers if they were to appreciate fully the nature of trade in all its aspects.

For writers on economic matters, Defoe's description of the distributive process and his insistence on its value was sufficiently revolutionary for him to remain a solitary figure for some time to come. Economic thinkers of the eighteenth century did not develop these ideas to any extent and inland trade remained handcuffed to the priorities of overseas trade and to anxieties about

---

[24] Defoe (1726), *The complete English tradesman*, chapter 22.

[25] Defoe (1726), *The complete English tradesman*, p. 223.

[26] Defoe (1726), *The complete English tradesman*, pp. 225-30.

a surplus of shopkeepers. Malachy Postlethwayt, writing as late as 1757, was still convinced the road to success necessitated a favourable balance of payments between one's own nation and another. However, Postlethwayt does seem to have accepted that consumption made some contribution to the nation's wealth even if he was more concerned to explain how Britain could attain superiority through the regulation of her foreign trade. 'To attain this superiority', he argued, 'a society should have in proportion to it's populousness and the extent of its lands, a greater number of men able to consume the productions of art, than another has: 2dly, that it consumes less than the other does of the produce of foreign ingenuity'.[27] To achieve these idyllic conditions, it was the responsibility of government to regulate imports by raised duties and prohibitions so far as possible without provoking retaliation against exports. The effect of such raised duties and prohibitions on the retailing and distributive trades was not discussed. Throughout, Postlethwayt appears to regard the trading sector as an unfortunate necessity, although it was a pool of manpower that could be called upon, within limits, to furnish demand when agriculture expanded, and conversely to absorb labour when there was a surplus elsewhere.[28] That inland trade contributed directly to the national good he did not consider, nor did he discuss its mechanisms. Land and foreign trade, with manufacture a very poor third, were the foundations of national wealth.

A great leap forward in thinking about the distributive trades came in 1776 with the publication of Adam Smith's *Wealth of nations*. Although the book was almost entirely devoted to an attack on the mercantile system, Smith introduced two concepts that flew in the face of much previous thinking about retailing. His first challenge to orthodoxy lay in his argument that the costs of distribution were a component in the price of all goods, whether those costs were borne by the producer or by an intermediary. Because the producer was an expert in production rather than in distribution, he was likely to be less efficient, and therefore more expensive, if he attempted to dissipate his capital and his expertise over the two occupations. By contrast a dedicated distributor would be able to focus his resources on the one task. The widespread belief in the ideal of direct transaction between producer and consumer was shown to be a chimera. The retailing tradesman, along with all those involved in the distributive trades were accorded a positive role in the economy since it was they who ensured that what the farmer or the manufacturer produced came to the consumer most efficiently and at least cost.[29]

---

27  Postlethwayt (1757), *Britain's commercial interest*, vol. II, pp. 394-5.
28  Postlethwayt (1757), *Britain's commercial interest*, vol. I, p. 24.
29  Smith (1776), *Wealth of nations*, vol. II, pp. 28-32.

Smith's second reversal of orthodox thinking was that he made the consumer central to national wealth. Whereas previous thinkers had seen production as the source of wealth, which must therefore be nurtured and protected from foreign competition, Smith turned the conventional equation around.

> Consumption is the sole end and purpose of all production; and the interests of the producer ought to be attended to only in so far as it may be necessary for promoting that of the consumer ... But in the mercantile system the interest of the consumer is almost constantly sacrificed to that of the producer; and it seems to consider production, and not consumption, as the ultimate end and object of all industry and commerce.[30]

Although Smith did not link the two, the connection between the retailing tradesman and the consumer is obvious. He demolished those theories that recommended the protection and nurture of home production and the strict control of imports. Instead he placed the consumer on the pinnacle of trade and made the retailer the agent of choice, the one who made available to the consumer the full range of world production at competitive prices. The phrase appears elsewhere in the work, but his innovative perception of the nature of wealth made reality of the idea that policy should be directed towards making England 'a nation of shopkeepers'.

Government policy throughout the early modern period was largely in accord with those current economic theorists hostile to unnecessary imports and to the retailers distributing them.[31] Particularly before 1700, there were strenuous attempts to regulate those imported goods, many but not all luxuries, upon which the retailing tradesmen depended, either by high rates of custom or by outright prohibition. For example, there was a string of acts prohibiting the importation of silk goods such as girdles, ribbons, laces, stockings and gloves.[32] In 1698 Parliament disastrously prohibited the importation of lace,[33] and two years later the use of all decorative calicoes and other Indian cloths,

---

[30] Smith (1776), *Wealth of nations*, vol. II, p. 155. The importance of this idea in Smith's thinking has been challenged, but see De Marchi (1999), 'Adam Smith's accommodation', pp. 20-24.

[31] It is not the intention in this study to expand on official economic policy during the early modern period, but to concentrate on those aspects impinging on retailing. An exposition of other aspects of policy can be found in, for example, Thirsk (1978), *Economic policy and projects* and Wilson (1965), *England's apprenticeship*.

[32] The earliest noted was 33 HEN6 c. 5 (1455), the latest 5 GEO3 c. 48 (1765).

[33] 9 & 19 GUL3 c. 9 (1698). The act led to retaliatory measures by France and had to be repealed in 1700 by 11 & 12 GUL3 c. 11 (1700).

both in furnishings and apparel.[34] It also passed acts designed to reduce importation by the imposition of high duties. Here it is difficult to distinguish taxes intended to provide revenue rather than to discourage imports, but there are some in which the intention is made explicit, such as the further charge of one penny per ell on 'Sail-Cloth, or Canvas usually entered as Hollands-Duck or Vitry Canvas' imposed in 1713 'for the better Encouragement of the making of Sail Cloth in Great Britain'.[35]

A more subtle way to curb imports was to restrict those who could buy or who could wear certain types of goods. An early Elizabethan act prohibited the sale of any 'foreign Stuff or Wares, ... appertaining ... to the apparelling ... or adorning of the Body' unless for cash or short term credit or unless the buyer was a substantial property owner.[36] All such wares were the very lifeblood of the retailing tradesmen and their survival would have been seriously threatened if the authorities had been able and/or willing to enforce such restrictions. Intentionally or not, the retailing tradesmen were the victims of the economic belief that the wealth of a nation lay in a properly regulated overseas trade.

Action against the lower orders wearing articles of apparel appropriate only to their betters addressed two anxieties. It reinforced attempts to regulate trade to produce a favourable balance of payments and it satisfied the recurring anxiety that social distinctions were breaking down, particularly as they were demonstrated in dress. Regulations of apparel had a long history stretching back at least to the fourteenth century. From that time, a series of Acts and Proclamations attempted to impose a framework of social groupings and to restrict access to desirable fabrics and other items of adornment.[37] The Proclamation of 1574 summarized nicely the main intention of these regulations; the restriction to the smallest possible group of 'the superfluity of unnecessary foreign wares ... and other vain devices'.[38] The very frequency with which these regulations were introduced suggests that they were ineffective, at least partly because little provision was made for enforcement. Even so, the very existence of these restrictions was a threat to the retailing tradesmen whose livelihood depended on the sale of precisely those goods forbidden to many a potential customer. Defeat for the regulators was virtually admitted in the proclamation of 1597,[39] although all the acts were not repealed until 1604.[40] They were never replaced, but a series of Bills were introduced

---

[34] 11 & 12 GUL3 c. 18 (1700).

[35] 12 ANNE c. 16 (1713).

[36] 5 ELIZ c. 6 (1562).

[37] A full account of the Acts of apparel and the Proclamations can be found in Harte (1976), 'State control of dress', pp. 134-7, 149-51.

[38] Harte (1976), 'State control of dress', p. 138, quoting from Hughes and Larkin, *Tudor proclamations*, no. 601.

[39] Harte (1976), 'State control of dress', p. 148.

[40] 1 JAC1 c. 25 (1604).

during the seventeenth century suggesting that much anxiety remained about dress no less than the balance of payments. None of the bills were to pass into law.

The suspicion attached to foreign goods was particularly apparent in the debates preceding these bills, though few were so outspoken as the MP who averred that 'God did not attire our first parents with excrements of worms'.[41] Increasingly it became accepted that to restrict the way people dressed was impractical, even if the anxiety remained about the lower orders aping their betters. There was little legislation in the eighteenth century regulating dress, and what there was made blanket prohibitions covering all sections of the community, such as the Acts forbidding the wearing of imported calicoes and of French cambric and lawns.[42] Perhaps the most effective acts were those requiring burial in a woollen 'shirt, shift or sheet' and not in linen. The first act was passed in 1666, but the regulations were made far more effective from 1678 when the burying clergy were made responsible for enforcement.[43] The motive behind all these acts may have been to redress an unfavourable balance of payments or to encourage home manufacture, but their intended effect was no less hostile to the retailing tradesman.

Action to regulate foreign trade and the Acts of Apparel impinged only indirectly on the retailing tradesman. Other governmental action was focused directly on inland trade. The idealized interface of producer and consumer in the open market, where a fair price could be achieved through negotiation and public opinion, was perceived throughout the period to be under threat. As we have seen, this model had probably never been a reality and increasingly it became more unreal during the early modern period. But the authorities, both national and local, clung to their Utopias. The practices of 'engrossing' and 'forestalling', that is buying up goods wholesale or before they reached the open market, and then 'regrating' or selling them on profitably, were deemed evil and against the national interest. In the official mind there seems to have been little acknowledgement of the merits of a more complex market, only of its possible dangers. In 1548 Hales even went so far as to claim that regrating was one of the three principal causes of the 'Vnyuersall dearthe of vytelles in the Realme'.[44] Those who bought to sell again were variously and vituperously labelled; in the 1550s, for example, the 'Regrators of Tanned Leather' were 'greedy persons' who 'by covetousness' engrossed and regrated to sell on 'at

---

[41] *House of Commons Journal*, vol. III, p. 449.

[42] 11 & 12 GUL3 c. 10 (1700) and 7 GEO1 stat. 1, c. 7 (1721) prohibiting the wearing of calicoes, 18 GEO2 c. 36 (1745) and 21 GEO2 c. 26 (1748) prohibiting French cambrics and lawns.

[43] 18 CAR2 c. 4 (1666) and 30 CAR2 c. 3 (1678), quoted by Harte (1976), 'State control of dress', p. 152.

[44] Memorandum in Hales's hand, S.P.D. Edward VI, vol. v, no. 20, quoted in Tawney and Power, *Tudor economic documents*, vol. 1, p. 219.

excessive prices' while the engrossors of linen cloth were 'evil-disposed and deceitful'.[45] A draft bill in 1593 was even more explicit about the 'yarne choppers or Jobbers of woollen yarne', castigating them as 'wanting the feare of God, and caring onely for their owne private gayne'.[46] Although most invective and action were directed against the practices rather than the perpetrators, the result was the same. There was a serious attempt to create an environment hostile to the wholesaling tradesman, who was perceived as instrumental in upsetting the proper model of internal trade. Statutes against forestalling, engrossing and regrating in specific commodities date back to the fourteenth century;[47] local prohibitions and legal action continue until the end of the eighteenth.[48] Indeed as late as 1801 Samuel Waddington was fined £1000 and give a term of imprisonment of four months for engrossing hops.[49] Legislation regulating Billingsgate fish market illustrates well current concerns. The preamble to an Act of 1699 claimed that this market had been a free one for 'time out of mind' but that what today would be deemed acceptable practices of wholesale marketing had developed. The act reiterated the freedom of the market, unsuccessfully as it turned out and the regulations had to be spelled out in more detail in 1749.[50] As late as 1769, the famous legal commentator Blackstone referred to forestalling as 'an offence against public trade'.[51] Later still locally interested parties were still invoking the legislation to check what they saw as infringements of the law rather than changing patterns of marketing. In 1790 the Proprietor of Manchester Market placed an advertisement in the local newspaper castigating the practice of selling 'Provisions and other Articles' at 'Inns, Public Houses and Private Rooms ... by which the Public have been deprived of the Advantages of a legal open Market'. Although his motive was in reality to protect his profits from Market Tolls, he used the language of public interest to win support for his threats of prosecution.[52] Legislation abolishing the three offences of engrossing, forestalling and regrating was passed in 1772 though this did not cover the offence under common law. Total abolition was only achieved in 1844.[53]

---

[45] 1 ELIZ c. 12 (1558/59) 'against the deceitful Using of Linen Cloth'.

[46] 'Draft bill ... restraining speculation in yarn', S.P.D. Eliz., vol. CCXLIV, no. 128, quoted in Tawney and Power, *Tudor economic documents*, vol. 1, p. 375.

[47] For example, 27 EDW3 stat. 1 c. 5 (1353/54) against forestalling Gascony wine, 5 & 6 EDW6 c. 14 (1551/52) against regrating corn, wine and fish.

[48] See Chartres (1990), *Agricultural markets and trade*, pp. 168-9 for examples.

[49] Hay (1999), 'State and market', particularly p. 161.

[50] 10 & 11 GUL3 c. 24 (1699) and 22 GEO2 c. 49 (1748/49), quoted in Sterne (1976), 'Fish marketing in London', p. 71.

[51] Blackstone (1769), *Commentaries*, vol. iv, p. 148.

[52] *Manchester Mercury*, 30 March 1790.

[53] 12 GEO3 c. 71 (1772) and 7 & 8 VICT c. 24 (1844); Hay (1999), 'State and market' p. 102.

The attention of the Government was also directed towards reducing the number of shopkeepers, particularly those who set up business outside market towns where their activities could be little regulated and where they were less subject to the scrutiny of the public eye. In a move that anticipated the author H.N. Merchant in the City of London by over a century, Parliament in 1554 attempted to halt a perceived decay in towns, and hence a reduction in revenue from taxes, by prohibiting non-residents from selling woollen and linen cloth, haberdashery, grocery or mercery retail in towns.[54] The intention was to discourage two types of undesirable tradesman; the rural resident shopkeeper, who made a small living from his neighbours but depended on incursions into the town on market days for serious profits 'to the greate decaye and utter undoing of thinhabitantes of the same', and the itinerant chapman or pedlar, who carried his shop on his back, relying heavily on the crowds found in markets and fairs for his trade.

Eight years late the Act of Artificers attacked retailing through a different channel. Ostensibly the Statute of Artificers was intended to 'banish idleness' and to 'yield unto the hired person .. a convenient Proportion of Wages'.[55] The first part of the act dealing with so-called servants did not affect the retailing tradesman, but later clauses attempted to restrict apprenticeship in some trades to the respectable end of society so that any 'Mercer, Draper, Goldsmith, Ironmonger, Imbroiderer or Clothier' could only take as apprentice a child whose parents owned freehold property valued over 40s. in cities and towns corporate, and over 60s. in unincorporated market towns. It is presumably back to this perceived ideal that the seventeenth-century writers like Philanglus were looking when they inveighed against too many shopkeepers, in contrast to the author of *England's great happiness* dreaming of a time when 'many of our poor Cotagers children' would be 'turn'd Merchants and substantial Traders'. If the Act of Artificers had been effective the development of the internal market would have been severely hampered.

Another group of retailing tradesmen whose activities were viewed with suspicion was the itinerants. The economic and social upheavals of the sixteenth century provoked considerable anxiety about the stability of society, which found a focus on 'rogues and vagabonds'. Legislation and other official action throughout the period were designed to punish and deter. The legitimate travelling tradesmen, who were important agents in the effective distribution of goods, were inevitably entangled in efforts to control the activities of the less reputable. In an attempt to distinguish the two, a licensing system was introduced as early as 1551/52,[56] presumably with little effect since local officials were hostile; for example, in the 1580s 16 pedlars or tinkers were

---

[54]  1 & 2 PHIL & MARY c. 7 (1554)
[55]  5 ELIZ c. 4 (1563).
[56]  5 & 6 EDW6 c. 21 (1551/52).

arrested in Warwick under laws against vagrancy.[57] An act of 1597 included 'all Juglers, Tynkers, Peddlers and Petty Chapmen wandering abroad' among the rogues, vagabonds and sturdy beggars, and provided for their whipping 'until his or her body be bloudye' followed by their forcible return to their place of birth.[58] Prosecutions under this act continued well into the next century. As late as 1662 the Justices of Shropshire ordered that petty constables should 'punish all Scotch pedlars and other wandering rogues, and send them back according to law', an injunction repeated in 1690.[59] A further act of 1696/97 required chapmen and other itinerant tradesmen to license themselves, with a scale of charges depending on the nature of the business.[60] Either attitudes were changing or the new licensing system did provide an adequate protection for the respectable as there seem to have been less persecution during the eighteenth century.

The murky end of the retail sector as represented by the itinerant tradesmen and the out-of-town shopkeeper was not alone in attracting the attention of government. Although there never seems to have been an attempt to suppress the retailing tradesman *in toto*, a two-pronged attack was launched against him during the seventeenth and eighteenth centuries using both methods of control and taxation directly on the business rather than on the goods sold.

A scheme of excise duties payable on the sale of articles, was devised by Pym in 1643, probably on a Dutch model. Although castigated by one M.P. as 'an unjust scandalous and destructive project', it became one of the main sources of governmental revenue down to the Napoleonic era.[61] By the beginning of the eighteenth century the system already had considerable control over aspects of retailing activity, particularly over the production and sale of alcoholic liquors. Excise continued to be used in times of crisis to raise money on a whole range of mainly imported goods including grocery, drugs, paper, silks, linens and haberdashery.[62] Its continued use as a form of fund raising resulted coincidentally in an efficient nation-wide organization well adapted to the collection of revenue and other forms of control. To fund the war fought under the leadership of the Duke of Marlborough, first candles, and then soap and starch were bought under the control of Excise so that all places of production had to be registered and the officers informed before boiling could

---

[57] Beier (1974), 'Vagrants and the social order', pp. 11-12, quoted in Spufford (1984), *The great reclothing*, p. 8, and discussed, pp. 6-16.

[58] 39 ELIZ c. 4 (1597)

[59] Kenyon (n.d.), 'Quarter Session orders', pp. xxvi, 78, 133.

[60] 8 & 9 GUL3 c. 25 (1696)

[61] Wilson (1965), *England's apprenticeship*, p. 129. Receipts from Excise rose from just over £250,000 in 1662-63, to an average of *c*. £400,000. Ibid., pp. 211.

[62] See, for example, *Acts and Ordinances* dated 8 September 1643 and 24 November 1645.

commence.[63] Although retailing was only affected peripherally by these restrictions, an act of 1723 extended the policing activities of Excise to 'every Druggist, Grocer, Chandler, Coffeehouse-keeper, Chocolatehouse-keeper and all ... other Persons ... who ... shall become a Seller or Sellers, Dealer or Dealers in Coffee, Tea, Cocoa Nuts or Chocolate, either Wholesale or Retail' by requiring them to make entry of all such goods stored in any 'Warehouses, Storehouses, Rooms, Shops, Cellars, Vaults,' etc. and sending in the returns with frequent regularity.[64] The burdensome nature of the implementation of this act is laid out in the Instructions to Officers. All dealers, having registered themselves and declared all parts of their premises used for the purpose were obliged: to see that they had accurate weights; to expose no tea or coffee etc. for sale until notice had been given to the officer and a permit shown that duty was paid; to enter 'every night in books, which are sent for that purpose, the totals of all the small quantities under six pounds, by them respectively sold or consumed in each day' and in other books all sales of over six pounds; to keep records of green tea and black distinct; and to label stocks accurately. To see that these instructions were obeyed, the Officer was expected to visit each dealer every ten days, open all canisters, go into every room, weigh all stocks and check all books.[65] Although the number of tradesmen affect in the 1720s was relatively small, by the second half of the eighteenth century the situation was very different. The system of supervision and control, with of course its concomitant opportunities for taxation, had been considerably extended, and by then most retailing tradesmen were caught in Excise's net. The way lay open for a tax on shopkeepers as such.

The Seven Years War (1756-63) provided the opportunity and in 1757 proposals for a tax on shop signs, and then on 'all open shops and retailers' were presented to the Duke of Newcastle's government, though they came to nothing.[66] The following year a similar proposal surfaced again; this time in the form of a licensing system for 'all merchants, wholesale and retail dealers' which would have cost each tradesman between 10s. and £2 a year.[67] Significantly, 'Public Marts, Markets and Fairs', the elements of the retail sector so often perceived to be virtuous by the economists of the day, were to be left 'open for all sellers as before'. These proposals were taken further and

[63]  8 Anne c. 9 (1709), 10 Anne c. 19 (1711) and 10 Anne c. 26 (1711).

[64]  10 George I c. 18 (1723).

[65]  Anon. (1778), *Instructions for officers.*

[66]  BM Add. MSS 33,039, fols 57-63 and 95-6, quoted by Mui and Mui (1989), *Shops and shopkeeping*, p. 33.

[67]  According to Gregory King in 1688 the average income per family of the 40,000 shopkeepers and tradesmen was only £45 per annum. 10s. represents a tax of *c.* 1 per cent, £2 is more nearly 4 per cent. Neither would have caused ruin, but even the lower rate would have eaten into the profits of the small tradesman. The figures are quoted in Thirsk and Cooper (1972), *Seventeenth-century economic documents*, p. 781.

instructions were issued to each Excise district to collect information on the 'number of shops or houses wherein anything whatever is sold by retail exclusive of alehouses and farmers' and labourers' houses unless they keep shops' although 'Shops above stairs' were to be excluded, and 'double shops' counted as one.[68] The lists were produced, and survive, but the tax was never imposed. Even so their creation afforded Excise a powerful tool with which to impose more effectively the multiplicity of regulations already in force, particularly those relating to the sale of tea. The retailing tradesman had become documented and classified just as the itinerants had become in previous years.

William Pitt's Shop Tax of 1785 was based largely on the proposals made in the late 1750s. His motives were entirely financial, and so were directed towards those who, collectively or severally, were likely to add most to the nation's coffers. Unlike his equally unpopular Income Tax introduced in 1799, the Shop Tax was not a universal imposition subject only to a perceived ability to pay, but was instead directed against a particular group, those who kept shops. Interestingly Pitt directed his attentions away from those small shopkeepers that had so exercised the minds of economic thinkers and excluded them from the provisions of his proposed tax. The charge fell only on those paying a rent above £4 (raised in amendment to £5) on a sliding scale starting at 6d. in the £, but rising to 2s. in the £ of rent paid for those paying more than £25 a year in rent, not just on the shop, but on the building; a heavy tax on profits.

The Shop Tax threaded its way relatively untroubled through Parliament to become law,[69] but the progress of the associated provisions to abolish the licensed hawkers was a different matter. Threatened, abused and regulated from the sixteenth century on, itinerants had at last become a tolerated, if not a respected, part of the retail sector. To find themselves now thrown to the lions of the wealthy retailers was more than they could bear. The outcry came from a wide spectrum of society, the itinerants themselves, no less than the manufacturers who supplied them. One of the best articulated came from the hawkers of Alstonfield in Staffordshire. They claimed that they had 'conducted themselves with industry, reputation and propriety', and ended by declaring that 'it was particularly hard that out of the great number of different trades ... they only should be selected for destruction'.[70] Fair comment, and the outcry won a reprieve; instead of abolition, the licensed hawkers faced raised charges for their licenses. The matter did not end there, and the shopkeepers entered the

---

[68] BM Add. MSS 33,039, fols 161-2b; HM Customs Library, E/T, 5:14. See Mui and Mui (1989), *Shops and shopkeeping*, p. 34.

[69] 25GEO3 c. 30 (1785).

[70] *House of Commons Journal*, vol. 40, pp. 1054-5, quoted by Mui and Mui (1989), *Shops and shopkeeping*, p. 75-6.

fray to defend what they had perceived to have been a just *quid pro quo* for the Shop Tax. Among the petitions submitted in support of the victimized shopkeepers, the one from six towns in Cornwall most clearly shows how heavily shopkeepers perceived themselves to be taxed, the impositions including 'house tax, window tax, commutation tax, insurance tax, the tax on bills of exchange and receipts', besides the parochial rates and the new Shop Tax. None of these, the Cornish tradesmen argued, were paid by itinerants who had 'no settled abode'.[71]

Pitt had his way in the short term, but so it might be thought did the shopkeepers, who had the satisfaction of seeing the annual fee for a license doubled and the hawkers' more objectionable practices curtailed. For the hawkers there was the consolation that their livelihood was at least saved from annihilation. The annual licence fees were increased by £4 per annum for all hawkers with a further extra £4 per horse or other beast bringing the annual licence fee to £8 for all and to £16 for those travelling with just one beast. Furthermore the hawkers were forbidden to sell by auction under penalty of £50 for each offence or within two miles of any city or market town.[72]

In the long term, the attempts to mulct the retail sector proved unsuccessful. The Shop Tax was never so profitable as had been hoped, bringing in only £59,000 in 1787.[73] Ever sensitive to public opinion, particularly when the opposition consisted of such a powerful body as the London tradesmen, Pitt gave way and both acts were repealed in 1789.[74] Retailing tradesmen at the end of the eighteenth century were hampered by overmuch regulation and burdened by taxation, but at least they were largely free from the hostile thinking of the economic writers of former years. Free trade was for the future, but the debate had started and the fear of an adverse balance of payments was considerably abated.

At the end of the eighteenth century no less than in the middle of the sixteenth, most retailers were apparently able to ignore the disapprobation of the theorists; they followed the advice of the 'great Mauchant man called Dives Pragmaticus' who proclaimed in a splendid poetic extravaganza of 1563 that God had planted Man in order for him 'To bye and to sel'. Indeed Dives went further pronouncing that 'Now truly for to bye, and truly to sell, Is a good thyng' and 'Both God and man, in it doeth delyght'.[75] As Dives Pragmaticus saw it, his function as a merchant was to act as a intermediary between those

---

[71] *House of Commons Journal*, vol. 40, pp. 1084, 1107. The towns were Falmouth, Launceton, Penzance, Redruth and Truro.

[72] 25GEO3 c. 78 (1785).

[73] Mui and Mui (1989), *Shops and shopkeeping*, p. 85.

[74] For a much fuller account of the ill-fated Shop Tax, see Mui and Mui (1989), *Shops and shopkeeping*, chapter 4.

[75] Dives Pragmaticus (1563), *A booke in Englysh metre*.

overseas with goods to sell and money to buy and those in this country in like situation. As a consequence he made no attempt to divide British 'artificers' judgmentally into the three groups of W.S. but urged all to buy from him to sell on, whether they were 'Drapers and Mercers', 'Brewers, Bakers, Butchers, and Cookes', or the lowly 'women hosiers, and makers of slops'. Instead he proclaimed in language no less extravagant than Defoe's some two centuries later that the activities of retailing tradesmen were positively virtuous in the sight of God and contributed to the country's wealth. And his advice to all members of society was no less forthright; they should spend, spend, spend. Even Defoe never went so far as to use religion to support his arguments, but for Dives Pragmaticus there was no doubt: 'GOD the great gever of vertue and grace, hath planted man here ... to bye and to sel'.

Chapter 2

# 'Too great numbers of shopkeepers in this kingdom':[1] access to consumer goods, 1550-1800

Historians have been slow to acknowledge that some established conclusions about the spread of fixed shop retailing are mistaken. Jefferys, in his detailed and influential analysis of retailing in the nineteenth century, concluded that this sector of trade was slow to respond to the economic, social and cultural changes associated with the so-called Industrial Revolution.[2] His belief that fixed shop retailing did not really replace a system based on markets, fairs and pedlars until the second half of the nineteenth century dominated historical thinking for several decades, and even now has not been entirely eradicated.[3] Alexander in 1970 was still arguing that it was not until the nineteenth century that conditions were conducive to a complex retailing system and thus to a substantial number of shops, and while Deane accepted that the shop had begun to supplant the pedlar, she believed that this started only in the eighteenth century and then only in the larger towns.[4]

The images of towns produced by Samuel and Nathaniel Buck in the first half of the eighteenth century go some way to support Alexander's view.[5] Each town is set in Arcadia with trees, hills and rustic figures. The towns are generally dominated by their churches round which the houses cluster. No hint of trade has been allowed to intrude apart from the occasional forest of masts as in Bristol, which in itself adds to the imagery of the setting. Sometimes a discreet label identifies an industrial building or a market house, but of shops and shopping streets there is no indication whatsoever. The contemporary journeys of Celia Fiennes endorse the imagery in the Bucks' townscapes. It

---

[1]   Anon. (1681), '*Trade of England revived*', p. 394.
[2]   Jefferys (1954), *Retail trading in Britain*, pp. 1-13.
[3]   A useful summary of the historiography on retailing can be found in Benson and Shaw, *Retailing industry*, vol. II, pp. 1-2.
[4]   Alexander (1970), *Retailing in England*, chapters I and IV, especially p. 3; Deane (1979), *First industrial revolution*, pp. 257-8, quoted by Willan (1976), *Inland trade*, p. 58.
[5]   The first panorama produced by the Bucks was printed in 1721, the last in the 1750s. All are reproduced in Hyde (1994), *Prospect of Britain*.

appears that a street lined with shops was something either she did not find or she felt not worthy of comment.[6] Although the Bucks' prints portray the town, so far as we can tell, with visual accuracy and in a setting their customers wanted, the imagery is deceiving. Each of the towns portrayed in these images, and many more besides, was a centre of an active retail trade as this chapter will show.

In this chapter the distribution of provincial retailers in the early modern period is investigated from three angles. First, orthodox methodologies designed to establish ratios of fixed shops to population are explored. The quest is then broadened to look at variations in the relationship between market provision, population size and the presence of fixed shops. Secondly, the focus is shifted to look at the availability of consumer goods. Thirdly and most speculatively, the emergence of towns with superior shopping facilities is investigated.

## Orthodox approaches to the distribution of fixed shops

The debate on the rise of the fixed shop has centred round both the actual number of shops and the ratio of fixed shops to population. This, on a national scale, is a practical proposition for the nineteenth century when more or less reliable data can be extracted from Trade Directories, and from the decennial census returns starting in 1801. These show a relatively poor ratio of fixed shops to population at the beginning of the century improving steadily from about 1850 onwards. However, extrapolating back from these data has led some to assume (conclude is perhaps too strong a word) that there must have been even fewer fixed shops in the eighteenth century than there were by 1800, with progressively poorer facilities in the seventeenth century, and so on backwards. By implication, *reductio ad absurdum*, a time must be reached when there were no fixed shops outside London and virtually all trading, such as it was, occurred through pedlars, markets and fairs.

This assumption has been challenged for the eighteenth century, over the country as a whole by Mui and Mui using a number of contemporary estimates like those of Gregory King as well as data abstracted from the excise records,[7] and it has been emphatically refuted by Collins with regard to the two contrasting towns of Shrewsbury and Wolverhampton.[8] For these two towns, where there is sufficient evidence to create tentative figures back to the late seventeenth century, the evidence suggests a clear fall in provision in the

---

[6] Fiennes (1984), *Illustrated journeys*.
[7] Mui and Mui (1989), *Shops and shopkeeping*, particularly chapter 2.
[8] Collins (1993), 'Primitive or not', pp. 23-38. This is based on her work for her forthcoming Ph.D. thesis, University of Wolverhampton.

decades round 1800 in both these two towns, more marked in the rapidly industrializing Wolverhampton but evident also in a county town like Shrewsbury.[9]

Collins's methodology could be applied to other towns to provide a broader coverage of the country as a whole. The sources she uses to give figures of population for the late seventeenth century are well known and have been the subject of much study. The Hearth Tax returns, the Compton Census and calculations based on Parish Registers are each associated with established methodologies for calculating the size of communities.[10] To find convincing data on the number of fixed shops is more problematic but Collins has shown that the probate records can be used to provide figures for the late seventeenth century and the first half of the eighteenth, even if they must remain somewhat speculative. Unfortunately to apply her methodology to other towns is more easily written than done. Analysis of the probate records requires a survey of the whole source as it relates to a particular town, and a substantial study of many documents in detail.[11] This is not a conceivable proposition for all towns, so that the best that can be hoped for is corroboration from the study of one or two. Extending such work back to the period before 1660 is even more difficult, since the national records such as those kept for Excise do not exist, the data on population is less reliable and the probate records become increasingly defective.[12] It seems that a point of *ne plus ultra* may have been reached with this approach.

It must in any case be questioned whether the ratio of fixed shops to population gives helpful insight into the retailing system of the seventeenth century and earlier. Such data have certainly produced useful information about retailing in nineteenth-century towns. It has proved possible, and useful, in certain circumstances to apply the methodology to some towns as early as the late seventeenth century, as Collins has shown. However, the settlement patterns predominant in the early modern period are generally unlike those of the nineteenth and the twentieth centuries so that there are many problems

---

[9]   Mitchell (1981), 'Retailing in eighteenth and early nineteenth-century Cheshire', pp. 40-41 notices the same deterioration and improvement in two Cheshire towns.

[10]   For example by Clark and Hosking (1993), *Population estimates*, though they cover only small towns.

[11]   Collins's work covering the two towns of Wolverhampton and Shrewsbury was possible because all probate inventories for the latter located at Lichfield JRO from 1660 to 1750 had already been transcribed with extensive notes on wills and administrations. There are few, if any, other towns of comparable size in the country where this has been done.

[12]   For some dioceses, for example Hereford, there are no surviving probate documents before 1660, for others, particularly those in the North, occupations were more or less never recorded before then. A general survey of the probate documents is therefore useless and a meticulous study of each document is required to pick out retailers. Even then, only those for whom stock was listed can be included so that the data will inevitably compare unfavourably with the later period.

about attempting to abstract data on ratios for the period, quite apart from the deficiency in the sources. For example Alexander's work on the growth of shop retailing in the first half of the nineteenth century is based on London and ten representative towns. Each of these ten, including the smallest of them, had a population in 1851 greater than any town in the early seventeenth century apart from London, and perhaps Bristol and Norwich, and each covered an area huge beyond comparison with towns two centuries earlier. Whereas maps of nineteenth-century towns need a scale based on the furlong, if not the mile, in many of the town plans produced by Speed and published in 1611/12, a scale based on the pace was more appropriate. In Speed's day, for example, Lancaster, with a population of about a thousand, probably extended no more than 500 paces at its broadest point, Derby with about two and a half times as many citizens covered much the same area, while Newport on the Isle of Wight, with some 1700 citizens stretched only for 400 paces or so. Even Shrewsbury, among the twenty largest towns in England probably needed only 1200 paces from end to end, and this despite the flourishing suburbs of Frankwell, Coleham and Abbey Foregate outside the protective river Severn which almost enclosed the main town.[13] Modern reconstructions of the probable area of settlement in four small Shropshire towns in the sixteenth and early seventeenth century show the same pattern on a smaller scale.[14] No one living in a town had to walk far to market and shops.

Although some towns had expanded substantially by the eighteenth century, the townscapes produced by the Bucks show much the same. People may have had to walk further, but access to the market and the central shops remained in many towns a matter of a short walk. For urban settlements on this scale a dispersed system of corner shops and suburban shopping centres was an irrelevance likely to lead to a dilution in standards and choice. Since most citizens would wish to visit the market regularly for perishable supplies, a centrally placed shopping centre to be used in conjunction with the market was an appropriate arrangement for most potential town customers. What matters in this model is not the number of shops, or the ratio between population and shops, or their distribution, but the range of goods on offer and the prices compared with alternative sources of supply. As we shall see, any departure from this norm was likely to be based more on a desire for social exclusiveness than on the need for local services or on new social and economic circumstances that made the old pattern unworkable for some shoppers.[15]

---

[13] Speed (1611/12), *Counties of Britain.*
[14] Watts (1995), *The small market town*, Map 2.2.
[15] I am thinking in particular here of industrialization in very small towns like Madeley or Broseley in Shropshire where the establishment of provision shops serving strictly local communities may have been encouraged by the pattern of work well before the nineteenth century.

Another important difference between the early modern period and the nineteenth century was the much smaller proportion of the population that was wholly urban or wholly dependent on income from manufacture or trade. The probate records for many small towns suggest that most people had access to land and grew at least some of their grain and/or raised some stock. For example, just under half of those leaving estates appraised for probate in Wellington, Shropshire between 1660 and 1750, had owned cattle at the time of their death, and most of those had also harvested some grain as well.[16] Wellington was a small town set in a relatively large parish, but the area was developing rapidly as its rich coal seams were opened so that its setting was much less rural than many other small market towns. But it was by no means unique; another Midland town, Cannock, of comparable size and industrial development, affords similar data. Out of 330 inventories surviving for the period 1562-1791, over two thirds refer to cattle, and more than half to crops.[17] It is clear that both these towns, and many others like them, not only served as a place of exchange for the agricultural community in their hinterlands, but were also part of that community themselves. As such they may not have been greatly in need of those retailers like butchers, bakers and provision merchants who were central to servicing the more industrialized and urbanized settlements of later years. As a consequence, only five probate inventories for Wellington relate to butchers and only two to bakers.[18] For Cannock, the figures are respectively one and two.[19] It may be that each town only ever had a few active bakers or butchers at any one time. If this is true of these semi-industrialized towns, it is even more true for others whose main function was to service a rural hinterland. In Ellesmere, another small Shropshire town, but one with little or no industrial development, the probate records of the period 1630 to 1800 reveal but two butchers and one baker.[20]

In the larger towns, where there was presumably correspondingly less opportunity for citizens to be involved in agriculture, the pattern may more nearly have approached that of most towns in the mid-nineteenth century. As early as 1422 a single court session in the town of Ely, serving a population of

---

[16] Trinder and Cox (1980), *Yeomen and colliers in north Telford*, pp. 72-90 and Table 1.

[17] Adams etc. (n.d., *c.* 1975), *Probate inventories of Cannock*, Introduction.

[18] Trinder and Cox (1980), *Yeomen and colliers in north Telford*, pp. 64-5.

[19] Adams etc., (n.d., *c.* 1975), *Probate inventories of Cannock*, Introduction.

[20] Ellesmere was a peculiar jurisdiction outside the control of the Bishop's court and its regulations did not always conform to those of that body. The probate records for Ellesmere are very good. Inventories continued to be taken, and have survived, for the whole of the eighteenth century. This argument should not be developed too far, at least for the eighteenth century. Richard Latham, a Lancashire farmer, was apparently selling his surplus stock and buying in cheap cuts of meat; for example, during 1743 he bought 'head and pluck' 14 times, 'bief' 6 times, and 'mutton' once, as well as bread on one or two occasions, Weatherill (1990), *Account book of Richard Latham*, pp. 53-6.

3-4,000, dealt with cases involving three bakers and twelve butchers, not to mention 37 brewers, 73 ale retailers, 11 dealers in fish, two vintners and two cooks.[21] In Lincoln, the surviving probate records for the early modern period contain 21 inventories for bakers and 12 for butchers, while in Shrewsbury the comparable figures for the period 1660-1750 are 30 butchers and 45 bakers.[22] Those whose estates were appraised for probate represent an unknown but probably small proportion of the total, but even when this is taken into account, it is unlikely that the number of butchers, bakers and provision merchants in the larger towns of early modern England matched those for most middle-sized towns in the mid-nineteenth century.[23]

Alexander attempted a further breakdown of ratios by categorizing shops into ten broad headings and investigating how well each group served customers.[24] This created some problems even for the nineteenth century, and would have caused more if he had been able to look at the contents of the shops rather than just at the given occupations of the shopkeepers. An attempt to squeeze the retail system of the seventeenth century into the same classification would be highly misleading.

For example, much purveying of fresh foodstuffs in the early modern period took place in markets or through street traders, or in town gardens, so that the number of shops offering these goods was small. Greengrocers appear hardly to have existed in the seventeenth century, and have not been noted in small towns during the eighteenth.[25] Yet by the 1850s, there were 132 in Liverpool, 85 in Manchester and 13 in York. Fishmongers were not uncommon in the sixteenth century and the early seventeenth when eating fish on fast days apparently remained an accepted practice. However, they seem to have died out temporarily after 1660,[26] though preserved fish remained widely available from other types of shop. By 1851, this type of shop was also common in

---

[21] Dyer (1989), *Standards of living*, pp. 196-7.

[22] Johnston (1991), *Probate inventories of Lincoln citizens*, pp. xxxvi and xxxix. For Shrewsbury the figures have been abstracted from the transcriptions of the complete set of Shrewsbury probate records held at Lichfield Joint RO.

[23] Alexander's analysis for 1848 shows York with 40 bakers, 125 butchers and 229 shopkeepers; for Carlisle the corresponding figures are 37, 45 and 157, Alexander (1970), *Retailing in England*, pp. 253-4.

[24] Alexander (1970), *Retailing in England*, p. 95 onwards and Appendices 1 and 2. Alexander's categories were books and stationery, chemists and druggists, cloth and clothing, pottery, food trades, metal goods trades, leather trades, oil and colour, tobacco, miscellaneous.

[25] Alexander assumes that most perishable foodstuffs were purveyed through the market, even though the Trade Directories listed green grocers and the like. He assumes that they traded through stalls in the market, though gives no evidence to support this assumption, and therefore omits them. In the seventeenth century the term a greengrocer was apparently unknown. The first reference to one given in the *Oxford English dictionary* is in 1723.

[26] This tentative conclusion is supported by Barley (1962), 'Lincolnshire shopkeepers', p. 18.

Alexander's sample towns.[27] The cheesemonger was another type of retailer quite common in the nineteenth century. Although the term was used in the early modern period, it was not applied to specialist retailers selling cheese, and most cheese was sold in the market, or by fixed-shop retailers like grocers, mercers or chandlers. Therefore, even if it were possible to compile satisfactory figures, a comparison of ratios of fixed shops to population for the early modern period with those for the nineteenth century applying Alexander's methodology, would give distorted results.

A further complication lies in the prevalence of craftsmen/retailers like shoemakers, saddlers and tailors. Often there is no way of telling the proportion of such enterprises devoted to retailing rather than to manufacture. Before 1800 most probably sold some or all of their products retail, but some may have been solely occupied in making for others to sell. This was not a complexity of retailing peculiar to the early modern period, although it was to become increasingly less important during the nineteenth century so that Alexander felt able to dismiss it as a problem. However for the early modern period to omit such tradesmen entirely when calculating the number of fixed shops would distort the figures, while to include them all would be equally unrealistic. Collins chooses to operate a quite a rigorous policy of exclusion. Because she focuses on just two towns, her figures have a particular validity, though her methodology would need testing more widely before it could be applied nationally. Despite the severity of her exclusions, her ratios for *c.* 1700 are still more favourable than those for a century later.[28] However, the problems of handling craftsmen/retailers, and therefore the potential distortions, would be magnified for *c.* 1650 let alone for *c.* 1600.

### New approaches to the distribution of fixed shops in the seventeenth century

The investigation of retail provision in the early modern period needs therefore to move away from ratios and to adopt models more appropriate to the circumstances of the time and to the sources available. As will be demonstrated, to view the retailing system of this period solely as the primitive precursor of what was to come gives an entirely false picture of a dynamic and flexible system well adapted to serve a growing body of consumers. There remains, however, the problem of sources. Willan was the first to draw attention to two possibilities; the plentiful evidence relating to the distribution

---

27  Alexander (1970), *Retailing in England*, Appendix 1.

28  Collins, 'Primitive or not?', pp. 30-31 and Table 1, show 37 and 30 shops per thousand population in *c.* 1700 for Shrewsbury and Wolverhampton respectively, dropping to 19 and 16 in *c.* 1800 and only rising to 21 and 18 by 1891.

of markets, and the trade tokens issued in the middle of the seventeenth century.[29]

Willan observes that there were about 800 market towns in Elizabethan England, acting as centres of exchange between town and country. Furthermore, he suggests that 'the market and the shop were complementary rather than competitive'.[30] This symbiotic link needs to be explored further, but first it is necessary to establish how these 800 or so market towns were distributed and how that distribution changed over time. This was a matter of considerable interest to contemporaries and there were therefore several publications listing market towns. The accuracy of these lists must inevitably be called into question; there is some evidence of copying from one to another, new markets were not always noted, and old and decaying ones could stay on the lists well after their useful life was over. Nevertheless, the lists, which have been analysed by Everitt and Chartres, provide a solid base for further investigation.[31]

The distribution of markets in England before the Restoration was uneven. Cumberland, extending over about a million acres was served by 15 market towns; Lancashire, only marginally larger, by nearly double that number. Within the counties themselves, the distribution was also uneven. In Cumberland, for example, the coastal strip was well serviced, the interior less well so. In Sussex, there was a noticeable empty space corresponding to the Weald. Few counties had the even distribution of some eastern counties like Essex or Kent. The reasons are not hard to seek, being largely geographical, but the consequence for market-goers was that some had to travel much further to market than others and, if one accepts that shops were generally associated with the market place, they presumably had less opportunity for shopping.

Chartres suggests that the distribution of markets was not static, the actual number in most counties going down, though not necessarily by very much. In some counties, even when the number of towns listed in contemporary sources remained the same after the Restoration as before, the actual locations may have changed. However, many market towns remained active throughout the whole period from 1500 to 1800, and the maps produced by Everitt for the first half remain essential valid for the whole, even if there are changes in detail. For example, in Shropshire Hodnet and Tong both seem to have succumbed to competition from more attractive neighbours and virtually lost their markets during the eighteenth century. On the other hand Broseley, which may once have had a market since decayed, and Madeley, the two main settlements in the rapidly growing industrial region of the Severn Gorge, appear to have developed market facilities in the eighteenth century, as did some

---

[29] Willan (1976), *Inland trade*, pp. 53, 83-9.
[30] Willan (1976), *Inland trade*, p. 53.
[31] Chartres (1990), *Agricultural markets and trade*, pp. 17-24 for a list of markets.

industrializing towns in Lancashire.[32] In 1673, Blome, one of several makers of a town directory, declared that Chapel en le Frith in Derbyshire was 'formerly a market town, but now disused', whereas Winster, despite its proximity to Matlock was 'a place where there is a meeting for the Sale of Provisions but is no Market Town'.[33] Possibly it was a market in the making.

Despite the fluidity of market facilities in detail, there remained a solid core of market towns in every county, reasonably well spaced, and appearing in every directory throughout the period. These towns, not only offered markets, but also held annual or more frequent fairs, and most benefited from being designated a post town.[34] Willan suggests, and I would agree, that this allows us to assume an equivalent distribution of fixed shops.

The second source suggested by Willan that may throw light on the distribution of retailers in the seventeenth century is the token coinage issued during the 1650s and 1660s after the withdrawal of the copper farthings. Tokens were presumably intended to provide small change in the absence of any official provision. They were issued in denominations of ¼d., ½d., and in some localities such as Shropshire and Lancashire of 1d. Although little is known about who issued them or in what quantities, Willan was able to find evidence to suggest that the governing bodies of some large towns like Oxford and Norwich may each have issued as many as 100,000 tokens (quite apart from the numbers issued by individual tradesmen), while smaller places like Poole in Dorset, or Bewdley in Worcestershire may each have issued over 10,000. He argued that even if only 1000 tokens on average were issued of each of the 12,722 different varieties listed in Williamson's revised list of 1889-91 (an undoubted underestimate of the true number) the total would exceed 12 million.[35] There is little evidence on how these tokens were used. They could have been given to customers as change and become almost common currencies in the locality. Some may have entered circulation as a result of agreements between the issuer and a local employer of labour, or have been used to pay wages direct for use in a truck shop. They may have worked as a

---

[32] For a more detailed discussion of Shropshire markets see Cox (1993), 'Distribution of retailing tradesmen', particularly pp. 11-12, and Map 1; for new developments in Lancashire and elsewhere, see Chartres (1990), *Agricultural markets and trade*, pp. 24-5.

[33] Blome (1673), *Britannia*.

[34] Fairs are discussed and mapped in Chartres (1990), *Agricultural markets and trade*, pp. 171-93; the posting towns are listed by Blome (1673), *Britannia*, pp. 13-14. The post is probably a less reliable indicator of town status than the existence of a market or the survival of tokens. The post depended on the national road system, and convenient stopping points upon it. Hence in Cumberland the post towns included Muncaster rather than the nearby town of Ravenglass, and three substantial market towns, Keswick, Wigton and Whitehaven were also absent from the list.

[35] Willan (1976), *Inland trade*, p. 84; Williamson (1967 edn), *Trade tokens issued in the Seventeenth Century*. There are several local studies adding new finds to Williamson, such as Thurlow Leeds (1923), *Oxford tradesmen's tokens*.

form of credit among small purchasers. Tradesmen may have seen a high rate of failure in the redemption of tokens by customers as a potential source of profit. What is clear is that a large proportion of them, probably over half, were issued by retailers, especially by mercers, drapers, ironmongers, haberdashers and the like. This can be deduced from the tokens themselves. One of the most common formats was an inscription giving the occupation of the named retailer, or a representation of his/her trade by a significant symbol like the Mercers' arms or a sugar loaf. On this evidence alone, Lancashire may have had as many as 25 towns served by fixed shop retailers, Staffordshire 23, and Sussex 35. Even remote Westmoreland had three. With the exception of Cumberland where the token evidence is inexplicably poor, all the counties under particular review in this study had a respectable scattering of towns in which it would have been possible to buy a range of goods not produced in the locality. This evidence is the more noteworthy as it depends on the survival of very small artefacts and on the issuers' decision to use significant detail on their tokens. It is probable that the number of towns in which retailers issued tokens is much greater, though the tokens themselves are uninformative. (See Table 2.1 for the figures for all the selected counties.)

The tokens in themselves afford no information concerning the scale of retailing activity pursued by their issuers. Fortunately some of those tradesmen who issued tokens in the 1660s or early 1670s can be identified in other records with reasonable confidence. Three examples will suffice. The William Mall of Bishops Castle, Shropshire, who issued an undated farthing token, is probably the mercer of that name who died in 1668. His probate inventory shows he left a personal estate valued at £48, and a shop containing a wide range of goods, although some were 'moth eaten'. Given the unusual name, it seems likely that the Elizabeth Dore of Newport in the Isle of Wight, who died in 1685 leaving a varied shop and a personal estate valued at over £800 was the widow or other close relative of the Richard Dore of the same place who issued a farthing token dated 1654. More confidently linked are the James Hamar of Rochdale, who issued a farthing token in 1655, identifying himself with the symbolic Eagle and Child, and the mercer of that name who died in 1659. He left a personal estate valued at £348 (apart from the debts owing) and a shop and warehouse stuffed with goods worth over £200.[36] On this slight evidence it would appear that tokens were issued by quite ordinary provincial tradesmen, and not just by the most substantial.

Alongside the two sources that Willan suggested, there is a third factor that may act as a pointer to centres of retailing activity. This is the size of settlements in terms of their population. There is considerable disagreement

---

[36] Hereford RO, Mall 1668; Hampshire RO, 1685 Ad 32; Lancashire RO WCW·1661 James Hamar.

between historians as to what minimal population constitutes a town. Corfield from one end of the debate suggests that only settlements with a population in excess of 5000 can be regarded as indisputably urban, although those smaller may have some characteristics of a town.[37] Braudel from the other end of the spectrum dismisses numbers as of prime importance concentrating instead on the idea that a town 'has to dominate an empire, however tiny, in order to exist'.[38] Perhaps the most satisfactory stance for this study is to assume a population of 500 as the absolute minimum to warrant the status of 'town', while bearing in mind Braudel's concept of empire.[39] A recent study of small towns in north Shropshire indicates how crucial a minimal population may have been to the successful establishment of a trading empire as represented by market and shops.[40] However, further studies show that this can not be taken as a model applicable to all England. Table 2.1 shows there was no uniform pattern over the country as a whole, either in terms of distribution or of correlation between the characteristics of market, population and tokens. It will come as no surprise that some counties were relatively thinly populated and were poorly provided with towns however defined. What is surprising is that the provision in Shropshire does not provide a suitable model for the rest of the country. In that county the correspondence between the last three columns is quite close, suggesting that the economic and social environment encouraged the establishment of fairly well-spaced markets supported by retailing fixed shops in settlements with a population of 500 or more, but not elsewhere. By contrast Sussex had rather fewer centres of population than Shropshire, but rather more market towns and over twice as many settlements in which retailers issued tokens, while Cumberland had very few centres of population and (apparently) of settlements with retailing shops but it had nevertheless a good number of market towns.

The figures look rather different if the counties are compared in terms of the relationship between provision and area. Cumberland, Derbyshire, Westmoreland, all counties with much upland, were the least well served with markets, while three of the Midland counties, Warwickshire, Staffordshire and Leicestershire were the best. In between the best and the worst, the two southern counties Sussex and Hampshire were less well served than Lancashire in the North, and only marginally better than midland Shropshire. There is no

---

[37] Corfield (1976), 'Urban development', p. 221.
[38] Braudel (1981), *Structures of every day life*, pp. 481-2
[39] Clarke and Hosking (1993), *Population estimates*, pp. i-ix.
[40] Cox (1993), 'Distribution of retailing tradesmen'.

## Table 2.1
## Comparative figures for selected counties: acreage, markets, tokens and population

| County | Acreage: J.G.[a] | Acreage: modern[b] | Places with tokens[c] | Markets[d] | Towns with 500+[e] |
|---|---|---|---|---|---|
| **North West** | | | | | |
| Cumb'd | 1,040,000 | 1,000,960 | 3 ( 0) | 15 | 4 |
| Lancs. | 1,150,000 | 1,219,221 | 41 (25) | 26 | 21 |
| Westm'd | 510,000 | 505,864 | 5 ( 3) | 8 | 3 |
| **Midlands** | | | | | |
| Derby. | 680,000 | 658,624 | 33 (18) | 10 | 9 |
| Leics. | 560,000 | 514,164 | 23 (16) | 12 | 10 |
| Shrops. | 890,000 | 844,565 | 20 (15) | 15 | 13 |
| Staffs. | 810,000 | 748,433 | 29 (23) | 18 | 11 |
| Warks. | 670,000 | 563,946 | 31 (19) | 15 | 15 |
| **South** | | | | | |
| Hants. | 1,312,500 | 1,037,764 | 45 (27) | 16 | 19 |
| Sussex | 1,140,000 | 936,911 | 59 (35) | 18 | 10 |

[a]: As estimated by J.G., Gent. (1720), *Great Britain's vade mecum*. Although they differ from modern figures, they are useful as an indication of contemporary perceptions. In fact, with the exception of Lancashire, J.G.'s figures are over-estimates.
[b]: Taken from *Chambers' concise gazetteer*, (n.d., but pre-1914). No acreage was given for Cumberland and it was calculated by multiplying the given figure of square miles by 640.
[c]: Taken from Williamson (1967), *Trade tokens issued in the seventeenth century*. The figures in brackets estimate the number of places with trade tokens issued by at least one retailer, such as a mercer, a draper, an apothecary or a chandler, and those who used the arms or symbols of an appropriate Company (such as the arms of the Mercers' Company, a pair of scales or a sugar loaf). That others chose not to use any indication of trade does not preclude them from conducting a retailing business. Thus the number given will be an under rather than an over estimate of the number of towns that had retailing businesses which needed to issue tokens.
[d]: Chartres (1990), *Agricultural markets and trade*, pp. 17-24
[e]: Figures are calculated from Clark and Hosking (1993), *Population estimates*, using their recommended multipliers. Clark and Hosking derive their figures from several sources, some of which give somewhat variable results. Where available, figures for the township rather than for the parish have been used. Where there are no figures for the township, a problem particularly in Westmoreland, an assessment of probability has been made using the ratio of township size to parish in the 1811 census. Five additional towns have been included which exceeded the upper limits for population as set out by Clark.

simplistic North-west/South-east divide here, although this has often been suggested.[41] In terms of places for which tokens were issued by tradesmen, Sussex and Warwickshire are the best served, closely followed by Leicestershire and Staffordshire, with Lancashire, Shropshire and Westmoreland at the bottom of the table.

Such pattern as there is may be explained at least in part by the differing models of settlement. For example, in Shropshire outside the clearly defined, albeit small, towns with both markets and other retailing facilities, there were few nucleated settlements but rather a plethora of scattered hamlets - not for nothing is one parish called Ruyton XI Towns.[42] This may have discouraged the establishment of shops outside the towns. By contrast the Hearth Tax returns of 1670 and other sources giving data on population suggest there were at least 15 settlements in Sussex with populations below 500 but with sufficient urban characteristics to qualify as a definite or possible towns by Clark *et al*. There were also villages like Harting, Kirdford, and Tillington that were not considered by contemporaries to be towns but nevertheless had substantial populations comparable with some of those that were so considered.[43] With this in mind it is not surprising that the correspondence between population, the existence of a market and of retailing facilities is lower in Sussex than in Shropshire. Whereas in Shropshire there are less than ten settlements which fulfil some but not all three criteria, of having 500+ population, a market and surviving tokens, in Sussex there are well over 40 such settlements, while in the neighbouring county of Hampshire there are over 30. In these two counties it would seem that the presence of a market and/or a certain level of population were not essential for a settlement to sustain other retailing facilities in the second half of the seventeenth century.

The data given in Table 2.1 challenges the notion of a poorly developed retailing system before the late eighteenth century or the early nineteenth. In this it extends the conclusions of Mui and Mui back in time to the mid seventeenth century and adds a new dimension to the work of Collins who looked only at two towns. Furthermore, the data suggest different patterns of distribution in different parts of the country, rather than a simplistic divide of poorer provision in the North than the South.

There is a twofold weaknesses in relying too heavily on these data. Firstly, with the exception of those concerned with the distribution of markets, they are focused heavily on the second half of the seventeenth century with little

---

[41] Taking the country as a whole the divide is rather more obvious, though not absolute; see Chartres (1990), *Agricultural markets and trade*, pp. 46-7.

[42] 'Town' in the name of this parish means 'settlement' and was applied to hamlets and villages no less than to towns in the modern sense.

[43] Clark and Hosking (1993), *Population estimates*, pp. ii-vii, 169-74; Whiteman (1986), *Compton census*, pp. 136-53.

continuity. Secondly, the data provide no evidence about the quality of the retailing provision, unless one assumes those who thought it worth while to issue tokens must have been tradesmen of some substance. The evidence needs then further contextualization both over time and in relation to quality of provision.

## Approaches to the distribution of fixed shops before 1700

Willan discusses the distribution of retailing outlets in Elizabethan England, but is conscious that he has failed to produce more than indicative and anecdotal evidence. He concludes that 'None of the sources available for the study of shops and shopkeepers in this period gives any detailed picture of the distribution of shops throughout the country',[44] though he could have added that the known distribution of markets is highly suggestive of other retailing facilities. Once on the seventeenth century he found himself on more solid ground though the difficulties remained to some extent.

It must be asked to what extent other studies can correct or support data given here. This presents a challenge. There are a number of studies which superficially appear to address issues relating to retail provision, but each has its own agenda and methodology and each is narrowly confined both in time scale and in area surveyed. The overall effect of these studies adds weight to the general propositions that retail activity had a presence in the provinces at least from the sixteenth century onwards and that provision shops were numerous in the eighteenth century. But the evidence each study offers needs to be contextualized by the others, and they all need synthesising together to produce a possible overall model of the distribution of fixed shops before the Restoration.

Two studies, the one by Patten and the other by the Tawneys, do afford insight into possible changes in the distribution of retailing activity during the sixteenth century, that difficult period for which Willan found no satisfactory sources other than the anecdotal. Both studies were based upon Muster Rolls, that is lists of able-bodied men and available arms. Such rolls are not uncommon, though relatively few have been published. Most are relatively uninformative except for population studies. However, the two used by Patten and the Tawneys exceptionally include the occupations of a high proportion of those listed and so makes it possible to use them to analyse occupational structure and retail provision. The two muster lists concerned are usefully separated in time, but unfortunately they do not cover the same parts of the country. Patten uses the Muster Rolls of 1522 for the hundred of Babergh,

---

[44] Willan (1976), *Inland trade*, p. 59.

probably the wealthiest area in Suffolk, which was itself one of the wealthiest counties of the time. As he cautions, his findings may not therefore be representative of the country as a whole.[45] By contrast the Tawneys base their study on the Muster Roll for the whole of Gloucestershire compiled in 1608 by the antiquary and lawyer, John Smith.[46] The two then are substantially different in scale. The Suffolk Muster Roll covers 32 settlements of which three were market towns. Listed are some 2000 men for 82 per cent of whom an occupation is noted (i.e. about 1640 men) out of a total population estimated at *c.* 10,500. The area covered by the Gloucestershire Muster Roll of 1608 is in every way more substantial. It surveys about 400 manors and boroughs of which 34 were market towns. Listed are some 20,000 people, mostly able-bodied men, for about 17,000 of which an occupation is given. Using the same multiplier as Patten, this gives a total population of about 100,000.[47] The Gloucestershire roll thus presents data based on a population about ten times the size of that in the Suffolk area. These Gloucestershire people lived in rather more than ten times the number of settlements and were served by about ten times the number of market towns.

Apart from this difference in scale, there are other considerations that make comparisons difficult. Gloucester was a far more substantial town than any of the three in the hundred of Babergh. Furthermore Gloucestershire was served by, and its settlements serviced, one of the most important arterial waterways in the country, the river Severn. Although both areas were important centres of a well-established cloth industry, Gloucestershire had in addition coal and iron industries that were matched by no comparable development in Suffolk. All these factors suggest that Gloucestershire would have supported a greater variety of retail provision than Babergh, and this is indeed the case.

Patten finds 66 occupations in Babergh Hundred, 30 of which only appear once and another five twice. Only the market town of Sudbury shows solid evidence of a retailing presence with a grocer, several retailing craftsmen like a pewterer, a glover, a goldsmith and a tallow chandler, several food retailers like fishmongers, butchers and bakers, some providers of services like tailors, smiths and tanners, cloth finishers like shearmen, dyers and fullers, and representatives of some 35 other trades. Even here there was no mercer, the archetypal purely retailing tradesman of the early modern period. The other two market towns, Lavenham and Nayland, were less well served, with some food retailers, a few providers of services and some cloth finishers. It is clear that

---

[45] Patten (1972), 'Village and town'.

[46] Tawney and Tawney (1934-35), 'Occupational census'.

[47] Patten (1972), 'Village and town', p. 7, explains his suggested multiplier. Earlier (p. 2) he suggests a population for Babergh of 10,500, which is not in accord with this multiplier. Because of this uncertainty a multiplier of five has been used for Gloucestershire, which will give figures at the low end of the possible range.

these two served some urban functions but the provision of goods from outside the region does not appear to have been one of them.[48]

The methodology deployed by the Tawneys differs fundamentally from that of Patten and thus complicates comparison with the Suffolk results. They estimate that 4.2 per cent of adult males were involved in 'dealing and retail trade'. This is high compared with what can be estimated from the Suffolk data. Even excluding Gloucester and the two largest market towns, Tewkesbury and Cirencester, the figure is still 3 per cent.[49]

What is more significant is a breakdown of the Gloucestershire occupational structure in ways not attempted by the Tawneys. Firstly there is a substantial number of craftsmen making the sort of consumer goods that found their way into the shops of retailing tradesmen; 145 glovers (compared with one in Babergh), and 37 metal workers such as cutlers, pewterers, braziers and goldsmiths (compared with three in Babergh) as well as 14 workers in paper and cardboard, seven pinmakers, three tankard makers, two each of point makers, hosiers and bottle makers, and one each of knitter, bonelace maker, starch maker and embroiderer, none of which were represented in Babergh at all.[50] Secondly there were 112 designated mercers in Gloucestershire, excluding their servants and relatives, that is taking the county as a whole a rough ratio of one mercer to every 1000 people. In addition, there were 40 travelling retailers such as chapmen and pedlars, 20 chandlers, 12 haberdashers, five apothecaries, three woollen drapers and a linen draper, and a grocer. With those added the ratio becomes roughly one retailing tradesman to 500 inhabitants. Compared with this there were no mercers in Babergh, and only three chandlers, one grocer, one haberdasher and three 'pedders'. This makes a comparable ratio of 1:1300, substantially less favourable than the figure for Gloucestershire.[51] Thirdly, the Gloucestershire mercers were well spread out and were trading in no less than 33 settlements. Although nearly a quarter of market towns, mostly small, did not support a mercer, three quarters of them did along with ten other settlements. No settlement in Babergh supported a mercer and it seems likely that its inhabitants had to travel to Bury St Edmunds for many goods not produced in the locality. Fourthly there is a marked

---

[48]  Patten (1972), 'Village and town', pp. 11-16.
[49]  Tawney and Tawney (1934-35), 'Occupational census', Table X, pp. 59-63. The Tawneys selections in this category are curious to say the least, including for example butchers, barbers, and inn keepers.
[50]  This is in accord with the idea of 'projects' to encourage home industries as developed by Thirsk (1978), *Economic policy and projects*, particularly chapter 2.
[51]  It is acknowledged that not all chandlers were retailers, but for most, retailing seems to have been a part of the business almost equally as important as candle making. If the braziers and pewterers were included among the additional retailing tradesmen - and they seem to have had a balance similar to the chandlers - then the ratio of one to 500 becomes even more solid. Such an inclusion would improve the Babergh ratio to 1:1050.

difference in the complexity of urban provision, if not proportionally in the number of such centres. Whereas Babergh had one town supporting more than 30 occupations and two others supporting more than 20, Gloucestershire (excluding Bristol) had three with over 60, another six over 30 and 13 over 20. There are dangers in concluding from these figures that there was a substantial development in the retailing of consumer goods over the period of 80 years. Laughton and Dyer show that Gloucestershire was well endowed with small towns in the later Middle Ages, likewise with markets, and that the population of the county was more highly urbanized by the 1520s than any other midland county.[52] Although they do not discuss fixed-shop retailing, it is probable that this also developed early. Even taking this into account, and factors like the size of the population base, the presence of a large town like Gloucester, and the effect of the river and the iron and the coal industries, it still seems probable that the Gloucester figures as compared with those of Babergh do show development. The figures cannot be extrapolated to apply to the country as a whole with any confidence, as the evidence is not yet available, but it is probably safe to say that by the early seventeenth century there was a significant presence of retailing tradesmen scattered over the country, similar to the pattern demonstrated in Table 2.1, whereas a hundred years before such activity was probably confined to major towns in many parts of the country. In addition this presence was probably serviced by a growing number of craftsmen, many of them rural such as glove makers, saddlers, cutlers and the like.

The Barleys' study of Lincolnshire tradesmen supports this tentative conclusion. Their study also covers the sixteenth and the seventeenth centuries. It thus overlaps the data both from trade tokens and from the Muster rolls, but it offers a different approach being based on a survey of probate records.[53] The Barleys base their findings only on those whose occupations were actually declared in the inventory, so some will have been missed, including many women traders (who were invariably defined by status) and all minimalist shopkeepers (who were frequently given no status or occupation at all). The source however provides advantages not found in sources like Muster Rolls, in that the probate inventory provides evidence of what was actually sold as well as of the occupational structure of the area.

Unfortunately the Barleys' methodology prevents direct comparison with the studies by Patten and the Tawneys, since their analysis is focused primarily upon the goods offered for sale, they provide no overall population figures for the area, and little breakdown of the occupational structure in each settlement. However, their analysis shows considerable retailing activity stretching right

52  Laughton and Dyer (1999), 'Small towns', especially tables 1-3.
53  Barley and Barley (1962), 'Lincolnshire shopkeepers'.

back into the sixteenth century. Before 1600 they find evidence for 29 mercers, 17 drapers, seven chandlers, two grocers, one haberdasher and one chapman. Most of these died in the last four decades of the sixteenth century. For the seventeenth century, numbers had increased substantially, with 66 mercers, 26 drapers, 14 chandlers, nine chapmen, five grocers, five ironmongers and four haberdashers.[54] There can be no certainty, but these figures probably indicate an increase in trading activity. However, with no data on the total numbers of surviving inventories for the two periods, and no indication whether there was a greater tendency to record occupation, as there was for example in the North, this conclusion must remain tentative.

Although the Barleys give little information on the location of retail activity, their discussion indicates that most retailing tradesmen operated from market towns, although there were some with substantial shops in apparently quite small settlements. The Barleys suggest this can be attributed to the remoteness of such outlets, though it seems implausible. A great swathe of land down the western side of the county was ill-served by markets, but of the villages mentioned as supporting a retailing tradesman, only Haxey lies in this area. The other places are located in the eastern half and are each less than five miles from their nearest market town.[55]

The tentative conclusion that over the country as a whole retailing activity probably increased during the late sixteenth century and the first half of the seventeenth is given some solidity by Watts's doctoral study of four small Shropshire towns, using not one but several different sources. Her figures show that as a percentage of all surviving inventories the number of craftsmen in Whitchurch rose by 50 per cent while in Wellington, Wem and Shifnal the increase was over 200 per cent. These increases were felt, not only in the towns themselves, but also in the rural hinterlands within the parishes.[56] The craftsmen of particular interest are those that helped to furnish the retailing tradesmen, such as 21 glovers, five hosiers, three capmakers, a pointer and a button maker, mostly from the period after 1600. In so far as the retailing tradesmen themselves were concerned, the probate record supplemented from other sources show that all four towns were centres of some retailing activity. Even Shifnal, the smallest and least town-like of the four, had a mercer after 1600. Of the others, Wem had a grocer before 1600 and five mercers, a draper, a chandler and eight chapmen thereafter; Wellington had three mercers before 1600 and five mercers and three drapers thereafter; and the largest town Whitchurch had five mercers, two chandlers, a chapman and an ironmonger before 1600, with 15 mercers and 16 drapers, two chapmen, a grocer and an ironmonger thereafter. Given that the number of probate records for the two

54  Barley and Barley (1962), 'Lincolnshire shopkeepers', pp. 7-8.
55  Barley and Barley (1962), 'Lincolnshire shopkeepers', p. 21.
56  Watts (1995), *The small market town*, Tables 7.2 and 7.4.

periods are comparable, although the first period covers 65 years while the second covers only 40, the increase is undoubtedly significant.[57] Watts's figures support the conclusions drawn from the Muster Roll of Babergh for 1522 and of Gloucestershire for 1608. They suggest an increased number of craftsmen supplying some of the required goods to an increased number of retailing tradesmen. Although clearly not all these tradesmen were active simultaneously, Watts considers that there were three mercers in business at the same time in Whitchurch in the early seventeenth century and no less than ten in the mid-seventeenth century.[58] Her study only deals with the four towns and not the parishes lying in between. However all four lay in the centre of extended parishes and in none of their rural parts were retailing tradesmen noted. This goes some way to support the findings earlier in this chapter that in Shropshire generally, virtually all retailing activity was located in the market towns.

Two further studies covering the period after the Restoration contextualize retail provision in areas already investigated for the sixteenth century and the early seventeenth. Both are based on probate evidence, but each unfortunately takes a different approach, not only from the other, but also from those covering the earlier period. The first, by Ripley, is based on Gloucester's hinterland that, he suggests, extends about ten miles and thus affords some direct comparison with the Muster Roll of 1608.[59] This area includes the market towns of Cheltenham, Newent, Painswick and Tewkesbury, which each had a substantial retail base before 1660, as well as Bisley and Stroud which had increased in importance since 1608. The area also included the small boroughs of Newnham and Kingstanley and ten villages with populations of between 500 and 1000. However, except for the four substantial market towns, none of these settlements show evidence of retailing tradesmen in 1608 and none do in this later period. Ripley concludes that in this part of Gloucestershire for all but their basic needs country people were dependent on the market towns, although he notes two village retailing tradesmen, a mercer at Birdlip and a chapman at Rodborough.[60] Neither settlement had been of importance in 1608. His study sheds no light on the questions raised by the 1608 Muster Roll and the presence then of mercers in quite small settlements like Abenhall, Blakeney and Lydney since all lie outside the area under review.

The second study, by Holderness, investigates rural tradesmen in the 50 parishes of eastern Lindsey. The area is no more exactly defined than this, but it can be assumed to cover a broad coastal strip closely studded with market

---

[57] Watts (1995), *The small market town*, Table 7.8.

[58] Watts (1995), *The small market town*, p. 390.

[59] Defined as the area from which those came who sued or were sued for recovery of debts before the Tolsey court in Gloucester, Ripley (1984), 'Village and town', p. 170.

[60] Ripley (1984), 'Village and town', p. 172.

towns, in contrast with the sparsely furnished western half.[61] His findings suggest that many, if not all, of the market towns must have had a substantial retailing presence, though he notes that the eighteenth century sees the appearance of village shopkeepers such as George Cowin of Candlesby (1725) and William Plant of Ingoldmells (1747). It is not clear whether these were the only two found or whether they are quoted as examples. Even if the latter the finding is significant as by that date the number of inventories is tailing off and two may represent but the tip of an unrecorded iceberg.[62]

The development of the village and the corner shop is particularly contentious. There was considerable anxiety towards the end of the seventeenth century concerning the number of shopkeepers establishing themselves outside towns, but there is little if any evidence to support these anxieties. The most telling evidence relates to the eighteenth century. This has been analysed by Mui and Mui in detail, and they conclude that in the mid-eighteenth century shops were numerous, with a marked difference between the South-east and the North-west.[63] However, the records of Excise, which supply the most reliable data for this period, only provide aggregates for each district of collection with no details about distribution at the level of the settlement. The danger of such data lies in what may be extrapolated from them. For example Mui and Mui suggest that there were just over three shops to the square mile in the South-east and between one and two for the rest of the country.[64] To assume from this that there was therefore a widespread presence of shops in villages would be quite unjustified, although the assumption is sometimes made. It could equally well be assumed, with equal lack of justification until more evidence is found that most of the shops were in towns.

Martin's study of 'village traders' in the Feldon of Warwickshire[65] goes some way to address this issue. He suggests that in the eighteenth century a substantial proportion of the population of this area were involved either part time, or indeed full time, in some trading activity and that the number was growing. However, he lumps together under a general heading of 'those engaged in some activity other than farming', the craftsmen and dealers of all sorts with those who fulfil his definition of a retail shop. In this sense his findings do not suggest a situation much different from that revealed in the 1608 Muster Roll for Gloucestershire. Tradesmen like tailors, smiths, carpenters, shoemakers, were not uncommon in 1608 Gloucestershire villages. Even in tiny settlements with under ten men named in the Muster Roll 10 per

---

61 Holderness (1972), 'Rural tradesmen'.
62 Holderness (1972), 'Rural tradesmen', pp. 80-81.
63 Mui and Mui (1989), *Shops and shopkeeping*, chapter 2 and Appendix 1.
64 Mui and Mui (1989), *Shops and shopkeeping*, pp. 40-41.
65 That is, that part of Warwickshire that was largely agrarian in character, as opposed to the more extensively wooded part called Arden.

cent were classified as craftsmen, while for those manors with between 30 and 40 men the proportion had risen to nearly 20 per cent. The Tawneys found only seven manors, all small, out of nearly 400 where there was no evidence for any but agricultural activity. Out of the 152 small manors, 54 per cent had tailors, 52 per cent workers in wood and 35 per cent workers in metal.[66] What appears to be significantly different is that the Feldon in Warwickshire had large numbers of food and beer shops, a group relatively inconspicuous in Gloucestershire.[67]

Martin does not distinguish between retailing activity in market towns, however small or decayed, and advantageously situated villages like Dunchurch where there was no market, or the smaller villages with little to recommend them as a site of economic activity. He implies the village 'shopkeeper' was quite common, but refers directly only to one (though whether so called in the document is not clear), who died in the small village of Oxlip. It is probably safe to conclude from his analysis that in the Feldon of Warwickshire there were a number of minimalist retail shops during the second half of the eighteenth century. There may have been some prior to that, but that is uncertain.[68]

This rather long section has attempted to establish how far Willan's speculation is correct that most of England was well served by retailing tradesmen like the mercer, who sold goods otherwise not obtainable in the district during the second half of the seventeenth century. Of this there seems little doubt. Three studies in different parts of the country show that this was also true for the sixty or so years prior to the Restoration, but that there were probably rather fewer places thus served during the sixteenth century. Although the association of retailing tradesmen with market towns is strong, this was not uniform over the country as a whole. The link was noticeably weak in the southern counties of Sussex and Hampshire, but there were also shops in settlements without market status in parts of Gloucestershire at least as early as 1608. The presence of petty shopkeepers in village or corner shops before 1700 remains a matter of speculation.

## The availability of consumer goods

A different approach to retail provision can be made by using probate records to focus on the substantial body of shopkeepers who made their living primarily by retailing and who sold goods largely produced outside the

---

[66] Tawney and Tawney (1934/35), 'Occupational census', pp. 40-41.

[67] Martin (1984), 'Village traders', pp. 181; Tawney and Tawney (1934/35), 'Occupational census', p. 36.

[68] Martin (1984), 'Village traders', pp. 180-82.

immediate locality. This group is typified by the provincial mercer,[69] but retailers qualifying for inclusion are also found under a variety of designations such as shopkeeper, grocer, chapman, ironmonger, and linen draper, under indications of status like yeoman, husbandman and widow, and with no given occupation or status at all. They range from those whose personal estates at probate were valued at well over £1000 with several hundred different wares in their shops and warehouses, down to the poor widows who offered for sale two or three items of grocery and haberdashery. Although some members of this group may be identified by their designated occupations, others can only be picked out from the wares they offered for sale. Despite the range in their wealth and status they do form a coherent group that has an importance out of all proportion to their numbers.[70]

Quite apart from the importance of this group to the social and economic fabric of towns in the early modern period, for the historian there is an additional reason for studying this type of retailer. An understanding of the distribution of consumer goods is crucial to the debate concerning the growth of consumerism, since much of the argument hinges on changes in consumer behaviour initiated by the availability of new and fashionable goods. It was this group of retailers more than any other who were responsible for the dissemination of such goods to the public. The most cursory study of the contents of their shops shows their importance as distributors of consumer goods. Their shops are stuffed with household items like glass and earthen ware, cooking pots and tools, needles and soap; quality fabrics like broad cloth, stuffs and holland; crape for funerals and ribbon favours for courtship; and exotic imports like sugar, tobacco, spices and dried fruits, not to mention tea, chocolate and coffee. A few of these items correspond with Weatherill's list of

---

[69] The term 'mercer' needs to be defined. In London and probably in other large towns like Bristol, the primary meaning pertained of 'One who deals in textile fabrics, especially a dealer in silks, velvets, and other costly materials' (*OED*). However, in provincial towns, particularly small ones, the term was used by the leading retailing tradesmen of high social status and economic importance, who sold a wide range of goods not produced in the locality. Tradesmen adopting this designation had probably served an apprenticeship. In many ways they were more comparable with a small proto-department store than with the nineteenth-century village shop with which they are sometimes misleadingly compared. This definition is not given by *OED*. The secondary definition given there of 'a small-ware dealer' is of little importance. The mercer may be contrasted with other retailers who were sometimes defined as 'shopkeepers'. They had probably not served an apprenticeship, but they sold similar goods, albeit usually of a lower quality and with less choice. Still lower down the scale of prestige were retailers who were given no designation at all, but who sold a few lines. Many of these tradesmen were probably not full time and may only have served their community in this way for quite short period. Little is known about such tradesmen, though there are clues in Stout (1967), *Autobiography*.

[70] Berger (1980), 'Development of retail trade', is a short study on the distribution of this type of tradesman before 1700. Although based on quite a small set of data drawn from probate records, its findings suggest the value of more extensive investigation.

'key' goods used by her to plot changes in her book *Consumer behaviour and material culture* during the hundred years after 1660,[71] but many more are consumables that do not feature in her main source, the domestic inventory. Such goods perforce were not a feature of Weatherill's analysis, yet they are no less crucial to a full understanding of consumer behaviour than those goods she selected. To study the outlets were such goods were available is a useful alternative approach.

For a variety of reasons this group of retailers is well represented in the probate records,[72] although obviously representation is not universal. The records themselves are of variable quality and quantity before 1660 and deteriorate after *c.* 1720 in many dioceses. This need not be a matter of concern if the question to be answered is not expressed in terms of how many retailers of this type were there, but whether this type of retailer was represented in a given community at all or whether consumers had access to goods not produced locally. From the consumers point of view it may have mattered little whether a choice of several hundred different wares was offered through a number of more of less specialist outlets or through only a single general one. A town with a haberdasher, a draper, an ironmonger and a grocer could be recorded as having four retail outlets, but if each had a monopoly in their own sphere then the customer may have had no greater choice in that town and have benefited from no more competition than in one served by a single all-purpose provincial mercer, who sold haberdashery, drapery, ironmongery and grocery, as many did.

Surprisingly, when relating these issues to those who lived in a town's hinterland, the crucial question may not be how far was it necessary to travel in order to buy goods originating outside the locality. The farming communities of early modern England had to attend an agricultural market regularly in order to dispose of stock and produce. There would have been few people in rural England who did not at times have to attend market, and for most it was almost a weekly necessity. This may have made a shop accessible even though it was patently many difficult miles away. On her' Great Journey' of 1698, Celia Fiennes commented of Penrith that 'its a long way for the market people to goe but they and their horses are used to it and go with much more facility than

---

[71] Weatherill (1988), *Consumer behaviour*, particularly Appendix 1. The items she selects for especial study are: tables, cooking pots, saucepans, pewter, earthen ware, knives and forks, china, utensils for hot drinks, window curtains, table linen, looking glasses, pictures, books, clocks and silver plate.

[72] Probably anxiety about the extent and scale of the deceased's debt is one of the main reasons for an executor or administrator to submit an estate to probate. If so, then the estates of provincial mercers and others of his ilk were more likely than most to be found in the records, because most such tradesmen were dependent on credit both given and received. See chapter 5 below for a discussion of retailing debt.

strangers'.[73] The *Account book* of Richard Latham (1725-58) tellingly illustrates this point. Latham was a small yeoman living in the plains north of Liverpool where communications were notoriously poor. His account book records visits to a surprising range of market towns and in some instances his accounts suggest that he combined a business visit to the market with shopping for the home. However, since his records were concerned only with monetary outgoings, it is by no means a complete record of his trips to market towns. Though his financial circumstances limited the scale of his purchases, he did buy goods like sugar, spices, haberdashery and cloth.[74] It would appear that difficult travel did not necessarily deny a small yeoman like him access to shops.

The records of some of the horse and cattle markets confirm, as Latham's accounts suggest, that distance was not such a barrier to rural trade as might be supposed. Regular weekly markets were held at Bridgnorth in Shropshire, primarily for horses. The toll books show that a would-be purchaser could have expected to find a good choice of animals of moderate quality - the sort that can be noted in probate inventories all over Shropshire, probably bought for £3-£4 and, after a year or two of hard work, valued at about £2 when the owner died. It is clear from the surviving toll books that men travelled substantial distances to attend. Several men from Kynnersley, a tiny village in north Shropshire well over ten miles away, have been noted. These were not necessarily horse dealers like William Bell, but ordinary yeomen farmers. In choosing to go to Bridgnorth, they were spurning much nearer markets at Newport and Wellington. What attracted them to the more distant market town is not clear, since its facilities were only marginally better. It is nevertheless significant that they were prepared to travel for what, to us, may appear fairly trivial advantage.[75] Their apparent preference at times for more distant markets corresponds closely with the pattern of travelling exhibited by Latham.

For Shropshire, where a substantial proportion of the probate record has been transcribed for the period 1660-1750, this approach is particularly valuable.[76] Its study supports the conclusions drawn from the data contained in

---

[73] Fiennes (1984), *Illustrated journeys*, p. 169.

[74] Latham (1990), *Account book*. Although some of his purchases may have been made from itinerants, it is unlikely all were, particularly items like sugar. A fuller discussion of Latham's shopping activities can be found in chapter 4. Weatherill (1988), *Consumer behaviour*, pp. 114-23 analyses his purchases.

[75] Bridgnorth Horse Toll books 1644-1720. Other books survive but were not searched. A full discussion of the networks in the horse trade can be found in Edwards (1988), *Horse trade*, chapter 2.

[76] The Shropshire probate records have been transcribed by adult education classes run by Dr Barrie Trinder over a number of years, under the auspices initially of Shropshire County Council and subsequently of Birmingham University. North-eastern Shropshire lies in the Diocese of Lichfield, where the practice of taking probate inventories continued until *c.* 1740. Even more fortunately the towns of Bridgnorth, Ellesmere and Shrewsbury (in part), as well as

Table 2.1 in that it offers little evidence of retailing activity outside the towns for the second half of the seventeenth century, or indeed for the whole of the early modern period from *c.* 1540 to 1750. Such rural retailing activity as there was seems to have been on a very small scale and probably ephemeral in nature. The most substantial village tradesman noted was Richard Jones of Baschurch, who died in 1739, leaving a personal estate valued at £66.[77] He had agricultural tools like plough and harrow as well as stock, while his cheese press shows that he was capable of processing the milk. His inventory also lists about 40 commodities including hand tools, earthenware, haberdashery, hardware, grocery and tobacco. Despite the variety, these shop goods were valued at only about £12. The spelling in the rest of the inventory is no worse than that in many others from rural Shropshire, but the appraisers appeared to have been floundering when they came to the shop goods and the spelling is notably bad for a retailer's inventory.[78] It suggests that among Jones's fellow villagers there was no one familiar with handling such stock except as consumers. The appraisers clearly knew what the commodities were, but they were not familiar with writing the terms down. As for other village tradesmen noted in north-east Shropshire, their activities as recorded in their inventories were so slight that they would almost certainly pass unnoticed without careful scrutiny of each document.[79] Typical inventories of minimalist retailers are those of Elias Tylor of Leighton (1686) who had three boxes in the shop and two more respectively of 'linings' and 'small linings' valued at 21s., and the spinster Susan Stephens, also of Leighton, (1680) who had three trunks 'with thread tape and old ribbon &c' valued in all at 13s. 4d.[80]

The Shropshire towns with populations over 500 in the early modern period, with established markets, and with issuers of tokens, are all represented by substantial retailing tradesmen in the probate records for both the second half of the seventeenth century and the first half of the eighteenth.[81] For the period

---

some rural areas, were peculiars where the practice continued until 1780 and beyond. Those parts of Shropshire south-west of the river Severn lay in the Diocese of Hereford. All probate records are missing before 1660, but the taking of inventories continued at least until 1760. Given the overall excellence of the probate records in the county, and the scale of work on them, Shropshire provides a good subject for analysis. See Cox (1993), 'Distribution of retailing tradesmen'. A small area west of Shrewsbury lay in the Diocese of St Asaph. The records from this section of the county have not been investigated in this study.

[77] Lichfield Joint RO.

[78] There is considerable evidence that appraisers of retailing tradesmen were usually fellow retailers; see Trinder and Cox (1980), *Yeomen and colliers*, p. 28; Cox and Cox (1984), 'Probate inventories 1', pp. 134-7. This inventory appears to be an exception.

[79] For a fuller analysis of small shopkeepers in north-east Shropshire, see Cox (1993), 'Distribution of retailing tradesmen', pp. 13-14.

[80] Both Lichfield Joint RO.

[81] Much Wenlock is apparently the exception. However, the probate records for that town are very thin.

before 1660, for which less has been transcribed, the pattern is little different, though there are indications that the smaller towns like Wem and Shifnal may have had few fixed shops, with most retail activity being confined to the market.[82]

Turning from Shropshire to other parts of England presents a challenge, because so much less of the probate record has been transcribed. However, for Sussex at least, the distribution of retailing tradesmen as indicated in the rather scrappy probate evidence, fits well with the data in Table 2.1 and presents a very different picture from Shropshire. Although by no means all the probate records for the towns and villages represented in Table 2.1 have been surveyed, let alone transcribed and analysed, there is sufficient to suggest that all market towns had substantial retailing tradesmen but that they were by no means confined to such places. They have been noted at two villages who also had issuers of tokens, but at no less than nine villages for which Table 2.1 provides no other indication of likely retailing activity. Such retailing tradesmen have been noted over a long time span stretching from 1632 until the mid-eighteenth century.[83] Furthermore their shops were comparable with those of mercers, ironmongers and the like found in market towns and quite different from the minimalist tradesmen found occasionally in Shropshire villages. Seven, like William Silverlock of Westbourne (1678), William Lintott of Harting (1710) and William Boxall of Kirdford (1754) were designated with prestigious occupations like mercer or grocer.[84]

For the eighteenth century the diary of Thomas Turner of East Hoathly in Sussex lends support to these findings. He was a shopkeeper from a family of shopkeepers. Details about his education are lacking but he probably served an apprenticeship like his brothers. His papers show a twofold continuity; firstly of his family which remained in the trade from the 1730s at least until the end of the century, and secondly of retail provision in Sussex villages generally. In Framfield, a substantial village, the Turners, father and son, kept a shop over several decades. In East Hoathly, a village with a population of about 350, Turner himself succeeded a mercer and was followed by his own son.[85] His diary is fairly uninformative about retailing activity in surrounding villages, though there are some references including several to a shop at Ninfield which he considered taking over himself, and to George Beard, his former servant and now a shopkeeper in the village of Chailey.[86] Turner's own shop, and the others

---

[82] The whole probate record of Wem has been transcribed and analysed for the period 1535-1660; see Watts (1995), *The small market town*, particularly chapter 7.

[83] 1632 should not be taken as a significant date. The probate records of West Sussex for the period before 1660 are more difficult to search than those of the later period. The retrieval of representative data is thus more uncertain.

[84] All can be located by name, place and date in the calendars at West Sussex RO.

[85] Turner (1984), *Diary*, pp. xvii-xx.

[86] Turner (1984), *Diary*, pp. 327, 111-12.

mentioned in his Diary, all seem to have been relatively substantial general shops comparable with those of some eighteenth-century urban shopkeepers like Henry Norman of Midhurst who died in 1769.[87]

If retailing in Shropshire seems largely to have been confined to the market towns, while in Sussex it flourished in many villages otherwise without any urban characteristics, the evidence from the midlands counties of Derbyshire, Leicestershire, Staffordshire and Warwickshire falls somewhere in between the two extremes. The provision of markets in these four varies considerably, with Warwickshire one of the best endowed in the Midlands, and Derbyshire one of the worst. Yet there is a marked similarity with regard to retailing activity. In each of them the probate record supports evidence from trade tokens that the market towns had retailing shops, but so did some villages with no market. Some of these shops were substantial, like those of William Webb, mercer of Brailsford (1674), Robert Beeley, shopkeeper of Eyam (1752), both of Derbyshire, or Joseph Hyde of Wednesbury (1743) in Staffordshire.[88] None have been noted like the minimalist shops of Shropshire.

The evidence from the North is more equivocal. Lancashire was well endowed, being moderately well furnished with markets and on the evidence of token survival, with a number of places, which supported a retail shop. Only one or two places without a market but with a shop have emerged from the probate records. On the other hand the autobiography of William Stout of Lancaster shows that in the last two decades of the seventeenth century it was not difficult to set up shop. Two of Stout's fellow apprentices set up shop with the assistance of his former master, the one in Cockerham, and the other in Tarporley in Cheshire, while Stout himself was sent, still not out of time, to attend his master's shop at Bolton.[89] The Bolton shop proved unprofitable and was closed; the other two were also apparently unsuccessful and did not survive many years. Whether this was due to the inherent risks of retailing or to the inefficiency of the men involved is not known, though Stout clearly thought it was the latter.

Further north in Westmoreland and Cumberland, the probate records are particularly valuable as they go some way to rectify the deficiencies in the evidence of trading tokens. Most retailing tradesmen appear in market towns, but two, Lancelot Jefferson of Westward (1685) and Anne Hall of Warwickbridge (1670) each lived in a small village close to a market town

---

[87] West Sussex RO. The evidence from Hampshire has not been fully analysed here but it supports the data and Table 2.1 and suggests, like Sussex, Hampshire was well furnished with retailing tradesmen outside the market towns.

[88] All Lichfield Joint RO. Marie Rowlands in her seminal study of Staffordshire in the early modern period reveals little evidence of retail activity outside the larger towns. It is not clear, however, whether she was looking for small and minimalist shops. See Rowlands (1967-68), 'Industry and social change', pp. 37-58.

[89] Stout (1967), *Autobiography*, p. 79 (1682).

(respectively Wigton and Carlisle). Neither were typical village shopkeepers. Jefferson appears to have been more of a merchant (though he may have had a retailing shop as well) whose main interest was iron and who operated in both Wigton and Carlisle as well as from his home. Widow Hall was probably a milliner, though she was not so called, and her small stock of made up clothing, and the haberdashery, trimmings and cloth needed for future work, are not dissimilar to that of another widow, Margaret Justice of Wellington, Shropshire (1685). Presumably her proximity to Carlisle afforded her a ready market.[90] Apart from these two atypical examples no village shopkeepers have been noted, though the market towns were obviously busy centres of retailing trade, at least from 1660 when the evidence becomes more accessible.

Approaching the subject of provision by investigating access to consumer goods rather than numbers of shops and ratio of shops to population suggests that most if not all people had access to a wide choice of goods even if the number of shops was limited. Access undoubtedly increased. Although there were shops in the sixteenth century, there were probably some market towns without. By 1700 and into the eighteenth century, there was probably no town with an active market that did not also have a mercer-type shop, and in some areas, there were many outlets in other settlements.

## The development of select shopping areas

Since at least the Middle Ages the location of certain types of shops in large towns had been based on the idea of the association of like with like. Surviving street names like 'Mercers Street', 'Butchers Row', 'Shoemakers Lane', testify to an arrangement that had served many generations well. Even in the market, regulations by the town authorities often required a similar arrangement. For example, in Whitchurch, Shropshire, an inquest of the manor in 1666 restated the appointed places in the market for the sale of each type of commodity.[91] The Great Fire of London in 1665 gave an opportunity for the City to break away from some of the traditional patterns of retail selling leading to a rearrangement of space. Other towns, such a Warwick after the fire in 1694, which destroyed much of the commercial centre of the town, also rebuilt along new lines, as was Northampton after one in 1675.[92]

---

[90] The Cumberland probate records are in Cumbria RO; that of Margaret Justice at Lichfield Joint RO.

[91] Watts (1995), *Small market town*, p. 297, based on Bridgwater collection 212/446/48.

[92] Borsay (1989), *English urban renaissance*, pp. 18-19, 90-95.

Even into the eighteenth century, and after the development of a modernized City, Defoe thought it necessary to advise young tradesmen to ensure that they set up business in an appropriate area of the town:

> Some, especially retailers, ruin themselves by fixing their shops in such places as are improper for their business. In most towns, but particularly in the city of London, there are places as it were appropriated to particular trades, and where the trades which are placed there succeed very well ... ; as the orange-merchants and wet-salters about Billingsgate, and in Thames Street; the costermongers at the Three Cranes; the wholesale cheesemongers in Thames Street; the mercers and drapers in the high streets, such as Cheapside, Ludgate Hill, Cornhill, Round Court, and Grace-Church Street, &c.[93]

There was, however, a different sort of urban differentiation based on social rather than occupational criteria. As Borsay points out, some towns, such as Exeter, Newcastle upon Tyne, Norwich, Worcester and York, had long been 'socially zoned' with the more prestigious parishes forming a central core.[94] The eighteenth century was an age of civic improvement, intended to enhance the prosperity and comfort of the better off and to enrich the whole community. Many towns benefited from rebuilding, from paving and street lighting, and from the introduction of new amenities like theatres, libraries and assembly rooms as shown in Table 2.2.[95] Such improvements would undoubtedly have led to some exclusion of the less desirable from select areas, if by no other mechanism that that of increased property values and higher rents.

As Table 2.2 shows, the pace of civic improvements quickened during the eighteenth century, but there are signs of it before 1700. The data in Table 2.2 are taken from Borsay's study, which is based inevitably largely on anecdotal evidence. As he himself admits his data were 'the result of combing through a variety of sources, and collecting a number of stray references'.[96] His theme was not retail development so he has not trawled for evidence of élite shops, but whether intentionally or not, civic improvement also created an environment conducive to the pastime of shopping.[97] A feature of some of these improvements was the growth of shopping areas away from the traditional market place, offering a degree of exclusiveness to the social élite. These areas were characterized by pavements, separating the pedestrian from

---

[93] Defoe (1726), *Complete English tradesman*, p. 61.

[94] Borsay (1989), *English urban renaissance*, pp. 294-5.

[95] Borsay (1989), *English urban renaissance*.

[96] Borsay (1989), *English urban renaissance*, p. 355.

[97] There is a good deal of evidence that shopping was seen as a social and leisure activity by some sections of society. This is not to deny that under different circumstances, shopping was a serious activity and part of 'women's work'. See Vickery (1998), *Gentleman's daughter*, pp. 163-5, Barker-Benfield, *Culture of sensibility*, pp. 156-9.

the hazards of the street itself, and by street lights, extending shopping opportunities and romanticizing the scene with reflections and sparkle. A new dimension was thus introduced into town planning, if that is not too strong a phrase to describe what happened in a piecemeal and unplanned way. Two distinct, but not mutually exclusive, retailing patterns emerge, the one with the

**Table 2.2**
**The development of amenities in selected towns**

| Town | Theatre | Musical performances | Assemblies | Gardens or walks |
|------|---------|---------------------|------------|------------------|
| **North** | | | | |
| Carlisle | | | | |
| Kendal | | | | |
| Liverpool | Yes | | 1726 | By 1750 |
| Manchester | c. 1753 | 1744 | Early C18 | |
| Preston | By 1750 | | 1682 | 1680s |
| Warrington | | | | |
| Whitehaven | 1769 | | 1736 | |
| | | | | |
| **Midlands** | | | | |
| Birmingham | 1740 | 1720s | 1703 | Mid C18 |
| Coventry | | 1740s | Mid C18 | 1697 |
| Derby | | | Early C18 | |
| Leicester | | | 1747 | |
| Lichfield | 1736 | By 1742 | 1733 | |
| Matlock | | | 1757 | |
| Shrewsbury | | 1720 | Early C18 | By 1698 |
| Stratford | | | 1755 | |
| Warwick | | | Early C18 | |
| | | | | |
| **South** | | | | |
| Chichester | | | | 1689 |
| Lewes | | | 1738 | |
| Portsmouth | c. 1750 | | | |
| Southampton | 1765-66 'new' | | 1767 | |
| Winchester | | 1703 | Early C18 | Late C17 |

*Source*: Borsay (1989), *English urban renaissance*, Appendices 3-6, pp. 329-54.

**2.1** Shops in the Strand, London, *c*. 1750. The difference between Figure 2.1 and Figure 2.2 (facing) is marked. In the view of Cheapside in the 1750s, pedestrians are separated from the carriageway only by bollards, which will give protection from traffic, but none from mud and wet, and shops are identified by substantial hanging signs (a practice declared illegal in 1762). In the second, a pavement has been built for pedestrians, the shops, though not the whole street, are lit and the shop windows are of lighter structure and better adapted to display.

**2.2**  Shops in the Strand, London, *c.* 1790

shops clustered round the market, the other with a pattern of streets where those shops selling wares likely to attract an élite were generally located together. Such shopping areas designed to fit particular social desiderata became more common.

Finding the right area to match the social aspirations of the envisaged clientele was important for an tradesman setting up his business, particularly in London where the Great Fire of 1666 had upset established patterns of retail trade and made available a huge swathe of land for redevelopment - a process that continued apace into the eighteenth century. As fashionable London extended westwards, areas only slightly less desirable socially were developed farther east. Two eighteenth-century entrepreneurs, Josiah Wedgwood, the manufacturer of fine china and earthenware, and the tailor Francis Place, each wrote at some length about the selection of area for their respective enterprises. Each indicates that social considerations were at least as important as commercial ones. In a letter to his partner before the opening of their second London showrooms in 1767, Wedgwood dismissed Pall Mall as 'too accessible to the common Folk ... for as you know that my present Sett of Customers will not mix with the Rest of the World'.[98] Eventually he settled for the corner of Newport Street and St Martin's Lane. Although planning to attract what was a rather less select clientele, Francis Place also demonstrated the same concern. He described how in 1795 he decided to take the plunge, to leave the safety of a journeyman's job and to set up his own business in partnership with a Mr Wild. His wife, he wrote some thirty years later in his autobiography, had 'found two or three shops in streets which ran into Holburn, from the window of any one of which she thought I could scarcely fail to sell as much as would pay the rent and perhaps to something more, but my ambition had risen considerably and I no longer contemplated a shop in a bye street. I now looked forward a shop in a principal thorough fare or in a street of good name where a large quantity of business might be done'.[99] Six years later in 1801, with the partnership in tatters and himself near to financial ruin, Place set up on his own. Again his chief concern was the selection of a good area and the implications of failure to do so. 'The customers I had before we came to Charing Cross had all left us, and our new customers were gentlemen who would not deal with a man in a garrett, and even if any of them shold be disposed to do so, the having left a good shop and gone into poverty would be conclusive evidence that he was a rogue'.[100]

Evidence concerning fashionable shops outside London is more difficult to come by. Most commentators like Defoe or Campbell focused on the

---

[98] Wedgwood Museum MSS, E.18149-25, quoted by Adburgham (1979), *Shopping in style*, p. 64.
[99] *Autobiography of Francis Place*, vol. II, p. 56.
[100] *Autobiography of Francis Place*, vol. II, p. 108.

metropolis,[101] while diaries or correspondence from provincial retailers comparable with those of Place or of Wedgwood have not emerged. To some extent their place is taken by descriptions of fashionable resorts given by travellers. One of the most informative for the later eighteenth century was written by Johanna Schopenhauer. Her tour of England and Scotland in the 1790s shows how extensively London practices had spread to the fashionable resorts a hundred miles and more from the capital. The spa town of Buxton, for example, had a magnificent crescent with the 'appearance of one single fine building, with some three hundred windows in its facade. The ground floors contain elegant shops, some lending libraries ... and a few coffee shops, while a covered columned walk protects the strollers from the rain which is so common here'. Other towns inspired similar comments. Cheltenham's single main street had 'elegant houses, handsome shops, lending libraries and coffee shops', Bath showed 'all that luxury and comfort can invent ... on display behind the glass windows of the beautiful shops', and Brighton was the place for 'elegant little shops where London merchants sell their prettiest and most exclusive fashions'.[102]

While offering no survey of the distribution of such shops over the country as a whole, Schopenhauer did provide a number of vignettes of fashionable provincial shopping areas. The more exhaustive travelogues of Fiennes and Defoe, written towards the beginning of what Borsay terms the Urban Renaissance might be expected to be more informative. Unfortunately their eyes were focused elsewhere so that their references to retail provision were neither frequent nor systematic. Fiennes commented on the Exeter Exchange, which was 'full of shops like our [London] Exchanges are'. Other shopping facilities only won a comment in relation to fashionable spa town, like Epsom, where shops selling 'sweetmeates and fruite' and millinery and china could be found, and Tunbridge Wells with 'a row of buildings on the right side which are shopps full of all sorts of toys, silver, china, milliners and all sorts of curious wooden ware'.[103] Defoe is even less informative apart from on Warrington, which was 'full of good country tradesmen'.[104]

The terminology used by Defoe is nevertheless useful as his occasional comments illuminate phrases used elsewhere. In several places he seems to imply that gentry and trade do not mix. For example, Derby was 'a town of gentry rather than trade, Chichester was 'full of gentleness families, and Lewes 'of gentlemen of good families and fortunes.[105] What he meant by 'a town of gentry rather than trade', may be explained by his entry for York, where 'is no

[101] Defoe (1726), *Complete English tradesman*; Campbell (1747), *London tradesman*.

[102] Schopenhauer (1988), *A lady's travels*, pp. 34, 105, 118, 130.

[103] Fiennes (1984), *Illustrated journeys*, pp. 238 and 126.

[104] Defoe (1724-27), *Tour*, vol. III, p. 138.

[105] Defoe (1724-27), *Tour*, vol. III, p. 29; *Tour*, vol. I, pp. 149, 146.

trade indeed, except such as depends on the confluence of the gentry'.[106] Here
he seems almost to be assuming that the gentry generated a particular sort of
trade appropriate to their requirements. Elsewhere he seems to associate the
gentry with those urban improvements that were conducive to cultural and
social activities. Winchester 'had its share of mirth' and 'the abundance of
gentry being in the neighbourhood, it adds to the sociableness of the place',
while Shrewsbury was 'a beautiful large, pleasant, populous and rich town; full
of gentry and yet full of trade too'. It was also 'full of mirth and gallantry' and
according to Defoe's contemporary 'with the most coffee houses round it that
ever I saw in any town', most apparently of poor quality but there
nonetheless.[107]

It would seem then that Defoe rather sporadically attempted a social
classification of towns in which the phrase 'full of gentry' may have been a
shorthand code intended to include social facilities and appropriate retail
outlets. If so his work suggests that what Schopenhauer described in the 1790s
had its beginnings a long time before, albeit only in a few provincial towns.
Blome in his descriptions of English towns published in 1673 was much more
systematic than Defoe but he seems to have used much the same code and
seems also to be identifying improved towns, perhaps with improved shopping
facilities. Although he never laid out a plan as such he seems to have identified
five categories of town from the terms he used.[108] Blome described the majority
of towns with adjectives such as 'indifferent' or 'mean'. Others he
distinguished only by their 'good market'. He can hardly have made it more
plain that towns thus described were not likely to attract fashionable shoppers,
though they may have attracted many people in from the countryside on market
days. Of other towns he recorded cultural advantages like libraries, schools and
the like, or administrative facilities such as Assize Courts, borough and city
councils, or cathedrals. Although these would have attracted professionals and
hence probably some additional crafts and shops, it would seem that on their
own they were not likely to have had fashionable shopping areas of the sort
already described. A fourth group of towns he distinguished by the quality of
their buildings and streets by such terms as 'fair', 'well built', 'open' and 'well
ordered streets'. Although a few of these, like Lancaster, were 'not much
frequented, nor inhabited by Tradesmen, but chiefly by Husbandmen', Blome
implied, if not actually stated, that most of the towns in this group were centres
of a thriving retail trade, albeit not of a fashionable sort. If that had been
Blome's highest praise, it could be concluded that in the 1670s there were not
yet any fashionable shopping centres outside London.

---

[106] Defoe (1724-27), *Tour*, vol. III, p. 109.

[107] Defoe (1724-27), *Tour*, vol. I, pp. 20, 203; *Tour*, vol. II, pp. 213, 214; Macky
(1722), *Journey through England*, vol. II, p. 140.

[108] Blome (1673), *Britannia*.

However, Blome reserved his highest encomiums for just a few towns, for which he reserved the phrases 'well inhabited and frequented' and, best of all, much 'frequented by gentry'. It goes without saying that he also deemed these towns physically attractive, like the fourth group. It is suggested that Blome was using these terms in the same way as Defoe was later to do and that in these towns, or at least some of them, there were already some of the requirements for a new style of shopping, such as a select, exclusive area and an attractive environment.

In the 1670s Blome found very few fashionable towns in the two southern counties of Hampshire and Sussex. Brighton was still small, 'ill-built' and its 'inhabitants chiefly Fishermen'. Only Lewes received high praise 'for fairness of buildings and streets, populousness of Inhabitants, both of gentry and Trades-men'. It was, Blome considered, 'one of the best towns in the Country'. The description of Chichester began well, but it becomes clear that most of the retailing sector was round the market place and thus hardly a possible venue for the fashionable to shop in comfort. In Hampshire, Blome regarded Southampton and Portsmouth as too maritime to rate highly, and only Winchester and perhaps Newport on the Isle of Wight would have had any attraction to the socially élite looking for a good shopping area. A foreign visitor touring England in 1661-63 provides some corrective to Blome's unfavourable view of seaports. William Schellinks wrote of Portsmouth having a 'very fine long street full of shops'.[109] Unfortunately Hampshire is the only county he visited under particular review in this study. Apart from his more favourable report on Portsmouth, his comments are otherwise similar to those of Blome and support the accuracy of his descriptions.

The western Midlands were better served, and here he used more ecstatic terms, though the entry for Birmingham was somewhat ambivalent. It was a 'large and well built town, very populous and much resorted unto'; a phrase with slightly different overtones from his usual way of describing a fashionable town. Two cities in the region stand out; Shrewsbury 'for ... neatness of buildings, both public and private, largeness (and variety) of streets and in populousness may be ranged in the number of cities in the first rank', while Derby had 'few inland towns equalling it'. Lichfield's streets were 'kept sweet and well-ordered', while Wolverhampton, had 'streets handsomely paved and the houses reasonably well built'; both were 'much frequented by the gentry'. Stafford streets were also 'paved and well ordered' so that it was 'well inhabited and frequented'. Coventry was a 'fair, neat and large city ... beautified with good buildings, and well ordered streets' and 'more than ordinarily frequented and inhabited'. Midland gentry thus probably had

[109] Exwood and Lehmann (trans. and eds) (1993), *Journal of William Schellinks' travels*, p. 145.

relatively easy access to superior shopping facilities, at least so far as the environment was concerned. Only Leicestershire was ill-served.

Of the 50 market towns Blome surveyed in the North-west, most were in the lowest category, but for a surprising number there are indications of the development of select shopping facilities. Although Liverpool suffered the same disadvantages as Portsmouth and Southampton, other towns were viewed by Blome in a more favourable light. Carlisle was 'fair, its houses well built ... a place of good trade' and 'well inhabited'; Kendal was 'very fair, large, well built, inhabited and frequented'; Manchester 'a large, beautiful and well inhabited town much resorted to', Warrington 'a very fine and large town'; while Preston was 'a great, fair, and well inhabited and frequented Borough town ...[with] a very large Market place, and the other streets ... very open, large and evenly paved, and the houses well built'.

If this interpretation of Blome's descriptions is correct, then by the 1670s the prerequisites for a select shopping area away from the market, such as wide paved streets, modern buildings and good cultural and leisure facilities were to be found in a sprinkling of large and middling sized towns, particularly in the Midlands, but also in the North-west and to a less extent along the south coast. Some may even have had some shops designed for the élite away from the market place. Possibly there were even some towns improved to such a degree that shopping could become part of the social round. However, Blome intended to give an accurate description of all towns, and for him this apparently meant viewing them as centres of a trade based on the market. He focused therefore on those factors that contributed to success in this context and it is only almost incidentally that he referred to developments heralding a new style of shops positioned in streets away from the market place, an environment attractive to the gentry trade. For this reason the existence of élite shopping streets before 1700 must remain a matter of speculation.


## Conclusion

A full study of the distribution of shops and of access to consumer goods still needs to be written. This chapter has done no more than to suggest some ways of tackling the subject and to reach three tentative conclusions.

First, the pattern of retail provision was uniform over the country neither in concentration nor in how it related to other identified urban characteristics such as the presence of a market and the size of population. The pattern is complex, and the different approaches give somewhat conflicting results, but they challenge to some extent the conclusions of Mui and Mui in their study of eighteenth century. Their findings concerning the number of shops in 1759 indicate that the further away from London, the poorer was retail provision.

Abstracting data only for the counties selected in this study, Mui and Mui found in Hampshire and West Sussex there was roughly one retail outlet to every 35 people, in Shropshire, Staffordshire, Derbyshire and Warwickshire one to 45, and in Cumberland, Westmoreland and Lancashire one to 75. Using other approaches this conclusion becomes less firm. Secondly, consumer goods were available nation-wide throughout the whole early modern period, though before 1600 a less well-developed retail sector may have reduced opportunities for some. Thirdly, by the late seventeenth century, the urban renaissance had provided the foundation for the establishment of provincial shopping areas serving a social élite. By the end of the eighteenth century, there were a number of towns with such areas. It is now time to turn to the shop itself, its design, structure and mode of operation.

## Chapter 3

# 'Their shops are Dens, the buyer is their prey':[1] shop design and sale techniques

*Nancy Cox and Claire Walsh*

For the eighteenth century there is a range of sources through which to study the interface between shopkeeper and customer. Personal diaries, account books and novels, provide insights into contemporary perceptions of shopping and into the relationship between shopkeeper and shopper as seen from the public's side of the counter. Surviving tradesmen's account books, covering a variety of trades and a range of social contexts, present the retailer's side, while several autobiographical works flesh out the bare bones of the records of sale and credit. Such sources encapsulate individual and personal experiences, but contextualization for these sources can be found in several ways. A few eighteenth-century topographical prints and townscapes of fashionable shopping streets furnish useful evidence of former practice. Newspaper advertisements surviving in their thousands, and many bill heads and trade cards offer opportunities for a different sort of analysis from the more personal records. One of the most valuable sources is the probate records of tradesmen, especially the inventories of their stock and equipment, although the number of inventories taken after 1720 fell, particularly in the South-east, and after 1750 dropped almost to nothing over the country as a whole.

Fewer sources survive for the period before 1700. Not many newspapers and their advertisements exist, and trade cards and bill heads were either more limited or have not survived in quantity. Shopkeepers' business records likewise survive only in limited numbers. By contrast, probate inventories are actually more informative for the seventeenth century than for the eighteenth, and they remain almost the only source covering the whole period back to 1550. Despite this scarcity of sources, it is possible to provide a broad outline of retailing in the sixteenth and seventeenth centuries, even if detail is lacking.

---

[1]    Dryden (1682), *The medall*, p. 192.

Retail histories of the early modern period have tended to stress the use of shop premises for production at the expense of examining the processes of selling and of enticing customers. While many shops in the period were sites of making and/or of preparing goods, this does not mean that they may not also have been carefully constructed for the task of selling. Indeed, a reference in the *Oxford English Dictionary* to the use of a shop as 'a building or room set apart for the sale of merchandize' rather than as a workshop for the preparation of goods, appears as early as the fourteenth century.[2] An examination of this interface between retailer and customer seeks to understand the different ways retailers used the space they dedicated to sales. Retailers could manipulate this space in a variety of ways; they could speed up the process of selling and make it more effective, or they could attract customers and display wares attractively.

## Selling through the window

It is likely that in the early modern period most fixed retail shops were constructed from the front room of a residential house. Those at ground floor level would have had the most immediate appeal to customers, but in busy towns shops would have been established on upper floors of buildings as well. For ground floor shops it would not have been difficult to enlarge a domestic window to signal retail trading, and early photographs of village shops show that this was the key structural change which marked out the shop from domestic houses, rather than the use of signs or fascia boards.[3] Reminiscences from the twentieth century show how easy it could be; 'my wife caught the craze for shop keeping, so I made a counter and shelves and our front room was a shop'; 'most of the selling was done in houses that had converted their front rooms into shops'.[4] In the sixteenth and seventeenth centuries shops could also take the form of semi-permanent wooden structures, often propped up against permanent buildings, though many of these were cleared away in the course of

---

[2] 'Marchaundes ... Bi-Souȝten him in heore schoppe to sullen heore ware', Langland (1362), *Piers ploughman*, ii, 189. Keene (1990), *Shops and shopping*, p. 31, gives instances of the use of the term 'shop' well before the earliest example in the *OED*, but he does not discuss the distinction between the two meanings of the word, except to suggest, like the *OED*, that the root has links with words meaning 'shed'. He does, however, note a use of the term 'sceoppa' to denote the Temple Treasury in a translation of Luke's Gospel into *Old English,* in a context where the exchange of money was a key element in the building's function.

[3] For example, see the photographs in Brown and Ward (1990), *Village shop.*

[4] Coombes (1930), 'Those poor hands', quoted by Benson (1983), *Penny capitàlists,* p. 114-15.

urban improvements in the eighteenth and nineteenth centuries when retailing from fixed shops increasingly became the norm.[5]

In the sixteenth century many small shops might have been of a simple form, with selling taking place on a board or counter let down in front of an opening in a wall or from the front of a wooden bulk. Shops of this type would have been cheap and easy to set up and secure when closed for the night. Such shops are possibly represented in probate inventories such as that of Richard Fitzherbert, a haberdasher of Coventry, who died in 1580. His shop had a desk in the window, vallans, shelves and canvas, and four great chests. His stock, though of good quality, was minimal and could easily have fitted in quite a small room.[6]

The unglazed shop window could be used in different ways. Particularly for smaller shops, the open window was an important area for transacting sales and through it, the retailer could sell directly to customers on the street. In the parlance of the time, to close the window was to close the shop. For example, draft rules for the Barber Surgeons drawn up in 1529 ordered that 'no persone presume to opyn his Shoppe wyndowes before he hath presented hymself to & before the Maysters or Gouerners of the sayde mystere for the tyme being', while in 1646-47 the Borough of Nottingham ordered 'The shopp windowes of all persons that trade in this Towne whoe are not sworn burgesses shallbee forthwith shutt vpp'.[7] An Ordinance of 1647 'concerning days of Recreation' ordained that on those days 'all Windowes of Shops, Ware-houses, and other Places, where Wares or Commodities are usually sold, shall be kept shut up'.[8] These examples discuss the opening and shutting of the shop, for which even today, 'putting up the shutters' is a recognized term, though probably it was trading through the window at issue. However, the several acts regulating the rebuilding of London after the Great Fire of 1666 were more explicit. Encroachment onto the street was prohibited 'save only that in the high and principal streets it shall be lawful for the Inhabitants to suffer their Stall-boards (when their Shop-Windows are set open) to turn over and extend eleven Inches and no more ... for the better conveniency of their Shop-windows.'[9]

Shopkeepers in the sixteenth and seventeenth centuries used the shop window in a way which clearly related their enterprise to the traditional

---

[5]   For example, Warwick was not merely rebuilt, but redesigned after the great fire of 1694, see Borsay (1989), *English urban renaissance*, p. vii. See also Stout (1967), *Autobiography*, pp. 220-21 for rebuilding in Lancaster in 1737.

[6]   Lichfield Joint RO.

[7]   1529 'Barber-Surg. Draft Rules 13', in Vicary, T., *A profitable treatise of the anatomie of mans body*, 1548 (1577, E.E.T.S., (1888), p. 254); 1646-47 *Records of the Borough of Nottingham, 1155-1760*, vol. V, p. 248. These two references are each taken from the *OED*.

[8]   *Acts and ordinances*, 28 June 1647.

[9]   19 CAR2 c. 3 sect. 14 (1667).

technique of selling from a market stall. Setting up a trestle board or stall board in front of the shop or the shop window, lowering a flap from the window to provide an immediate display and selling area, or simply using the window ledge as a point of exchange, were ways for shopkeepers to compete with the immediacy of the market and the array of pedlars and local produce sellers who lined the streets. Probate inventories of retail shops from all over the country confirm the ubiquity of stalls used in conjunction with the shop. For example, Robert Ellis, a mercer of Oxford (1597) had 'two stall cloths'; John Couldham, a linen draper of Great Yarmouth (1613) 'two tilts and an old stall' apart from extensive wares in his 'shop'; William Gilly of Bury St Edmunds (1716) with a shop stuffed full of pewter had also 'stall stuff[10] and tilt'; and Thomas Boyle, pinmaker of London had 'two stall grates a stall board a sign & sign Irons' worth £3, as well as two shops.[11]

Although glass manufacture had begun in England in 1557, domestic glazing was adopted only slowly before 1700. Shops in key shopping streets in London seized upon improvements in glass technology during the latter half of the seventeenth century to glaze their windows, thus keeping up with domestic fashions despite the expense.[12] However, probate inventories of provincial shopkeepers in which items of window furniture appropriate to unglazed frames, such as lattices, were recorded and valued, suggest that many shopkeepers outside the capital chose not to follow this trend immediately. They may have been discouraged by the cost, or may have been less driven by competition than London shopkeepers. Particularly for small shopkeepers selling through the window, this may have been an effective mechanism which they were reluctant to abandon. An oil painting of East Street, Chichester, in 1815, reveals an unglazed butcher's shop with joints of meat displayed in the window next to other shops that were glazed.[13] Even in London, certain trades chose not to enclose well into the nineteenth century, despite the fact that the technology of glass manufacture had put panes of glass within the reach of the most humble shopkeepers.[14] Some butchers' shops were apparently still unglazed in the 1860s.[15] The use of open windows at such a late date may

---

[10] Probably in this instance, 'stuff' in the sense of 'appurtenances', 'apparatus', though it may mean 'fabric draped for display'.

[11] Respectively Oxford RO, MS WILLS Oxon 164/4/3; Norwich RO, INV 26/252; ibid., 73/111; Corporation of London RO, Orphans inventories, 3107.

[12] Rees (1819-20), *Manufacturing industry*, vol. 3, p. 80; Trinder (1992), *Industrial archaeology*, p. 302.

[13] *East Street Chichester 1815*, a painting by Joseph Francis Gilber in West Sussex County Archives.

[14] For example, plate glass was made in this country from 1773, see Trinder (1992), *Industrial archaeology*, p. 302.

[15] For example, the watercolour by J.L. Stewart (*c.* 1860) of 76, Aldgate High Street, London, shows the unglazed windows of the butcher's shop of J.W. Archer and Hickinbotham. [Guildhall Library collection, no. 284].

reflect traditional associations of hygiene with fresh air, or simply more conservative approaches in certain retail trades. Certainly the tradition of the open shop window was long and well established.

The display of goods in the shop window was an obvious method of attracting customers' attention and signalling that a shop was open and trading. The frequent early references to 'shop windows' in probate inventories confirm they were an important tool for shopkeepers. For example, in 1671 the appraisers of the personal estate of Richard Butler, a woollen draper of Basingstoke, Hants., recorded that he had 'rowles of Cloth at window'.[16] In 1668 Sylvester Widmere the elder, mercer of Marlow, Bucks. had in his shop '5 Wyer grates to the Windows' and '8 Shuttings to the Windows'[17] and Joshua

**3.1** Lattice window. A lattice window similar to those referred to in the text, in this case apparently to protect the interior from interference by those outside.

---

[16] PRO, PROB 4/21215. The cloth will have been draped for display.

[17] Reed (1988), *Buckinghamshire probate*, p. 23.

Johnson, mercer of Wellington, Shropshire, had '2 lettices for ye Shop windows' in 1695. Valued at 12s. they must have been substantial pieces of equipment.[18] Clearly these windows were unglazed and the lattices and grates may have been used to protect the stock inside the shop while the shutters were open, or to hang wares upon so that they could be viewed by passing customers. A watchmaker used a lattice when he opened his new shop in Exeter High Street in 1814, though this time behind a glazed door.

'small as the front was, some ingenuity was required to extend my small stock over that small surface ... I made use of the door to gain, apparently, more frontage, by covering it on the inside with green wire lattice, on which I exhibited my spoons and other small silver articles'. [19]

In the sixteenth and seventeenth centuries, even without the availability of glass to enclose the window the display of wares using a lattice would have been possible and desirable, though only during the hours when the shutters were open.

Other evidence confirms the importance of sales through the shop window. The Lancaster shopkeeper, William Stout, described how, during the exceptionally hard frost of 1683, he 'attended the shop in winter with the window open, without sash or screen till nine in the evening, and with the windows shut and the dore open till ten a'clock without coming into the house except to our victuals or to the fire ...'.[20] The Customer Ledger of William Wood of Didsbury, Lancashire, (1786-91) indicates that the window continued to be used for selling throughout the period. Wood mainly recorded his credit sales, entering each item in the customer's own section.[21] However, this practice was largely abandoned in his last year of life. Instead he distinguished two types of sale, 'bill out of shop' and 'goods out of window'.[22] While quantitative evidence is hard to obtain, the ease of construction, cheapness, immediacy and relationship to the tradition of the stall, would suggest that selling through the window remained a common retail technique throughout the early modern period.

The benefit of selling directly through the window was that sales could be concluded quickly and thus turnover could be high. This was appropriate when customers did not need to spend much time selecting goods, or when the

---

[18] Lichfield Joint RO.
[19] Ellis, 263 High Street, Exeter opened May 1814, Ponsford (1978), *Time in Exeter*, p. 130.
[20] Stout (1967), *Autobiography*, p. 80.
[21] Wood's Customers Ledger (1786-91).
[22] Noted by Mui and Mui (1989), *Shops and shopkeeping*, p. 211, but they miss the significance of the distinction.

**3.2** Selling through the open window. Although Rowlandson's print is intended as a satirical attack on electoral practices, he would not have used the image of a shop selling through the open window if that were not still a recognizable feature of London in the 1780s.

retailer only had a limited range of wares for sale. Selling through the window had advantages for the shopkeeper over the trader selling from the market stall. The shopkeeper could have reserves of stock to call upon in the shop behind him and the opportunity to prepare or to organize stock when there were no customers. Shopkeeper and stock were better protected from the weather and the flow of business past the window was not hindered if there were numerous customers. As opposed to glazed shops, which needed to encourage customers to go inside, it was easier to capture those passers-by who preferred not to enter the shop. They could also decide quickly whether or not they were interested in buying and examine goods by natural light.

## Cash sales

It seems likely that many sales made directly through the window were for small quantities ready packaged, and that the possibilities of negotiation between customer and retailer were more limited than selling from within the shop. For these reasons and because the transaction was completed quickly, it is probable that most sales made through the shop window were for cash and involved goods at fixed prices. Providing small quantities and ensuring there was sufficient small change produced some problems for the retailer. One solution was to use trade tokens as an alternative to coinage, and surviving tokens from the mid-seventeenth century suggest that much was sold in units of ½d. or ¼d.[23] With little opportunity for display beyond what could be seen in the window, choice for the customer must have been limited, but the flow of trade swift. Stout's comments already noted on packing goods for market day, may indicate what was most commonly sold in this way, that is sugar, tobacco, small hard ware and dried fruit. Occasional entries in retailers' probate inventories also hint at ready packed goods for sale, though the rarity of such entries should not be taken to reflect a rarity of such packaging. From the appraisers' point of view it was easier to enter, say, '4 lb. ginger' than '64 one ounce papers of ginger'. Even so certain items, particularly pins and nails were not infrequently listed as packaged in small lots as if for sale like the '26 papers yellow & wt Nayles ijd paper' of John Ballard of Bewdley in Worcestershire in 1676.[24] Other commodities ready packaged include the 'odd papers w'th peper in' in the shop of the Macclesfield mercer James Oldfield in 1634 and some 70 lb. of 'Tobacco in papers' at 10d. and 8d. per lb. belonging to William

---

[23]  Williamson (1967), *Trade Tokens*. Tokens for ¼d. and ½d. are common, while those worth as much as 2d. are rare.

[24]  Hereford RO, AA20 Box 65.

Hockenhall of Newcastle under Lyme in 1733.[25] In fact the goods listed as already weighed and packaged are much the same as those mentioned by Stout.

## The concept of an open market

The long standing practice of selling through the shop window was probably supported by ideas developed by the Church in the Middle Ages to establish an ethic of trade. Central to this was the concept of a just price 'that the buyer was willing to pay and the seller was willing to accept'.[26] In this definition the just price appears to represent little more than the current price fixed in a free market, but the Church also accepted that when the just price was severely abused by fraud or misrepresentation, either the buyer or the seller should have remedy in the civil courts.[27] Furthermore, following Roman Law the canonists developed a doctrine of the unjust price by which one party to the deal took advantage of weakness or necessity on the part of the other. They therefore condemned such practices as monopoly or artificial price-fixing, forestalling, regrating and engrossing.[28] Perhaps rather illogically, canonists included in the doctrine of the just price, control by a competent authority, whether the municipality or the state.[29] Parliament adopted these ideas, regulating some prices,[30] and enacting that most retail sale took place only in the open market where onlookers could challenge abuse.[31] Although Parliament was primarily concerned about the loss of revenue from illicit sales in unauthorized places, the phraseology reflects a genuine distaste for sale beyond the public gaze typified by the Act of 1553 to 'avoid the great Prices and Excess of Wines', which refers to 'Many Taverns of late newly set up in very great Numbers in Back-lanes, Corners and suspicious Places'.[32] On the other side of the coin, when attempting to regulate the production of wax, Parliament exempted from the terms of an Act of 1581 all those 'selling the Wax of their own Bees in open Markets ...',[33] implicitly acknowledging that such selling practices were sufficient protection in themselves against fraud. Perhaps the clearest

---

[25] Respectively Chester RO, WS 1635 and Lichfield Joint RO.

[26] Brundage (1995), *Medieval canon law*, pp. 75-6, 237-8.

[27] Gilchrist (1969), *Church and economic activity*, p. 59.

[28] Gilchrist (1969), *Church and economic activity*, p. 61.

[29] Gilchrist (1969), *Church and economic activity*, p. 59.

[30] For example, 21 HEN8 c. 9 (1529), caps; 28 HEN8 c. 14 (1536), wine. The price of staples like bread and beer were controlled throughout the period.

[31] Acts requiring sale in the open market only include 6 HEN8 c. 9 sect. 3 (1514), coloured wool and yarn; 13 & 14 CAR2 c. 7 (1662), red tanned leather. There are many more when it is implied, for example, 11 HEN7 c. 19 (1495), upholstery; 19 HEN7 c. 6 (1503), pewter.

[32] 7 EDW6 c. 5 (1553).

[33] 23 ELIZ c. 8 (1581).

expression of Parliament's preference for shops and markets open to public scrutiny, lies in the Act for rebuilding London after the Great Fire of 1666. This categorized streets into four types, but shops were apparently expected only in the 'high and principal streets', and not in the 'By lanes' or 'streets and Lanes of Note',[34] presumably because these were not open to public scrutiny.

This attitude to retail sale was not conducive to the establishments of glazed shops or those engaged in interior sales, since any sale in them would have taken place as it were behind closed doors and without witnesses. However the undoubted advantages of sale on the premises could not be gainsaid. There was added security against theft and the wares were better protected against the onslaughts of weather. Sale through the shop window was thus a compromise in that it allowed for the purchaser to stand outside in a public thoroughfare where the transaction could be witnessed by passers-by, but it afforded the retailer all the advantages of fixed premises at the point of sale.

The use of open shop windows as a sales method makes sense in the context of the clustering of retail shops round the market place in market towns that was observed in chapter 2. The shop windows opened out not just onto a public thoroughfare, but onto the market place itself, so that sales could take place in the market with all the protection to the customers that this was supposed to afford. This made the shopkeepers' position reputable in the eyes of authority, while also giving them access to customers attracted into town by the market. Throughout his *Autobiography*, William Stout of Lancaster stressed the importance of market days to his trade. So under 1682 he wrote that he was 'mostly imployed in the shop in the weekdays, in making up goods for the market day, as sugar, tobacco, nayls and other goods, and particularly prunes', and again in 1688 'My sister came ... on the market days - and was as ready in serving retaile customers as a young apprintice could have done'. That he was not unique is also clear; for example, his neighbour Thomas Green had a second shop in Kendal 'which he attended evry market day there'.[35] Roger Lowe, another seventeenth-century shopkeeper in Lancashire, makes the same point about the importance of such opportunities for intermittent sale, though for him it was apparently a fair not a market that was good for his business. 'being Warrington faire, he wrote, 'I kept shop all day'.[36]

### Varieties of selling and complex shops

While shops selling to customers directly through the window must have been very common in the early modern period, both because of their easy

---

[34] 19 CAR2 c. 3 sect. 14 (1667).
[35] Stout (1967), *Autobiography*, pp. 79, 90, 143.
[36] Lowe (1968), *Diary*, p. 48.

**3.3** London shops in 1736

construction and because of their potential for fast selling, other types of shop serving customers from inside the shop existed, though this could take different forms. A topographical print of Bishopsgate in 1736 depicts a range of shops using different sales methods. In the centre of the print, a fully glazed shop with an elaborate fascia board is represented, which would have provided customers with a secluded environment away from the social mix of the street. Here customers would probably have expected attentive service and would have been allowed the time to make decisions about purchasing. In contrast, at the unglazed butcher's shop preparation, and probably also the sale, of meat is shown carried out on the street in front of the shop. On the left is depicted what appears to be an open food shop in which sales are negotiated over a counter but with a limited space provided for customers. Here there is no room to browse or to examine merchandise, and the assistant would not have come from behind the counter to attend to them. This structure of shop would have been ideal for rapid sales, rather like a modern fish and chip shop, with little opportunity for display and selection. Presumably sales were by cash only.

This print points to different approaches to selling in different outlets and to their co-existence. Small shops must have predominated, but even in the sixteenth century, complex premises within a single establishment also existed. It would have been easy for a successful retailer with a single-room shop to expand into another room, like the Tamworth mercer, William Allen (1604), who had a shop and a nether shop.[37] Mercers' shops had long been amongst the most important in any town, and Keene points to the large scale of these 'great shops' in London during the medieval period, ranging from one room to many.[38] Evidence for big shops in the provinces also survives in probate inventories. For example, John Moyseley, a mercer of Coventry, Warks. (1545) had a hall, kitchen and shop, and a chamber over. His goods were divided into wares and grocery. The premises of the Hampshire tradesman, John Beald, (1587) appear to have extended back from the shop through a hall and a kitchen, each with its own parlour off. Above there was a chamber over the shop, and another over one of the parlours. It seems at least possible that the shop itself was as wide as the hall and parlour combined since it contained stock that took ten pages to itemize. It was truly a large shop if not a particularly complicated one in terms of its premises.[39]

For shops concentrating on selling inside, the shopkeeper's counter was an important focus for the selling process and there are illustrations of its use

---

[37] Lichfield Joint RO.
[38] Keene (1990), 'Shops and shopping in medieval London', pp. 42-3.
[39] Respectively Lichfield Joint RO and Winchester RO, 1568A 8/2.

dating from the mid-fifteenth century and beyond.[40] Probate inventories, so vital as evidence for some shop practices, are a challenging source for use in plotting the development of selling over the counter. There are two reasons for this. Firstly, some counters (as the term is most commonly used today) may have been fixtures and so not recorded at all. Secondly, although many counters were listed in the early modern period, by no means all records refer to a table or board over which sales were made. This is because the primary meanings of the term 'counter' all relate to the activity of counting money; a counter may be either a small disc used in counting operations, or a devise like an abacus to assist in counting, or a table on which money is counted. Although counters in the first sense are easily distinguished from counters in the modern sense, the other two are not. Randle Holme provided an engraving of a counter in the sense of a table for counting in the mid-seventeenth century in his illustrated book of objects appropriate for armorial bearings.[41] It is used in many inventories in this sense, particularly before 1700. For example, Elizabeth Hurt, a mercer's widow of Coventry (1578), had a counter table in the great parlour and Richard Maries, feltmaker of Norwich (1590), had a counter valued at 4s. in the Parlour Chamber.[42] In neither of these cases can there be much doubt of the meaning of the term, but there are many others for which interpretation is less easy. John Shearman, a London trader specializing in linens (1723) had counters in both the Counting House and the Shop. Whereas the one was almost certainly for dealing with money, the other could have served either in the same way or as a table over which goods were sold.[43] The extensive furniture listed in the shop of the Shropshire mercer Joshua Johnson of Wellington (1695) conveys similar ambiguities. In all, three counters are listed; the one with '3 boards on ye side' was valued at 13s. and had six drawers under and a 'Joint Box' nearby,[44] while the other two were listed together further on. Whereas the first is suggestive of over the counter sale with a cash box handy, the second at 6s. 8d. is more doubtful and the third at only 1s. could have been a piece of simple equipment like an abacus to aid computation.[45]

---

[40] For example, the perfumer's shop illustrating John Lydgate's poem 'Pilgrimage of the life of man', British Library, Cotton MS Tiberius A VII, f. 93, reproduced in Basing (1990), *Trades and Crafts*, p. 51

[41] Holme (1688), *Academy of armory*, book III, p. 259a and Plate 5/cxliv.

[42] Respectively Lichfield Joint RO and Norwich RO, INV7/188.

[43] Orphans Inventories 3109.

[44] That is, the box was joined or properly made. Johnson's Inventory is kept at Lichfield Joint RO.

[45] The term 'abacus' has not been noted in inventories or in any of the sources used by the University of Wolverhampton's Dictionary Project. It is suggested that the term 'counter' was used instead, since it is accepted that computational aids of this type were employed.

## Dual selling systems

Whether provincial shopkeepers sold directly through the window or from within the body of the shop, the evidence of probate inventories suggests that stock was flexibly arranged, possibly to facilitate dual selling systems, where one area was used for the sale of small items in frequent demand and others for items which required more consideration by the customer and more salesmanship by the retailer. The inventory of Samuel Stores of Warbleton, Sussex, who died in 1711, provides an example of this.[46] Warbleton was not large, and did not even rate as a small town in contemporary publications.[47] It also appears not to have had a market and, if any tradesmen issued tokens, none have survived. Nevertheless, it had this substantial shop, comparable with those owned by tradesmen called mercers elsewhere. The appraisers referred to the shop and the warehouse but they listed the goods for sale without indicating their location. They started with the cloth, which they mostly itemized and valued separately, followed by a couple of entries relating to haberdashery. There is then a single entry covering a range of grocery and miscellanea very typical of village shops valued in all at about £30, followed by a list of the retailer's equipment, which does not include a counter. The layout of this inventory is replicated in many others and is best explained by assuming that the appraisers moved from the warehouse, in which the cloth and perhaps the haberdashery were stored and displayed, into the shop where a miscellany of goods were kept in small quantities perhaps to be sold for cash.

Other listings of a slightly different type point to a similar conclusion, for example the inventories of two Shropshire tradesmen, Walter Turner, ironmonger of Newport (1746), and Benjamin Boucher, grocer of Bridgnorth (1741).[48] Boucher's shop in Bridgnorth fronted onto that part of the High Street in which the market took place. The exact site of Turner's shop in Newport is unknown. However the linear nature of the town's development along the one main street in which the weekly market took place more or less precludes any but a shop fronting onto this active trading area.[49] Turner's stock was scattered over several rooms. Some goods, mostly in fairly large quantities were in the warehouse including five casks of sugar worth over £28, £37 worth of tobacco stems and dust and £23 worth of rum and spirits. Then he had a 'shop' full of small ironmongery and a 'Lase' of larger items like pots and furnaces, cart

---

[46] East Sussex RO, W/INV/195.

[47] Clark and Hosking (1993), *Population estimates*, lists what they adjudge to be small towns and Warbleton is not included. Their sources are listed and discussed in pp. ii-vii.

[48] Both Lichfield Joint RO. Turner's inventory is in the main series. It was not dated, but probate was granted in April 1746. Boucher's inventory is in the Bridgnorth Peculiar series.

[49] I thank Dr Malcolm Wanklyn for information about Boucher and Bridgnorth.

bushes, wire and cord, while on 'the Bulk' were substantial quantities of goods not itemized 'in ye Pedlars Trade' (£7) and 'in the Milleners way' (£50). Before the appraisers finally left the trading premises they returned to the shop, or entered a second one. After recording a grate worth 15s., they went on to list some grocery, including sugar and some spices, and more ironware, finishing with a counter and shop equipment worth £10. The grate is far too valuable to be for a fireplace and is more typical of window furniture. From Boucher's inventory it appears his business was conducted in a similar way, though there was a less clear division between trade and household. In the shop itself was grocery, mostly in small quantities, along with 25s. worth of odd things.

Both Turner and Boucher were substantial tradesmen for northern Shropshire, and their inventories suggest that they each had a complex business with many lines. Each of their inventories show that different types of goods were stored in different parts of the premises, a distinction being made between small and fancy items in one area and bulkier and more mundane items elsewhere. These divisions, most notably the small and fancy items in Turner's outside Bulk, all point to different patterns of selling for different types of goods.

## Service oriented selling: the example of London

Selling within shops could take different forms, ranging from the speedy processing of payment of goods over a simple counter as seen in the food shop to a concentration on service and comfort for the customer. For this latter method more space for customers was required inside the shop. References to the conscious manipulation of the interior décor to create a particular shopping environment appear in the early eighteenth century, the most out-spoken being Daniel Defoe. In 1726 he was castigating the young tradesman who set up shop and planned 'to paint and gild it over to make it fine and gay'. He recognized, and disliked, the fact that some retailers were exploring new ways of using the shop premises themselves to entice in the passer-by. 'Never', he wrote, 'was such painting and gilding, such sashings and looking-glasses among the shopkeepers as there is now'.[50] He believed he was witnessing a fundamental change in style, which he put down to the influence of the French, who were 'eminent for making a fine outside';[51] an interesting comment in view of Miller's belief, quoted earlier, that the French tradesmen had made no progress in marketing skills before the second quarter of the nineteenth century.[52]

---

[50] Defoe (1726), *Complete English tradesman*, pp. 182-3.
[51] Defoe (1726), *Complete English tradesman*, p. 184.
[52] Miller (1981), *Bon Marché bougeois culture*, p. 24.

**3.4** Tradecard of Dorothy Mercier

Some trade cards and hand bills give an indication of what such shops may have looked like inside, though the pictorial evidence needs to be viewed with caution.[53] Trade cards were intended to impress potential customers, so the actual level of furnishing in high class shops is hard to assess. Even so, the trade cards must have borne some relation to real examples or they would have been ineffective as advertising. The one of Dorothy Mercier, printseller and stationer in the 1750s includes in the image of a supposedly successful shop all the trappings of a fashionable living room; carpeting, lights, seating, pictures, while only the counter and the storage racks betray the shop.[54] Defoe's description of extravagant furnishing intended 'to make a show to invite customers', though also exaggerated, must have had some basis in reality. He claimed that the fittings of a pastry cook's shop cost £300 in 1710, including sash windows, galley tiles 'finely painted in forest-work and figures', several looking glasses, including one over a fireplace, two branch candlesticks, three great glass lanterns and 25 sconces, plus painting, gilding and carving to the tune of £55.[55] Despite the polemical nature of Defoe's writing and the idealized images in trade cards, probate inventories for high class London retailers confirm the reality of a sophisticated level of interior decoration. William Monsford, a draper who died in 1721 had in his shop a pier glass and three glass sconces, four leather stools, two chairs and cushions, a silk curtain and ten Indian pictures.[56] The shop of Henry Ackerman, a China dealer who died the following year was even more lavishly furnished. His shop contained six cane chairs, a painted card table, 16 canisters, a looking glass, a pair of glass sconces, four pair of scales as well as the counters, drawers and racks.[57] By the early eighteenth century some of the more expensive London shops were already offering the shopper an environment so attractive that it became part of the appeal of shopping for the wealthy.

Searching for evidence of such decoration in earlier periods is more difficult but the mid-sixteenth-century diatribe, supposedly by W.S., but more probably by John Hale, against those 'mercers, grocers, vinteners, haberdashers, mileyners, and such as doe sell wares growing beyond the seas, and doe fetche oute oure treasure of the same' gives an indication of what an enticement well stocked shops could present. The author described how 'from the towere to westminster alonge, euerie streat is full of them; and their shoppes glister and shine of glasses, aswell lookinge as drinckinge, yea all manor vesselles of the

---

[53] Such documents varied enormously in size, from that of a modern visiting card to a broad sheet. For the sake of simplicity, all have been termed a trade card here, although one or two of those cited are quite large.

[54] Banks collection, 10.69.

[55] Defoe (1726), *Complete English tradesman*, p. 181.

[56] Walsh (1993), *Shop design*, p. 78, referring to Orphans inventories 3178.

[57] Orphans inventories 3157.

same stuffe; painted cruses, gaye daggers, knives, swordes, and girdles that is able to make anie temporate man to gase on them, and to bie soumwhat, though it serue to no purpose necessarie.'[58]

The size of shops and the level of sophisticated interior decoration increased throughout the course of the eighteenth century as more retailers became attuned to the importance of ambience and the profitability of attentive service. The most important development for high class shopkeepers was the showroom where customers were allowed the time to browse amongst carefully laid out displays. Josiah Wedgwood's showrooms in Portland Square were famous in their day, but followed the trend of other shops catering for the social élite. 'We must have an Elegant, extensive & Conven't shewroom', he wrote in 1767. Wedgwood possessed a particularly astute sense of marketing, but the way he displayed his wares, laying out table services as if for use in a domestic setting, belong to the continued history of the manipulation of a domestic atmosphere in shop interiors evident in the inventories of Monsford and Ackerman. Wedgwood's scale of display, however, was new and the implementation of it more subtle. A straightforward permanent display of china would have done little to stimulate desire or to extend the horizons of his potential customers. Instead he ordered that displays should 'every few days be so alter'd, revers'd, & transform'd as to render the whole a new scene, Even to the same Company, every time they shall bring their friends to visit us.'[59] In particular Wedgwood targeted female customers, aiming 'to do the needfull with the Ladys in the neatest, genteelest, and best method'. Since his display rooms were in line with those of the largest and most fashionable London shops, he could afford to be extravagent with his displays such as 'a much greater variety of setts of Vases' decorating the walls. His policy was to encourage customers to visit regularly and to be entertained by new styles and the atmosphere of his shop. In order to succeed, London retailers looking for customers towards the upper end of the social spectrum needed to be sensitive to the potential of shop architecture, display and general ambience to encourage sale, though each had to exploit these elements in a way appropriate to their own location and type of stock.

**Ambience and display in the provinces**

It is more difficult to gather evidence for the manipulation of interior decoration by provincial retailers. On the whole decoration in provincial shops must have been more limited than in smart London shops. But provincial retailers who catered for aristocratic customers used to shopping in London

---

[58] W.S. (1581), *Discourse of the common weal*, pp. 67 and 91.
[59] Wedgwood Museum MSS E.18149-25, quoted in McKendrick (1982), 'Josiah Wedgwood', p. 118-19.

would have been made aware of retail techniques there from their own visits to purchase stock. Robert Owen in his *Autobiography* records the fine manners and expert salesmanship of McGuffog's, a high class draper of Stamford in Lincolnshire, whose shop was 'a kind of general rendezvous of the higher class nobility'.[60] Particularly in tourist resorts where London shopkeepers often kept branch shops, the level of decoration may well have matched London standards. Johanna Schopenhauer, the young German tourist of the 1790s, commented upon the 'handsome shops' in Cheltenham, the 'elegant little shops where London merchants sell their prettiest and most exclusive fashions' in Brighton, and the Crescent in Buxton 'with more than three hundred windows in its facade' behind some of which were 'elegant shops'.[61]

In the absence of visual material, probate inventories, are once again the most important source for investigating the interior of provincial shops and their fittings. In the early eighteenth century, as had been the practice for generations, appraisers almost invariably started their valuations in the shop with the stock, and added the furnishings and fittings almost as an afterthought. These items were often listed only in general terms like 'the scales and all other lumber in the shop', as if to highlight their relative unimportance. As the century progressed, the appraisers' attitude appears to have changed; more furnishings and fittings were recorded and they were given more prominence in the inventory. This alteration in positioning is a valuable pointer to changes in attitude. In other respects the changes are easily missed since the opulence of furnishings and fittings in provincial shops was lower than in London shops.

When Thomas Horne, grocer of Arundel in Sussex, died in 1719, his appraisers valued some 150 items of stock, mainly drapery and haberdashery. Their systematic listing suggests a well-ordered interior, presumably with fixed shelves since none were appraised, but nothing to indicate the paraphernalia of comfort designed to encourage shopping for pleasure. Fifteen years later when his widow Susan died, the situation was different. She had apparently continued to sell the same sort of stock on the same scale, but the shop itself had been transformed, since it now had sash windows, one large and another middle-sized looking glass with six painted ones, as well as counters, shelves and boxes. Significantly one of the appraisers valued both inventories which suggests a uniform policy on the two occasions.[62] Twenty years later in 1754, in Henry Peirce's tailor's shop in Harting, Sussex, the appraisers started with the shop fittings, including a well-equipped fireplace, several tables and chairs, four candlesticks, the shelves and the shop board. Only when all this had been listed and valued, did they turn their attention to the stock.[63]

---

[60] Owen (1857), *Life*, p. 13.

[61] Schopenhauer (1988), *A lady's travels*, pp. 105, 130, 34.

[62] West Sussex RO, MF835 1719 and MF835 1735.

[63] West Sussex RO, MF842.

The goldsmiths were amongst the retailers with the most elaborate display in London and this fact may be reflected in the inventory of the midland watchmaker, Isaac Stretch, who died in 1716, which recorded he had a sash window, one glass press with lining and shelves, 'the glass case that stands upon the window', shop partitions and chests, and chairs, as well as 'the watch out of doors' worth £2 10s.[64] Even in a large town with a substantial retail trade like Birmingham, among less prestigious trades change seems to have been slower in coming. The toyman John Edwards died in 1733 leaving a huge stock of small attractive items, many intended for the better off. Apart from his stock, he had apparently nothing to attract the passer-by inside, nothing for the shopper to sit on, and no lighting nor fire place.[65] In contrast, the appraisers of Thomas Heely, so called button and toymaker who died in 1764, started their list with his fittings, including several glass cases for display, a half-sash door, several counters and various canisters for his tea and groceries.[66]

One of the earliest examples of a provincial shop interior designed to stimulate sale comes neither from a big town like Manchester or Birmingham nor from a fashionable spa like Tunbridge Wells, but from the small posting town of Newport in Shropshire. This was a small market town with limited facilities, comparing unfavourably with other nearby towns like Wellington, Bridgnorth or Whitchurch and in a different league from Shrewsbury or Wolverhampton. Yet the shop of Richard Motley (1709) suggests a sophisticated awareness of salesmanship not unlike that of Wedgwood several decades later. From his inventory it is almost possible to reconstruct his shop, with some of his stock stored in a desk and a chest of drawers, the rest presumably on shelves fixed to the walls since they were not listed. In addition the scene was set with a looking glass and some small pictures, two cane chairs, two small trunks and six silk cushions. Clearly his customers were expected to browse, select and purchase in some comfort and at leisure.[67]

## Nurturing different types of customer

The *Autobiography* of Francis Place, who was setting up shop in London in the 1790s, provides an example of the complex approach some retailers took to the development of their business in the early modern period, both nurturing

---

64  Lichfield Joint RO.

65  Lichfield Joint RO. It is possible that such items were not recorded by the appraisers, but in an otherwise carefully constructed inventory, this seems unlikely. It seems equally improbable that fittings would have been removed prior to the inventory when in other respects it appears complete.

66  Both Lichfield Joint RO.

67  Lichfield Joint RO.

regular custom and encouraging passing trade at the same time.[68] Place was an independent tailor with an associated retail business. His trade depended on account customers who bought from him regularly and were given credit. His *Autobiography* makes it clear that the appearance of his shop was crucial in first drawing such customers to the business. Once the relationship had been established, Place would often visit them in their own homes, but the shop remained as a business front for his activities, confirming his reputation and convincing potential new customers of his standing.

For Place, the shop front with a glazed shop window was a significant element in achieving this impression, as for many other shopkeepers who focused on service orientated selling. The glazed window offered the customer seclusion from the noise and bustle of the street and the shopkeeper the opportunity to sell to a captive audience. Glazed windows also allowed the permanent display of goods. The widespread use of glazing was a matter for comment by one foreign visitor as early as 1728, who wrote of glass that the 'shops are surrounded with it, and usually the merchandise is arranged behind it, which keeps the dust off, while still displaying the goods to passers-by'.[69]

Since the introduction of glazing into London shops in the late seventeenth century, improvements in the manufacture of glass were made, the panes increasing in size. By the end of the century, plate glass was available in panes up to two feet high. With thin glazing bars of brass a mere ¾" thick, the impression that Cheapside in the 1770s made on one observer was that the shop fronts 'seem to be made entirely of glass'.[70]

The glazed windows and shop door with their surrounding frames, and the sign and fascia board were important in signalling to potential customers that this was a retail shop in a busy street. The shop front gave shopkeepers the opportunity to exploit the latest architectural fashions which in turn reflected on the fashionability of their stock. Windows filled with enticing displays set in fashionable and neatly painted exteriors proclaimed financial security and good taste. Such windows and displays are evident in shops seen in topographical prints from the early eighteenth century onwards.[71] Place described how he consciously managed the physical environment of the street and the shop front to improve its impact on potential customers when he opened his new shop in 1801.

---

[68] *Autobiography of Francis Place*, vol. II.

[69] *Voyage en Angleterre*, (1728), V&A, 86NN 2, fol. 29, quoted by Braudel (1986), *Wheels of commerce*, pp. 69-70.

[70] Lichtenberg (1938), *Lichtenberg's visits to England*, p. 63; Walsh (1993), *Shop design*, p. 44.

[71] See, for example, Figures 2.1 and 2.2, where the shop windows are clearly visible, and the comments of two eighteenth-century visitors quoted below on p. 219.

> I pulled out the Shop front, closed the doors in front under the shop to the vaults and paved the places where there were wooden flaps in the footpath in front of the shop. I put in a new front as elegant as the place would permit, each of the panes of glass cost me three pounds, and two in the door, four pounds each.[72]

Place's comment, stressing the extravagance involved in fitting out the shop in this way, indicates that, despite the expense, he saw it as necessary to cultivate the level of clientele he aimed at.

Although the nurturing of account customers was crucial to Place's trade, he was already alert to the potentially significant value of passing trade when he opened his first shop in the 1790s. 'We shall scarce fail to succeed', he wrote, 'for we have business enough between us to feed and clothe us, and the sale of Gloves, Slings, Breeches balls, Boot garters, waistcoats and an occasional customer which a shop cannot fail to bring will certainly pay the rent and taxes'.[73] For this he saw the display of certain fashionable goods in the window as an important strategy to attract customers in from the street. Place claimed that his shop window more than paid for itself by attracting in the passer-by who would make a one-off purchase. The window was used mainly to display fashion accessories amenable to quick sales for cash, like gloves, handkerchiefs and ribbons, though he also experimented with more ambitious displays of fashion garments, like waistcoats. Although not always successful, his attempts suggest that he saw window display as an important tool in attracting custom, and that customers were accustomed to using window displays to inform themselves about new products. Window shopping after dark was also a well established practice. Place kept the shop and window lit at night with 'five large argand lamps in the shop besides the candles to make the windows and every part of it as nearly equally light as possible'.[74] Johanna Schopenhauer, the young German tourist of the 1790s, was particularly impressed with their glass windows and attractive displays of London shops, remarking on 'the splendour of the shops and larger stores', their 'richness and elegance', 'the brilliant displays of precious silver ware' and 'the beautiful draperies ... the merchants show to the public behind large plate glass windows'. She observed the 'fairy glitter of the crystal shops' and the apothecaries whose windows gleam 'like an Aladdin's cave' at night as well as attractive displays by candle

---

[72] *Autobiography of Francis Place*, vol. II, p. 123.

[73] *Autobiography of Francis Place*, vol. II, p. 82.

[74] *Autobiography of Francis Place*, vol. II, p. 123. See also Patent No 1425, 15 March 1784, 'Lamp producing neither smoke nor smell, and giving more light than any known before', Woodcroft (1854), *Alphabetic index of patentees inventions*, p. 11.

makers, fruit sellers and cake shops and by the engravers whose windows are 'always surrounded by a crowd of inquisitive people'.[75]

The attraction of the shop window display in the eighteenth century lay in the presentation of a plethora of choice. Salters & Co., hat makers of London produced at least two different bill headings illustrating their shop front, respectively in 1794 and 1804. In each the double-fronted windows are depicted as stuffed full of hats in various styles; 26 in the one and no less than 40 in the other. The trade card for Gill's Hat Warehouse (1798) was similar, with 36 different hats of various types depicted in his bow window. Further afield the bill head of Sarah Bedford & Co., cut glass makers of Birmingham (n.d.), confirm that enticement through the image of choice was not confined to London. Her shop is depicted on her bill head with large double square bay windows with an object in each pane.[76] Window display was clearly valuable to provincial retailers, as revealed earlier in the chapter. However, it is important not to exaggerate the extent to which the new glass technology brought new practices to shops, in the provinces. While the technology for making large glazed windows was available, retailers may have chosen not to deploy it for financial or practical reasons. Topographical views of thriving provincial town centres around key areas such as the market square, reveal widespread glazing of shops,[77] but the use of glass remained a matter of comment well into the nineteenth century. For example, in Newcastle upon Tyne, a writer in 1827 commented that the shuttered shop windows had been replaced with glass as if it were a fairly recent event.[78]

## Two-tier selling

Within each town of any size there were some streets that served a more fashionable clientele than others. For retailers aiming to appeal to high-class customers, the position of the shop was a crucial factor. The location of a shop on a particular street signalled to potential customers which level of market was

---

[75] Schopenhauer (1988), *A lady's travels*, pp. 138-9. Although it is always necessary to be cautious about translations when nuances of meaning can be lost, this is hardly a problem here for the main gist of Schopenhauer's description. It should be noted, however, that the use of the word 'store' in a British context at this date is an anachronism.

[76] Banks collection, 72.196 and 72.197; 72.81; 66.5. Bedford's bill head is undated but belongs to the eighteenth century.

[77] For example, the watercolour of Norwich Market Place by Robert Dighton (1799), Norfolk Museums Service, Castle Museum, Norwich.

[78] Mackenzie (1827), *Descriptive account*, p. 162 quoted by Alexander (1970), *Retailing in England*, p. 9. There is a range of comments on both improvements, and the lack of them in provincial towns in the first half of the nineteenth century on that and the following page, mostly taken from contemporary guide books.

intended. The value of this for retailers was that they maximized their chances of dealing only with customers who were interested in their wares and could afford their prices. The level the shop traded at was also signalled by the design of the shop front, the wares placed on show in the window and the dress and manners of the shop staff. For large shops, the behaviour of the shop staff was crucial because they represented the shopkeeper and had the potential to damage his or her reputation. Fanny Burney, in the words of her naïve heroine, Evelina, satirized the behaviour of drapers' assistants in London:

> But what most diverted me was, that we were more frequently served by men than by women; and such men! so finical, so affected! they seemed to understand every part of a woman's dress better than we do ourselves; and they recommend caps and ribbands with such an air of so much importance, that I wished to ask them how long they had left off wearing them.[79]

That Burney's satire was not too much of an exaggeration is indicated by Robert Owen's more factual description of the elaborate preparations made by the counter salesmen, including hair powder, before they were allowed into the shop belonging to Messrs Flint and Palmer, 'an old established house on old London Bridge'.[80]

However, while some shops geared themselves to a distinct market, others seem to have maximized their potential to draw on different levels of the market at the same time. Some possible evidence was presented earlier suggesting provincial shopkeepers may have used different areas for different kinds of sales, such as fast or slow selling, and these may well have exploited this potential. More substantial evidence for London relating to shops at the top end of the market serves to explore these different approaches more closely.

Wedgwood's London shop was divided into areas for browsing and sociability and areas for the processing of sales with counters and shop staff. An area was even set aside for self service.[81] Francis Place was anxious that his shop would look busy, stating that it 'looked well that there should be several people employed about the shop', and eventually when the business had expanded enough, he put the care of customers into the hands of an employee described significantly not as an apprentice or journeyman tailor but as 'a young man who understood the trade as a shopman'. Meanwhile Place concentrated on his customers, 'dancing attendance on silly people, to make myself acceptable to coxcombs to please their whims, to have no opinion of my

---

[79] Burney (1778), *Evelina*, p. 25.
[80] Owen (1971), *Life*, vol. I, p. 18.
[81] Wedgwood Museum, MSS, E.17677-96. Wedgwood to William Cox, 7 April 1769, quoted in McKendrick, 'Josiah Wedgwood', p. 119

**3.5** Shop interior, *c.* 1800. The print shows the interior of a genteel (but probably not highly fashionable) draper's shop with counter, chairs for customers, pieces of cloth draped for display and fashionably dressed assistants. The image corresponds closely with both the fictional account of such shops by Evelina herself and the factual observations by Robert Owen.

own but to take especial care that my customers should be pleased with theirs'.[82] This division of labour suggests that Place was able to deal with different levels of customer within one establishment, perhaps taking customers to a different area of the shop than that used for passing trade.

It seems that some shops in eighteenth-century London were divided into a front shop with counters and a back shop with a more domestic ambience. The trade card of Benjamin Cole from the 1710s makes a feature of a door and a window into a back room with a fire blazing in the grate.[83] Back shops, or in smaller shops the parlour, could have been used to pamper more prestigious customers or to use a more intimate atmosphere to build up relations with a customer who might be offered long-term credit. In this way shops could maximize their potential to attract different levels of customers. This would be particularly appropriate in small towns where high spending customers may not have been numerous, but would have been important to court.

While shopkeepers had to dance attendance on customers, they also had to be alert to the possibilities of theft. Already by 1699 an act was passed to address the 'Crime of stealing Goods privately out of Shops and Warehouses, commonly called Shop-lifting' which, it declared, was 'of late Years much increased'. It is clear from the careful wording of the act that the problem of stealing from shops was not satisfactorily dealt with by the law as it stood and it was therefore necessary first to define it as distinct from other property offences. Shoplifting consisted of stealing from a shop or warehouse, 'by Night or in the Day-time ... although such Shop ... be not actually broken open ... and although the Owners of such Goods ... be or be not in such Shop' and whether or not they 'be put in Fear'. It is significant that pressure for such an act (which did no more than deny benefit of clergy to offenders) came as early as 1699 and that already the problem had been clarified to such an extent that the nature of the offence could be clearly articulated.[84]

One of the best descriptions of how shop-lifters operated is fictional, although its author claimed it was based on a true story. Daniel Defoe's *Moll Flanders*, the story of a woman who fell into misfortune and thence into crime, draws on his own experience as a journalist and as a bankrupt tradesman. He described how Moll, destitute and desperate, was rescued by a woman she called her 'governess', who introduced her to shop-lifting:

> I was very shy of shop-lifting, especially among the mercers and drapers, who are a set of fellows that have their eyes very much about them. I

---

[82] *Autobiography of Francis Place*, vol. II, pp. 123-4, 99.

[83] See below Figure 4.1. Heal (1925), *London tradesmen's cards*, p. 81, suggests a date of 1710-20. The reference is Heal collection, 70.39.

[84] 10 & 11 GUL3 C23 (1699), 'Act ... for the better apprehending of Felons that commit Burglary, Housebreaking or Robbery in Shops ...'.

made a venture or two among the lace folks and the milliners, and
particularly at one shop where I got notice of two young women who
were newly set up, and had not been bred to the trade. There I think I
carried off a piece of bone-lace, worth six or seven pounds, and a paper
of thread. ... Our principal trade was watching shopkeepers' counters,
and slipping off any kind of goods we could see carelessly laid
anywhere, and we made several good bargains, as we called them, at this
work.[85]

Some time later Moll saw her partner apprehended while she herself was
already preparing her next crime:

As for me, I had very luckily stepped into a house where there was a lace
chamber, up one pair of stairs, and had the satisfaction, or the terror
indeed, of seeing the poor creature dragged away in triumph to the
justice, who immediately committed her to Newgate.
   I was careful to attempt nothing in the lace chamber, but tumbled the
goods pretty much to spend time; then bought a few yards of edging and
paid for it.[86]

The significant features of Moll Flander's fictional experiences are the type
of shop most vulnerable to shop lifting; sale over the counter, the use of cash,
the obvious presumption that some customers at least will be unknown to the
assistants and that not all will buy. Historians of nineteenth-century retailing
have tended to assume that customers in the early modern period were under an
obligation to make a purchase once they entered the shop, but Defoe's account
is supported by court records of shoplifting cases. One shopkeeper in his
Deposition at the Old Bailey in 1794 related how the accused 'said they wished
to look at some ribbons, in consequence of that I took out the drawer ... the
other woman said, she did not like blue ribbon at all, and asked me if I would
show here some white ones? in consequence of that I took out the white
drawer'.[87] This report reveals type of exchange that must have been common in
shops in the period, since the shopkeeper noticed nothing unusual in it with the
customer in a position of demanding to see a range of items at will.

## Cash sales and fixed pricing in newspaper advertisements

The use of fixed prices and cash sales is certainly evident and probably
widespread well before the period of so-called 'modern retailing' after 1850.

---

[85] Defoe (1722), *Moll Flanders*, pp. 203 and 209.
[86] Defoe (1722), *Moll Flanders*, p. 214.
[87] *Old Bailey Proceedings*, December 1794, p. 101, quoted by Walsh (1993), *Shop design*, p. 82.

The techniques can be traced back at least to the beginning of the eighteenth century when they are manifest in the early advertisements placed in national and provincial newspapers. At this time examples noted of sale by fixed price do not relate to the stock of a fixed-shop retailer but to patent medicines sold through, though not entirely by the newspaper printers.[88] Some of these medicines emerged before the end of the seventeenth century, but on a big scale their production and distribution developed hand in hand with that of the provincial newspapers. For example 'The Golden Snuff Famous for many years' was advertised in the *Norwich Gazette* in 1707.[89] By 1741 when *Aris's Birmingham Gazette* started almost every edition of a provincial newspaper carried advertisements listing patent remedies against all ills, and Aris's was no exception. The seventh number proclaimed the virtues of Daffy's Elixir and stated that it was sold not only by the printer but also at 26 other outlets scattered over the Midlands, all selling at a uniform price. These outlets were not just the booksellers so often associated with marketing patent medicines, but included five so called shopkeepers, five grocers, three ironmongers and a glover, a druggist, a cutler, a hatter, a milliner, a baker, a surgeon, a watchmaker and a mercer.[90] This technique of sale through retail outlets linked to the provincial newspapers remained predominately the preserve of the makers of proprietary drugs. However, since in the late seventeenth and early eighteenth centuries the dividing line between medicaments, foodstuffs and beverages was fine, the concept of branded[91] goods sold at fixed prices, often imposed nation-wide, spread into the grocery and confectionery trades, and to some extent into the drinks industry, such as Howes Genuine acid for making punch, lemonade, jellies etc., and Lemery's new invented powder for cleaning paint.[92] Sir Hans Sloane, who had gone out to Jamaica as personal physician to the Governor of Jamaica in 1682 and observed there the natives drinking chocolate, came back to England to make his fortune marketing a chocolate

---

[88] The subject of patent medicines is exhaustively covered by Porter (1989), *Health for sale*. It is not our intention to deal with it here except in so far as selling practices in other fields were influenced by the way patent medicines were advertised and distributed.

[89] *Norwich Gazette*, 7 June 1707.

[90] *Aris's Birmingham Gazette*, 28 December 1741.

[91] The term 'branded' is a difficult one and is not always appropriate to eighteenth-century terminology, though there is no satisfactory alternative. Many goods were defined by the place of origin, like 'London porter', 'Durham mustard', 'North Clay hops'. It is impossible to determine at what point these designations ceased to indicate place of origin and came to refer to an identifiable type. In this sense these terms had some of the characteristics of brand names and the commodities were probably no different from some so called branded goods like Daffy's Elixir that was pirated and made by other than the authorized manufacturer.

[92] Both *Aris's Birmingham Gazette*, respectively 12 November 1770 and 2 June 1780. Other examples of brand name goods have been noted including 'Morgan's genuine Sago Powder', 'Churchman's Fine Chocolate' and 'Hill's Worcester Porter', all from *Aris's Birmingham Gazette,* respectively, 7 June 1790, 8 July 1751 and 26 April 1790.

branded with his name. The mechanisms used to market this new commodity after his death are not known, but it was widely stocked by eighteenth-century grocers and tea dealers at a price well above that of ordinary chocolate.[93] Some of these tradesmen advertised it along with other grocery at what seems to have been a price applied nationally. The purpose of these advertisements was no doubt to establish brand names in the public's mind, but also to lay down standard prices to be expected, usually in a number of named outlets. The risks for the retailer to stock such products and to take up the mode of selling by standardized fixed prices were presumably offset by the advantages. An implicit part of the deal with the newspaper printer seems to have been that the goods would be regularly advertised at his expense rather than at the shopkeeper's. There may also have been an established acceptance of sale or return, though this has only been noted spelled out in one advertisement.[94]

The *Norwich Gazette*, started in 1706, shows how rapidly the practice of selling at fixed price for cash only spread beyond proprietary medicines to individual tradesmen who advertised their own stock. Advertisements of this type appeared in the newspaper giving fixed prices for tea and coffee in 1707, Beer vinegar in 1708, and best Cherry Brandy in 1709.[95] By the 1750s the sale of some alcoholic liquors by fixed price was becoming commonplace in the Midlands including rum, London porter and even a range of wines.[96] Although the early selling of tea and coffee at a fixed price may have been precipitated by direct competition from London,[97] the practice was gradually extended to other groceries, as is shown in the advertisement for the sale of the stock in trade of the late Mr Richard Lutwych of Birmingham.[98] This advertisement is interesting because, although the groceries were offered at fixed prices, the haberdashery and drapery were not. Both of these were notoriously sold by haggling.[99] In 1780 John Green, druggist and grocer of Birmingham advertised the prices of over 40 items.[100] Two years later the Manchester 'Chymist, druggist, and oilman', G. Browne, advertised 29 items of drugstery, grocery and saltery, many of them at several different qualities, again all apparently at

---

[93] For example, *Piercy's Coventry Gazette*, 22 August 1778; *Aris's Birmingham Gazette*, 7 June 1790.

[94] In the *Leicester and Nottingham Journal*, 12 January 1760 the assurance was given to retailers both of future advertisement by the printer and an offer of sale or return.

[95] Respectively, *Norwich Gazette*, 8 March 707 and 4 October 1707; *Norwich Advertiser* 28 August 1708 and 15 January 1709.

[96] For example, *Aris's Birmingham Gazette*, 22 October 1750.

[97] For example, *Aris's Birmingham Gazette*, 27 January 1752.

[98] *Aris's Birmingham Gazette*, 26 February 1750.

[99] For example, the Swiss visitor Cesar de Saussure, in England during the 1720s, related a story about a Quaker shopkeeper that assumes haggling was the norm when buying drapery; Saussure (1902), *A foreign view*, p. 324.

[100] *Aris's Birmingham Gazette*, 3 January 1780.

fixed prices.[101] In contrast is the advertisement for Mr Macaulay's tea of Manchester placed by G. Keary in a Liverpool newspaper in 1760. Unlike those for most branded goods, this one was apparently simply to inform his customers of new supplies in his own shop, but at specific prices.[102]

By the late eighteenth century there is further evidence of large establishments using techniques of fast selling. Some trade cards confirm the practice, like that of the London saleswoman, Hannah Tatum.[103] The firm of Messrs Flint and Palmer, for which Robert Owen worked for a while and which he called old-fashioned was certainly not so in its methods of selling haberdashery; indeed Robert Owen claimed that it was 'the first house to sell at a small profit for ready money only'. In this establishment 'not much time was allowed for bargaining, a price being fixed for everything, and compared with other houses, cheap ... the article asked for was presented, taken at once, and paid for all with great dispatch, and a large business was thus daily transacted'.[104] Newspaper advertisements and trade cards suggests that the style of selling described by Owen, rather than being innovatory as he claimed, was becoming commonplace so that a woollen drapery business for sale in Manchester was recommended because its 'situation is inferior to none, it stands particularly well for the Ready Money Country Trade, being in the Heart of the Market and an old established shop'.[105]

More threatening to traditional retailers than fixed prices and sales for cash only were the aggressive tactics of entrepreneurs, usually from London, who descended on Birmingham, other big towns and quite small villages to offer their wares, not only at fixed prices but also for ready money, in sales lasting but a few days. Like the production and distribution of patent medicines, this sort of salesmanship probably depended on advertising in newspapers with a substantial readership and it appears to have been of little significance before the middle of the eighteenth century. The advertisements suggest a growing expertise on the part of these operators in manipulating the market. Early examples are often quite straightforward like the rather bald advertisement placed by J. Whitfield Yates in *Aris's Birmingham Gazette* in 1757 for a range of linen drapery and haberdashery.[106] Others at about the same time were exploiting specific opportunities, or at least suggested they were, like S. Cole, a

---

[101] *Manchester Mercury*, 2 April 1782.

[102] *Williamson's Liverpool Advertiser*, 12 December 1760.

[103] Oxford, Bodleian Library, John Johnson collection, Box 6, reproduced in Lemire (1991), *Fashion's favourite*, Fig. 8. The card is undated, but its style suggests the first half of the eighteenth century. Written on it by hand is the figure 1740, which is possibly the date. No other example of a trade card advertising fixed prices and/or sale by cash only has been noted earlier than 1740, though newspaper advertisements show the practice was not new.

[104] Owen (1971), *Life*, vol. I, pp. 18-19.

[105] *Manchester Mercury*, 6 July 1790.

[106] *Aris's Birmingham Gazette*, 8 April 1757.

silk mercer from London, who was trying to unload his fashionable silks 'upon account of the present mourning',[107] or the 'Person from London' who came to Manchester with 'all sorts of India Goods' selling prize captures by commission.[108] His advertisement was skilfully constructed in terms of its language, making its appeal to 'the Public in general' by addressing, in the usual terms of eighteenth-century politeness, the 'Nobility, Ladies and Gentlemen'. The commodities on offer and their prices however, suggest a broad rather than an aristocratic market. It becomes clear that a brisk sale of goods was expected to a substantial body of customers crammed into the 'large commodious Room' in Market Street Lane. The impression of elegance and fashion is in line with the dressed up Owen and his fellow salesmen, but the salesmanship as revealed in the statement that 'To prevent Trouble, every Piece of Goods' had 'the lowest Price mark'd on it, from which no Abatement can be made' is in line with the decidedly inelegant pressurized selling that Owen also described.

Such salesmen did not confine their activities to large towns. Thomas Turner, the shopkeeper in the village of East Hoathly in Sussex, described the arrival of one of these salesman, and the anxiety the visit engendered:

> This day came to Jones's a man with a cartload, of millinery, mercery, linen drapery, silver, etc., to keep sale for two days. This must undoubtedly be some hurt to trade, for the novelty of the thing, (and novelty is surely the predominant passion of the English nation, and of Sussex in particular) will catch the ignorant multitude, and perhaps not them only, but people of sense who are not judges of goods and trade as indeed very few are ... [109]

This salesman typified many others in that linen drapery and haberdashery remained the most popular lines in such short term sales for ready money and at fixed prices. This may be because such goods were generally sold by haggling and there was an unsatisfied demand for cheapness and speed so long as they were combined with an illusion of elegance. However sellers of other commodities also took advantage of what was clearly a successful technique, like the 'Manufacturer from Kidderminster' with 'A great Variety of Wilton and Scotch Carpets, of the best Quality and most elegant Patterns and Colours', who came to Birmingham in 1780 for four days.[110] Others are more unexpected, like Mr Campione, a self claimed Italian, who was offering an

---

[107] *Aris's Birmingham Gazette*, 10 November 1760. The Court mourning for George II required the wearing of suitably sombre colours, rendering other fashionable silks slow moving in London.

[108] *Manchester Mercury*, 8 October 1782.

[109] Turner (1984), *Diary*, 6 September 1764.

[110] *Aris's Birmingham Gazette*, 1 May 1780.

extraordinary range of prints and statues in 1770, including 'Busts and Monumental Ornaments of Kings, Queens, Princes, Poets, Philosophers, Physicians, &c, in fine Paris Plaister Work, after the Italian Manner'.[111]

The significance of these numerous entrepreneurs, who did much to ruffle the serenity of provincial retailers, was twofold. Firstly it spread abroad the techniques of fast selling and thus probably speeded up their adoption by those trading from fixed shops, and secondly they must have played an important role in accustoming the public to this retail method.

In the later eighteenth century, some London firms specializing in mercery and haberdashery apparently relocated themselves permanently to provincial centres. It is not clear whether these tradesmen were those who had previously travelled round who now settled down, rather like some chapmen did later in life.[112] Nor is it known how common the practice was, since the only evidence lies in the newspaper advertisements of those who chose to publicize their arrival, nor what advantages they expected to gain from relocation. Possibly the experiences of travelling salesmen, either directly or through hearsay, alerted other London tradesmen to the opportunities of fast selling in the provinces. Be that as it may, some tradesmen did relocate. In 1770 Messrs Salked & Wilson, linen drapers, haberdashers and hosiers, moved from London to Shrewsbury to open a shop on College Hill offering a 'genteel and fresh assortment' for ready money on reasonable terms. Twelve years later Needham, Locke & Bushell opened up as linen drapers, mercers and haberdashers in St Mary's Gate, Manchester with a 'large and elegant Assortment ... having taken Care to select the choicest Articles and from the best Markets', again for ready money.[113] Such examples could be replicated from all over the country, particularly in linen drapery and haberdashery where previously haggling had been the accepted mode of sale.

## Shopkeepers' advertising techniques

Advertising is a marketing technique that has too often been associated with the mass markets of the late nineteenth century and the twentieth; Jefferys even goes so far as to claim that eighteenth-century shops 'were not designed and planned to attract customers and create wants'.[114] Recent work on newspaper advertising in the second half of the eighteenth century has challenged this, In the *Birth of the consumer society* McKendrick shows how well the principles of advertisement and display were understood and exploited in the eighteenth

---

[111] *Aris's Birmingham Gazette*, 20 August 1770.
[112] Spufford (1984), *Great reclothing*, p. 45.
[113] *Aris's Birmingham Gazette*, 19 March 1770; *Manchester Mercury*, 1 January 1782.
[114] Jefferys (1954), *Retail trading in Britain*, p. 37.

century by manufacturers like Josiah Wedgwood and George Packwood,[115] and Mui and Mui in *Shops and shopkeeping* have looked at the evidence newspaper advertisements provide of new sales techniques.[116] However neither study looks at the distinction between different types of retailing tradesmen and their relative use of newspaper advertising.

Along with the nationally available London newspapers, by 1750 most large towns had their own newspaper, with its own effective system of distribution. The midland newspaper, *Aris's Birmingham Gazette*, for example, had a network of distribution covering many towns in Derbyshire, Leicestershire, Staffordshire, Warwickshire and Shropshire by 1743, only two years after its inception, whereas the *Manchester Mercury* covered much of Lancashire, the west side of Yorkshire and the north of Cheshire.[117] A superficial survey of newspaper advertisements suggest that their value was increasingly recognized by tradesmen. However, Mui and Mui's analysis of the use of advertisements by retailers shows not so much that this played an important part in a retailer's marketing strategy as they claim, but rather that it was a medium used by very few. For example, in London, only eight woollen drapers or mercers advertised in *The Times* during the first half of 1790.[118] The Returns produced for Excise in 1759 indicated there were about 3500 shops in the Lancashire collecting area.[119] During 1760 in the weekly *Manchester Mercury* there were only about a dozen advertisements of retailers of which two were for the stock sales of shops closing down, one announced the dissolution of a partnership and another a change of address. Of the rest, one offered services rather than goods and two at least were retailing manufacturers. Apart from a wine dealer, the rest offered drugs and/or chemicals for sale. During 1790 the number of advertisements of retailers increased to about 30, but of those six announced the succession of widow, son or former 'servant', three a change of address, three a new outlet and three the stock sales of shops closing down. Of the strictly promotional advertisements six were for tea dealers and/or grocers, two for chemists and one each for a fruiterer and a confectioner. The rest were primarily manufacturers.

Although once established the provincial newspaper did indeed become a vehicle for advertisement used by a wide variety of customers, well-established retailers using convention methods of selling were generally not among them, unless they were announcing changes in circumstances such as a removal or

---

[115] McKendrick (1982), 'Josiah Wedgwood' and 'George Packwood', pp. 100-196.

[116] Mui and Mui (1989), *Shops and shopkeeping*, chapter 12.

[117] The area of distribution for the two newspapers has been deduced from the lists of retailers from towns in the area who sold proprietary medicines on behalf of the printers.

[118] Mui and Mui (1989), *Shops and shopkeeping*, p. 238. For their general analysis of newspaper advertisements see pp. 225-48 and Appendix 1.

[119] See Mui and Mui (1989), *Shops and shopkeeping*, Appendix for how the number of shopkeepers was arrived at.

death. However, there were several types of distributors who found the placing of newspaper advertisements as an appropriate medium for promotion. Above all it served those who needed to sell across a large area, and who were able to set up a good network of distribution. Thus they were useful for manufacturers of patent medicines and similar products, who were able, through their associations with the printers of newspapers, to refer customers to a range of outlets (including shops).

A second group of distributors who clearly valued the placing of newspaper advertisements were those starting up in an expanding or newly developing trade like the grocers and tea dealers or the chemists and druggists. These trades were ones where competition was fierce and price fixing commonplace. To some extent retailers involved in the fashion trade found themselves pressured in a similar way. Although there happen to be none in the two years reviewed, there was a scattering of advertisements in other years announcing new spring stock or the latest fashions from London.[120]

For retailers courting high-class customers, newspaper advertising was associated with pushy sales techniques and was thus a sensitive issue. Wedgwood had written in 1771, 'I would much rather not advertise at all if you think the sales are in such a way as to do without it',[121] though he later overcame his reluctance. After the appearance of two unsolicited 'puffs' in 1770 by his competitors he wrote to his partner urging that they too should 'get another article in the next paper to complete the Triumvirate'.[122] Wedgwood was not alone in his reluctance to use newspaper advertisements. In the first issue of the *Liverpool Chronicle* in 1757, the editorial was 'a dissertation on the Utility of News Papers'. A considerable section of this was devoted to an apologia on newspaper advertisements which contained the comment that:

> It is not many years since it was thought mean and disreputable, in any tradesmen of worth and credit, to advertise the sale of his commodities in a public Newspaper, but as those apprehensions were founded only on custom, and not on reason, it is become now fashionable for very eminent tradesmen to publish their business, and the peculiar goods wherein they deal, in the News Papers, by way of Advertisement; nor can any one make appear what disgrace there can be in this, for do not the great trading corporations apprize the public of their sales in the public News Papers? In a word Advertisements in these papers form, on the general, to be of no less utility to the public in the concerns of real

---

[120] For example, Mrs Barney, a milliner of Wolverhampton announced she was 'Just returned from London with a compleat Assortment of the most fashionable Good for the ensuing Spring', *Aris's Birmingham Gazette*, 1 May 1780.

[121] Wedgwood Museum, MSS, Leith Hill Place, Wedgwood to Thomas Bentley, quoted by McKendrick (1982), 'Josiah Wedgwood', p. 123.

[122] Wedgwood Museum, MSS E.18325-25, Wedgwood to Thomas Bentley, quoted in McKendrick (1982), 'Josiah Wedgwood', p. 125.

business, to the trading and busy World, than the Common news is to people of more leisure, ... [123]

Curiously Wedgwood also strongly objected to an widely used alternative form of advertisement, the trade card or hand bill, which he forbade to his showrooms on the grounds that 'We have hitherto appeared in a very different light to common Shopkeepers, but this step (in my opinion) will sink us exceedingly ... it being a mode of advertisement I never approv'd of ...'.[124] This form of advertisement was nevertheless attractive to many a shopkeeper who was interested in appealing to consumers in the immediate area accessible to his shop for whom the widespread dissemination of a newspaper advertisement had little attraction.

Dating survivals is usually impossible, although few seem to belong to the seventeenth century. By the late eighteenth many retailers used them, and engravers like Matt Darly advertised on their own cards their willingness to execute this type of work.[125] Whatever Wedgwood felt about them they were part of the normal marketing apparatus of retailers, especially those catering for the élite. Trade cards conveyed messages at many levels which would have been well understood by potential customers at a time when all, the illiterate no less than the educated, were attuned to visual and symbolic expression. Take, for example, the trade card issued by Mrs Holt's Italian warehouse.[126] The vignette is enclosed by olive trees, a traditional symbol of plenty and a component of the sign that hung above her shop. With nice economy of expression the idea of plentifulness is thus linked pictorially with her address, which is more fully laid out in the text. Five small sub-pictures represent five Italian towns, each the source of well-known luxury goods. Though most of these were in this period also made in Britain, the evocative nature of their foreign origins was still powerful. Again the image is re-inforced by text; *Leghorne* Hats, *Venice* Treacle, *Florence* Cordials and *Bolognia* 'Sausidges'. The classical figures suggest a discerning public capable of understanding the allusion, while the coat of arms portrayed on the back of the ship implies royal patronage of the highest order. Everywhere there are signs of the good things available, which the sturdy seamen strain to carry on board. Written in elegant hand, the script is no less evocative and reinforces the images, cataloguing the wares and culminating in that '&c' to promise more bounty than can be listed. A subtlety of advertising easily missed is the signature of the man who

---

[123] *Liverpool Chronicle*, 6 May 1757.

[124] Wedgwood Museum MSS E.18427-25, quoted in McKendrick (1982), 'Josiah Wedgwood', p. 124.

[125] For example, Matts Darly, Banks collection, 91.7.

[126] Heal collection, 126.10. Olive trees were also a sign commonly used by Italian warehouses, see Larwood and Hotten (1866), *History of signboards*, p. 242.

**3.6** Tradecard of Mrs Holt

designed and printed the card, William Hogarth, the great artist and engraver. No doubt he signed it to advertise his own work, but the choice of a fashionable engraver by Mrs Holt would hardly have been missed by her customers. Such attention to detail may appear excessive to modern eyes, but the number of trade cards that were claimed falsely to have been the work of the great artist suggest that some at least of her contemporaries were appreciative of his skill and prestige if unwilling to pay the price.[127]

Although Mrs Holt's trade card is one of the most sophisticated of surviving trade cards, there are many others of a similar standard. The hat-maker Charles Paget's trade card operates no less cleverly, though in a different way.[128] The manufacture of top quality hats required beaver and cony fur, plucked not from the living animal, but from the skin taken from a corpse. Even at a time when death was treated more as a matter of fact, this was not a comfortable image to present to the public. On Paget's trade card the beaver and the cony were represented as living happy creatures, rather as a smiling pig or a laughing chicken is used today to advertise the products of their own flesh, so that the happy porker or the happy chukka chuke somehow becomes identified with the Happy Eater. In the same way, Paget's trade card portrays, not the dead skins which were the raw materials of his trade, but attractive, almost cuddly animals. Even the camel represented on the card looks approachable. Yet at the same time, Paget reminds his customers of his quality products made only of the best materials.

Trade cards and hand bills, printed on sheets of paper or card of an appropriate size, were distributed on the street in front of the shop, handed to customers inside or even used as the reverse side of a bill. They were also intended as aides memoires to those who had already given their custom to remind them not only what was on offer, but also the whole ethos and ambience of the relationship between themselves and the retailer. In all likelihood they were useful to country customers who had to shop by post or through a local agent or the medium of other people. The needs of those shopping at a distance were also met by a development of catalogues towards the end of the eighteenth century. Relatively few survive but those that do show well how these documents too were intended not just to inform, but to create an ambience. For example, the cover of 'Bettison's Catalogue' of London and Margate dated 1794, is in the same form as many simple trade cards, but with the royal arms prominently displayed. The 24 page catalogue itself starts with a poetic address 'TO THE NOBILITY and GENTRY OF MARGATE, AND ITS ENVIRONS' beginning thus:

---

[127] Heal (1925), *London tradesmen's cards*, suggests a number of false attributions in his collection; for example, Richard Hand, p. 68 and No. V.
[128] Heal collection, 12.283.

**3.7** Tradecard of Charles Paget

WITH due respects all friends we greet,
Whose bus'ness leads them down High-Street,
And beg they condescend to stop
And view the goods in BETTISON'S shop;
Where humour, taste and sense display
The various follies of the day.
Walk in, and view, enough you'll find
To please the eye, inform the mind;[129]


## Conclusion

The study of retail provision through fixed shops in any part of the early modern period shows activity and diversity, with the retail sector flourishing at the beginning of the period, no less than at the end. In the sixteenth century, despite an apparent official preference for selling in the open street, the evidence suggests a range of shop styles, while the view held by many that the luxury trade was undesirable for the economic health of the country was belied by a flourishing sale of luxury goods from fixed shops.

It is evident that numerous different types of retail outlets co-existed, and that shopkeepers deployed different methods to sell their wares dependent upon the type of customer and the type of wares. The same range of shops could be found in the provinces as existed in London, but in the provinces the small serviceable shop was more common as was the larger one designed to cater for a socially mixed clientele. The attractive interiors and seductive displays of glass in fashionable London shops were occasionally replicated elsewhere, but there were plenty of successful provincial mercers, haberdashers, ironmongers and pewterers, who made their living by selling not only necessaries but also wares that gave comfort or convenience, or were desirable to possess or to consume.

This emphasis on a lively retail sector throughout the early modern period is not to suggest there was no change. Retailing was, as it still is, inextricably caught between production, transportation and wholesale marketing on the one hand, and the consuming public on the other. Increased spending power for a broad spectrum of people was matched by industrial innovation and newly discovered imported consumables. These are but two of the pressures for change. And change there was. The most dramatic and the most discernible was triggered by new possibilities in the use of the printed word. Newspapers, hardly of widespread significance before 1700, became a medium for advertisement and a vehicle for creating networks through which branded

---

[129] Banks collection, 93.8. Another example is the '*catalogue of various goods, imported, manufactured and sold by Jasper Taylor, Oilman*', of London. It is not dated but belongs to the eighteenth century also from the Banks collection, 89.39.

goods could be marketed on a national scale. For some types of goods this was to change the nature of their retailing. Print also enabled retailers to advertise themselves through trade cards and bill heads and to attract a clientele shopping from a distance.

The effects of all these changes were contradictory, both encouraging fixed prices and cash sales in some areas of trade, while extending the use of credit in others. The increased use of such techniques, for none was entirely new, called for changes in shop lay-out. The effect on customers was considerable, and will be discussed more fully in the next chapter.

# Chapter 4

# 'For a tradesman ... his customers are to be his idols':[1] the relationship between the retailer and his customers

The idea that there was once a self-sufficient society dies hard.[2] If such a society ever existed it had certainly disappeared in England by the Middle Ages, and had probably gone long before. Even those who still hold to the idea of a largely self-sufficient rural society would accept that the aristocracy lived at a far higher and more complex level than their inferiors. Few would be surprised by Dyer's description of an aristocratic way of life in the late middle ages transcending geographical differences and resulting in a largely international society with a common culture. He suggests that there is plenty of evidence of a cosmopolitan repertoire of dishes recorded in medieval cookery books involving not only local staples but also imported items like wine and spices. Such a diet involved substantial purchasing. For example, during 1452/53 the Duke of Buckingham's household consumed no less than 2lb. of spices per day on average through the year.[3] Most aristocratic and gentry accounts of the period reveal also a heavy expenditure on fabrics, and though much of this was produced locally, there was at least some outlay on imported silks and linens.[4] Metal goods made of silver, pewter and the copper alloys were also important elements in the household expenditure, and virtually all must have come from specialist producers.[5] Although some purchasing, maybe most of it, was through fairs and markets, some was undoubtedly from shops, as revealed in the formidable shop inventory of a Southampton merchant who

---

[1]  Defoe (1987), *Complete English tradesman*, p. 71.

[2]  For example, Holderness (1972), 'Rural tradesmen', p. 82, avers that before 1870 'The shift from a rural society which was largely self-sufficient for all its common wants, to a community dependent on retail supplies of one type or another had *begun* to be apparent' (my italics).

[3]  Dyer (1989), *Standards of living*, pp. 63, 66-7.

[4]  Dyer (1989), *Standards of living*, pp. 78-9.

[5]  See for example, Hatcher and Barker (1974), *History of British pewter*, chapter 2.

died in 1447.[6] There can be no doubt then that for the upper echelons of society, purchasing from shops in some form or another was a pre-requisite of the standard of living (in its broadest sense) appropriate to their station.

What has been less broadly accepted is that some people towards the other end of the social scale also had access to purchased goods. Although the peasantry used goods rather than made profits, some, though probably not all, had a small cash surplus in some years, allowing the acquisition of a few items like salt, herrings, clothing, furnishings and kitchen utensils. Most townsmen, like some of their country cousins, must have had access to the market. In the large towns at least, there appears to have been 'quite a rich material culture' in which clothing accessories of metal, bone and wood, household fittings and other equipment were commonplace. Many of these artefacts must have been bought and it is at least probable that some came from shops.[7]

In the mid-sixteenth century the polemic poem by the so-called Dives Pragmaticus supports the thesis of a broadly based material culture dependent on a healthy retail sector. His 'callyng of people to sale of his marchaundyse' apparently assumed that a wide spectrum of society would be able to take advantage of his wares from the pope to the lowly sexton, and from emperors, kings and lords down to husbandmen and craftsmen. Furthermore he included women among those who he assumed had money to spend, addressing not only gentleman, master and tradesman, but also gentlewoman, mistress, good wife, mother and fair maid.[8] Nevertheless, it can not be gainsaid that all his potential customers had some status in society. Dives does not appear to have been addressing those whose spending power was minimal; and like any merchant he did not even stop to consider those who had no money at all. Those with no surplus cash at the end of the year had to do without even the near essentials like a cooking pot, a knife and salt, while the occasional luxury of a yard of decorative inkle[9] or a pair of buckles must have been beyond their wildest dreams. Thus although a great many could participate in the consumer market from the beginning of the early modern period, it would be quite wrong to equate this with a mass market. It is also unfortunately impossible to estimate the proportion excluded.

What is only a hint of a consuming market well down the social scale contained in the poem of Dives Pragmaticus in mid-sixteenth century, becomes increasingly solid evidence over time. Weatherill's study of material culture in the century after the Restoration provides firm statistical evidence of the level of comfort in the home, much of which depended on purchased goods. Even in

---

6   Richard Thomas, 'mercator' of Southampton (1447), transcribed and translated in Roberts and Parker (eds) (1992), 'Southampton probate inventories', vol. I, pp. 2-9.
7   Dyer (1989), *Standards of living*, pp. 109-16, 170, 196-9, 205-7.
8   Dives Pragmaticus (1563), A *booke in Englysh metre*.
9   A tough tape, often decorative, used for such purposes as making apron strings.

the poorest group in her sample, 52 per cent had cooking pots, 76 per cent had some pewter, 17 per cent had earthenware and 14 per cent even had looking-glasses, while 6 per cent had books, 5 per cent pictures, 2 per cent knives and forks and 1 per cent china, suggesting that the group may have included some relatively well-to-do living in the home of a relative.[10] Although this may suggest that the figures are somewhat high, it does not invalidate her findings overall with regard to this group. All these objects found by Weatherill must have been purchased at some time indicating some surplus cash beyond basic living needs. Most of these people were not the poorest of the poor, but by no standard can most of them be regarded as of the middling sort.

Occasional pieces of evidence are telling. For example, one argument brought forward against the 1692 bill for regulating hawkers was that if chapmen and pedlars did not come to the door, servants would go out to the shops and risk moral corruption.[11] It is significant that it was assumed servants would be buying the sort of things that itinerants sold, such as ribbons, buttons, personal accessories, even linen and the like; what was at issue was merely where they would make the purchase. Those who had access to the kitchen door were purchasing consumers who, if one point of access to the market were denied to them, would find another. It is unlikely that the acquisitive aspirations of such people were substantially different from their own families or from those of similar social and economic status. Even if it was the act of becoming a servant that broadened horizons, then each servant must have acted as a missionary bringing new products and new dreams to the unenlightened when they returned home. And when they left service, as many did, they would have carried habits of consumption and acquisition into their new life.

A different sort of evidence for the first half of the eighteenth century concerning the purchasing activity of those at the lower end of the middling sort is furnished by the account book of the small yeoman farmer, Richard Latham of Scarisbrick, who began to keep a record of some of his outgoings shortly after his marriage in 1723. His accounts show that although he was not poor, he was certainly not well-to-do, indeed he appears to have struggled at times. Nevertheless, a breakdown of his expenditure year by year from 1724 to 1740 shows that he never made less than five purchases of groceries a year, and no year passed without at least one purchase each of utensils, clothing and haberdashery. Even books and medical items were purchased virtually every year.[12] Latham's minimal accounts suggest outings, probably of himself accompanied by members of his family, to buy quite a range of goods even if the total expenditure was small. For example, between 3 August and 10

10  Weatherill (1988), *Consumer behaviour*, Table 5.1. The poorest group concerned those dying with a personal estate valued at under £5.

11  Thomas (1983), *Man and the natural world*, p. 247.

12  Weatherill (1988), *Consumer behaviour*, Table 6.1.

September 1748, he bought a new coat for one daughter and handkerchiefs for two of the others, some flax and some meat, treacle, a new sickle, a besom, candles, venice turpentine, nails, spices, sugar, salt and soap all costing just under 8s.[13] Whether this represents one family outing or several opportunistic purchases whilst attending the market is unknown, but something was probably bought for each of the children still living at home, as well as several items for the household.

By the eighteenth century it is rare to find a substantial retailing tradesman who did not sell sugar, the odd spice like ginger and pepper, thread, inkle and buttons, handkerchiefs and tobacco; even the smallest shop had at least two or three. Those items had become the stock in trade of the minimal retailers, carried by them because there was a ready sale among the nearly poor. A good illustration of a shop servicing the lower end of the market may be found in the accounts of William Wood of Didsbury in the 1780s. Typical items for sale were in part similar to those purchased by Latham half a century early, like sugar, treacle and spices, though Wood also sold provisions like flour and bacon which Latham had little need to buy. The way that Wood defined some of his regular credit customers suggests that they were of lower social standing than Latham, like 'ould William Chase', while others are known to have been labourers, menial servants or shoemakers.[14]

One suspects that the wretched inmates of any poor-house of the late eighteenth century would have frequented shops like Wood's in better times. As it was their life in old age was made marginally more tolerable by a few comforts. Sugar or molasses were bought regularly by some poor-house officials, suggesting these commodities were regarded as an acceptable part of the diet of the poor. Even in others when the regulations banned the provision of tea, tobacco and spirits for fear of being accused of offering luxuries to the indigent, such items did appear, though they were often disguised as medical necessities. Complaints that inmates spent their tiny earnings on these forbidden luxuries also suggest that old habits died hard and that many of the poor had become accustomed to the consumption of these so-called luxuries and were not willing to forego the pleasure even when confined in the poor-house. [15]

To define the point below which the market did not reach is not the purpose of the argument here. Although it may merely be that the evidence becomes more solid over time, it seems more likely that that there actually was an increase in the number of people who could afford to purchase both consumables and durables. There was certainly also an increase in shops

---

[13]  Weatherill (1990), *Account book of Richard Latham*, p. 72.

[14]  Mui and Mui (1989), *Shops and shopkeeping*, pp. 212-13, based on Wood's Customers Ledger.

[15]  Shammas (1990), *Pre-industrial consumer*, p. 144.

intended to serve the lower end of the market. Be that as it may, what is undoubtedly true is that the market as a whole had to address the challenge of serving a socially mixed spectrum of society. For many fixed shop retailers it must have been a particular challenge to solve the problem of the great unwashed rubbing shoulders with the elegant and the refined within the confines of a small shop. For the customers, there was the challenge of finding what they wanted to buy in outlets that did not offend their own sense of position in society.

The subject, then, of this chapter is the relationship between customer and retailer and the strategies each party adopted to resolve the tension inherent in a dynamic market. Rather than a survey of the use of shops chronologically in all its facets, some aspects of this complex subject will be discussed in turn under three broad headings; exploiting different levels of provision, social aspects of shopping and shopping as a leisure activity.

### Customers using a variety of retailing outlets

A breakdown of the purchases of Richard Mitford, bishop of Salisbury, in 1406/07 shows that out of a recorded expenditure of £143, he spent £59 or roughly 40 per cent in London, mainly on preserved fish, wax, jewellery and spices (including almonds and dried fruits), £51 at large sea ports like Bristol and Southampton, mainly on imported wines, fish and iron, with a mere £5 at Salisbury itself spent largely on fresh fish and horseshoes. The rest was spent either locally, sometimes in small towns like Devizes, more rarely in villages on the estate like Potterne, or at distant specialist centres like Oxford. The accounts of less peripatetic households with similar incomes show much the same pattern. In 1466/67 King's College, Cambridge, used London tradesmen either directly or through their agents at Stourbridge fair to buy pewter, bells and fish. The last was also bought more locally from ports like Lynn, while cloth came from as far afield as Salisbury and Winchester. Relatively little was bought in Cambridge itself.[16]

The shopping activities of John Willoughby between 1644 and 1646 may have been constrained by the Civil War. Nevertheless he shopped widely in the principal towns of East Devon, though his accounts show no record of purchases in London. Unfortunately his accounts are not always informative about where he was purchasing; more common are entries like 'for pepper and standing the horse, 8d.', making clear that the outlet was at some distance.[17] Nevertheless a number of the towns he used are recorded; Honiton for fish and

---

[16] Dyer (1994), *Everyday life*, p. 260. See Laughton and Dyer (1999), 'Small towns', particularly pp. 36-9 for further evidence of similar activity by others in the same period.

[17] Gray, Todd (ed.) (1995), 'Devon household accounts', pp. 111-65.

meat, Seaton for pans and larks, Exon (i.e. Exeter) for fish, fruit, spices and salt, Ottery for beef and soap, and Taunton for unspecified goods. In addition there is the occasional tradesman named, like the mercer Mr Cullen (for silk, lace, buttons, cloth, trimming and tailoring), and Mrs Masie, from whom a barrel of raisins of the sun was purchased costing £2 with an additional 3s. for wrapping and carriage.[18] However impossible it may be to establish a precise picture of his shopping habits and the reasons for them, it is nevertheless certain that he had a range of options and used them.

   Almost a century later, the surviving records of the Purefoy family of Shalstone in Buckinghamshire (1735-53) tell much the same story of a mixture of distant and local shopping, though for them London suppliers may have played a greater part than those living more distantly. Fish as much 'as will come to 3s. or 3s. 6d.' was delivered weekly from James Fisher of Newgate Market, London, though he was by no means the only fishmonger patronized.[19] Wine and spirits in variety also usually came from London from a Mr Moulson, though a local tradesman was used on occasions.[20] Sugar, coffee, tea were frequently ordered from London, usually, but by no means always, from the Willsons near St Paul's churchyard.[21] Other grocery came from Brackley, a local market town, usually from the grocer Mr Yates, who also acted as a go-between to supply goods he either did not stock at all or not of the required quality.[22] Other tradesmen recorded among the published letters include a ropemaker and a gardener of Brackley, an ironmonger, a brushmaker and a chandler of Buckingham, and a purveyor of pickled mushrooms of Deddington. Razors were sharpened in Oxford and blankets obtained through circuitous negotiations from Witney.[23]

   Most furnishings also came from London, but some quite expensive goods were obtained locally, for example from a chairmaker and a clockmaker of Bicester, a brazier and a carver of Buckingham and a clockmaker of Helmdon.[24] Much the same pattern of purchasing applies to the acquisition of clothing. Mostly the tradesmen were London milliners, mercers, drapers and the like, but 'a fashionable pair of Russia leather tops for half Jack boots' were ordered from Buckingham, and 'blew Cloath' from Brackley, while tailors from Brackley, Tingewick and Chipping Norton were employed, although perhaps not for the more fashionable clothing. A mercer from Bicester supplied

---

[18]   Gray (ed.) (1995), 'Devon household accounts', p. 151.

[19]   Eland (1931), *Purefoy letters*, pp. 61-5. Similar evidence could be extracted from Mitchell (1973), *Purefoy letters*, which contains a different selection of documents, but in the matter of purchasing practices reveals little new.

[20]   Eland (1931), *Purefoy letters*, pp. 70-80.

[21]   Eland (1931), *Purefoy letters*, pp. 67-70.

[22]   Eland (1931), *Purefoy letters*, pp. 66, 70.

[23]   Eland (1931), *Purefoy letters*, pp. 82-92.

[24]   Eland (1931), *Purefoy letters*, chapter V.

some of the materials and saw to the making up of several garments.[25] Most of the tradesmen were sited either in local villages or market towns, but there was a considerable extension of the range towards Oxford in the south west, which was itself some twenty miles away.

Nicholas Blundell was a contemporary of the Purefoys, but he lived more remotely from London and used it correspondingly less. Even so, he bought silks, haberdashery, tea and coffee regularly from the metropolis, as well as making occasional purchases of other items like snuff and garden seeds. For most purposes, Liverpool satisfied his requirements for high-quality goods while some more mundane goods like candles, physic and soap were bought at Ormskirk.

Beyond this regular framework of a distant London, an accessible large centre and a local market town, his shopping strategy seems to have been fairly chaotic, depending largely on circumstances and chance. Certainly the established retailers in Liverpool could not have afforded to be complacent, since there was a variety of other salesmen operating in different ways that competed for, and sometimes gained, his custom. For example, he attended Chester fair more than once despite its awkward position for him south of the Mersey, and while there bought items that one would have thought he could have acquired more easily in Liverpool, including some made to measure stays.[26] He also used Preston, and Ashbourne in Derbyshire, in a similar way. Most local fairs, like Salford, Weeton and Prescot were visited and goods purchased. He was attracted to a visiting scotchman 'who had a chamber ... of rich goods', and to another 'Rich Pedlor' who sold him some silver hafted knives and forks.[27] Visitors to his door were often successful, including a woman with flint glass, a pedlar with fustian called 'holland strip', Betty Thomas, who came out of Liverpool to sell 'some Forraine goods and 'One from Ormskirk [who] was here to acquaint me he had Muslins &c to sell'.[28] Interestingly he recorded the purchase at the door of some 'Indian Chink Callico', which, if it was really the genuine imported textile, was illegal, as well as some chairs from Ireland.[29] On those occasions when hostility to Roman Catholics flared up, he discreetly removed the family to Flanders and on the way visited the New Exchange in London as well as buying lace and a calico night gown in Dunkirk.[30]

---

[25] Eland (1931), *Purefoy letters*, chapter XII.

[26] For example, Blundell (1968-72), *Great diurnal*, 26 January 1726.

[27] Blundell (1968-72), *Great diurnal*, 21 September 1726; 2 March 1726.

[28] Blundell (1968-72), *Great diurnal*, 24 September 1712, 7 December 1712, 1 November 1720, 23 March 1710.

[29] Blundell (1968-72), *Great diurnal*, 23 March 1715, Statutes 11 & 12 GUL3 c. 10 (1700) and 7 GEO1 c. 7 (1720); Blundell (1968-72), *Great diurnal*, 11 February 1723.

[30] Blundell (1968-72), *Great diurnal*, 19 November 1716, 2 July 1723.

Purchasing from such a variety of outlets depended upon a network of reliable carriers. The *Carriers Cosmographie* of 1637 indicates that there was reasonably well-organized and extensive carrier services by the early seventeenth century.[31] From the Restoration it was much improved, particularly when it became possible to advertise in newspapers and hand bills. Where Willoughby in Devonshire seems to have relied upon his servants to fetch and carry, the Purefoys and the Blundells in less disturbed times could exploit an efficient and competitive service of carriers. Through them even such perishables as fish and oysters could be relied upon to arrive in satisfactory condition, barring a few disasters. The Purefoys used at least four carriers. Scattered references suggest that goods could be sent or delivered on practically any day of the week either through Brackley or through Buckingham. For the Blundells carriage was a more complex matter, but they seems to have had few problems about arrangements, though it is sometimes difficult now to establish the full mechanisms used until more is known about the people involved. Goods purchased in London were boxed up, usually by a Mrs Aldridge, a friend and tradesman in London and probably connected with an upholsterer of that name in Liverpool, and sent up to Liverpool or Ormskirk for collection.[32] Carriage from the metropolis was not cheap. Usually the cost seems to have been a few shilling, but on one occasion, when boxes were sent down to pack the goods, the total cost of carriage on a consignment worth only £6 came to 8s. 11d., and on another some London pewter was charged at the rate of 1d. per lb.[33] Similar arrangements were made to get goods home purchased at Preston or Chester, though on one occasion some stays made to fit were brought over from Chester by the staymaker himself, while on another the purchases made at the time of the fair, mainly of groceries, involved the purchase of 'Mugs, Box & Bag to hold the goods' as well as the carriage.[34]

Blundell's shopping range was extensive, considerably larger than that of the Purefoys, and it is not easy to see why. Liverpool was an excellent shopping centre and it seems unlikely that dearth of choice could have been a factor. Yet in an area notoriously ill supplied with good roads, Blundell chose to go to Preston some 25 miles to the north, to Salford about 30 miles to the east and to Chester some 40 miles to the south, besides many outlets in between.[35] Many of these visits may have been necessitated by estate business,

---

31 Hey (1980), *Packmen*, pp. 211-24, discusses the development of the carrying trade, although he focuses particularly on Derbyshire and southern Yorkshire. See also Gerhold (1993), *Road transport*, chapter 2.

32 For example, Blundell (1968-72), *Great diurnal*, 28 March 1711.

33 Blundell (1968-72), *Great diurnal*, 28 March 1711, 20 May 1718.

34 Blundell (1968-72), *Great diurnal*, 26 January 1726; 19 July 1710.

35 For example, Blundell (1968-72), *Great diurnal*, Chester, 19 July 1710, 26 January 1727; Preston, 2 July 1708, 10 July 1727; Salford, 25 June 1724.

but the fact remains that Blundell chose to combine business with domestic and personal shopping in distant places despite the hassle involved.[36]

It would be a mistake to suppose that a purchasing strategy of this complexity was the exclusive prerogative of the rich, though information on the lesser sort of customer is sparse. The accounts of even a small yeoman like Richard Latham suggest he was a substantial shopper. As a farmer, Latham was not dependent on a weekly wage, with all the implications of that type of income on the pattern of purchasing. Instead sporadic sales of stock and crops would have given him relatively large but equally sporadic amounts of cash to spend. One would expect this pattern of income to be reflected in a similar pattern of expenditure, with large outgoings on domestic needs at sporadic intervals. This is not quite what the accounts show. Instead Latham is revealed as a regular shopper, buying sugar, for instance, in the 1740s in smallish quantities two or even three times a month, probably being offered credit by his regular supplier.

Latham referred only incidentally and sporadically to the places he visited. It is thus impossible to draw up a definitive list of places, let alone of retail outlets, patronised by him. Despite this paucity of information in the accounts, he recorded visits not only to Ormskirk, the nearest market town of any size, but also to Skelmersdale, Preston, Wigan and Liverpool. Besides these substantial - and relatively distant - centres of retailing trade, he and his family regularly attended fairs, often only recorded because they involved expenditure on fairings like gingerbread. The fairs he named include those at Bursko (presumably Burscough), Prescot , Ruffert and Standish, not all by any means local.[37] It would be unwise to assume that all the recorded visits involved shopping, but some indubitably did. For example, the mention of Preston on 24 March 1750 was associated with expenditure on an iron pan and possibly with the purchase of '2 littel books'.[38] Some town visits seem to have been recorded because the actual journey itself involved expenditure, so that it may be assumed that other visits were made without mention because no actual travelling expenses were incurred. Indeed the number of records for a particular town is almost inversely proportionate to its distance from his home, with Ormskirk, his nearest market town hardly mentioned at all, unlike Liverpool and Preston, although these were some distance away and can only have been visited occasionally. Latham's use of such a range of commercial centres may in part be explained by the specialized nature of some markets and fairs. For

---

[36] A similar pattern of purchasing revealed in the papers of a woman from Lancashire, Elizabeth Shackleton, is discussed in Vickery (1993), 'Women and the world of goods', p. 289.

[37] Weatherill (1990), *Account book of Richard Latham*, p. 18 (Burscough), p. 67 (Prescot), p. 60 (Ruffert), p. 18 (Standish).

[38] Weatherill (1990), *Account book of Richard Latham*, p. 78.

example, Preston was noted as a market for linen and hemp, which could account for at least one of his visits to that town.[39] Be that as it may, it seems probable, though it cannot be proved, that Latham and his family availed themselves of a wide range of outlets from fair and market stalls to the shops in several different commercial centres. It is certain that he was nowhere near self-sufficient and his business interests as a farmer afforded him at least the opportunity of shopping at various levels. Even his rather uninformative accounts suggest a large range, albeit smaller than Blundell's, but still stretching to about 17 miles in all directions but to the west where the sea intervened.

People like Latham may have gone quite far afield on business, usually to visit markets, and it appears to have been widely assumed by the trade that they might well also visit the shops. This awareness had its effect on the siting of shops. William Stout of Lancaster, for example, referred to a shop 'being situate in the best of the market place'.[40] Advertisements in local newspapers show the degree to which certain types of retailer were located in or near the market place and therefore easily accessible to those in town primarily for other reasons. For example, the grocer and hosier, John Armson, took a shop in the market-place, Leicester in 1760, while in 1770 the saddler John Whitaker, who already had premises in Stourbridge, opened a Shop 'near the Town-Hall in Bridgnorth ... where he duly attends every Market Day'.[41] Other shopkeepers trading from less favourable sites, were prepared to move. For example, the Nottingham bookseller, John Ireland, announced in 1760 that he was removing from Eastgate 'to the Shop late Mr Barnard Thickpenny's ... in the Market-Place'.[42] John Scoles spelled out more explicitly the reasons for his move in 1790 when he transferred his Tea Warehouse from Deansgate in Manchester 'to a more central situation ... near the Bottom of Market-street Lane'.[43] Those letting or selling shop premises were quick to point out the advantages of a site near or in the market place. The situation of one 'good-accustomed SHOP' was 'inferior to none ... being in the Heart of the Market' while another 'very desirable shop' 'fronted to two different Aspects of the ... Market' which was therefore in 'a good Situation, if not the best of any in Town for a Retail Business'.[44] The advertisement of the leases of two messuages in Congleton, Cheshire in 1760 highlight the importance attached to a market site for the

---

[39] For details of market specialists see Chartres (1990), *Agricultural markets*, pp. 138-41. Latham's visit to Preston in 1729 was associated with flax; see Weatherill (1990), *Account book of Richard Latham*, p. 15.

[40] Stout (1967), *Autobiography*, p. 220, the entry for 1737.

[41] *Leicester and Nottingham Journal*, 29 November 1760; *Aris's Birmingham Gazette*, 16 April 1770.

[42] *Leicester and Nottingham Journal*, 6 September 1760.

[43] *Manchester Mercury*, 22 June 1790.

[44] *Manchester Mercury*, 6 July 1790; *Aris's Birmingham Gazette*, 19 June 1780.

retailer; the one is a 'handsome sash'd house, situate in the Corn Market, with a large Shop ... very commodious for a Grocer, Ironmonger or Mercer', whereas the other, although 'a good house ... in the middle of the town' was apparently for non-retailing tradesmen such as the previous occupant who was a 'Jersey Comber and Stuff Maker'.[45] The evidence is overwhelming that shopkeepers were well aware of the possibilities of a site in the market place. For some shoppers this close associations of two different types of outlet made regular shopping more convenient, but for those who found themselves on matters of business in more distant locations, it must have been almost a necessity.

For Londoners there was no need for much locational diversity, the metropolis being sufficient for all their needs. At the top end of the retailing hierarchy were the pure retailers like the mercers, some of whose shops were already designed and furnished for genteel shopping in the latter half of the seventeenth century. The Royal Exchange and the New Exchange, opened respectively in 1571 and 1609, each had a gallery of small shops or stalls selling largely fashionable goods and operating through as it were the shop window, but for the social élite. A plethora of producer/retailers supplied customers in rooms opening onto the street behind which lay their workplaces. For food and mundane goods there were several markets and a growing number of food shops and petty chandlers, while the streets swarmed with hawkers and street traders of every description. The diary of Samuel Pepys shows that he used all of the types of outlet listed above, showing something of the complexity of shopping for an upwardly mobile Londoner.

His diary shows something more. It opens when he was at the beginning of his career and when for him appropriate and extravagant dress was an adjunct to progress. He described each acquisition in some detail, and his diary conveys something of his excitement in the process - the choice of cloth, the fittings, the first appearance and his anxieties about spoiling the new finery. What is frequently absent is the name of his suppliers. Presumably his father, who was a tailor, was able to satisfy most of his requirements of dress, but Pepys also patronized others, ranging from the anonymous mercer in Lombard Street, from whom he purchased 'a suit of lute-string' for his wife, to the named Mr Pym who was also the tailor to his patron, Lord Sandwich.[46]

The idea of using particular tradesmen as a means to social advancement is supported not only by Pepys's attitude to Mr Pym the tailor, but also by his more overt comments on visits to other shopkeepers. Pepys was at pains to record visits to two noted tradesmen, although he was obviously unacquainted with either; 'Truelocke, the famous gunsmith' and Turlington, the spectacles maker, and 'it seems, ... famous for them'.[47] It may be significant that on each

---

[45] *Manchester Mercury*, 18 March 1760.

[46] Pepys (1985), *Diary*, 18 February 1660/61, 14 October 1661.

[47] Pepys (1985), *Diary*, 29 March 1667, 18 October 1667.

occasion he used the term 'famous'. Another tradesmen of like genre was Mr Greatorex, the mathematical instrument maker. He was no less notable in his day, and Pepys's motives for visiting him initially may have been entirely in terms of social advancement. However, Pepys became so interested in his products that the first visit became one of a series and the records of such occasions were less of fame than of desirable curiosities.[48] The acquisitive rather than the emulative emotions came to the fore.

## Social aspects of shopping

Nowadays it is commonplace to speak of the importance of the retail sector to the economic well being of the country at large, as well as to specific communities. However, apart from the dying breed of village and corner shops, shops and shopkeepers are rarely considered as being integral to the social, as opposed to the economic, life of a community. Shopping is perceived as an important economic activity, perhaps with leisure implications for individual shoppers, but it is not considered as central to the social fabric. In the early modern period shopping was for some embedded in a social relationship from which both sides, shopkeeper and customer, benefited. Although such ideas were by no means fundamental to all shopping or to all shoppers in the early modern period, for some, and some shopkeepers, social cohesion was part of the relationship and an important element in the success of the business. It must be stressed that it was not inherent in all shopping and in some types of business association it was more important than others.

### (a) Selling to the socially superior

The large household of the social élite is a case in point. Here it is unlikely that there would have been any sort of personal relationship between the master or mistress of a grand establishment and most of the tradesmen who serviced it and whose business benefited from it. Such personal relationships as did develop were at a different level. It was the steward and the other officials in a noble household who arranged most purchasing, not the person who paid the bill and it was with those people that the tradesman had to forge a profitable understanding.

The Household Accounts and Disbursement Books of Robert Dudley, Earl of Leicester, in the late sixteenth century and the Diary of the shopkeeper Thomas Turner in the mid-eighteenth suggest that the shopping habits of the great did not alter much over the years. Although the two sources are quite

---

48  For example, Pepys (1985), *Diary*, 24 October 1660.

different, the practices portrayed are not. Dudley's accounts show most transactions were conducted through his steward or other officials of his household, as recorded in the reimbursement of the servant Robert Pitchford 'the same day which he paid for iiij paire of dry perfumed gloves for your lordship at ijs iiijd a paire'. A distinction was sometimes made between the regular tradesmen and the occasionally visited. So one named Cokke was designated as '*your lordship's* haberdasser', while another, Shepperde, was no more than '*a* haberdasser' a month or two later. Whereas Cokke was supplying 'blacke silke nightcaps' at 6s. each, Shepperd contribution was 'wassht gloves' at 3s., so perhaps the difference lay in the quality of goods supplied; the one who supplied the expensive and the unusual was rewarded with an acknowledged patronage, whereas the purveyor of more ordinary wares had to be satisfied with the odd casual sale.[49] It is, however, at least possible that the steward had formed relationship with Cokke beyond that of buyer and seller and he had not with Shepperde. The range of suppliers named in these accounts confirms the complexity of supplying a noble household in London. Any idea of a high degree of self sufficiency from his Lordship's estates must be abandoned; virtually everything was purchased

The implications of this type of second-hand relationship between servant and tradesman elusively implied in Dudley's accounts are all too apparent in the diary of Thomas Turner, the Sussex shopkeeper, although the two lived two centuries apart. The biggest potential custom in the district for Turner lay at Halland House, the Sussex mansion belonging to the Duke of Newcastle. Although its owner visited only occasionally, Turner was assiduous in fostering a relationship with the steward, Christopher Coates. At times the two of them appear to behave as if social equals, though Turner felt it necessary to oblige Coates, and their business transactions were more often than not negotiated at Halland rather than in the shop.[50] The presence of the Duke himself at Halland used to cause a flurry of visits by Turner. Before the public day in April 1761 Turner was 'To and fro at Halland' and on the day itself 'At Halland almost all day'. The following year, after another visit by the Duke, Turner was again at Halland to receive 'payment of Mr Coates in cash 18s. 2d. for a bill delivered the 14th for goods delivered to Halland for the use of the Duke of Newcastle this last time of his being here'.[51] Such details suggest that in strictly monetary terms, the association was not particularly profitable, though to be a supplier to the Duke, in however small a way, no doubt brought less easily definable benefits.

---

[49] Adams (1995), *Household accounts ... of Robert Dudley*, p. 180, 2 October 1584, and p. 225, 11 February 1585.

[50] For example, Turner (1984), *Diary*, 3 April 1759 and 31 July 1759.

[51] Turner (1984), *Diary*, 4-5 April 1761, 23 August 1762.

The association with such a grand neighbour, even at second hand, did not oblige Turner to extend or improve his premises to a level appropriate to a high class customer, since the Duke himself never had occasion to visit them. Turner manifested no anxiety about his shop and domestic quarters *vis à vis* the steward. They were apparently of sufficient quality to stand up to an occasional visit,[52] and in any case Turner was apparently able to contrive that he normally met Coates in the houses of other customers with some social status.[53] The relationship was nevertheless not entirely easy. For example on one occasion when Turner was at home settling accounts with one of his London suppliers, 'about 7.30 word came that I must go down to Halland; so I was obliged to leave Mr Collison alone'.[54] Halland was ever an imperative.

Halland was not the only socially superior establishment with which Turner did business. There were several other families of some status in the district whom Turner could not afford to offend by expecting them to call at the shop. Instead Turner took his wares to the customer. The strategy of active visiting was obviously successful. One visit to John Vine, a substantial tenant farmer and Turner's landlord for the schoolroom he rented, resulted in the sale of 'a frock and two waistcoats'.[55] Turner did not relate whether this visit had been preceded by one to show off patterns but this was obviously one of his selling methods; for example, on another occasion he called on Mr French, the biggest farmer after the Duke of Newcastle, with 'some patterns for Mrs French for a gown'.[56] Since the French and the Vine families mainly did their shopping from their own home, again there was no need for Turner to bring his shop up to the standard they might have expected, and indeed would have found, in establishments aspiring to exclusivity like London firms such as Harding, Howell & Co. or Morgan & Sanders, for whom a promotional prints were published in Ackermann's repository of 1809.[57]

The trade card of the Millinery warehouse, West's of London, illustrates another facet of the tradesman's approach to providing a service for the élite. His stock suggests fashionable goods, if not of the highest quality, but he offered 'A Back Door in Bear Street for a Coach';[58] possibly service at the coach door as an alternative to service at home and offering some of the same advantages to each side. Whereas the customer remained in the comfort of a home environment, the shopkeeper was not obliged to tie up capital in premises and fittings, because the customer did not enter the shop.

---

52 For example, Coates 'drank tea' at the Turner's household on 14 March 1758, then stayed on to play brag and to take supper, Turner (1984), *Diary*, p. 142.

53 For example, Turner (1984), *Diary*, 7 March 1758.

54 Turner (1984), *Diary*, 9 January 1759.

55 Turner (1984), *Diary*, 8 August 1754.

56 Turner (1984), *Diary*, 17 April 1755.

57 Reproduced in Walsh (1999), 'The newness of the department store', pp. 54, 61.

58 Attingham MSS, 112/6/Box 34/139.

*(b) Charades of gentility*

A recognition by tradesmen of the status of gentility ceased to be an exclusive prerogative of those accepted as genuine gentry during the eighteenth century. New style retail outlets, often using aggressive selling techniques, advertised wares certainly not intended for the gentry but in language that suggested they were. The plebeian or country customers likely to have been attracted to these wares were seduced by an assumed gentility. 'Gentleman' and 'Lady' became terms applied to all customers, though there was often an implied assumption that there were others of a lower status outside. A newcomer in 1750, for example, addressed himself to 'all Gentlemen, Ladies, Dealers and others'.[59] An advertisement for Stoughton's Elixir gave advice on how it should be taken in the form 'Gentlemen drink it in their Wine, Ladies in their Tea, and others in Beer'.[60] Edward Gibson, up from London to Birmingham, informed potential customers that 'The Tea-Kettle being always ready, Gentlemen and Ladies may try the teas', while J. Farror, just returned from London, invited his customers to try his teas and to view his 'rich and elegant Assembly of China Ware'.[61] An incomer in 1782 selling cheapish fabrics in a short term visit addressed his advertisement to 'Nobility, Ladies and Gentlemen and the Public in general'. He was selling only priced goods with no abatement, a common indication of low quality, but he promised 'Ladies and Gentlemen waited on with any of the above Goods at their own Houses and thought no trouble, buy or not'.[62] It is doubtful if a home visit was a reality for many, but the illusion was already beginning whereby all shoppers could imagine themselves esteemed and pampered, an illusion that was to find its full expression in the department store.[63]

*(c) Service through the window*

At the other end of the social scale, the nearly poor were using shops, though the privilege of going into the shop itself was often not for them. Although there is plenty of evidence of the non-élite using shops of all types, some of which sold over the counter, for many of the poor who were insufficiently respectable in appearance and certainly not creditworthy, the facility of the shop window gave them access to goods not available in other outlets like the market or the itinerant. This would particularly have applied to grocery. The

---

[59] *Aris's Birmingham Gazette*, 10 December 1750.
[60] *Aris's Birmingham Gazette*, 4 January 1742.
[61] *Aris's Birmingham Gazette*, 27 January 1752, 23 August 1790.
[62] *Manchester Mercury*, 8 October 1782.
[63] For a series of studies on the department store, see Crossick and Jaumain (1999), *Cathedrals of consumption*.

day book of William Wood of Didsbury is one of the few sources giving some insight into shopping through the window. Unlike inventories, his records give no indication of the shop layout, and there are only indirect clues on who bought through the window. The most distinctive feature of these purchasers was their anonymity. Even if known to Wood, they were not named and it is probably fair to assume that many were unable to gain credit, that it was inappropriate for them or that their presence was unwelcome to him. Probably most were of lower status, who in market towns combined their shopping with a visit to the regular weekly market or the annual fair. The use of assistants on market day, which is well documented, such as inferior workers, apprentices, or female relatives, was not necessarily to provide extra help as such. Stout, for example, often took the opportunity of these events to get out and collect in outstanding debts, leaving his sister in charge. This suggests that he expected most sales to be through the window and for cash and that assistants under these circumstances were not given the responsibility of deciding who was credit worthy.[64]

Sales through the window was an acceptable part of a retail system based on the weekly market, though it was found elsewhere as well, and it probably operated in a similar way; crude display, raucous shouting to attract buyers and negotiation of price. At what point if at all in this period market stall holders turned to fixed prices is not known, but as these became more acceptable to shopkeepers it seems likely that sales through the window fell into line with shop practice. However, this remains conjecture. What is certain is that the window in this sense remained a feature of retailing practice throughout the period, though some shops abandoned it altogether, and others incorporated it into a more complex selling strategy.

*(d) Dealing with the socially equal: service in the shop*

Whether a tradesman was doing business at a distance with social superiors or selling through the window to chance customers, he did not need much in the way of a shop. In the former case all he needed was a small room, often furnished with little more than a chest for keeping the stock secure, in the latter only display facilities out front similar to a market stall. Minimal premises of this type may be found throughout the early modern period, but they were most common in the sixteenth century, and to some extent died out subsequently. Such shops and their development in London were described briefly by John Stow in 1598. They were formerly 'sheds or shops with solers over them' but now were 'largely built on both sides, and also upwards, some three, four, or

---

64   For example, Stout (1967), *Autobiography*, p. 90 (1688).

five stories high'.[65] The change can probably be explained by an alteration in the balance of social mix among the customers, with a greater number expecting to be served from within the shop itself. As tradesmen became increasingly dependent on customers of equal or near equal social status, one solution was to modify the shop to provide adequate facilities. The transition from the almost bare lock-up premises characteristic of the sixteenth century to what would be recognizable as a shop to modern eyes is illustrated by the probate documents of two mercers from Wellington, Shropshire, each of whom died towards the end of the seventeenth century. The stock of Benjamin Wright (1700) suggests he served largely a market of relatively low social status, though the parts of his premises devoted to trade were quite extensive. His house was comfortable and fairly modern for the time, but his shop and warehouse were sparsely furnished. There was a coffer in the workhouse and a cupboard but, unless they were fixtures, no counter and no chairs. There is some evidence that Wright had some commerce with the local gentry,[66] but most of his trade was probably conducted through his shop window so that he had little need of expensive fittings. For this trade, his shop was sited advantageously, almost certainly being in the market square.[67] By contrast the stock of his fellow mercer, Joshua Johnson (1695/96) suggests he catered for a market somewhat further up the social scale from most of Wright's customers and his shop was commensurately furnished. He had a 'large glass', a counter 'with 3 boards on the side' under which there were six drawers. Along with these there were two other counters, some wainscoting in the shop and several nests of drawers and boxes. All that was obviously lacking for leisured shopping within the shop were some chairs. The listing of the lattice for the window suggests that, like Wright, only some of his customers came into the shop while others may have conducted their business through the window.[68]

Once the inside of the shop itself became the selling area, a new sort of relationship seems to have developed with customers in which some degree of intimacy and the offering of credit became important. The earliest noted clues to this new relationship appear in the 1660s, though this is not to say that the practice may not have been well established by then, but with no surviving evidence. As an avid reader and owner of books, Pepys's book sellers were almost personal friends. For example, in January 1660/61 he visited more than once 'my bookseller in St Paul's churchyard'.[69] Later he recorded the death of

---

[65] Stow (1598), *Survey of London*, p. 263.

[66] For example, on 6 October 1691 Wright was paid for supplying William Forrester for hops via another tradesmen (and probable connection), William Doughty, Forrester MSS, Box 296.

[67] Trinder and Cox (1980), *Yeomen and colliers*, pp. 23-6 and 314-21.

[68] Trinder and Cox (1980), *Yeomen and colliers*, pp. 22-3, 30 and 302-8.

[69] Pepys (1985), *Diary*, 5 January 1660/61, 18 January 1660/61, 23 January 1660/61.

Kirton, 'my bookseller', in November 1667 and not long after referred to 'my new bookseller'. In each case the use of 'my' is surely significant, and contrasts sharply with the impersonal 'mercer of Lombard Street' quoted earlier.[70] His provincial contemporary, the shopkeeper of Ashton in Makerfield, Roger Lowe, hinted in his diary of similar relationships. Twice in November 1663, he recorded that he kept shop all day, once with the comfort of a fire.[71] It seems a curiously inactive process, but for the following year an entry suggests that keeping shop had its companionable side, possibly serving the practical purpose of fostering relationships with customers. Lowe recorded in April 1664 that 'old Peter Lealand came to me, and sit in shop a good while, and att night I went to bringe him towards home, and we talked of times and about Mr Woods'.[72] This social bond also brought its problems. Lowe recorded some less comfortable social pressures he experienced;[73] ones that he was often unsuccessful in resisting. A drink was, and has remained, an established way of sealing a bargain, but in Lowe's case it all too often involved time he could ill afford away from his business. So when 'Old Jenkins this day came and payd me 11s. 9d.', Lowe allowed himself to be taken to the Ale house where Jenkins 'spent his 6d. on me'.[74] On another occasion when he tried to refuse an invitation, the threat of loss of custom was not just implied:

> This night I was envited to goe to Gawther Taylor's to drink Braggod, for wife bought her commodities of me, and she said if I would not come, then farewell; so I was constrained to goe, but I stayd but for a short time.[75]

The diary of the Sussex shopkeeper Thomas Turner gives a similar impression of long periods of inactivity punctuated by visitors. For many of his customers, who were more or less his social equals, shopping was combined with social intercourse, often in the form of drinking tea or of staying to share whatever meal was appropriate - breakfast and dinner are each mentioned more than once.[76] Some ostensible visits to the shop turned into extended social occasions, with Turner not altogether consenting, like the day that 'the curate of Laughton, came to the shop in the forenoon, and he, having bought some things of me (and I could wish he had paid for them), dined with me and also

---

[70] Pepys (1985), *Diary*, 11 November 1667, 10 January 1667/68.

[71] Lowe (1938), *Diary*, 16 and 25 November 1663.

[72] Lowe (1938), *Diary*, 7 April 1664.

[73] As is discussed in chapter 6, Lowe was an apprentice, keeping shop for a master whose main business was some distance away.

[74] Lowe (1938), *Diary*, 20 May 1664.

[75] Lowe (1938), *Diary*, 10 March 1664.

[76] For example, Turner (1984), *Diary*: 11 July 1764 Mrs Fuller, a widow (breakfast); 23 August 1762 Dame Roase, a widow and grocer of Lewes (tea); 29 October 1762 Jarvis Bexhill (dinner).

stayed in the afternoon till he got in liquor'.[77] Happier were some of the gatherings, particularly of women who came to buy, but stayed for the rest of the day to drink tea and play games like brag.[78] These long drawn-out social gatherings leave an impression of a shop where activities such as buying and selling were rare distractions, an impression confirmed by many entries bemoaning the lack of trade. 'At home all day, but very little to do' is a refrain that runs through page after page.[79] So often did he record that no-one had come to the shop, that one is left wondering how he managed to stay in business. This picture of a sadly decaying little shop is sharply dispelled by one entry in which he expands on what he actually meant by seeing no one. 'Not at all busy today,' he wrote for one autumn day in 1763, 'My spirits quite low, though I know not for what, unless it be for want of company, hardly ever seeing anyone but those who come to and from the shop'.[80] It is surely significant that he wrote of those who come *to and from* the shop, but not *into* it. It would appear that these were not people that counted, not even enough to come into the shop, and certainly not like those customers who passed through the shop to drink tea, eat dinner or play brag after their shopping was complete. Possibly these anonymous visitors to the shop purchased through the window.

Turner's experiences of the pressures of customer power were not dissimilar from those of Robert Lowe a century earlier. The need to avoid offence, however inconvenient had to be a priority. When Mr Sam. Gibbs called in to pay off his account, two other customers accompanied him. Turner wrote that 'common civility and gratitude obliged me to ask them all to walk in, which they did and stayed with me till near 7 o'clock'.[81] Time and again his resolutions to avoid drunkenness were broken. Although he was not always so explicit as Lowe, internal evidence suggests that good relations with customers, either real or potential, was a crucial factor in Turner's failure to control his drinking. The problem was probably exacerbated by one of his important customers, Jeremiah French, who seems to have been loud-mouthed and overbearing and who could best be kept sweet with '2 or 3 drams of old English gin'.[82] Turner's own wish that he could 'have the resolution to drink only water' was never fulfilled; another customer/friend would arrive and his resolve would fly out of the window. [83]

---

[77] Turner (1984), *Diary*, 25 November 1763.

[78] 'Fanny Hicks, James Marchant, Fanny Weller and Bett. Mepham drank tea with me, and they stayed and spent the even with me and played at brag. They all met by accident, coming to buy goods in the shop, Fanny Weller excepted', Turner (1984), *Diary*, 14 January 1763.

[79] For example, Turner (1984), *Diary*, 4 March 1760.

[80] Turner (1984), *Diary*, 28 September 1763.

[81] Turner (1984), Diary, 5 December 1757.

[82] Turner (1984), *Diary*, 1 May 1758.

[83] Turner (1984), *Diary*, 13 December 1761.

The accounts of the small Cheshire shopkeeper, William Woods of Didsbury show that he had about 30 credit bearing customers, some of whom came into the shop very frequently. Not a great deal can be deduced about these people except that they were apparently all known to Wood, though some were of lowly status, and one or two were identified only by how they could be contacted. There is some evidence in the accounts that shopping played a greater part in the lives of some of these customers than the satisfaction of mere material needs. There is little indication of bursts of shopping activity each week as the wages are paid. On the contrary shopping appears for some almost an excuse for social intercourse. Thus in only ten days starting on 3 January 1787 either Matha Chase or her son William made eleven visits to the shop missing only two days. One cannot escape the conclusion that for the Chase family, shopping was embedded in the social fabric of their lives no less than in those of the ladies who came to Turner's shop to buy but stayed to drink tea and play bragg.[84] The evidence given in depositions made before the courts supports the importance of the social element in marketing strategies suggested in the patterns of purchasing by Wood's customer, Matha Chase.[85]

## (e) Dealing with the socially equal: the home as a showcase

The trade card of the London linen draper, Benjamin Cole, illustrates another aspect of the complexity of serving a broad social mix. The picture displayed on the card of a shop interior, shows in the foreground a conventional shop with customers being served over the counter, while in the background a partially opened door reveals an inner room, warmed by a blazing fire in the grate.[86] Such images of shop interiors are rare, but they reinforce visually verbal images conjured up as in Turner's Diary. Some of his customers were too grand and too remote to visit his shop at all, others got no further than the shop window, but in between, there was a broad band who came into the shop, some of whom went further into the select privacy of the house. The idea that domestic space was divided into zones of increasing privacy were well understood by late seventeenth England,[87] and it is probable that the same concepts governed the way some shops were organized. Adjoining living rooms were undoubtedly only entered by esteemed customers, who were served personally by the master or mistress. By this separation, a shopkeeper

---

[84] Mui and Mui (1989), *Shops and shopkeeping*, pp. 212-16.
[85] For example, Northern Circuit Assize depositions cited by Styles (1994), 'Clothing the north', pp. 149-50 and footnote.
[86] Heal collection 70.39; Heal (1925), *London tradesmen's cards*, p. 81, suggests a date of 1710-20.
[87] Weatherill (1988), *Consumer behaviour*, pp. 8-13; Weatherill (1993), 'Meaning of consumer behaviour', particularly pp. 213-15.

was able to serve a wide social and economic range of customers from the same premises without offence, just as to this day many pubs offer different decors in the bar and in the saloon with drinks at different prices. This separation became even more important when the technological improvements and new products made available a great range of goods at prices ordinary people could afford, so that more people wished to enter the shop.

Nicholas Blundell fleshes out the visual image of Benjamin Cole's trade card. Given that Blundell was a Roman Catholic, which at times meant life in a hostile world, he may have had an unusually close relationship with his suppliers, though there is little evidence that he restricted himself to Catholic shopkeepers. Despite living in an isolated spot ill served with roads, Blundell appears to have needed little excuse to visit Liverpool. There he met and socialized with his shopkeepers, in between buying their goods; they also came out to his house.

Some of the meetings seem to have been initiated by the tradesmen concerned, and were part of the service normally offered to customers of high status. In this vein, Mrs Mary Gorsuch came over to bring a Powder Box made by her father for Mrs Blundell, but the relationship was close enough for the visitor to be invited to stay for dinner.[88] Some meetings happened at a neutral venue like the drink at the Woolpack with the haberdasher Mr Chorley when they 'discoursed about shearing and ordering of Rabet skins'.[89] Some meetings of this type followed directly from purchases at the shop premises like the day he and his friends bought some goods at Mr Cotton's and then went on with him to the Woolpack.[90] The most frequent event was some shopping by Blundell combined with a meal at the house of one or other of his favoured mercers, Mr Cotton and Mr Hurst; as when he bought some goods at Mr Cotton's shop and then 'he treated me at his Hous, and gave me a dooble Snuff Box'.[91] Even tradesmen who appear but occasionally in the *Diurnal*, and were therefore presumably less close, invited him to a meal like the day Mr Brownhill sold him some sweetmeats and gave Blundell a drink and then Mrs Lancaster treated him to a 'snap of a dinner' before selling him a sugar loaf.[92]

As with Turner and his customers, friendship probably played some part in the relationships between Blundell and the tradesmen he patronized, but it is unlikely that the motive for this generosity was entirely altruistic. Tradesmen clearly felt the need to bind customers to them with ties of loyalty, particularly when the customer was as free spending and as prompt paying as the Blundells. The freedom with which he was allowed to intrude into the private houses of

88  Blundell (1968-72), *Great diurnal*, 17 November 1706.
89  Blundell (1968-72), *Great diurnal*, 31 January 1708.
90  Blundell (1968-72), *Great diurnal*, 16 March 1714.
91  Blundell (1968-72), *Great diurnal*, 16 May 1718.
92  Blundell (1968-72), *Great diurnal*, 15 October 1710.

**4.1** Tradecard of Benjamin Cole

his suppliers suggests that they may have been using the premises, and possibly their own apparel, as showcases. There is little direct evidence for this hypothesis, but the diary of Samuel Pepys offers one example. He became increasingly friendly with Ralph Greatorex, a scientific instrument maker, and on one occasion at least Pepys did penetrate the house. The visit may have started in the shop, though Pepys did not specify where he saw some 'lamp-glasses, which carry the light a great way, good to read in bed by'. Not surprisingly Pepys declared his intention of having one. Subsequently the two men were apparently in the house since Pepys was shown a wooden jack 'in his chimney, that goes with the smoake, which indeed is very pretty'.[93]

The use of the home as a show case could explain some unexpected results in Weatherill's analysis of the ownership of goods by social status. Those she defined as gentry died possessed of substantially larger personal estates than those belonging to a trade or a profession. Yet, in spite of superior wealth and social standing, the gentry apparently were less likely than retailing tradesmen to own decorative goods such as pictures, looking-glasses, pewter, china and earthenware. It was in this group that ownership of the new decorative goods was relatively high; perhaps most significantly 10 per cent owned the utensils to serve hot drinks compared with only 4 per cent of the whole set under review.[94] The ability to offer hospitality in the form of tea or other drink or dinner seems to have been a necessary part of a successful tradesman's sales strategy. In this sense the paraphernalia of tea drinking, no less than for presenting a genteel dinner were as much part of his business equipment as the counter and chairs in the shop.

Probate inventories, the source of her data, proffer little evidence on new and fashionable fabrics and haberdashery ware, yet they too could have been displayed advantageously to the select customers. It is perhaps a manifestation of displaying one's wares on one's back that Johanna Schopenhauer observed when she wrote of the 'desire for a certain luxury in dress and the like' among shopkeepers, though she may have misunderstood their motives.[95] It is unlikely that direct copy was aimed for, but the spread of awareness about fashionable goods. Like Pepys and the jack that was very pretty, a sale might not have been forthcoming immediately, but the seeds of desire were sown. Once a fabric was safely on the back of the customer or, like the 'dooble snuff box' safely in his hand, the customer too became a display cabinet among the social set.

If this hypothesis is correct, and the tradesman's house, and indeed his own person, were the showcases by which he displayed his wares, it follows that he played a crucial role in giving significance to 'things' and in weaving 'them

---

[93] Pepys (1985), *Diary*, 24 October 1660.
[94] Weatherill (1988), *Consumer behaviour*, Table 8.1 and Chapter 8.
[95] Schopenhauer (1988), *A lady's travels*, 22 January 1790.

into a complex cultural conversation about the structure of ... society'.[96] He was a seller of wares, but also himself a consumer and a member of a set of consumers who were his customers. 'Things' found in his house for his own personal gratification and also in the shop for sale, thus served a double function. They made his own life more pleasurable or more comfortable and they served as advertisements to attract customers. It is not therefore surprising to find the rooms open to public view in a tradesman's house contained the sorts of goods that would create an ambience of gentility and fashion. Typical of many examples are William Faux of Lincoln (1708) and Benjamin Boucher, grocer of Bridgnorth, Shropshire, (1748). Faux had in his parlour, among other items of furniture, seven cane chairs, a little table, a large looking-glass, five pictures, a stove with its fender, and earthen ware and glasses in a closet. Elsewhere in his house he had a coffee mill and a coffee pot. Boucher's public rooms were even more obviously furnished for displaying fashionable comfort. In his little parlour were five chairs, five pictures, a cupboard with drawers, a corner cupboard, a set of china, a fireplace with fire shovel, tongs and fender, and a warming pan. The fore street chamber, despite the presence of a substantial bed, was also furnished for presentation, with 'Books of several Quallities', a chest of drawers, a writing desk with drawers, a round table, an easy chair and seven other chairs, a looking-glass, six large and nine small pictures all with gilt frames, two pair of window curtains and five cushions. Among his silver, kept in the same room, were seven small spoons, a pair of tea tongs, and buttons, buckles and clasps.[97]

## Shopping as a leisure activity

Looking at the point of sale with the eyes of the customer brings into the frame several new concepts, not least those of the 'shopper' and of 'shopping'. These terms are generally used to express different meanings from 'buyer' or 'customer' and 'buying', since elements of enjoyment are included. In the previous section, the problem addressed was how the retailer could provide customer satisfaction, to use a modern phrase. Customers, who it was assumed were willing to buy, were categorized, sorted, courted and treated according to their station. For their part, customers used their own powers of choice to select

[96] Breen (1993), 'Meaning of things', p. 250. Part III, 'Production and the meaning of possessions', in Brewer and Porter, *Consumption and the world of goods*, pp. 175-301, includes studies on various aspects of the way meaning is given to goods. Apart from the chapter just cited by Breen, Weatherill, 'The meaning of consumer behaviour', pp. 206-28, and Vickery, 'Women and the world of goods', pp. 274-301, are particularly pertinent here.

[97] Faux, Lincoln RO, L.C.C. Admon 1708/52; Boucher, Bridgnorth Peculiar series, Lichfield Joint RO.

appropriate sellers and to negotiate appropriate conditions. Even when the relationship contained within it bonds of friendship, there was the implied threat that customers could choose to go elsewhere.

Shopping in another sense of the word is a different type of activity. It is initiated and superficially controlled by the shopper, whose prime motive is enjoyment; shopping is a leisure activity even if it involves incidentally the purchase of essentials.[98] The first use of the term 'shopper' recorded by the *O.E.D.* appears in a quotation taken from *The Guardian* newspaper as late as 1862, thus supporting the widely held belief that shopping was a new past-time of the nineteenth century.[99] In it Paris is described as 'a city not only of pleasure seekers, but of keen and indefatigable shoppers', a revealing juxtaposition of two activities, seeking pleasure and shopping.[100] The term 'shopping' itself, other than in the sense of buying, appeared only a decade or so before and is likewise combined with pleasure in Thackeray's comment of 'the delightful round of visits and shopping which forms the amusement, ... of the rich London lady'.[101]

As a leisure activity shopping already had a long history by the time Thackeray wrote *Vanity Fair*. An essential element of the market and the fair was amusement. Although serious business remained at the core of activity in this type of marketing, round it huge crowds disported themselves, incidentally buying whatever was on offer appropriate to their purse. The fair remained a popular pastime throughout the period. Pepys took his 'boy' to Bartholemew Fair, where he showed him the best shows and then 'up and down, to buy combes for my wife to give her maids',[102] Blundells bought 'Spurs & buckles for Fairings'[103] and Latham bought gingerbread at the fair.[104] But as a place for pleasure and for buying little gifts for family and friends, it was joined by other outlets offering more refined and genteel facilities.

In the late sixteenth century a new business centre marked, so far as we know, a new style in shopping. The Royal Exchange was opened in 1571, followed in 1608/09 by the New Exchange in the Strand. Each was intended primarily as a place where business deals could be transacted and commercial news disseminated, but each was built with a gallery for retail sale. A depiction of the New Exchange in 1772 shows how this aspect of the two markets

---

[98] Emphasis here on shopping as a pastime is not intended to detract from other aspects of women and shopping. Vickery (1998), *Gentleman's daughter*, pp. 163, 164-7, emphasizes how women saw shopping as part of their work.

[99] See for example, Fraser (1981), *Coming of the mass market*, p. 110; Winstanley (1983), *Shopkeeper's world*, pp. 2-8, 58-9.

[100] *Guardian*, 847/2, 3 September 1862.

[101] Thackeray (1848), *Vanity Fair*, chapter xii.

[102] Pepys (1985), *Diary*, 2 September 1664.

[103] Blundell (1968-72), *Great diurnal*, 26 June 1722.

[104] Weatherill (1990), *Account book of Richard Latham*, p. 23.

**4.2** The New Exchange. Although the New Exchange is named neither on the print
nor in the accompanying text, the identification is generally accepted. Certainly
contemporary descriptions correspond closely.

operated and the degree to which they were designed for shopping as a leisure activity. Business through the shop window was transformed from a form of street or market trading into an opportunity for social engagement in which purchasing was incidental, though almost inevitable given the fashionable nature of the wares on offer. The picture shows the window extending across the whole frontage, with the small booths behind lined with shelves and other means of display. The lighting is cleverly arranged with clerestory windows and further sources of illumination at the back of each booth. The customers move in a protected environment with paving under their feet and a roof over their heads. The Exchanges gave little opportunity for shopping within a social relationship as shown in the last section. Instead it was the customers who gathered there, meeting friends, passing from booth to booth, and the booth holders stand separated and apart, service providers, not social acquaintances.

The establishment of the two Exchanges demonstrates how shopping as a leisure activity moved on as early as the late sixteenth century from the rough and tumble of the fair and market into an arena designed for particular groups, in this case an élite. Although illustrations of the inside of the Exchanges are later, the method of operation depicted seem to have been the same from the start. Certainly by the Restoration, Pepys painted a vivid picture of shopping as a leisure activity in which the Exchanges were frequently visited. Sometimes visits (and purchases) seem to have been en route to more important engagements such as the day Pepys and his wife went to the Old Exchange, then on to a Mr Fox who took them to the Queen's presence-chamber. Although they purchased a whisk,[105] which his wife put on there and then, there is no indication in the diary that a lack of such a garment had precipitated its acquisition. Visits more often than not appear to have been regarded as an outing, like the time his wife and 'Mrs Martha Batten, my Valentine', bought a pair of embroidered gloves and six plain pairs, or several years later at the New Exchange when he paid for a new year gift chosen by his wife. On other occasions he and his companions were merely window shopping as on a day at the New Exchange, they 'saw some new fashioned pettycoats ... very handsome' and his wife had 'a mind for one of them'.[106]

By the following century the habit was so well established, in London at least, that Defoe thought it necessary to instruct young tradesmen on how to handle shoppers, warning them of the dangers of incivility towards those 'ladies, and those, too, persons of good note, ... [who] divert themselves in going from one mercer's shop to another, to look upon their fine silks, and to rattle and banter the journeymen and shopkeepers, and have not so much as the

---

[105] That is, a neckerchief worn by women in the latter half of the seventeenth century [OED].

[106] Pepys (1985), Diary, 22 November 1660, 18 February 1660/61, 2 January 1667/68, 15 April 1662.

least occasion, much less intention, to buy anything'.[107] In 1747 Campbell, in discussing the talents required by a London mercer wrote that 'he must be a very polite Man, and skilled in all the Punctilio's of City-good-breeding; he ought, by no Means to be an Aukward clumsey Fellow, such a creature would turn the Lady's Stomach in a Morning, when they go their Rounds, to tumble silkes they have no mind to buy'.[108] Fanny Burney described this morning round as seen though the eyes of her naïve young visitor to London:

> We have been shopping, as Mrs Mirvan calls it all this morning, to buy silks, caps, gauzes, & so forth. The shops are really very entertaining, especially the mercers; there seem to be six or seven men belonging to each shop; and every one took care, by bowing and smirking to be noticed. We were conducted from one to another, and carried from room to room with so much ceremony, that at first I was almost afraid to go on.
>
> I thought I should never chose a silk; for they produced so many I knew not which to fix upon; and they recommended them all so strongly, that I fancy they thought I only wanted persuasion to buy everything they showed me. And indeed they took so much trouble, that I was almost ashamed I could not.
>
> At the milliners, the ladies we met were so much dressed, that I rather imagined they were making visits than purchases.[109]

In factual rather than in fictional terms, Johanna Schopenhauer, the German tourist, made a similar comment at much the same time. '... we set off shopping', she wrote, 'This means going into at least twenty shops, having a thousand things shown to us which we do not wish to buy, in fact turning the whole shop upside down and, in the end, perhaps leaving without purchasing anything'.[110]

Shopping as a leisure activity may have started in the metropolis and may always have remained more important there than in the provinces, but the practice spread. It was most manifest in spa towns and other fashionable resorts, like Tunbridge Wells, which already had shops bordering the walks of the Pantiles before the fire of 1687, and like Bath,[111] but to some extent it probably became an element in any town which had been sufficiently improved to make an outing on foot a pleasure. Parading along paved and lit streets and gravelled garden walks became part of town life, and the new style of shop window display was part of the visual scene.

---

[107] Defoe (1726), *Complete English tradesman*, p. 64.

[108] Campbell (1747), *London tradesman*, p. 197.

[109] Burney (1788), *Evelina*, p. 25.

[110] Schopenhauer (1988), *A lady's travels*, p. 150.

[111] Borsay (1989), *English urban renaissance*, pp. 35, 168-9; Fiennes (1984), *Illustrated journeys*, pp. 125-7.

**4.3** The Pantiles, Tunbridge Wells

Ironically it is only as this approach to shopping became available to more people, that social commentators and historians began to take notice, believing they were observing a new phenomenon. It was not a novelty of the mass market and it was not even new in the seventeenth century when the urban renaissance began. At fairs and markets, the stalls had long offered attractive wares and entertaining spectacles to the passers by who could spend money or merely enjoy the scene; in modern jargon, they could enjoy a shopping experience. Urban improvement, new shop designs and methods of display offered similar pleasures to those who might well have disdained the vulgar rough and tumble of the fairground.

## Conclusion

The quotation from Defoe used in the heading for this chapter reminded tradesmen of the importance of cherishing their customers, and it reminds us that shopping involves much more than merely buying things in a shop. Most importantly shopping involves choice. Customers in the early modern period had long passed the time when the only venue for purchasing goods was the local market, with little opportunity to exercise choice and even less of enjoying a pleasant experience. Already in the sixteenth century shoppers could choose outlets that best suited their needs or that provided an environment in which they felt comfortable. Customers used, and abused, their power and tradesmen perforce had to adapt their own tactics to the demands and inclinations of their customers. Some aspects of shopping like the open window or purchasing in the context of social intercourse, may have involved forms of interaction between retailer and customer with which we are now unfamiliar, but which were appropriate to the society of the time. Some of those forms may have helped to invest things with meaning and to spread acceptance of novelty, a topic addressed more fully in chapter 7.

Chapter 5

# 'It is the most dangerous state of life that a man can live in':[1] managing credit

As already noted in the previous chapter, when Defoe wrote his advice to a young tradesman, he suggested he regard 'his customers as idols; so far as he may worship idols by allowance, he is to bow down and worship'. Although Defoe did not make the connection explicit, one of the so-called allowances the tradesman would have to offer was credit. Selling for cash alone was virtually impossible and 'the tradesman that trades wholly thus, is not yet born, or if there ever were any such, they are all dead'. However, despite the assumption that sale through credit was inevitable, Defoe was quick to point to the dangers, warning that 'He that takes credit may give credit, but he must be exceedingly watchful, for it is the most dangerous state of life that a man can live in'.[2] Defoe seems in his advice to agree with a commonly held view today that credit is a facility offered solely for the benefit of the consumer and he never discussed its positive advantages for the tradesman. Yet the benefits were real. The offer of credit not only facilitated sale, it also helped to create a bond between buyer and seller, tying the one to the other. On a more mundane level it enabled the tradesman to hold a smaller reserve of cash in the shop.

Though the practice of giving credit must almost certainly be older, evidence for credit sales as recorded in a shop book date back only to the sixteenth century. The earliest noted is the entry of 'Such Sperat dettes as were owinge ... as appereth by the shoppe bokes' in the inventory of Thomas Harrison, girdler of Southampton, (1554).[3] Two other tradesmen in the sixteenth century have been noted with debts recorded in shop books; in 1583

---

[1] Defoe (1987), *Complete English tradesman*, p. 48-9. This chapter deals only with managing credit *vis-à-vis* customers. Credit as a tool for facilitating supply is covered, briefly, in chapter 6.

[2] Defoe (1987), *Complete English tradesman*, pp. 71, 188 and 48-9.

[3] Hampshire RO, B wills 1554/126-7, transcribed and printed in Roberts and Parker (1992), 'Southampton probate inventories', pp. 53-61. It should not be assumed that this is necessarily one of the earliest records of shop debts as such. Few inventories survive for any retailers before 1550 so conclusions on earlier practice must be tentative.

William Sharples, mercer of Warwick, had over £220 in shop debts out of an inventory total of £393 and John Beare of Ludham, Norfolk, trading in mercery (1589) had 'In the debte bookes xxxj li js vjd'.[4] During this period individual debts in number are not infrequently recorded in tradesmen's inventories, but not stated to be specifically shop book debts. It would seem that the idea of shop book debts as a distinct category of debt requiring its own systematic record developed only slowly. These early examples of shop books reveal a high proportion of retailers' estates tied up in shop debt. For Harrison it represented over one quarter of his personal estate, but for Beare it was nearly a half and for Sharples nearly two thirds. While these high figures suggest a certain inexperience in controlling the level of debt, they also indicate that under certain circumstances sale through the shop book was seen as a desirable sales strategy.

The use of a shop book to record debt was clearly open to abuse as a result of either incompetent bookkeeping or deliberate fault. Debtors could have been charged twice or the amount owing entered incorrectly. The possibilities for abuse by either party were increased by the death of the creditor when it became the task of his executor or administrator to call in the debts. Since the customer had not formally acknowledged the debt by his signature against the entry, and the testator or intestate was dead, the executor or administrator had little chance of proving his right to collect the money in a court of law. Parliament recognized there was a problem as early as 1609, though this was perceived largely as one for the customer who might be charged a second time by careless bookkeeping or fraudulent practice. The act laid down that the shop book could only stand as evidence for a debt for one year unless there was 'a Bill of Debt' - an unlikely eventuality for much shop credit.[5] Although by imposing a restrictive time limit on the recovery of debts recorded in the shop book, the act appeared to increase the difficulties of shopkeepers and their executors or administrators, this may not have been the case. For the first time the shop book was recognized, albeit with qualifications, as a legitimate record of debt.

The probate inventories of retailers confirm that the use of the shop book continued unabated, after the act of 1609. Indeed the practice appears to have grown and executors, administrators and appraisers were more ready to isolate shop debts from debt in general than their predecessors had been and to record those debts. Though an analysis of the shop debts so recorded may cause too much emphasis to be placed on the risks of the retail trade, nevertheless the damage to the business caused by the death of the owner and the subsequent difficulty of recovering debts at law is all too apparent. Since the executors or

---

4    Worcestershire RO 008:7 1583 no. 74a, William Sharples; Norwich RO, INV 5.139.
5    7 JAC1 c. 12 (1609), 'Act to avoid the double Payment of Debts'.

administrators had not been personally involved in the debt they could not speak with the authority of participants in the deal. Sorting out the books and collecting the debts of the deceased may therefore have been disproportionately delicate. The widow of Thomas Vallor, mercer of Harting, Sussex (1678) made more explicit than most the problems of collecting once the shopkeeper himself was dead when she wrote of 'the want of evidence of the said debts', despite being able to list the debtors as recorded in the shop book.[6] Some executors appear to have virtually abandoned hope, like those of the estate of Philip Capell, apothecary of Coventry, (1682), who recorded the £200 of debts as 'most bad that will be lost', and omitted them from the total value of £277, or those of Thomas Browne, mercer of Northwich, Cheshire, (1748) who left 202 book debts 'which are supposed to be lost & irrecoverable', though they were only valued in total at just over £10.[7] Others were perhaps right to view the shop books with despair. For example, the administrator of the estate of Henry Staker, mercer of Chichester in Sussex (1719), declared that 'In the Bookes & papers of the said Intestate there Appeared to be charged on sev'all persons sev'all sums of money but what thereof is certainly due or can be received is not yet knowne many of the said persons being insolvent & others unknown besides there is reason to believe that some of them are payd'.[8] Sometimes the more hopeful debts were divided from the less, as in the inventory of Edward Collis, a Northampton linen draper (1625), who had 'Debts sperate' (£190) and 'Debts desperate' (£99), though both were included in the total of £498.[9] Possibly here, as elsewhere, the distinction between the sperate debts and the desperate was that the latter were of more than a year's standing and thus no longer reclaimable at law.

Comments appended to some probate inventories of tradesmen suggest that many had only the most rudimentary idea of how to handle credit effectively. The inventory of Roger Hayward, a blacksmith of Watford, Herts. (1592) reveals what was probably common practice both in the sixteenth century and for many years to come among small businesses. His appraisers acknowledged £12 of business debts 'by divers p'sons as appeareth by his dett book, Taylis [tallies] and scores upon the walles'.[10] The undated account book of a 'Mr Tench' from Cheshire probably dates from roughly the same period. It consists of a jumble of entries, not all dated and apparently not in chronological order. It is virtually impossible to deduce even whether an entry recorded a purchase or

---

6   West Sussex RO, MF842 1678 VALLOR.
7   Lichfield Joint RO; Chester RO, Ws 1748.
8   West Sussex RO MF838 1719 STRAKER.
9   Northamptonshire RO, Volume AV No. 239.
10  Hertford RO, A25/1305.

a sale.[11] Over a century later matters had hardly improved in some cases. The administrators of Thomas Ruffe, a saddler from Oswestry who died in 1720 were clearly in despair of ever settling the books when they recorded that 'There are some small debts appear to be due to him by his Shop book which are so obscure to read and Imperfect not giving acc't where the parties Live, thus the Adm'rators cannot assertain or particularize the same'.[12] With this in mind, it is not surprising that much of Defoe's advice to a young tradesman was devoted to the management of credit. His improbable account of an illiterate and almost innumerate shopkeeper who 'made notches upon sticks for all middling sums and scored with chalk for lesser things', not to mention the six spoons used as an aid to counting, might seem a journalist's flight of fancy, but it was probably an apt illustration of many shop keepers' limited grasp of bookkeeping.[13]

These indications of tradesmen's inability to manage accounts are surprising given the concern expressed by some parents as early as the sixteenth century for their children to be taught accounting. The evidence is thin, as always for this period, but it is telling. It comes from the instructions given in wills for the upkeep and education of children after the decease of the testator. Although it was more common to stipulate an education in general terms, either for all the children or just for the sons, a few required skills in accounting to be taught. For example, William Butler, husbandman of Hawkwell, Essex (1589) wanted his son to have 'a good and godly education' including writing, reading and casting up. Much the same was required by John Edwardes of Foulness Island (1581) and by John Sawkyn, husbandman of Goldhanger (1594).[14] Licenses granted to schoolteachers in parts of Cambridgeshire suggest that these parental aspirations were not wholly unrealistic. Although there must be suspicions about any individual license, overall the fact that a clerk from Norwich was prepared to grant a license at all for a master to teach boys to 'write, read and caste an accompte' suggests at the very least that the practice was not unknown.[15]

By the second half of the eighteenth century, there is evidence to suggest bookkeeping, the essential skill for the management of credit, was becoming an accepted norm for shopkeepers, at least in London and other big cities. As Defoe expressed it, 'the tradesmen's books being so essential to his trade, he that comes out of his time [as an apprentice] without a perfect knowledge of the

---

[11] Chester RO, DDX 326. It has been labelled a mercer's account book, but there seems to be no information on who the Mr Tench was that wrote the book, or where he came from.

[12] NLW SA1720/163.

[13] Defoe (1987), *Complete English tradesman*, pp. 188-90.

[14] Emerson (1991), *Elizabethan life*, p. 120.

[15] Spufford (1974), *Contrasting communities*, p. 187.

method of bookkeeping, like a bride undrest, is not fit to be married'.[16] This involved at the very least basic literary skills and some understanding of arithmetic, two skills so obviously lacking not only in Defoe's imaginary tradesman, but also in real ones like Hayward, Tench and Ruffe. Based on data taken from ecclesiastic court depositions, Cressy suggests that evidence of basic literary skills among London and Middlesex tradesmen rose from 71 per cent in 1580-1640 to 92 per cent in 1720-30, and among East Anglian tradesmen from 45 per cent to 66 per cent. He cites further evidence from other sources that indicates levels continued to rise over the rest of the eighteenth century.[17] Writing books giving guidance on the acquisition of a 'fair legible hand' abounded for the late seventeenth century onwards,[18] so that by 1747 Campbell could assume 'Reading and Writing are so useful, that we need not ... use many arguments to recommend Children being well founded in these before they are bound'. Arithmetic and accounting were, in his view, more problematic, though no less important. He considered that 'A tolerable Notion in Figures is absolutely necessary to most Arts', and he advised 'all Parents to let their Children be taught at least common Arithmetic, before they are bound.[19] He would certainly have disapproved of the early and limited education received by William Stout in the 1670s, who had apparently struggled only with reading, writing and the classics, despite the fact that his 'father minded to get me constantly to school to get learning in order to be placed to some trade or other imployment'. After his father's death Stout had a brief period of more appropriate education lasting three weeks. He 'went to a scrivener, to learn to write, halfe, and the other to arithmetick. I got so good an entrance into arithmetick that by industry, I made good progress in it, without any instruction other than books'.[20]

It is unlikely that Stout would have had to struggle largely on his own if he had been born several decades later. The eighteenth century saw a large increase in the number of schools, many of them short lived. For example, in the 1770s and 1780s no less than eight commercial schools have been noted in Derby, a town with less than 10,000 inhabitants.[21] Schoolmasters exploited the new medium of provincial newspapers to advertise themselves and the skills

---

[16]  Defoe (1987), *Complete English tradesman*, p. 15.

[17]  Cressy (1993), 'Literacy in context', p. 316. See also Hunt (1996), *Middling sort*, pp. 56 and 58.

[18]  Money (1993), 'Teaching in the market place', p. 339.

[19]  Campbell (1747), *London tradesman*, p. 20. See also Hunt (1996), *Middling sort*, pp. 58-62, for a useful account of attitudes to accounting. She refers to one book on accounting written specifically for girls, Anon. (1678), *Advice to the women and maidens of London*. The anxiety expressed in this work about helpless widows is picked up by Defoe (1987), *Complete English tradesman*, chapter xxi.

[20]  Stout (1967), *Autobiography*, pp. 69-71, 74 (1670s).

[21]  Langford (1989), *Polite and commercial people*, p. 85.

they offered, like the one run by Sharp of Warwick who advertised that 'Young Gentlemen are genteely Boarded and carefully instructed in ... Arithmetick'.[22] An analysis of such advertisements from the four midland counties of Warwickshire, Worcestershire, Staffordshire and Shropshire in *Aris's Birmingham Gazette*, 1781-95, shows the importance attached to the acquisition of mathematical skills. Nearly 70 per cent of advertising schools offered writing, nearly 60 per cent arithmetic (the second most popular), about 40 per cent bookkeeping and accounting, and 30 per cent Mathematics.[23] The number of teachers (used in the broadest sense of the word) who chose to write books on mathematical subjects is also indicative of a growing acceptance by the educational establishment of the need to teach mathematics.[24] The improved instruction led to greater expectations by tradesmen. For example, in the 1790s an advertisement for an apprentice to a button maker specifically required that any applicant should 'know something of Accounts',[25] while a grocer in Shrewsbury was looking to employ 'a Serious active young Man' who was 'perfect in Accompts'.[26] Other advertisements suggest that more and more tradesmen were prepared to keep good accounts and wished to buy the books they needed. Newspaper advertisements by stationers and booksellers show shop books as a regular line of stock, presumably in sufficient demand for printers to make them in standard formats to suit different needs. Francis Place proposed a system that would use 'a day book or ledger, a cash book or order book and a stock book', all of which have been noted in advertisements.[27]

Defoe declined to instruct on methods of bookkeeping, averring that there were plenty on the market already. This was true. The most reliable, and the one used almost universally today, is the system of double entry, usually called the Italian method at the time. It had originated in northern Italy during the late thirteenth century and early fourteenth, it had become a basic tool of financial management in Italy by 1500 from which knowledge of the system spread slowly throughout Europe.[28] The first noted English work on double entry was published in 1632, but by the middle of the eighteenth century there were

---

[22]  Banks collection 104.71.

[23]  Money (1993), 'Teaching in the market place', pp. 343-5. Money's whole article gives a useful account of the spread of educational opportunities in the eighteenth century.

[24]  Money (1993), 'Teaching in the market place', Table 17.2.

[25]  *Aris's Birmingham Gazette*, 9 August 1790.

[26]  *Salopian Journal*, 11 July 1798.

[27]  *Autobiography of Francis Place*, vol. II, p. 81; for example, James McLeod, book seller and stationer, advertised 'all sorts of Shop Books, as Day-Books, Cash-Books, Bill-Books, Journals, Ledgers, etc., etc.', *Aris's Birmingham Gazette*, 25 February 1760; Wright and Ormandy of Liverpool listed on their trade card 'Bankers & Merchants Account Books in the completest manner', Banks collection 111.71.

[28]  Swetz (1987), *Capitalism and arithmetic*, pp. 12-13.

several, some running to many editions.[29] However, despite his earlier statement to the contrary, Defoe did set out a simple system for keeping accounts. Firstly, he recommended 'the ancient and laudable custom with tradesmen in England always to balance their accounts of stock and of profit and loss, at least once every year'.[30] This was indeed the practice of one tradesman, William Stout, who recorded the totals in his *Autobiography*, though even such a meticulous tradesman as he seems to have omitted the task on occasions as he included no figures for some years.[31] Secondly, Defoe recommended a day book in which all credit sales and other financial dealings should be entered as they occurred and from which the details should be transferred to the appropriate ledgers.[32] His recommended system was almost certainly based on established practice among the more organized tradesmen, although no contemporary account books of tradesmen are known to survive. This deficiency is in part made good by comments from Stout and Francis Place in their several autobiographies. On settling up the estate of the merchant, Augustin Greenwood, Stout remarked that he 'found his books were duely kept and posted, and even the last parsell of goods that he had delivered, the day he died upon, was posted from his day book or Jurnall to his ledger or debt book, in the manner he used'.[33] Place laid out the accounting principles on which on which his partnership should be based in the 1790s, though it must be doubted whether most businesses reached his standard:

> Fourth, we must have a day book or ledger, a cash book or order book and a stock book. The cash book must contain every item received or expended.
> Fifth, all the books must be examined by us jointly every week, compared with the bought book, a book containing an entry for every thing purchased for money or credit, and with the bill books.[34]

Some later examples were constructed on a similar system, albeit sometimes imperfectly. Thomas Turner, the Sussex shopkeeper, was less methodical. He appears to have entered sales in his day book regularly,[35] but the transfer to his

---

[29] Carpenter (1632), *A most excellent instruction*. Eighteenth-century manuals include: Webster (1721), *An essay on book keeping*; Malcolm (1731), *A treatise on book keeping*; Clare (1758, 8th edn), *Youth's instruction*.

[30] Defoe (1987), *Complete English tradesman*, p. 187.

[31] Stout recorded his annual casting up at the end of his first year of trading (1689), but then apparently not again until 1697. By 1704 he wrote of inspecting his affairs 'as usual yearly', Stout (1967), *Autobiography*, pp. 95-6, 119, 147.

[32] The system was discussed discursively in Defoe (1987), *Complete English tradesman*, chapter 20, particularly p. 190.

[33] Stout (1967), *Autobiography*, p. 133 (1701).

[34] *Autobiography of Francis Place*, vol. II, p. 81.

[35] For example, Turner (1984), *Diary*, 13 February 1755, 28 January 1757.

ledger was less systematic. For example, on the 19 June 1758, he admitted that he had not 'posted' his Day book since 25 May. The shopkeeper, Roberts of Penmorfa, Caernarvonshire, kept both a day book and a customer ledger, but he was even less systematic in their use, and some sales were initially recorded on 'scraps of paper'.[36] The apothecary and surgeon, William Elmhirst of Ouslethwaite, used a more primitive method of accounting. He appears to have kept a single book into which details were entered as and when a course of treatment was completed. Details such as when a customer paid off a debt are frequently missing.[37]

By the mid-eighteenth century tradesmen themselves were beginning to make their use of the shop book more secure in law. From 1750 a series of Private Acts each relating to a particular town or district was passed by Parliament to facilitate the collection of small debts. The earliest noted were for Westminster and Tower Hamlets in 1750 and over the next 25 years some twenty more were passed covering large towns like Liverpool and Birmingham, county towns like Shrewsbury, Exeter and Canterbury and places like Old Swinford and the Holland district in Lincolnshire.[38] In 1807 such Acts were extended to cover all debts up to £5.[39] Although the format varied somewhat depending on the particular circumstances of the place concerned, there was a considerable degree of uniformity. The preamble usually began by stating that 'a great Trade is carried on in the Town ... and the Inhabitants thereof have of late Years greatly increased'. It continued by expressing anxiety about two different types of debtor. Firstly there were the 'poor honest Persons' who were 'obliged to contract Small Debts' which they were unable to pay, and who were often treated unduly harshly by the courts under current law. Secondly there were 'many evil disposed persons' who took advantage of the slow and expensive processes to evade payment. Thus the acts continued to develop the concept first expressed in statute half a century earlier of the honest as opposed to the malicious debtor.[40] In an attempt to deal appropriately with both types of defaulters, a local 'Court of Requests' was set up composed of a quorum taken from a list of the good and the true in the town, (in Liverpool a

---

[36] Penmorfa shop ledger, noted by Mui and Mui (1989), *Shops and shopkeeping*, p. 217.

[37] Elmhirst (n.d.), *Ledger*. Only the one ledger survives.

[38] All Private Acts, respectively 23 GEO2 c. 27 (1750) Westminster; 23 GEO2 c. 30 (1750) Tower Hamlets; 25 GEO2 c. 43 (1752) Liverpool; 26 GEO2 c. 34 (1753) Birmingham; 23 GEO3 c. 73 (1783) Shrewsbury; 13 GEO3 c. 27 (1773) Exeter; 25 GEO2 c. 45 (1752) Canterbury; 17 GEO3 c. 19 (1777) Old Swinford and 17 GEO3 c. 32 (1777) Holland district. Each act set up a 'Court of Requests' in the town composed usually of the Mayor and several named commissioners who were to sit regularly and deal with small claims worth less than £2.

[39] 47 GEO3 Sess. 1 c. 4 (1806/07).

[40] 4,5 ANNE c. 17 (1705) and 6 ANNE c. 22 (1706). According to Earle (1989), *Making of the English middle class*, p. 129, the acts may have created more problems than they solved, as they appear to have encouraged more people to sue out commissions of bankruptcy.

## Table 5.1
### Retailers' debts as recorded in their shop books

| Date | Retailer's name | Place | Occupation | Total inventory in £ | Total shop debts | Bad shop debts | Mean debt owed | Number of debtors | Number owing less than £1 |
|---|---|---|---|---|---|---|---|---|---|
| 1554 | Thomas HARRISON | Southampton, Hants. | Girdler | 423 | 120 | 98 | 1.10 | 111 | 80 |
| 1583 | William SHARPLES | Warwick | Mercer | 392 | 221 | 206 | 1.60 | 192 | 140 |
| 1589 | John BEARE | Ludham, Norfolk | mercery | 78 | 31 | | | | |
| 1592 | Roger HAYWARD | Watford, Herts. | Blacksmith | 114 | 12 | | | | |
| 1621 | Edward MAYES | Manchester, Lancs. | Gent/mercery | 373 | 74 | | 1.30 | 55 | 24 |
| 1623 | John PARES | Rochdale, Lancs. | mercery | 57 | 11 | | 0.20 | 61 | 61 |
| 1623 | William ROTHWELL | Bolton, Lancs. | Chapman | 634 | 104 | | 2.20 | 47 | 26 |
| 1623 | George YEONG | Norwich | Pewterer | n.t. | 104 | | | | |
| 1624 | Kenrick EYTON | Chester | Mercer | 214 | 40 | | | | |
| 1626 | Ann BAKER | Ipswich, Suffolk | Widow (wine) | 84 | 33 | 8 | | | |
| 1634 | George SELDON | Liskeard, Cornwall | Mercer | 360 | 54 | | | | |
| 1645 | John JAMES | St Ives, Cornwall | Mercer | 90 | 1 | | | | |
| 1648 | Robert WILSON | Carlisle, Cumb. | Glover | 321 | 123 | | 2.70 | 45 | 19 |
| 1649 | Lawrence NEWALL | Rochdale, Lancs. | Mercer | n.t. | 33 | | 1.00 | 33 | 27 |
| 1665 | Robert ADDISON | Carlisle, Cumb. | saddlery | 370 | 207 | | 0.70 | 306 | 269 |
| 1665 | Benjamin MARSHALL | Lincoln | Mercer | 1204 | 254 | 121 | | 32+ | |
| 1667 | Thomas WOOTTON | Bewdley, Worcs. | mercery | n.t. | n.t. | | | c. 200 | |
| 1667 | Robert GREEN | Shrewsbury, Shrops. | Chapman | 307 | 3 | | | | |
| 1667 | Charles SLANNE | Newbury, Berks. | mercery | 709 | 88 | | | | |
| 1670 | William RICHMOND | Penrith, Cumb. | Grocer | 236 | 23 | | | | |
| 1670 | Thomas SMITH | Shrewsbury, Shrops. | haberdashery | 77 | 60 | | | | |
| 1671 | Henry HOLBEY | Norwich | Haberdasher | 1380 | 110 | 7 | | | |
| 1671 | John RUMNEY | Penrith, Cumb. | Pewterer | 143 | 21 | | | | |
| 1674 | Joan BOURNE | Bridgnorth, Shrops. | hats | 248 | 61 | | | | |
| 1677 | Edward WARRE | Tenbury, Worcs. | Mercer | 190 | 7 | 7 | | | |
| 1678 | Thomas VALLOR | Harting, Sussex | Mercer | n.t. | 401 | 225 | 3.00 | 135 | 87 |
| 1681 | Alexander JOHNSON | Woodstock, Oxon. | Mercer | 702 | 129 | | | | |
| 1685 | Lancelot JEFFERSON | Westward, Cumb. | general | 261 | 51 | | | | |

| | | | | | | | | |
|---|---|---|---|---|---|---|---|---|
| 1688 | Richard ASHLEY | Worcester | Mercer | 624 | 105 | | | 1.20 | 57 |
| 1689 | Edmund JOHNSON | Woodstock, Oxon. | Mercer | 1006 | 72 | 25 | | | 85 |
| 1692 | Ann HORSLEY | Bedwardine, Worcs. | general | 424 | 8 | | | | |
| 1700 | Robert MILLWARD | Newport, Shrops. | Mercer | 252 | 30 | | | | |
| 1702 | George WRIGHT | Lincoln | Chandler | 357 | 42 | 20 | | | |
| 1706 | Samuel LUCK | Steyning, Sussex | Mercer | 1406 | 217 | 33 | | 1.80 | 46 |
| 1710 | William LINTOTT | Harting, Sussex | Mercer | 629 | 194 | 100 | | | 121 |
| 1711 | Thomas BYSSHE | Petworth, Sussex | Mercer | 1637 | 508 | 61 | | | |
| 1713 | William COYNEY | Manchester, Lancs. | Mercer | 56 | 28 | 10 | | | |
| 1716 | Thomas ALLEN | Midhurst, Sussex | Linen Draper | 576 | 64 | | | | |
| 1732 | William HOCKENHALL | Newcastle, Staffs. | Grocer | 1128 | 733 | 180 | | | |
| 1748 | Thomas BACKSHELL | Broadwater, Sussex | mercery | 753 | 63 | | | | |
| 1748 | Thomas BROWNE | Northwich, Cheshire | Mercer | n.t. | n.t. | | | | 203 |
| 1754 | William BOXALL | Kirdford, Sussex | Mercer | 1825 | 202 | | | | 119 |
| 1754 | Richard MALPAS | Bridgnorth, Shrops. | Glover | 154 | | | | | |
| 1781 | James WALKER | Leeds, Yorks. | Dry Salter | 543 | 590 | 5.20 | | | 47 |

*Notes*: Occupation: when as given in the original, the initial letter is capitalized; when deduced from stock, it is given all in lower case. The inventory of Kenrick Eyton was not totalled; the total given here does not include debts. The inventories of William Coney, Richard Malpas and James Walker were totalled excluding debts and have not been adjusted here.

*Sources*: Harrison, Hampshire RO, B wills 1554/126-7; Sharples, Worcestershire RO, 008:7 1583 n. 74a; Beare, Norwich RO, INV 5.139; Hayward, Hertford RO, A25/1305; Mayes, Lancashire RO, WCW 1621 Edward Maes; Pares, Lancashire RO, WCW1623 John Pares; Rothwell, Lancashire RO, WCW 1623 Wm Rothwell; Yeong, Norwich RO, INV 26/93; Eyton, Cheshire RO, WS 1624; Baker, Norwich, RO INV/33 Box 42 No 239; Seldon, Truro RO; James, Truro RO; Wilson, Carlisle RO, 1642; Newall, Lancashire, RO WCW 1649 Laurence Newall; Addison, Carlisle RO, Richmond, Carlisle RO; Marshall, Lincolnshire Archive Office, L.C.C. Admon. 1667/131; Wootton, PRO, C5 582/120; Green, Lichfield Joint RO; Slanne, Berkshire RO, D/A1/120/155 6; Richmond, Carlisle RO; Smith, Lichfield Joint RO; Holbey, Norwich RO, INV 57A/33; Rumney, Carlisle RO Bourne, PRO, PROB 4/12502; Warre, PRO, PROB 4/3221; Vallor, West Sussex RO; Johnson, A., Oxford RO; Jefferson, Carlisle RO; Ashley, Worcestershire RO, 008.7BA 3585 Feb. 1686/87; Johnson, E., Oxford RO; Horsley, Worcestershire RO; Millward, Lichfield Joint RO; Wright, Lincolnshire Archive Office, L.C.C. Admon. 1702/1; Luck, West Sussex RO; Lintott, West Sussex RO; Bysshe, West Sussex RO; Coyney, Lancashire RO WCW 1713 William Coyney; Allen, West Sussex RO; Hockenhall, Lichfield Joint RO; Backshell, West Sussex RO; Browne, Cheshire RO, WS 1748; Boxall, West Sussex RO; Malpas, Lichfield Joint RO; Bridgnorth Peculiar, 1754; Walker, Borthwick, York, TEST CP 1781/7.

selection of Aldermen, common Councillors and 'most substantial and discreet Gentlemen, Merchants, Housholders, or inhabitants, shopkeepers or trades-men') who were to meet frequently and settle claims for under £2.[41] The fact that so many acts were passed suggests they met a real need.

It is difficult to generalize from the probate record how great a proportion of their assets retailers were prepared to sink in book debts for the sake of their trade or whether this changed over the period. As well as these sixteenth-century tradesmen, several others have been noted whose book debts apparently represented a high proportion of their moveable wealth, including Thomas Smith of Shrewsbury (1670) with £61 of book debts out of a total moveable wealth of £77 and William Hockenhull, a grocer of Newcastle under Lyme (1733) with £553 out of £1128.[42] Probably more common was 10-20 per cent. The *Autobiography* of William Stout, the Lancaster ironmonger, is pertinent here. At the end of his first year of trading in 1689, he analysed his business and found that he had 'sould goods for ready money about £450 and upon credit about £150'. This is considerably higher than what is typically found in inventories and Stout himself clearly felt that the balance was wrong and that he had been 'too forward in trusting and too backward in caling, as is too frequent with young tradesmen', a sentiment echoed in general terms by Defoe some years later.[43] Stout's comments at the end of nine years trading highlight the problems of a conscientious tradesman. In 1697, when he inspected his books he found he had 248 insolvent debtors in his books, owing £220. Just as in shop debts listed in inventories, Stout's individual debtors must each have owed very little, but collectively these debts represented a substantial sum that had made a heavy inroad into his profits. His own judgement repeated what he had written several years before, namely that he was 'too credulos and too slow in caling, and seldom made use of atturney, except to write letters to urge payment'.[44] It would seem that as time went on he became less tender hearted.

It is particularly useful when the appraisers chose to list the book debts in detail. This affords extra information in several ways two of which are pertinent here; the scale of each individual's debt and the social structure of the set of customers paying through credit as recorded in the shop book.

In the retailers' inventories noted where full details are given, overall 70 per cent of shop book debts were for less than £1. Some were tiny, and apparently

---

[41] The quotations are taken from Private Acts 4 GEO3 c. 41 (1764) Kendal, and 25 GEO2 c. 43 (1752) Liverpool.

[42] Both Lichfield Joint RO.

[43] Stout (1967), *Autobiography*, p. 96; Defoe (1987), *Complete English tradesman*, p. 46.

[44] Stout (1967), *Autobiography*, pp. 119-20 (1697).

for single items, like the 4d. for currants owed by William Clegge in 1649. [45] Assuming that most were running accounts, (and the evidence from the few surviving shop books is that this was common practice as we shall see below), then most retailers appear to have been successful in keeping these customers under reasonable control with regular, but partial, repayments. Both parties were thus using credit. For the customer it increased flexibility when cash was temporarily short; for the retailers it bonded customers to them and reduced the pressure on the supply of small change. At the same time, if managed properly it incurred little risk unless some disaster rendered customers unable or unwilling to pay. In this respect, the death of the retailer could have been just such a disaster as it made it more difficult to enforce payment through the courts.

An analysis of surviving shop books confirms the evidence of the probate inventories. Mui and Mui have studied the accounts of two eighteenth-century retailers. The ledger of the one, William Wood of Didsbury, Cheshire, covers a period of about five years from 1785. Wood sold largely grocery and had about 30 credit customers, who each bought between 5s. and 30s. worth of goods a month and about £10 worth in the year. Wood's customers mostly settled by paying a round sum and leaving a debit balance. There is some evidence, despite the apparently poor quality of his bookkeeping, that Wood kept a firm hold on the credit he allowed. Firstly, the purchases declined of those customers who failed to pay off part or all of their debt, perhaps because they were refused further credit for the time being. Secondly, when Wood died, there were very few bad debts.[46] Roberts of Penmorfa, Caernarvonshire, whose account books cover the 1790s, had a much more varied stock including some grocery, hardware, medicinal products, drapery and haberdashery. Given the nature of the area and the distance between market towns, it is not surprising to find that he served an extensive catchment area. This must have had implications for managing credit making it more difficult for him to assess the credit worthiness of potential customers living at a distance. Even so, he had a substantially larger credit trade than Wood, with about 200 customers most of whom payed off their debts in part each spring and autumn.[47]

A few accounts in the ledger of William Elmhirst, the surgeon and apothecary of Ouslethwaite, near Barnsley, Lancashire (1769-73) show a similar pattern of managing credit to that of Wood and Roberts, including settlement by instalment and in some cases payment in kind. For example,

---

[45] Lancashire RO WCW 1649 Lawrence Newall. Other customers of Newall owed respectively 4d. for long pepper and 7d. for tobacco.

[46] Mui and Mui (1989), *Shops and shopkeeping*, pp. 211-16, particularly pp. 212 and 215, based on Wood's Customer ledger.

[47] Mui and Mui (1989), *Shops and shopkeeping*, pp. 216-19, based on the Penmorfa Ledger.

Joshua Shay's account was opened in October 1770 and had reached over £3 by April the following year, when he paid off £2. A few months later £1 3s. 0d. was remitted in return for three sheep, leaving a balance of 6d. A further debt of 1s. was incurred, but no more repayments were made before Elmhirst's death in 1773.[48] There are several other examples of debtors using goods rather than money, including payment with livestock, cloth, coal and candles.[49] Accounts of this type are atypical in Elmhirst's ledger. Most customer accounts were paid in full when treatment for a specific problem was no longer required, perhaps because the goods and services offered by a medical man like Elmhirst were required only sporadically. Others, particularly those for customers of status, ran for some time without any interim payments. For example, Francis Edmund Esq. already owed nearly £37 when his account was transferred in 1768 from another ledger (now lost). Over the next year it rose to over £50 before settlement in full, with no partial repayments in the interim.[50]

Both Stout at the turn of the century and Turner some fifty years later expressed concern about the dangers of granting credit to customers. Each seems to have been of rather a pessimistic outlook, making it difficult to assess how typical is their picture of small businesses. As a Quaker, Stout's own inclinations were re-enforced by the beliefs of his Society. Trading beyond one's means was to be condemned at all times. Stout described many business failures and he invariably attributed them to careless living or to mismanagement, rather than to circumstances beyond the tradesman's control. The cryptic comments on indebtedness contained in the diary of his near contemporary, Roger Lowe, lend weight to Stout's strictures. It would seem that Lowe's indebtedness had begun before the start of the diary and that the so called 'Prentisshipp' may have been a form of indentured service as a way of paying off a debt.[51] The frantic struggles between his 'freedom' in November 1665 and his engagement in service to Thomas Peake in October 1667 are mirrored time and again in Stout's autobiography - 'he bought the shop, but did not manage it to profit, by his extravigant living and carelessness in his business became insolvent', he ended up 'a servant in a draper and mercer's shop in Richmond'.[52] His own career suggests he had a considerable acumen for retailing and wholesaling himself, though much less for overseas trade. His profits may never have been great in his own eyes but they mounted up to give him a substantial estate by his death. And if selling by credit gave him much

---

48 Elmhirst (n.d.), *Ledger*, p. 10. It is possible the account was continued on p. 91+, in which case it was paid in full. However, this may relate to another person of the same name.

49 Such payments are discussed by Sigsworth and Brady in Elmhirst (n.d.), *Ledger*, p. iv.

50 Elmhirst (n.d.), *Ledger*, pp. 8, 28, 33, 46.

51 See particularly Lowe (1938), *Diary*, 27 April 1664, 6 May 1664, 17 November 1665.

52 Stout (1967), *Autobiography*, pp. 99-100 (1690).

pain when one of his customers defaulted, he clearly recognized that the shop book, if properly managed, was an essential part of successful trading.

However, the diaries of both Stout and Lowe, his near contemporary, show how difficult the management of debt could be. Lowe wrote frequently of his problems, but his experiences with one customer, Humphrey Starbotham, a pedlar living near Wigan, epitomize the challenge faced by all retailers. Lowe's first attempt to collect what was obviously an already long-standing debt owing by Starbotham was in the summer of 1663 when a visit failed to secure payment, but success did not come for nearly another year.[53]

Stout's detailed account of the doings of his nephew, also called William Stout, shows how sharp was the knife edge between success and failure and how crucial was strict vigilance over debt. Stout had taken on his nephew as an apprentice in 1721, despite some reservations about his suitability for the trade. By 1728, the apprenticeship complete and himself aged 63, Stout with some reluctance made over the shop to his nephew. The transfer involved goods worth £370, plus £32 in cash with which 'he [the nephew] went to Sheffield to buy goods' together with the use of equipment and premises rent free. By 1731 Stout's worst fears had been realized. His nephew 'was in great straits with his creditors, who, observing his prodigalety, threatened to sue him'. On investigation it emerged that in three years the younger Stout had run up debts of nearly £1000, while those owing to him amounted to but £240. Stout took over charge again, cleared the debts within a year, and re-established his nephew in a rejuvenated though rather smaller business with goods valued at £240 but with cash totalling over £400. By 1737 bankruptcy again loomed with debts totalling more than £500, being over £100 in excess of the assets.[54] Again Stout had to intervene. There is no question that the shop was viable; Stout had after all run it himself successfully for years. What he contributed to the shop was an eye for a trading opportunity and an unremitting attention to careful accounting and the collection of debts.

Thomas Turner's Diary mirrors Stout's *Autobiography*. Trade in Turner's eyes was almost always uncertain; bankruptcy threatened round every corner. Yet throughout all his vicissitudes, like Stout, Turner survived. His reflections on the debt of some £18 owed by a 'Master Darby' in 1758 encapsulate both the dangers and the advantages to the small tradesman of trading by credit:

> Oh what a confusion and tumult there is in my breast about this affair! To think what a terrible thing it is to arrest a person, for by this means he may be entirely torn to pieces, who might otherwise recover himself and pay everyone their own. But then on the other hand let me consider some of this debt hath been standing above 4 years, and the greatest part of it

---

[53] Lowe (1938), *Diary*, 28 August 1663, 22 July 1664.
[54] Stout (1967), *Autobiography*, pp. 184-5 (1721), 208 (1731), 221-2 (1737).

above three years. I have tried very hard to get it these two years and cannot get one farthing. They have almost quite forsaken my shop, buying nothing from me that amounts to any value, but every time they want anything of value, they go to Lewes. And I have just reason to suspect they must be in debt at other places'.[55]

This extract is valuable because it shows what Turner expected of his credit customers. They should be credit worthy, they should pay off some of their account at regular intervals and they should continue to patronize his shop. When all three broke down he was prepared to put the matter into the hands of a lawyer despite his dislike of going to law. However, this does not seem to have been a frequent occurrence. Mostly debt was a nagging sore with regular complaints that trade was 'very dull' and that it was 'almost next to impossible to get in any money due on book.'[56]

It would be reasonable to suppose that the credit worthiness of customers bore some relationship to their social status, but the evidence does not support this supposition unequivocally. Thirteen inventories have been noted in which details of customers' social status were recorded, presumably copied from the shop book. In one other no such distinctions were made, but this could be because none of the customers merited honorific title in the eyes of the retailer rather than because of a disinclination to record such information. The significance of these social classifications is unclear but the evidence from this tiny sample suggests that retailers did attach some importance to the status of credit customers since they went to the trouble of recording it, although other factors like their own status, the nature of their wares and the location of their shops must each have had some bearing on how successful they could be in acquiring such customers. The mean indicates that some 28 per cent of customers in the books of those who did record status were designated as 'Mr' or higher, the median is lower at 17 per cent, a difference that suggests the sample is somewhat unbalanced by high-status tradesmen like Richard Ashley and Samuel Luck.[57] Surprisingly in this sample there is little evidence of a chronological trend towards the granting of credit down the social scale. The figure was high throughout the period, ranging from 41 per cent up to 96 per cent, or as high as 100 per cent if Rothwell is included.

Very little is known about the various mechanisms of credit for eighteenth-century people of little or no status, such as pawnbroking or petty money lending, though they were probably common. Styles suggests that credit

---

[55] Turner (1984), *Diary*, 22 May 1758.

[56] Turner (1984), *Diary*, 18 February 1758.

[57] These figures are based on the ten retailers whose books show differentiation by status and includes only the one list of debtors recorded in Thomas Wootton's inventory, that is, the one containing those recorded in his shop book.

**Table 5.2**
**Social status of indebted customers as recorded in retailers' shop books**

| Date | Retailer's name | Superior | Mr/Mrs | Goodman/ Goodie | Unspec. |
|---|---|---|---|---|---|
| 1554 | Thomas HARRISON | 0 | 6 | 12 | 95 |
| 1583 | William SHARPLES | 3 | 55 | 11 | 123 |
| 1621 | Edward MAYES | 0 | 8 | 0 | 47 |
| 1623 | John PARES | 0 | 6 | 0 | 55 |
| 1623 | William ROTHWELL | | | | 47 |
| 1626 | Ann BAKER | 0 | 6 | 0 | 26 |
| 1648 | Robert WILSON | | 3 | | 42 |
| 1649 | Lawrence NEWALL | 0 | 4 | 0 | 28 |
| 1665 | Robert ADDISON | 5 | 40 | | 263 |
| 1667 | Thomas WOOTTON (shop)* | 4 | 44 | | 111 |
| | (other) | 1 | 81 | | 59 |
| 1688 | Richard ASHLEY | 2 | 45 | 3 | 35 |
| 1706 | Samuel LUCK | 6 | 54 | 6 | 55 |
| 1748 | Thomas BROWNE | | 32 | | 194 |
| 1781 | James WALKER | 1 | 4 | | 109 |

* Some of the list is illegible and about 40 names are unavailable for analysis.

granted by tradesmen on the purchase of goods was widespread. It was probably universal among smaller outlets, the fastest growing sector in the retail trade and the one that largely served those of low status.[58] One cause for this may have been the shortage of cash, particularly of small coin for change.[59] Frequent small purchases required either plenty of small change or the acceptance of payment by credit. The most likely to have been faced with this dilemma were the petty tradesmen, and they are also the most likely to have left no records. It can only be assumed that their customers were expected to fulfil the same criteria as were required by Turner; that is, to be credit worthy within the context of their place in society and their purchasing aspirations, to pay off part of their account regularly, and to demonstrate loyalty by frequent purchasing. Whether all or even most of these petty tradesmen were able to keep adequate accounts is another matter, though the small scale of their operations may have meant that a book sporadically maintained and supplemented by tallies and scores on the wall, would have sufficed.

[58] Styles (1994), 'Clothing the north', p. 150.
[59] Mui and Mui (1989), *Shops and shopkeeping*, pp. 215-16.

## Conclusion

The management of credit by retailing tradesmen is an area in which the early modern period witnessed considerable change. Ironically contrary to the assumptions of some historians, granting credit appears to have been a normal part of the shopkeeping practice even in the sixteenth century and it remained so throughout. What did change, possibly as a consequence of the Act of 1609 was that debts recorded in the shop books began to be seen as a distinct genre to be handled separately. Bookkeeping and accounting remained primitive and, from the very limited sample available, it would appear that double entry was not widely adopted, despite a number of instructional manuals on the subject. On the other hand, Defoe's simplified system does seem to have been based on the practice of better tradesmen and account books designed for the purpose were widely available by the eighteenth century, as were facilities for learning the necessary skills.

Nevertheless, debt remained a two-edged sword. Despite its advantages to the retailing tradesmen, it was a nagging anxiety ever threatening to bring ruin. The 1609 Act brought recognition to the shop book as a record of debts acceptable under certain circumstances to a court of law, and the string of private acts in the second half of the eighteenth century made the collection of small debts more expeditious in some towns, but the retailing tradesman neglected the proper management of credit at his peril.

## Chapter 6

# 'A settled little society of trading people who understand business':[1] networking among retailing tradesmen

In the last three chapters the focus has been on the shop itself and on the relationship between retailer and customer. It is now time to turn to the broader setting in which the retailer operated, and to the networks of family and fellow tradesmen which made for success in business. The chapter draws heavily on the experiences of three early modern tradesmen, whose autobiographical material spans over a century from the Restoration to the 1760s. Roger Lowe, of Ashton in Makerfield, Lancashire, wrote a *Diary* that covers the eleven years from 1663 to 1674, while William Stout's *Autobiography* covering his family background, his education and apprenticeship, and his career as a 'Wholesale and Retail Grocer and Ironmonger' in Lancaster effectively spanned 60 years from about 1670 to the early 1730s. The third, Thomas Turner of East Hoathly, Sussex, kept a diary from 1754 to 1765.[2] When contextualized by other anecdotal evidence, these three extensive sources give a reasonably comprehensive picture of the way the provincial retail sector functioned in the second half of the seventeenth century and through the eighteenth. For the period before 1660 there are no comparable sources, so that in this chapter only fleeting and conjectural references can be made to that period.

That the successful retailing tradesman operated within a complex network of support is amply demonstrated by both Stout and Turner. Each of them, though with different degrees of emphasis, demonstrates the importance of the family in his business and the significance of an appropriate apprenticeship. In addition each has something to say about the local trading community and links with their suppliers, and each reveals, though rather fortuitously, the importance of those who bought to sell again as a profitable component of his trade. This chapter looks at these elements in turn, starting with the family and the apprenticeship; although looked at separately, the two were in fact often inextricably intertwined. The importance of the local trading community is then

---

1    Defoe (1987), *Complete English tradesman*, p. 35.
2    Lowe (1938), *Diary*; Stout (1967), *Autobiography*; Turner (1984), *Diary*.

discussed, followed by the establishment of an effective network of suppliers and the place of those who bought to sell again.


## The family

Apart from ensuring the child had an adequate education, which has already been discussed in chapter 5, the most obvious contribution the family could make to the aspiring tradesman was to provide a ready-made business. Records like the Apprenticeship records of guilds and the Borough records of the admission of freemen give some instances of this but not so many as might be expected. For example, the Admission books of the Mercers' Company of Shrewsbury show most apprentices were the sons of outsiders, but a few served with their fathers like Richard Taylor, Timothy Seymour and Hugh Jones, admitted respectively in 1613, 1695 and 1719, and a few others apparently served under a member of the family such as the two boys from Montgomery, Samuel Thomas, who served under John Thomas (1662) and Owen George, who served under Edward George (1662).[3]

However, although this method of acquiring a business with all the appropriate networks in place was available for the fortunate, the dynastic element in shopkeeping was by no means so commonplace as may be supposed. The situation in Wellington, Shropshire, in the second half of the seventeenth century may be unusual in this respect. There was already one mercer, whose family participation in the trade stretched back at least to the 1620s and lasted into the 1701s. Three, possibly four, more were able to establish themselves successfully in the 1660s. Two, Benjamin and Stephen Wright,[4] were the sons of the non-conforming vicar, but the other two, Joshua Johnson and Andrew Socket, were incomers.[5] Benjamin Wright, Johnson and Socket were each able to establish a dynasty, though in each case it was of short duration. Wright's son, though a mercer like his father, moved to Cheshire, Johnson's grandson apparently disposed of the shop when he became a landed gentleman,[6] and the Socket business seems to have been moribund before the death of the last member of the family designated as mercer in the 1720s.[7] Other Wellington tradesmen were less successful dynastically. None of

---

[3]   All from *Admission of freemen*, except Taylor from *Admission of brothers*.

[4]   There is little evidence of Stephen. A trade token was issued in the name of Stephen Wright, mercer, in 1668, Williamson (1967), *Trade tokens*, p. 964, and he appeared briefly in the Parish Register. He may have moved away or died young.

[5]   A fuller discussion of the Wellington mercers and other tradesmen may be found in Trinder and Cox (1980), *Yeomen and colliers*, pp. 20-26.

[6]   See, for example, Orleton Trustees MSS, 999/Y4, Lease dated 5 and 6 January 1720/21.

[7]   Trinder and Cox (1980), *Yeomen and colliers*, pp. 25-6, 362-3.

the three apothecaries and surgeons appears to have handed on his business to a member of his family.[8]

Dynastic failure was generally more typical than the experience of Wellington mercers, who at least maintained a business over two or more generations. The evidence from elsewhere in the country suggests that dynastic success was not common. For example, while a few Coventry tradesmen did found retailing businesses lasting over several generations, notably the Kilbees and the Kervins, most were not thus successful.[9] Stout's business was to all intents and purposes single generational. His family was of yeoman stock, he himself was childless and neither of his two nephews who attempted to take over the shop were successful. For Turner there was continuity in shopkeeping over the generations although this continuity did not apply to one specific business. Though he himself did not inherit the family business, Turner was the son of shopkeeping parents and two of his sons took up the trade, one of them eventually acquiring the shop in East Hoathly.[10] However, for both Stout and Turner, as will be discussed shortly, the most important contribution made by their family lay in a different direction from a ready-made business.

For those parents seeking to establish a child in a business other than their own, works like Campbell's *London tradesman* were invaluable. This publication, and others like it,[11] were intended to give information and instruction to parents and to young tradesmen who were unfamiliar with good practice. Campbell's title page made clear his intended readership. His work was 'CALCULATED for the Information of PARENTS and Instruction of YOUTH in their Choice of BUSINESS', H.N.'s book contained 'all things absolutely necessary to be known by all those who would thrive in the ... whole Art and Mystery of TRADE and TRAFFICK', while Defoe provided 'a collection of useful instructions for young tradesmen'.[12] Most of Campbell's specific advice was contained in one chapter. The rest of the book (except for a chapter on how the apprentice should deport himself) was devoted to descriptions of individual trades and to the costs a parent must expect to incur. Campbell was adamant that funding an apprenticeship was not enough, and that the costs of setting up must be considered, delivering a 'caution that can never be too much inculcated, that unless a Lad had a rational Prospect of setting up for himself in any of these Branches of the Retail Business, it is more than Madness to serve an Apprenticeship of seven Years'.[13] In trades where fashion

---

[8]   Trinder and Cox (1980), *Yeomen and colliers*, pp. 41-2, 348-9, 369, 374-5.

[9]   Berger (1993), *Most necessary luxuries*, pp. 278-80.

[10]  Stout (1967), *Autobiography*, pp. 67-8; Turner (1984), *Diary*, Footnote 1 on p. xvii and Appendix.

[11]  For example, H.N. (1684), *Compleat tradesman*; Defoe (1987), *Complete English tradesman*.

[12]  Defoe (1987), *Complete English tradesman*, Preface.

[13]  Campbell (1747), *London tradesman*, p. 283.

played a part or customer choice was a requirement, (like the mercer or the linen draper), setting up and stocking a London shop could run into several hundreds of pounds, if not thousands.

The figures in Table 6.1 relate to London in the mid-eighteenth century and probably for shops at the top end of the market. Although referring to the previous century, figures quoted by Earle of actual premiums paid by parents suggest that Campbell's figures were probably in accord with current practice. Earle gives the cost of apprenticeship to a Levant merchant as £100-£860, to a woollen draper or a mercer as £100-£120, to a yarn seller as £40 and to a milliner (for a boy) as £30.[14] In the provinces, figures were lower but they could still represent a substantial proportion of parental assets, which also tended to be lower. For example, Richard Acherley, a yeoman in the parish of Wem, Shropshire, left £50 in his will to the unborn child if a boy 'to set him apprentice to a good trade' with a further £100 when he reached the age of twenty-two.[15]

As noted in chapter 3, the increasing requirement of an appropriate shop setting did not come cheap and it was to their family, or to a lucrative marriage, that most young tradesmen had to look for the costs of setting up in trade. The most useful connection for an apprentice was marriage to his master's daughter. Out of his sample of 375 tradesman, Earle was able to locate six cases of this, and there may have been more which have gone unnoticed.[16] The Shropshire mercer, Benjamin Wright of Wellington, probably helped his career in this way. His apprentice master is unknown, but his marriage at about the time his apprenticeship must have ended to a member of the Coventry dynasty of shop retailing tradesmen, is suggestive.[17] Lowe gave much time and thought to a possible marriage. The degree to which he associated marriage with progress in business is suggested by his account of meeting a mercer from Warrington at the Ashton alehouse, where they 'talked about tradeinge and how to gett wives'.[18] One he considered, but did not act upon, was to a girl he did not even know, the daughter of a Lancashire clothier with a portion of £120.[19] Stout gave several instances of advantageous marriages. For example,when his apprentice, John Goad, finished, he set up and shortly after

---

[14] Earle (1991), *Making of the English middle class*, p. 94.

[15] Lichfield Joint RO, where Acherley is given as of Overley. Probate 26 September 1672.

[16] Earle (1991), *Making of the English middle class*, pp. 192, 394-5.

[17] Holy Trinity, Coventry, parish register, 6 August 1668, Mr Benjamin Wright of Wellington, Shropshire, mercer, to Mrs Ann Kervin o.t.p.

[18] Lowe (1938), *Diary*, 8 October 1663.

[19] Lowe (1938), *Diary*, 27 June 1665. This was proposed to him by a respectable Presbyterian divine, who offered to negotiate for him.

**Table 6.1**
**Costs of setting up in a selection of trades in London, 1747 and 1761[20]**

| Trade | Apprentice-ship £ | Setting up 1747 £ | Setting up 1761 £ | Annual wage £ |
|---|---|---|---|---|
| Apothecary | 20-200 | 50-200 | 100 | |
| Book seller | 20-100 | 50-100 | 100-200 | 15-20 |
| Brazier | 5-20 | 100-1000 | | |
| Chandler shop | - | - | | |
| China shop | 5-100 | 100-2000 | | |
| Colour shop | 5-20 | 200-1000 | | 20-25 |
| Confectioner | 10-40 | 100-30 [sic] | | 39-52 |
| Earthenware shop | 5-20 | 100-300 | | |
| Grocer | 20-100 | 500-2000 | 500+ | 15-20 |
| Haberdasher | 10-50 | 100-2000 | | |
| Hosier shop | 20-200 | 500-5000 | 500 | |
| Ironmonger | 30-100 | 500-2000 | | |
| Linen draper | 20-100 | 1000-5000 | 1000 | |
| Mercer | 50-200 | 1000-10,000 | 2000-3000 | 25-40* |
| Milliner | 5-20 | 100-1000 | | 13-15 |
| Oil shop | 40-70 | 500-1000 | | |
| Perfumer | - | 100-200 | | |
| Pewterer | 20-40 | 300-1000 | 500 | |
| Slop shop | up to 5 | - | | |
| Stationer | 20-30 | 100-2000 | 50 (retail) | |
| Tobacconist | 30-100 | 100-5000 | | |
| Woollen draper | 50-200 | 1000-5000 | 1000-5000 | 12-20* |

\* For book-keeping

'married a very agreeable young woman with a good portion', while Stout's nephew, William, when he restarted in 1732, had £160 from his father-in-law.[21]

Turner's *Diary* opened when he was already in trade, so there is no information on what was spent on his education and setting up in business.

[20] Campbell (1747), *London tradesman*, pp. 331-40; Collyer (1761), *Parents and Guardians Directory*, quoted in Earle (1991), *Making of the English middle class*, p. 107.

[21] Stout (1967), *Autobiography*, p. 183 (1721), p. 210 (1732). Ben-Amos (1991), 'Failure to become freemen', gives other examples of family assistance in setting up during the seventeenth century.

Stout, on the other hand, made much of his parents' sacrifice, first in schooling (though that was interrupted by the pressures of the farming year), and then the payment of £20 for an apprenticeship. His father had also intended to pay for the freedom of the proposed apprentice master who, as a Quaker, was not prepared to take the required oath, so that in turn Stout himself would be able to become free without the payment of a heavy entry fine. This scheme came to nothing. In addition Stout's father made provision in his will for his son to establish himself in trade by leaving him property and bonds worth about £150.[22] In 1738 Stout gave £300 to nephew, John, to stock his shop, more, as Stout observed somewhat wryly, than he himself had had at the same point in his career.[23] These figures are considerably in excess of those suggested by H.N. in 1684 for setting up and stocking a shop of £100 for London and £60 in the provinces.[24]

The saga of Gualter Brunskill, who married Stout's niece Margaret, further illustrates the importance of family support and how many people were sometimes involved in supplying it. For 'want of other business' Brunskill had served as a factor to a merchant in Barbados. Appointed executor in the will of his brother, a grocer and ironmonger, and having in his own view some knowledge in the trade, he decided to take on the shop and the apprentice. Stout spent upwards of £200 in rebuilding the shop for his niece and her husband and, when their apprentice was killed, arranged (and by implication paid for) the son of another niece to replace the dead boy.[25] Hunt in her study of the 'middling sort' shows the degree to which families expected to support quite distant relatives as well as their own children, just as Stout did. She concludes that 'Early modern English business activity relied upon the willingness of ordinary families to shoulder risks that most middle-class people today would view as unacceptable'.[26]

Stout relied, not only on family assets to pay for setting up in trade, but also their assistance in running the shop. Stout never married, so was unable to look for his wife to serve at the counter while he was busy elsewhere but he certainly contemplated so doing first to Bethia, the daughter of his fellow tradesman, Thomas Greene, and then to other 'young women of discreet behaviour and good fortune'.[27] These tentative moves came to nothing and Stout was thus deprived of a wife's assistance in the shop. There seems to have been a long tradition of wifely co-operation in running a shop, apparent from the letters written in the early seventeenth century by the London tradesman,

22  Stout (1967), *Autobiography*, p. 68 (1672), pp. 70-73 (1677-79), p. 89 (1687).
23  Stout (1967), *Autobiography*, p. 223 (1738).
24  H.N. (1684), *Compleat tradesman*, p. 21.
25  Stout (1967), *Autobiography*, pp. 218-20 (1735).
26  Hunt (1996), *Middling sort*, pp. 22-9, particularly p. 23.
27  Stout (1967), *Autobiography*, pp. 141-2 (1702).

Robert Gray, to his wife right through to the observation by Johanna Schopenhauer in the 1790s.[28] For Stout, his sister was a more than adequate substitute and he emphasized the value of her assistance again and again. She came first on fair days and market days when she was 'as ready in serving retaile customers as a young apprentice could have done' and she was 'diligent ... to overlook and assist the apprentice in my absence'.[29] When her health failed Stout had to employ a man on market days and he himself had to spend more time in the shop to oversee the apprentices. When Stout's nephew, William, took over the shop, he too depended upon the services of a sister.[30]

Turner's family network was also complex and supportive. His father had set up shop in Framfield in 1735 and, subject to his wife's interest, apparently intended it for Turner in due course. However, by that time Turner had taken over the shop of a deceased mercer in the village of East Hoathly some three miles away from Framfield. As a result, Turner's younger brother Moses took over the family shop when their mother died.[31] The operations of the two shops were closely intertwined. Moses frequently 'stood shop' when Turner was elsewhere engaged,[32] each lent stock to the other when required and bought stock likewise, though relationships were not always without friction.[33]

Turner's first marriage was disastrous so far as the business was concerned. His wife, Peggy, was sickly and capricious and there were frequent rows which Turner believed affected the business.[34] Only once did he do more than imply she was of little assistance, but the occasions are rare when he records constructive assistance, like the days she helped by sewing up some bed linen for an order, or by packaging tobacco, or by 'putting up goods for the audit'.[35] Not once did Turner refer to his wife attending the shop in his absence; it was always his brother who came over to stand shop. Peggy sounds much like the wife of Thomas Green, described by Stout as one who 'minded the house and entertained some flatering, disembling women, who were chargeable to them, and drew out their children to excess in victuals, apparel and vanety in conversation'. She seems to have been quite unlike the ideal image of the wife sitting behind the counter as portrayed by Schopenhauer.

---

[28] The letters are stored in the House of Lords RO and are discussed in Willan (1976), *Inland trade*, pp. 122-6; Schopenhauer (1987), *A lady's travels*, 27 January 1790.

[29] Stout (1967), *Autobiography*, p. 90 (1688), p. 105 (1691).

[30] Stout (1967), *Autobiography*, p. 105 (1691), p. 200 (1726), p. 204 (1729).

[31] Turner (1984), *Diary*, p. xix.

[32] For example, Turner (1984), *Diary*, 3 July 1756, 27 August 1764.

[33] For example, Turner (1984), *Diary*, 28 July 1756, 28 January 1758; 22 April 1757, 9 October 1758; 5 March 1764; 4 January 1758.

[34] For example, Turner (1984), *Diary*, 30 August 1755, 10 February 1756; 21 April 1758.

[35] For example, Turner (1984), *Diary*, 30 July 1754, 14 January 1756, 24 October 1757.

When Turner started to look for another wife, a good portion was something he hoped to obtain just as Stout had hoped in his tentative searches, and indeed Turner's new partner did have expectations.[36] An interest in his business affairs seems to have been something further her hoped to find in his new wife, but may not have found in Peggy. In this she may have been representative of a change that was receiving some comment, with some wives supposedly distancing themselves from business affairs in an attempt to appear genteel. Defoe was scathing about the wives who scorned 'to be seen in the counting house, much less behind the counter'. In their own interest, he thought, they should take an interest so that they would not be helpless if left widowed, though he did think some occupations were unsuitable for women, including the mercer, the woollen draper and the linen draper.[37]

Other evidence suggests that Defoe perceived a change taking place more rapidly than it really was. Campbell, writing some twenty years later, still apparently assumed that wives and daughters would 'do all the business of the shop'.[38] Evidence concerning practice confirms Campbell's view of things. Probate records paint the same picture. For example, as noted in chapter 3, Susan Horne of Arundel continued the grocery shop after the death of her husband for fifteen years while Elizabeth Sherwyn of Shrewsbury kept up her husband's business as a brazier and pewterer for about a year after his death in 1686.[39] During the second half of the eighteenth century, the provincial newspapers carried many advertisements of widows determined to carry on, like Mary James with a business of grocery, chandlery and soapboiling (1770) or Margaret Barnett, goldsmith and jeweller (1794), although the latter accepted she would need 'proper assistance'.[40] What Defoe claimed to have observed may have been true in some instances, there is little evidence of a widespread decline in wifely participation.

## Apprenticeship

If the family was the bedrock on which most successful businesses depended, apprenticeship was the gateway in most towns to the local trading community. Earle suggests that in London this was the most common mode of entry during the sixteenth century and the early seventeenth, but the practice, though never collapsing entirely, subsequently ceased to be the only starting point for a

---

[36] Turner (1984), *Diary*, 31 July 1765.
[37] Defoe (1987), *Complete English tradesman*, pp. 201, 205.
[38] Campbell (1747), *London tradesman*, p. 189.
[39] Lichfield Joint RO, Humphrey Sherwyn, probate 15 February 1686/87, Elizabeth Sherwyn probate, 19 October 1687.
[40] *Aris's Birmingham Gazette*, 22 January 1770; *Salopian Journal*, 28 January 1794.

business career.[41] Although increasingly under attack both from writers and by the many tradesmen who preferred to set up shop without this training, the apprenticeship system survived. For all its failings, this was probably because it gave certain types of tradesmen an advantage in establishing themselves.

Experiences of apprenticeship in the second half of the seventeenth century were varied. Already there were signs of change. William Stout mostly recorded positive experiences for himself and his contemporaries. He was apprenticed to Henry Coward, an ironmonger and grocer of Lancaster, for a premium of £20. Coward seems to have taken seriously his responsibilities as an apprentice master. Although Stout was occupied in his early years mainly in packing up goods for sale and in serving on market days, in the later stages of his apprenticeship he was encouraged to take a more positive role in the business, as were his fellow apprentices. For example, Stout was sent over to Ireland in 1687 on Coward's business, but he was also allowed to trade on his own account while there.[42] He acted in the same way when his own apprentices were reaching the end of their term. For example, in 1714 he encouraged John Baynes, 'a bould and enterprizing youth' to buy and sell various goods that Stout himself did not deal in.[43]

Similar practices were not uncommon in London, though few probably received the favoured treatment of Simon Mason, indentured to a London apothecary in 1715. Mason shows apprenticeship at its best. He had a good master, he was able to learn about the medicines and ingredients in use at the time and in the later stages he was permitted to attend St Thomas's Hospital and to treat patients on his own. As a result by the end of his apprenticeship he was already earning about £50 a year, enough if he had no other resources to set up on his own in a small way.[44] However, an apprentice to an apothecary in London was probably in a favoured position. The London Apothecaries were one of the few companies that monitored the progress of enrolled apprentices. On at least two occasions, they refused to grant candidates more than conditional freedom, because they had been given insufficient opportunities for learning - a serious warning to parents to see that they chose a reliable apprentice master for their sons.[45]

Stout's apprentice master, Coward, also helped his apprentices to gain experience, while forwarding his own business interests by opening shops in neighbouring settlements and putting one of the youngsters in his care in charge. Stout's predecessor ran a subsidiary shop in Cockerham for a time,

---

[41] Earle (1991), *Making of the English middle class*, pp. 85-6.

[42] Stout (1967), *Autobiography*, p. 73 (1679), pp. 79-80 (1682-83), pp. 86-7 (1687).

[43] Stout (1967), *Autobiography*, p. 171 (1714).

[44] Mason (1754), *Narrative*, quoted by Earle (1991), *Making of the English middle class*, p. 99.

[45] Burnby (1983), *English apothecary*, pp. 79-80.

while Stout was sent over for two days a week to one in Bolton. Neither experiment was an enduring success.[46] Roger Lowe had a less happy experience of running a subsidiary shop in Ashton in Makerfield for his apprentice master in Leigh. Lowe seems to have spent virtually the whole of his term of nine years in this shop, not altogether happily, although relations with his master do not appear to have been bad and he was given plenty of opportunity to gain experience in relative safety. 'I thought it sad', he wrote, 'for me to be ingaged 9 yeares to stay in Ashton to sell my Master's ware of and get no knowledge'.[47] At the end of his term, he felt his best chance lay in employment rather than in independence. In 1667 he committed himself to serve Thomas Peake of Warrington for three years for £20. Later he returned to Ashton where he died in 1679. He was apparently then the master of a small shop.[48]

Stout's *Autobiography* also reveals the importance of the apprenticeship in strengthening the ties between members of the local trading community. In any town of reasonable size, and in particular in incorporated towns where freedom of the borough was the gateway to respectable trading, apprenticeship was the essential step in the road to fortune. At any one time there must have been a substantial number of apprentices in a town. For example, Dyer estimates that in Worcester there were several hundred apprentices in the city at any one time in the sixteenth century, out of a total population between 4000 and 8000.[49] Even in small towns like Wellington, Shropshire, there must have been a couple of dozen. These apprentices, although each bound to a master, must have felt some identity of interest among themselves. For example, the London apprentices were sufficiently united in 1641 to organize a petition protesting against high property prices.[50]

Apprentice solidarity may have manifested itself undesirably in at times in high spirits and lawlessness, but it had its good side as well as its bad.[51] Stout demonstrates this. Some of the boys who were serving apprenticeships at the same time became fellow tradesmen in Lancaster. Much of Stout's concern devolved round the many disasters and deaths that befell his fellows, but the

---

[46]   Stout (1967), *Autobiography*, p. 79 (1682).

[47]   Lowe (1938), *Diary*, 16 October 1664.

[48]   Lowe (1938), *Diary*, 18 September 1667, 28 October 1667. The probate inventory of his personal estate is transcribed on p. 133 after the main text of the *Diary*.

[49]   Dyer (1973), *City of Worcester*, pp. 26, 153-4.

[50]   Ben-Amos (1991), 'Failure to become freemen', p. 164.

[51]   Mendenhall (1953), *Shrewsbury Drapers Company*, pp. 102, refers to some examples in Shrewsbury in the mid-seventeenth century. An example of what amounted to licensed disorder was the tradition for Shrove Tuesday when London Apprentices used to 'assail houses of dubious repute, and cart the unfortunate inmates through the city', Chambers (1888), *Book of days*, vol. I, pp. 238-9. Pepys mentioned several instances of disorder by apprentices, the most serious starting on 24 March 1667/68.

survivors, all at roughly the same stage in their career, had some interests in common and to some extent worked in co-operation. It must be significant that Stout thought it worth mentioning that John Bryer, who became his close neighbour and trading friend, had been an apprentice at precisely the same time, though under a different master.[52]

Another positive aspect of the apprenticeship was that it gave the young man the opportunity of establishing links within the trading community. Stout apparently assumed that a young man setting up would have the support of his former apprentice master, as he had had from his own.[53] When one of his former apprentices 'broke' (that is, went bankrupt), he set out what he saw as the lasting responsibilities of an apprentice master. As 'he had been my apprentice', he wrote, 'and the beginning of his creditt by my recommendation, I thought myself obliged to use my endevours to make the most for the crediters'.[54] He had similar exalted views on the reciprocal obligations of the apprentice and poured scorn on those who spent their term ingratiating themselves with their master's customers and suppliers, 'a practice much then used but by me always detested as being contrary to the golden rule to do to others as I would they should do to me'.[55] Stout's Quaker principles may not have found common acceptance. Establishing an interest with his master's customers was a practice Defoe recommended, though by customers he meant, not the chance buyers in the retail shop, but those who bought to sell again. 'If a young man comes from his master, and formed no acquaintance or interest among the customers whom his master dealt with, he has ... lost one of the principal ends and reasons for his being an apprentice, in which he has spent seven years and perhaps his friends given a considerable sum of money'.[56] Certainly the tailor, Francis Place, apparently had no inhibitions endeavouring 'to procure customers of my own, intending as soon as I had procured enough to keep us from starving to give up journeywork altogether'.[57]

Even if Stout disapproved of poaching his master's customers, he was in no doubt of the dangers of starting up where you were not known. When his nephew, John, who against his advice had gone to Kendal to serve his apprenticeship and then decided to return to Lancaster to set up in business, Stout was dismayed and recommended that an opening be sought in Kendal 'where he was known', but to no avail. John Stout did eventually establish a successful business in Lancaster, but only with substantial family support.[58]

---

52  Stout (1967), *Autobiography*, p. 88 (1687).
53  Stout (1967), *Autobiography*, p. 89 (1689).
54  Stout (1967), *Autobiography*, p. 149 (1704).
55  Stout (1967), *Autobiography*, p. 90 (1688).
56  Defoe (1987), *Complete English tradesman*, p. 14.
57  *Autobiography of Francis Place*, vol. II, pp. 3-4.
58  Stout (1967), *Autobiography*, p. 222 (1738).

Neither Campbell nor Defoe were entirely convinced of the merits of the system that governed such a large proportion of the life cycle. Campbell recognized that apprenticeship was the accepted requirement of many trades, leading to the freedom of the City of London and of other incorporated towns, but he questioned its educative value. Too often, he suspected, the master saved himself the expenses of a servant, while the apprentice 'spent the most precious Part of Life, in learning to weigh and measure out a Pound of Sugar or a Yard of Ribbon'.[59] Referring to apprenticeship to an Oilman he declared it was 'worth no Lad's while to slave seven years in this dirty shop for any knowledge he can reap from his Master on his practice', while apprenticed to a Stationer a lad would have to 'be Ignorant to the last Degree if he cannot learn all that is to be known of this Trade in a few Months conversing with any communicative Man of the Trade'.[60]

Defoe was only slightly less condemnatory. He was convinced that the first few years of an apprenticeship, which normally lasted seven years in the retail sector, were little benefit to youngsters, except to teach them 'submission to families, subjection to their masters, and dutiful attendance in their shops'. Defoe assumed during the last couple of years, the apprentice, now in his late teens or early twenties, should be able to learn if properly guided to be master of his business and capable (his financial circumstances permitting) to set himself up, for 'as buying indeed is the first, so selling is the last end of trade, and the faithful apprentice ought to be fully acquainted with them both'.[61]

Defoe's ideal of a shortened apprenticeship served during the late teens and employed in acquiring a thorough grounding in all aspects of the trade, was very different from the reality as seen by Campbell. There is support for both points of view in the evidence, though the experiences of one of Turner's younger brother rather endorses Defoe's point of view.

Whereas Turner's younger brother, Moses, was apparently apprenticed in the conventional way to a Lewes retailer and then took over the family shop at Framfield, the youngest brother, Richard appears to have been treated less favourably. He was apprenticed to George Beard, a shopkeeper of Chailey, and former servant to Turner, on terms that suggest that Richard was to be little more than a shop assistant. Contrary to usual practice, which was for the master to pay a premium for the expense and trouble of training the boy, Richard, who was only eleven, was nevertheless paid wages from the start; 10s. for the first year rising to £3 10s. in his last, the whole to be paid as a lump sum at the end of the term. At the end of his seven years, and still only eighteen years old, the Turners did not attempt to set him up in business, but arranged another bonded term, this time for three years, as 'a servant to serve in his shop' of John

59  Campbell (1747), *London tradesman*, pp. 282, 127.
60  Campbell (1747), *London tradesman*, p. 283
61  Defoe (1987), *Complete English tradesman*, pp. 10, 15.

Madgwick, a linen draper in Lewes and one of Turner's principal suppliers. For this Richard was to be paid £21 if retained for the full term, but £10 10s. only if he left after two years. In addition he was to be taken to London and Maudling Hill Fair at least once. Thus from the age of 11 years to 21, Richard was paid but £35 in all. Subsequently he appears to have become a yearly servant in Cuckfield. Whether Richard ever came into a share of the family businesses, set up independently or remained a servant, is not known. He died in 1774.[62] His experiences have similarities with those of Roger Lowe a century earlier. He too had spent much of his apprenticeship serving in a shop, in his case somewhat away from his master, and he too, initially, went into service.

Evidence from eighteenth-century newspapers suggests that Stout's experiences of a constructive apprenticeship had not entirely vanished. Advertisements for apprentices were common in a variety of trades, but those requiring no premium were probably offering terms similar to those served by Richard Turner, that is the apprentice would be no more than a poorly paid assistant.[63] More commonly a premium was required, sometimes in terms that suggested it might be substantial.[64] Although apprentice masters were expected to teach their apprentices the trade, few if any checks were made, and explicit assurances to this effect were rare. Almost the only two noted were the advertisements of a mercer, grocer and chandler in Cleobury Mortimer, Shropshire and of a druggist and chemist in Birmingham, who promised applicants 'an opportunity of seeing the nature of Drugs in general'.[65] The occasional advertisements also reveal that some apprentices took over their masters' business, like Talbot Waterhouse, a London confectioner, who had succeeded his apprentice master by 1743 and John Oakley, grocer and tea dealer of Shrewsbury who did likewise in 1794.[66]

There is also evidence of difficult relationships between the apprentice and his master. The unhappy or venal apprentice who broke his indenture and ran away was also not uncommon. In Bristol during the seventeenth century there was a steady sprinkling of apprentices who ran away or were dismissed, often with no official recognition of the fact.[67] Lowe had told of one such a century earlier, but all provincial newspapers published a fairly regular scattering of advertisements describing such runaways, apparently in the hopes of their

---

62 Turner (1984), *Diary*, 9 April 1754, 27 December 1760, 16 June 1665; Appendix A.
63 For example, one from an ironmonger in Leicester, *Leicester Journal*, 5 March 1790.
64 For example, a 'genteel premium' was required by a milliner advertising in the *New General Advertiser*, 1 May 1722.
65 *Aris's Birmingham Gazette*, 11 March 1751 and 24 January 1780.
66 Attingham MSS 112/6, Box 35/137; *Salopian Journal*, 9 July 1794.
67 Ben-Amos (1991), 'Failure to become freemen', pp. 166-7.

apprehension and return. Most concerned manufacturing apprentices, but a few involved the retail trade.[68]

## The local trading community

In medieval towns the trade guilds provided the environment in which a tradesman operated and a firm, and possibly stultifying control, over economic activity. This was already under attack before the end of the sixteenth century. A *Discourse of corporations*, probably written in 1587-89, averred that 'Private Societies, and Companies suche as concerne misteries and Consiste in buyinge and sellinge, as mercers, grocers, etc., bringe more harme than good to publique wealth'.[69] At this date, the attack was probably provoked as much by an ethical dislike of the goods such tradesmen sold as by the suspicion that these institutions were operating in restraint of trade, but the focus was to shift towards the second argument before the end of the period. Adam Smith's charge against the trading corporations was simple; they did indeed act in restraint of trade. This was achieved first by limiting the number of apprentices and requiring them to serve long terms, and secondly by restricting the right to trade to those who had freedom of the town. If all controls were removed, Smith argued, tradesmen would have to face more competition and journeymen might have to accept lower wages, 'But the public would be the gainer'. He even expressed doubts about the innocence of associations ostensibly for 'merriment and diversion' since 'the conversation aids in a conspiracy against the public'.[70]

It might be thought that Smith's attack on trading corporations came too late, since by the second half of the eighteenth century such institutions had lost much of their economic power and much retailing was taking place in towns and villages which had never been incorporated. In one respect this view is mistaken. In many places incorporated companies and boroughs fought a rearguard battle to retain their privilege of exclusive rights to trade. For example, the apprenticeship laws continued to be observed into the 1760s in Leeds even though the guilds had lost their economic significance by the early eighteenth century, and the situation was not dissimilar in Exeter.[71] The Corporation of York also made unremitting attempts to stem the tide of unfree tradesmen. For example, in 1775 a committee was appointed to address this

---

[68] Lowe (1938), *Diary*, 27 March 1664; for example, *Aris's Birmingham Gazette*, 17 September 1750, 11 October 1790.

[69] British Library, Harl. MSS 4243, ff. 60 seq., quoted in Tawney and Powell, *Tudor economic documents*, vol. III, p. 276.

[70] Smith, *Wealth of nations*, vol. I, pp. 107-17.

[71] Langford (1989), *Polite and commercial people*, pp. 180-81.

problem and it found no less than 164 shopkeepers in the distributive trades who had not obtained their freedom, including six each of milliners, hatters and glovers, and five each of drapers and hardwaremen.[72] Elsewhere such attempts had been given up long before. For example in Evesham, never a town of distinction, it was admitted in 1671 that 'By the interrupcion of the late times itt hath beene omitted to enrole and sweare many persons within this borough', and an attempt was made to rectify the situation. Three years later the corporation made a similar admission about apprenticeship enrolments. Nothing seems to have come of either attempt.[73] In Shrewsbury, on the other hand the Mercers continued to attempt control over all retail trade in the town down to the 1830s.[74]

Although the incorporated companies were concerned primarily in protecting the interests of their members by restricting competition, this was not their sole function. Mendenhall suggests that during the seventeenth century the Drapers of Shrewsbury developed a 'new dynamic corporate spirit, based on trading activity', with the Company not only providing a rallying point for collective action but also taking the lead in advancing the common interests of the group.[75] Some companies, both in London and the provinces, had in the past played some part in maintaining standards of fair trading, hygiene and safety.[76] In London, a number of the Livery Companies had powers granted either by Statute or by charter to enforce standards. Most of these powers were given to craft companies, like the Plumbers and the Founders, both of which had the right to regulate weights, but a strictly trading company like the Mercers had had during the early part of the sixteenth century the right to measure, not only silk, its principal commodity, but also canvas and linen.[77] Some provincial companies and the governing bodies of many boroughs had standard weights and measures.[78] Some claimed the right to search, though most of these powers had been lost by 1700. A few London

---

[72] Mui and Mui (1989), *Shops and shopkeeping*, pp. 130-33.

[73] 'Evesham borough records', no. 475 (19 April 1671) and no. 497 (6 February 1674).

[74] Mendenhall 1953), *Shrewsbury Drapers Company*, p. 85.

[75] Mendenhall 1953), *Shrewsbury Drapers Company*, pp. 112-13.

[76] For a brief account of the adulteration of food, see Burnett (1979), *Plenty and want*, pp. 99-120. Burnett suggests (p. 99) that the problem was probably at its worst in the first half of the nineteenth century, that is after all vestiges of guild control had disappeared.

[77] Connor (1987), *Weights and measures*, pp. 236-7, 329-30.

[78] For example, Evesham had its own measures for the ell and the yard for a while, and the standard weights and bushel were punctiliously handed over from one mayor to the next, Roberts (1994), *Evesham Borough records*, record no. 197 5 December 1634 for the standard ell and yard; record no. 212 8 December 1637, for the first mention of the weights. The standard measures disappear from the records in the 1640s, but the weights and the bushel continue until almost the last record in the surviving book for 21 December 1683. Buckingham retained control over a set of standard weights and measures into the nineteenth century, Elliot (1975), *Buckingham*, pp. 210-12.

livery companies remained active into the eighteenth century. The Apothecaries, one of the seventeenth-century creations, was assiduous in promoting the education and the business interests of its members. The educational competence of would-be apprentices was investigated before enrolment and again at the end of term. The company instituted regular herbalizing excursions, which the apprentices were expected to attend, it established its own elaboratory in 1672, and a Physic Garden at Chelsea the following year.[79] Provincial companies probably sank into inertia more readily, but examples of corporate activity can be noted occasionally.

Charitable activities like the relief of widows or elderly tradesmen, and loans for young tradesmen setting up or established ones experiencing temporary difficulty, continued to be undertaken even when the companies had lost all economic power. For example the London Fishmongers were responsible for St Peter's Hospital at Newington, Surrey, in which 42 men and women free of the company were cared for. Apart from this there was a continual drain on funds earmarked for charity to provide outdoor relief. London companies continued to grant loans, at least through to the end of the seventeenth century. For example, the Grocers lent £3660 to 81 individuals in 1635-36 and the Fishmongers £2755 to 77 in 1690.[80] Most provincial companies were probably not very different though on a much smaller scale. For example the Coventry Mercers, with very limited resources except for a £40 bequest from Thomas Whealtey in 1566, nevertheless loaned small amounts, typically ranging from £2 to £4, not only to impoverished tradesmen and their widows, but also to newly enfranchised freemen and others in need of temporary accommodation.[81] In sixteenth-century Worcester, the Clothiers administered a revolving fund of about £200 to assist tradesmen setting up with temporarily loans.[82] The administration of such charitable funds often continued when in other respects the company was moribund and provided in a small way a community of interest for the tradesmen concerned.[83]

The dangers inherent in the decay of the guilds did not pass unrecognized. As the number of shopkeepers increased after 1660, with no control over how they were trained or where they practised except for the competition of the market place, alarm bells started to ring. H.N. was not alone in attacking the growth of unregulated retailers, advocating compulsory universal apprenticeship and retailing confined to members of trading companies

---

[79] Burnby (1983), *English apothecary*, pp. 79-80; Earle (1991), *Making of the English middle class*, p. 253.

[80] Earle (1991), *Making of the English middle class*, pp. 258-9, note 8 on p. 361.

[81] Berger (1993), *The most necessary luxuries*, pp. 208 and 240. The Company had other small resources that they used in a similar way.

[82] Dyer (1973), *City of Worcester*, p. 116.

[83] For the relief of the poor by trading companies in Scotland, see Sanderson (1996), *Women and work*, pp. 145-9.

established in every market town.[84] This alarmist and retrograde approach came to nothing in the tide of deregulating thought that culminated in Adam Smith, but it is an indication of how strongly perceptions of an idealized former world can govern views of the present.

Although Stout as a Quaker was excluded from many of the activities of Lancaster as an incorporated borough, his *Autobiography* shows that co-operation among tradesmen was a reality that did not depend on membership of a guild. Instead it was of an informal nature operating in much the same way as Defoe was to recommend, though Stout was caustic about the dangers of overmuch drinking and tittle tattle.[85] Defoe was sure that success depended on becoming part of a trading community even if it did only consist in convivial meetings and chat. 'A settled little society of trading people who understand business, and are carrying on trade in the same manner with himself ... teach the tradesman more that his apprenticeship ... there he learned to trade, here he is made a Complete tradesman' and 'The tradesmen's meetings are like the merchants' exchange, where they manage, negotiate and, indeed, beget business with one another'.[86] Most of Stout's 'society of trading people' in Lancaster consisted of his former apprentice companions like John Bryer, and his close neighbours like Thomas and Richard Green, Augustin Greenwood and John Hodgson. It was with these, or some of them, that Stout went to London to buy supplies; it was from one of them, the merchant John Hodgson who shared the same house, that Stout bought his refined sugar and molasses; while another, Augustin Greenwood, was both 'a good customer in the ironmonger way' and allowed tobacco to the young tradesman on favourable terms. By implication it was Greenwood who taught Stout much of what he knew about tobacco.[87] Stout apparently also felt that he belonged to a wider community of tradesmen in Lancaster. This shows itself partly in his many accounts of what happened to other tradesmen but also in his frequent use of the collective pronoun. When the ship from Virginia failed to arrive in 1691/92, Stout wrote 'we were obliged to go to Liverpool for tobacco'.[88] Elsewhere he commented that 'We had now no carriage from London but by land', and 'there being no coporas works in Liverpoole ... we formerly had [it] from London and foreigne parts'.[89]

This sense of corporate identity based on self-interest, which could find expression alongside the normal competition of trade, was found in the non-

---

[84] H.N. (1684) *Compleat tradesman*, p. 17 seq.

[85] Stout (1967), *Autobiography*, pp. 103-4 (1691).

[86] Defoe (1987), *Complete English tradesman*, pp. 33, 35.

[87] For example, Stout (1967), *Autobiography*, p. 97 (1690), p. 109 (1693); p. 95 (1689); pp. 105-6 (1691/92). Some of these close associates were Quakers like Stout.

[88] Stout (1967), *Autobiography*, p. 106 (1691/92).

[89] Stout (1967), *Autobiography*, p. 95 (1689),

incorporated towns no less than in the corporate ones. This is demonstrated by a curious string of events in the western midlands in 1760. It began when the 'Grocers, Druggists and Tea Sellers of Birmingham' announced that due to the poor state of trade they were not going to give Christmas boxes that year. This initiative was followed by similar notices from Kidderminster, Stourbridge, Wolverhampton, Deritend, Shrewsbury, Bridgnorth, Newport, Dudley, Newton in Montgomeryshire and Wem.[90] Several of these towns were unincorporated with no system of town government above that of the parish. Clearly tradesmen in these towns were able, and did, get together to take concerted action when they felt the need.

Sometimes it is easier to see what external pressures provoked this sort of action. When the London tea dealers combined in the 1770s in an attempt to protect legal trade in that commodity, their actions provoked the dealers in Bristol and in Hull to collective action in protest.[91] The proposed Shop Tax and regulating of hawkers in the 1780s provoked a storm of collective protest from around the country. In the four weeks from 16 June 1685, there was a series of collective petitions concerning the Government's change of heart over hawkers from retailers in Kendal, Lancaster, Warrington, Wolverhampton, Carmarthen, Exeter and several other places besides. The following year shopkeepers were again organizing themselves, this time against the proposed rates of tax. In less than two months 41 petitions from all over the country were presented to Parliament from groups of tradesmen.[92]

The value of the urban community, however fragile it was, is made plain by events such as these and by Stout in his *Autobiography*. For the shopkeepers set up in smaller settlements like Lowe in Ashton in Makerfield and Turner in East Hoathly there was no such support. Their social life depended on those who were also their customers with all the problems that could bring. Their trading life could lack the support of communal experience and identity of interest found in Defoe's 'settled little society of trading people who understand business'.

## Suppliers

The simple model of the movement of goods going from the producer or importer, through the wholesaler and then the retailer, to the end consumer has questionable relevance for the early modern period. Yet, with the exception

---

[90]   *Aris's Birmingham Gazette*, 24 November, 1, 8, and 15 December 1760.

[91]   Memorials to the Lords of Treasury from Bristol and Hull dealers, both dated 1 January 1783, and more fully discussed and quoted in Mui and Mui (1989), *Shops and shopkeeping*, p. 20.

[92]   Mui and Mui (1989), *Shops and shopkeeping*, pp. 77-8, 81-4.

perhaps of the term 'consumer', which was rarely used, each of the terms did have meaning in the early modern period, and tradesmen who performed each of these functions can easily be identified in the records.

As is so often the case, Defoe made a perceptive analysis of the classic structure of inland trade and those involved in it. Beneath the merchant:

> who carry on the great foreign *negoce*, and who ... import the growth of all countries hither ..., we have a great number of considerable dealers, whom we call tradesmen, who are properly called warehouse-keepers, who supply the merchants ... for exportation; and also others who are called wholesalesmen, who bring and take off from the merchants all the foreign goods which they import; these, by their corresponding with a like sort of tradesmen in the country, convey and hand forward these goods, and our own also, among the country tradesmen, into every corner of the kingdom, however remote, and them to the retailer, and by the retailer to the last consumer, which is the last article of all trade.[93]

The career of Stout both draws attention to the dangers of simplistic labelling and modelling and explicates the meaning of terms used around 1700. At the start of his autobiography Stout called himself a 'Wholesale and Retail Grocer and Ironmonger,[94] but even this double dual role does not describe adequately what and how he bought and sold. He served his apprenticeship with an ironmonger, but one who had 'a full trade for groceries, ironmongerware and sevra[l] other goods'. No doubt when Stout set up himself as the fifth ironmonger in Lancaster, he sold a similar mix.[95] Whether initially he sold wholesale as well as retail is not clear, but by 1704, having sold his shop several years previously, what 'imploy' he had 'was by selling grocery goods by wholesale to country shopkeepers, without keeping open shop'. Elsewhere he makes clear that this meant he kept a warehouse.[96] Stout also took to 'merchandizing', that is either foreign or coastal trade,[97] before returning in later years to sell retail by keeping open shop.[98] His career highlights two features of retailing tradesmen that appear to have been widespread throughout

---

[93] Defoe (1987), *Complete English tradesman*, p. 8.

[94] Stout (1967), *Autobiography*, p. 67.

[95] Stout (1967), *Autobiography*, pp. 73-4 (*c.* 1680), p. 96 (1689).

[96] Stout (1967), *Autobiography*, p. 148 (1704); p. 131 (1700), p. 133 (1701). This is a use of the term that was by no means universal in the eighteenth century, when the warehouse seems often to have been a second room in a retail shop or a designation for a supposedly upmarket outlet.

[97] Stout (1967), *Autobiography*, p. 121 (1698), p. 131 (1700). Defoe (1987), *Complete English tradesman*, p. 5, suggested that ventures into merchandizing were not uncommon among tradesmen in coastal towns. Other Lancaster tradesmen apart from Stout also made investments in foreign trade, including Stout's former apprentice, John Troughtwood, see Stout (1967), *Autobiography*, pp. 29-30.

[98] Stout (1967), *Autobiography*, p. 150 (1704), p. 208 (1731).

the early modern period. Firstly, retailers often dealt in a variety of goods well outside what might be expected from their designated trades. This had implications in the way retailers were supplied. Secondly, although tradesmen made a distinction between wholesale and retail trading, many retailers were involved in wholesaling and even in merchandizing as well.

### a) Multiplicity of suppliers

The first feature, that of a broad variety of goods in many retailing shops, is only relevant here because it complicated the supply side of the business. Stout sold grocery and ironmongery, but many a provincial tradesman, particularly the mercer, also sold haberdashery, linen and woollen draperies and much else as well. For example, in 1544 a Coventry tradesman specializing in upholstery with a shop and a warehouse, was selling, not only coverlets, bedding, and soft furnishings with the materials for making them, but also haberdashery, small wares, saltery, paper and grocery.[99] This lack of specialization was not just a feature of the earlier part of the period, or later of village shops. The huge inventory taken of the stock of a Wolverhampton mercer in 1701 was divided up under the headings; Linen drapery, Mercery, Haberdashery, Grocery and Woollen drapery, almost as if each were a separate department.[100] This shop seems to have been particularly well ordered, but it was by no means exceptional in the range of goods it contained.

Lowe's experience indicates that the problem of supply was no less acute for many small retailers. Although most of his goods came from his master thus simplifying the matter of supply, Lowe does seem to have been responsible some times for negotiating on his own with Warrington tradesmen and local producers.[101] Right at the end of his apprenticeship he was even dealing with more distant suppliers like the Chester merchant who dealt in Bristol goods, and whom Lowe met in Liverpool.[102] Fleeting references occur that highlight the importance of personal contacts and recommendations. For example, when he bought hour-glasses from one Henry Feildinge, Lowe wrote a letter of introduction and recommendation to John Chaddocke, a former fellow apprentice.[103] Stuck out on his own, possibly the only shopkeeper in the village, Lowe received little training during his apprenticeship. As his apprenticeship neared its close his expressions of anxiety increased and he

---

[99]  Lichfield Joint RO, probate inventory of Roger Palmer of Coventry (1544).

[100]   Lichfield Joint RO, Peculiar series, probate inventory of Jonathan Hickman of Wolverhampton (1701).

[101] For example, Lowe (1938), *Diary*, 4 April 1664, 6 June 1665; 3 May 1664, 27 June 1665.

[102] Lowe (1938), *Diary*, 27 March 1666.

[103] Lowe (1938), *Diary*, 4 May 1664.

complained that after nine years of service he had got no knowledge.[104] Reality bit more sharply when, free of his indentures at last he felt 'sadly troubled for fear of miscarryeinge' and ignorant of 'how to get cloth and things'.[105] The problem of buying cloth was resolved temporally, but it is not surprising that he decided to opt for the safety of employment rather than remaining independent. However, he did come back to keeping his own shop later,[106] possibly because he had been able to rectify his lack of 'knowledge' while serving the Warrington tradesman, Peake as a journeyman. At least such service would have given Lowe the chance to create his own 'little society of trading people'. His experiences must have been common even if those apprentices who turned journeymen have left no record.

The complexity of Stout's purchases was complicated by the fact that he chose to combine trips to London on business with the annual general meeting of the Society of Friends. When he first set up shop, he was obliged to go to London for grocery to tradesmen he 'was recommended to', that is presumably carrying with him letters of recommendation. He was thus able to buy £200 worth of goods paying only for half in cash 'as was usual to do by any young man beginning trade'.[107] Apart from supplies acquired through his 'correspondents', in 1704 Stout was instrumental in arranging the apprenticeship of a cousin to a dry salter in London, thus providing himself with a family trading link in the metropolis. Once this was in place he ceased going to the capital, using his cousin as agent.[108] This form of networking may have been common, but until more family reconstitutions are done for retailers, this must remain a matter of speculation. One retailing dynasty that lasted for over a century is the Phillips family in Wellington, Shropshire. They seem to have done precisely what Stout did, apprenticing one member of the family in Shrewsbury, and establishing family connections in London and in Manchester. They thus had trading links in all the main areas of supply, London for linens, silks and grocery, Manchester for linens, threads, ribbons and fustians and Shrewsbury for cheap woollens.[109]

---

[104] Lowe (1938), *Diary*, 16 October 1664.

[105] Lowe (1938), *Diary*, 20 December 1665.

[106] Lowe (1938), *Diary*, 21 December 1665, 10 February 1667/68.

[107] Stout (1967), *Autobiography*, p. 89 (1688).

[108] Stout (1967), *Autobiography*, p. 166 (1712) and p. 169 (1713).

[109] PRO, P.C.C., Will of William Phillips the elder, of Wellington, gent., probate 1685 and Lichfield Joint RO, will of Richard Phillips, probate 1705; the connection with Manchester is the most tenuous, but a Robert Phillips, draper of Manchester was associated with William Phillips on several Wellington deeds, for example, Eyton collection, vol. I, 665/132-33 Orleton trustees MSS 999 ki. 2 November 1714. The Shrewsbury Drapers were particularly assiduous in setting up links with London, though this was largely for wholesale trade, see Mendenhall (1953), *Shrewsbury Drapers Company*, p. 91.

A similar pattern developed for Stout's trade in Sheffield, where he bought 'Sheffield and Birmingham manufactories' though it took longer to establish suitable links.[110] For the first few years he went himself, but in 1691 he arranged with Obadiah Barlow, probably a fellow Quaker, to buy goods in Stout's absence. This was made easier through a further arrangement he made in 1693, when he left money with the landlord there, Joseph Downs, to pay for what he had ordered. In 1709 he went a step further, taking the names of makers so as to order direct and arranging for an ironmaster and factor there to pack up his order so that he himself did not need to go again.[111] Of his other supplies, iron and tobacco were most vexatious. Tobacco could normally be obtained from Furness or Cartmel, but Swedish iron had to come from Leeds or York.[112] Both tobacco and sugar depended crucially on the market and on whether or not war was hindering the usual links. In the early days Stout bought these from his neighbours; sugar from the refinery at Lancaster, and tobacco from a wholesaler. Later Stout seems to have gone further afield for these goods to suppliers in Liverpool and Bristol, where he was able to 'settle a correspondence'.[113]

Stout's dealings in cheese demonstrate how great a part serendipity could play in early modern trade. From the start of his career, he had bought his cheese at Preston fair and thus became acquainted with the cheese wholesalers who dealt there. At the same time he inevitably became involved with the coastal traders and merchants who carried cheese from Lancashire and Cheshire to London bringing back groceries and other merchandize on behalf of Stout and his fellow shopkeepers. Stout himself became actively involved in this trade by 1715. Perhaps because of these associations with the trade in cheese, Stout was able to win the tender for supplying cheese to the rebels imprisoned after the 1715 rebellion - a brief but profitable enterprise involving two or three hundred weight a week.[114]

Turner had much the same experience since he too sold a variety of goods. Located in Sussex, it is only to be expected that most of his suppliers were based in London. Mui and Mui believed that one of the principal changes occurring in the eighteenth century was that the wholesale and the producer became more active in seeking customers rather than the retailer seeking out a supplier. Though there is some evidence of this, Turner, like Stout several decades before, still visited London to see his suppliers, to place orders and to pay bills. On one trip in March 1759, he settled his accounts with nearly thirty

[110] Stout (1967), *Autobiography*, pp. 89-90 (1988-89).

[111] Stout (1967), *Autobiography*, p. 106 (1691-92), p. 109 (1693), p. 160 (1709)

[112] Stout (1967), *Autobiography*, p. 95 (1689)

[113] Stout (1967), *Autobiography*, p. 95 (1689; p. 114 (1695)

[114] Stout (1967), *Autobiography*, p. 106 (1691-92); p. 95 (1689); p. 172 (1715); p. 176 (1716).

suppliers including two linen drapers, two haberdashers. and one each of tobacconist, druggist, horse-milliner, grocer, ironmonger, hosier, woollen draper, hat-warehouse and a hatter, metal button and hardware warehouse, distiller, pewterer, cheesemonger, and oilman and one who designated himself specifically as a wholesale mercer.[115] These were by no means his only suppliers used during the eleven years of the diary. Apart from several other Londoners, he bought supplies from tradesmen in Lewes and Maidstone, two Kentish paper makers as well as producers of locally made items like beehives, clogs and gingerbread from eight nearby villages. Like Stout, who had bought up bankrupt stock when the opportunity arose, Turner frequented sales of captured and condemned stock held by the Customs House.[116]

One of Turner's most important suppliers did represent an eighteenth-century development in wholesaling, though it was not entirely new. Samuel Ridings and Son of Manchester seem to have visited Sussex regularly, apparently staying over Monday night at the White Horse in Lewes. Here the local tradesmen, including Turner met for breakfast and to do business.[117]

Turner's methods of paying his suppliers were as varied as his stock. Locally, and only occasionally, he used barter. For example in 1760 he offset a book debt of one of his superior customers with the butter she had packed up and supplied him on commission for Thomas Scrase, a Lewes tradesman. Scrase then paid in part for the butter Turner had supplied him in 1758 with three wigs, leaving outstanding a debt for the butter supplied in 1759. Similar complicated arrangements were made over rags for the paper maker.[118]

The extensive use of bills of exchange, particularly between himself and his London suppliers depended upon trust, which occasionally broke down. For most purposes Turner could depend upon the mercer, Samuel Durrant of Lewes to act as his local banker and the Southwark haberdashers, Margesson and Collison, to act in the same way in London.[119] In this respect he was not dissimilar to Stout who had also made arrangements for the payment of his bills in Sheffield through an agent.[120] But whereas Stout appears to have carried large sums of cash with him, especially in the early years before he

---

[115] Turner (1984), *Diary*, 21 March 1759 and pp. 344-5.

[116] For example, Stout (1967), *Autobiography*, p. 100 (1690); Turner (1984), *Diary*, 21 February 1764. See also advertisements for these sales in the *Sussex Weekly Advertiser* like the one on 12 April 1790.

[117] Turner (1984), *Diary*, 1 May 1756, 23 February 1762, 5 March 1764.

[118] Turner (1984), *Diary*, 21 January 1760 and 5 October 1759.

[119] Turner (1984), *Diary*, a full discussion of Turner's financial dealings can be found in Appendix C.

[120] Stout (1967), *Autobiography*, p. 109 (1693).

established bonds of trust with his suppliers,[121] Turner was able to make greater use of the bill of exchange as a devise for dealing with credit.

The problem of stocking a multiplicity of wares and the consequent necessity of dealing with many suppliers was not new. The confused and disorderly accounts of William Wray, mercer of Ripon, Yorkshire, which cover the last two decades of the sixteenth century suggest he had about twenty suppliers in the 1590s, when his accounts are at their fullest. Apart from some goods supplied by his 'brother', Walter Dougell, his supplies came mostly from about six major sources, one located in Ripon itself, two in Beverley over fifty miles away, and three from the same family but whose location is unknown. Other wares came either directly from the producers, mostly local people, or from more distant tradesmen such as the pepper from a York alderman, the thread and fringe from a 'Coventre man' and various items from Norwich. Although Wray mentioned paying debts at Beverley fair, he does not seem to have used it for stocking up since his purchases were spread evenly throughout the year. For some goods Wray 'paid and quit', but it was more usual for him to use credit or part credit. This was paid off in times varying from one week to a year, though such a long term was not common.[122]

Right at the other end of the period, Francis Place was also using several suppliers, including at least three mercers and two woollen drapers. He found the market highly competitive and chose to use several suppliers in order to encourage them to compete against each other for his custom. It is not known how many suppliers Stout used (though he referred to 'tradesmen' rather than to 'a tradesman'). It was probably several in London and the same in Sheffield. Turner over eleven years used at least eight grocers, five mercers, four haberdashers, three woollen drapers and two linen drapers, some local some from London and one from Manchester. It seems probable that both he and Stout used much the same technique as Place to encourage competition.

The retailers discussed here each had different circumstances and experiences, but these are less noticeable than what they had in common suggesting that they may provide insight into the way retailers were supplied generally over the period. Each of them, even Lowe, used a number of suppliers consisting partly of local producers and partly more distant tradesmen dealing in wholesale. They all too acquired some stock from local tradesmen probably not dissimilar to themselves. Although not apparent in all sources, it seems that recommendation and networking played an important part in the

---

[121] Stout implied he took the cash with him on his first visit to London, but in his last visit to Sheffield he certainly did, see Stout (1967), *Autobiography*, p. 89 (1688); p. 160 (1709).

[122] Willan (1976), *Inland trade*, p. 67.

supply side of the business, as, of course, did credit, Defoe's 'most dangerous state of life' but also 'as good as stock, and ... as durable'.[123]

An important development of the eighteenth century hinted at only fleetingly in Turner's diary, and in the other sources addressed not at all, was the increasing use of trade cards, pattern cards, catalogues and samples as a form of communication between the wholesale and the retailer. This was in itself only an extension of the 'correspondence' so often mentioned by Stout. The use of this term was probably an innovation of the seventeenth century and may have resulted from a different approach to commercial negotiations which encouraged the setting up of relationships at a distance. Stout, for example, tended to refer to correspondence when he was first establishing contact and before he was known personally to the supplier, and he tended to replace it with closer links based on agents at a later date.

The extensive use of trade cards, pattern cards, catalogues and samples had to wait for the increased availability and consequent lower cost of paper as well as the coming of the printing press to the provinces in the eighteenth century. The use of these devices was applied to the whole spectrum of inland trade and involved the relationship between retailer and consumer no less than that between wholesaler and retailer. In all cases it encouraged trade at a remote rather than at a personal level. The order could be selected from samples, price lists and catalogues sent by the many suppliers and then delivered by one of the many options of carriage. The travelling salesman, agent or employee of the wholesaler or manufacturer also became more common, carrying the samples and delivering by word of mouth what would otherwise have been on paper.[124]

It is difficult to know how significant these eighteenth-century developments were. Much is made of them partly because the sources most informative about their operation come from firms most involved in their use. Neither Turner nor Place say much about them and certainly do not give the impression of being swamped with promotional literature. Probably these innovations passed by many country and petty shopkeepers who continued to use traditional methods to obtain supplies. Certainly some provincial retailers were employing very similar methods at the end of the eighteenth century as Stout had been at the beginning. Elizabeth and Susannah Towsey sold millinery and haberdashery in Chester during the 1780s. Although they originally visited London themselves to make orders and pay bills, subsequently their forewoman went in their place. The minute instructions the two sisters issued have survived. These include references to more than a dozen London tradesmen, some whose bills must be paid, some whose stock must merely be examined and some others from whom

---

[123] Defoe (1987), *Complete English tradesman*, pp. 48-9.

[124] For example, Satchell et al. (1990), 'Kendal pattern book', describes the pattern book of the Crewdsons of Kendal in Westmoreland which contained nearly 500 samples, mostly of linen mixed with either worsted or woollen, or both.

goods could be ordered if they were suitable and the price was right.[125] Although haberdashery and millinery were trades well served by pattern cards and samples, the Townseys apparently preferred direct and personal contact with their suppliers, at least occasionally.

### b) Combining retailing with wholesaling

Stout implies that moving from retailing to wholesaling was welcome and that his subsequent return to retailing was done through a sense of duty. Certainly the diarists portray the disadvantages of running a shop with minimal help; the long hours and the necessity to open up whenever a customer called, the expectations of customers to be provided with a social environment along with the shopping, and the importance of an excessive patience and civility however unreasonable the person on the other side of the counter. Stout also seems to imply that to go from retailing to wholesaling was a step up on the trading ladder. Newspaper advertisements announcing such a move are rare and do not suggest that it was particularly common.[126]

Wholesaling as a distinct category of trade had a long history. In the sixteenth century some of the larger trading companies had been clear in their minds that their members were restricted to trading wholesale. Indeed, the very name of the Grocers indicates that they were intended to trade in gross or wholesale. There were two issues standing in the way of implicating such a policy. The first was one of definition; companies had some difficulty in deciding what constituted retail trading and therefore whom they should exclude from membership. Over the period the definition changed somewhat though this may have had little effect in practice. Whereas in the sixteenth century to deal wholesale was to deal in bulk, by the eighteenth it was more often to act as a middleman between the merchant and the retailer. The second issue concerned the members of such companies who were unwilling to be constrained by the dictats of their ruling bodies. One of the most substantial companies, the Merchant Adventurers, was successful in imposing its regulations only on members resident in London and the suburbs, while elsewhere members won the right to sell retail if they chose.[127]

In the provinces, there were some companies that attempted to restrict their members to wholesale trade, like the Drapers of Shrewsbury,[128] but for the

---

[125] Mass Observation (1947), *Browns and Chester*, pp. 14-25. The instructions are also reproduced with some discussion of them in Aldburgham (1981), *Shops and shopping*, pp. 8-9.

[126] An unnamed tradesman announced in 1790 that he was relinquishing retail trade to confine himself to wholesale. He was envisaging becoming an agent for one or more manufacturers, *Aris's Birmingham Gazette*, 20 July 1790.

[127] Willan (1976), *Inland trade*, pp. 50-52.

[128] Mendenhall (1953), *Shrewsbury Drapers Company*, p. 94, note 1, notes that in 1619 the Drapers claimed no more that five of their members supported themselves by retailing. An

most part provincial tradesmen were free to trade either wholesale or retail, or both, as they saw fit. Although in the seventeenth century there must have been specialist wholesalers in many large towns, many more substantial tradesmen were probably less particular in their mode of operation being happy to exploit any opportunity for profit. The grocer Thomas Wootton of Bewdley (1667) may be typical in this respect. From the huge list of his debtors it is possible to identify local and distant retailing tradesmen, craftsmen and retail customers.[129]

John Houghton in 1693 commented that his correspondent found no wholesalers in Derby as if this were unusual,[130] but, apart from occasional examples like the inventory of Wootton, the evidence is thin before the advent of newspapers and trade cards. Thereafter the situation becomes clearer, with those declaring themselves to be wholesalers more common among the London tradesmen than the provincial. Even so there were a substantial number that declared themselves ready to trade either wholesale or retail. Out of a set of nearly 500 trade cards and bill heads, 104 of the tradesmen involved, mostly Londoners, declared themselves to deal wholesale only, and 76 both wholesale and retail. A set of about 1400 advertisements, mostly from provincial rather than London newspapers, paints a similar picture, with 130 wholesalers and 104 with dual function. Other tradesmen can be noted who made no claims, but were in fact selling both wholesale and retail, such as Ralph Wood of Nottingham who offered 'Genuine Gallipoly Olive Oyl' for sale 'by the tun or in small quantities', the fruiterer Thomas Revett of Manchester with cider at 'prices according to Quantity', or Messrs Smith and Co., who addressed themselves to 'families, country drapers, haberdashers and milliners'.[131]

## Those who bought to sell again

Defoe assumed that the true customers, that is 'the country shopkeepers or others, who buy in parcels, and who buy to sell again', represented the central core of a tradesman's business.[132] Although he did not develop this theme, the reasons behind it are not hard to seek. Possibilities for expansion in a market

---

analysis of the probate inventories of Shrewsbury drapers suggests that the Company continued to discourage retailing which was regarded as the province of the Mercers. I thank Diane Collins for this information.

[129] PRO, C5/582/120. I thank David Lloyd for a transcript of Thomas Wootton's inventory, with his notes identifying many of the debtors listed. The Shrewsbury Mercers attempted to control all retail trade in Shrewsbury down to the 1830s.

[130] Houghton (1727), *Husbandry and trade improv'd*, vol. I, p. 105, Letter 37 dated 22 April 1693.

[131] *Leicester and Nottingham Journal*, 18 October 1760; *Manchester Mercury*, 18 May 1790; *Sussex Weekly Advertiser*, 15 February 1790.

[132] Defoe (1987), *Complete English tradesman*, p. 14.

town were limited and many retailing tradesmen appear to have diversified into alternative lines of business. For example, each of the known mercers in Wellington, Shropshire, during the second half of the seventeenth century had interests beyond the shop as diverse as malting, candle-making and coal-mining, not to mention the investment of surplus money in property, mortgages and loans and some small-scale farming.[133]

One alternative to diversification was to extend the customer base either socially or geographically by setting up subsidiary outlets. This form of expansion had considerable advantages. It lessened the risk by sharing it with other people and reduced the need to pack so much into small packets for retail sale. The master shopkeeper could site the new outlet where the customer base did not compete with his own, he could stock it largely on his own terms and he could withdraw support at his own convenience. For the secondary shopkeeper it could be the first step towards independence for those who lacked the resources to set up on their own, although at it could offer what was not far from bonded servitude.

Probate records show that a second outlet, usually in an adjacent market town, were not uncommon. Examples can be found spanning almost all the period and stretching across the whole country. Two of the earliest examples noted come from Manchester in the 1580s. Thomas Hardman, mercer, (1583) and Edward Hanson, mercer/grocer, (1584) each had a secondary shop, respectively in Warrington and Bolton.[134] In the Midlands early examples include Thomas Crychlow, a draper of Derby (1601) with a second shop in Ashbourne and the saddler, Roger Brownrigge (1604), with retail shops in both Coventry and Rugby. Another saddler Humphrey Castleton (1665) had shops in Shifnal and Wellington, while the brazier and pewterer, Elizabeth Sherwyn (1687) had a large shop in Shrewsbury with a much small one at Wem as well as goods with £10 at Newton.[135]

For some reason, as yet unexplained there are no examples of secondary shops noted in the probate records for the Midlands during the eighteenth century, though other sources indicate their existence as well as suggesting how many of them may have operated. For example, George Burbage, book seller, had a shop in Leicester, but opened another just for market days in Loughborough, while John Witaker, a saddler with a shop in Stourbridge, attended another near the Town Hall in Bridgnorth, again only on market days.[136] In 1790 a 'Saddle, Bridle and Whip Warehouse' was moved to more

---

[133] Trinder and Cox (1980), *Yeomen and colliers*, pp. 22-6 and Inventories nos 126 and 174.

[134] Both Lancashire RO, probate, quoted in Willan (1976), *Inland trade*, pp. 61-2.

[135] All Lichfield Joint RO.

[136] *Leicester and Nottingham Journal*, 21 June 1760; *Aris's Birmingham Gazette*, 16 April 1770.

commodious premises in Leicester, but the proprietor retained the old shop which 'He or his man will attend ... on Saturdays, that is market days'.[137] Other eighteenth-century examples taken from elsewhere in the country include the mercer Samuel Luck (1706) with shops at Steyning and Newhaven, another mercer, Richard Hartley (1729) with shops at Tadmarton and Swalcliffe, a merchant John Unthank (1735) with shops at Orton and Kirby and V. Close & Son (1810) advertising earthenware for sale in his shops at Hanley, Staffs., and Boston, Lincs.[138]

The diaries of Roger Lowe and William Stout suggest that the subsidiary shop was common in the north west and they show something further of the mode of operation. Stout and one of his fellow apprentices each had a brief period in such a shop, though both were closed when proved unprofitable. Lowe's master was more fortunate, since the shop lasted a large part of Lowe's apprenticeship and was possibly then taken over by another of his master's so-called apprentices.[139] More complex arrangements were made by the Lancaster draper and grocer, Thomas Green, who had a second shop in Burton, Kendal, 'which he attended evry market day there and William Huggin of Yeland on other days'.[140] Probably the secondary shops noted in probate were serviced in similar fashion, either being open only on market days, and/or being attended by an apprentice or an employee full time with the master attending only when business was brisk.[141]

The so-called independent petty or country shopkeepers, and the petty chapmen, are more difficult for the historian to fit into the networks of retail provision, though fit in they obviously did. At one stage in his career, Stout gave up keeping open shop and took to selling grocery goods by wholesale to country shopkeepers.[142] 'Country shopkeeper' and 'Petty shopkeeper' are terms that were widely used at the time and, it would seem, were widely understood since they are rarely defined. One polemic writer suggested that such retailers were to be found in every settlement with more than ten inhabitants;[143] no doubt a gross exaggeration, but with enough truth not to be laughed out of court. These shopkeepers were accused by other writers of paying no taxes, taking on no local offices and contributing little if anything to the local economy.[144] Clearly the respectable country shopkeeper like Thomas Turner of

---

[137] *Leicester Journal*, 30 July 1790.

[138] Respectively West Sussex RO; Oxford RO; Carlisle RO; Banks collection, 98.7.

[139] Stout (1967), *Autobiography*, p. 79 (1682); Lowe (1938), *Diary*, 7 October 1664 and 28 October 1667.

[140] Stout (1967), *Autobiography*, p. 143 (1703).

[141] For a brief account of women in Scotland selling for others, see Sanderson (1996), *Women and work*, pp. 143-4.

[142] Stout (1967), *Autobiography*, p. 147 (1704).

[143] H.N. (1684), *Compleat tradesman*, p. 26.

[144] Anon. (1681), *Trade of England revived*, p. 397.

East Hoathly was not what the writer had in mind. Turner did pay taxes, he did take local office and he had a business sufficiently substantial to make it possible for him to deal with London tradesmen.[145] He was far removed from the poverty stricken woman with a deserted husband, Elin Godsalve, whom Stout assisted. Even she was a respectable woman come down in the world, rather than an opportunist small timer on the make.[146] Stout set her up in a small shop in a part of the town likely to serve a different class of customer from his own, with '£10 value of grocery goods and other small ware at the first cost to pay me when she could'.[147] Although the initial £10 was paid back quite quickly, she may well have felt obliged to continue restocking from Stout with a rolling debt binding her to him. In this sense her shop was probably little different from those attended by an apprentice or a journeyman.

Judging by the small amounts found in the shops of some petty shopkeepers, it is unlikely they would ever have been in a position to buy wholesale.[148] They may also not have been in a position to do much in the way of the usual processing required of a shopkeeper since the equipment added costs, so that they may have had to rely on their retailing supplier to have done that for them.[149] In many cases they must have been supplied by local retailers who gave them slightly favourable terms in return for accepting goods in slightly bigger units than the average consumer. Like Stout and Godsalve, a symbiotic relationship may well have formed, usually with mutual benefit.

There is some slight evidence that some substantial tradesmen provided for these petty shopkeepers. Some advertisements seem to be directed towards them rather than to shopkeepers in general. For example, in 1760 Joseph Milward, a nailor from Belper, kept a stall at Leicester market to supply 'Country Shopkeepers, Carpenters and the like', while Messrs Smith of Bridgnorth advertised in 1790 that they were just returned from Manchester and London with some goods including bankrupt stock 'very cheap and ... well worth the Attention of all Country Shopkeepers'.[150] Although the distinctions

---

[145] Turner (1984), *Diary*, p. xxii; for example, in 1763/4 he was overseer of the poor, in 1764/65 church warden and in 1765 survey of the highways.

[146] She was the daughter of Stout's old apprentice master and her husband was a Lancaster tradesman who went bankrupt and was disowned by the Society of Friends in 1707, Stout (1967), *Autobiography*, footnote 183.

[147] Stout (1967), *Autobiography*, p. 165 (1711) and footnote 195.

[148] Then as now, buying wholesale meant buying in bulk; by the hundred weight or barrel for items like dried fruit and sugar, the piece for cloth and the gross for small wares, see Willan (1976), *Inland trade*, pp. 51-2.

[149] Benson (1983), *Penny capitalists*, pp. 114-15, suggests that running a small shop may have become easier as the spread of factory made products increased. Although this may be true, being supplied by a retailer rather than a wholesaler proper, may have solved that problem for the petty shopkeeper in the early modern period.

[150] Respectively *Leicester and Nottingham Journal*, 5 January 1760; *Aris's Birmingham Gazette*, 24 June 1790.

are fine, these advertisements do seem to be of a different nature from those designed for the attention of substantial shopkeepers, and they do suggest that some retailers, who did not see themselves as wholesalers, nevertheless acted as if they were by supplying even smaller outlets. This is confirmed by the reminiscences of a Bristol draper. Although the source is late, and he was remembering back to the 1820s, he recalled how it was usual for his shop to supply a small shopkeeper or even a hawker at lower rates 'for them to sell again'. This seems to have developed into quite a steady line of business extending the range of customers served, albeit indirectly.[151]

The link between the travelling chapmen and retailing tradesmen are even more difficult to establish, but there is enough scattered evidence to suggest that, like the petty shopkeeper, chapmen were sometimes bound to a shopkeeper by ties of mutual self interest. As noted in chapter 1, authority was often hostile to the chapman, who was not readily distinguished from the roving bands of vagabonds and beggars who took to the odd piece of trading when opportunity arose. Essex J.P.s in an attempt to resolve the problem decreed that 'all Pedlars or Petichapmen ... may goe to their usuall Markettes and Fayers the direct waye, not opening or shewing their wares by the waye, And returnyng within the space of fower dayes'.[152] If enforced, this injunction would more or less compelled chapmen to buy their wares from the place of residence. The decree in 1605 by the Spanish Company ordaining that those who 'keepeth oppen shop or warehowse in the streate and usually selleth wares to chapmen by retail shalbe accoumpted a retailer',[153] again supports the idea that retailers were supplying chapmen, as does the occasional comment in diaries and the like. For example Henry Best, wrote in 1741 that 'Hollands were imported by merchants and sold to Linen drapers 'at whose shops country pedlars furnish themselves'.[154] Defoe makes much the same point when he recommended the apprentice to acquaint himself with his master's chapmen of both kinds, 'as well those he sells to, as those he buys of'. Although he does not make himself quite clear to the modern reader, he seems to distinguish between the chapman and the country shopkeeper, while assuming that both were valued customers.[155]

Eighteenth-century advertisements suggest that substantial tradesmen were attempting to tap into a wider market by attracting chapmen as customers. As Spufford has shown, the chapman was one of the most effective ways of disseminating ephemeral literature round the country, so it is not surprising that

---

[151] Ablett (ed.) (1876), *Reminiscences*, p. 166, and extensively quoted.

[152] Harleian MSS no. 7020 Art. 33 fol. 267, reproduced in Tawney and Power (1924), *Tudor economic documents*, pp. 362-4.

[153] Quoted by Willan (1976), *Inland trade*, p. 55.

[154] Best (1857), *Rural economy*, p. 106.

[155] Defoe (1987), *Complete English tradesman*, pp. 13-15.

an early provincial advertisement was addressed to 'all Booksellers, Country Chapmen, Hawkers and others' offering 'Romances, little Histories, Story Books, Jest Books, Riddle Books, songs and Ballards'.[156] Although not conclusive evidence of a tradesman supplying chapmen and other itinerants, the goods 'in ye Pedlars trade' worth £7 'on the Bulk' recorded in the probate inventory of Walter Turner of Newport, Shropshire, in 1746 are certainly suggestive.[157]

The importance of the chapmen to the provincial retailing tradesmen found expression in the petitions sent to Parliament concerning the proposed abolition of licensed hawkers in the late 1780s. In one month of 1785 there were eighteen petitions in support of the hawkers, mainly from the Midlands and the North. Although most of the petitioners were manufacturers or wholesale dealers, some were shopkeepers. The debate divided the retailing sector, some in support of, and others strongly opposed to chapmen, hawkers and other travelling salesmen. These were seen as much as competitors as part of the retailing network.

Secondary outlets of a different sort from the country or petty shop or from the chapmen and hawkers were those opened in the provinces by London retailers, or by large provincial operators in the reverse direction. Tradesmen such as the confectioner, Keelings of London and Tunbridge Wells, Nodes, the goldsmith and toyman of New Bond Street, London and Brighton, and Bettison, the purveyor of perfumery, trinkets and toys of London and Margate, provided a service to the élite who spent part of the year in London and part in a fashionable resort.[158] Though few were on the scale of the potter, Josiah Wedgwood,[159] some other manufacturers also opened retail outlets in London, such as the Birmingham gun makers, Blair and Sutherlands (1802), The Norwich shawl manufacturer P.I. Knight (1785), and the washing-machine maker, R. Rogerson of Warrington (1789).[160]

## The fair

The fair was one arena where much of the networking between various sectors of inland trade took place. It was presumably for this reason that the agreement between Turner's brother, Richard, and the draper of Lewes, John Madgwick, stipulated that the boy should be taken at least once to Maudling Fair, where he

---

[156] Spufford (1985), *Small books*, chapter 5; *Norwich Gazette*, 28 December 1706.
[157] Lichfield Joint RO.
[158] Banks collection, 48.40; 67.141; 93.8.
[159] For a full account of Wedgwood's marketing activities, see McKendrick (1982), 'Josiah Wedgwood'.
[160] Banks collection, 69.06; 107.5; 58.36.

could be made known to other tradesmen congregating there.[161] Mui and Mui suggest that by the end of the eighteenth century the wholesale function of the fair 'had long since fallen into desuetude'.[162] There is, however, considerable evidence that the fair was remarkably resilient to the pressures of the new methods of distribution, although the evidence is elusive. Certain it is that towards the end of the seventeenth century and into the eighteenth, fairs were used by retailing tradesmen both to buy and to sell on. Stout, the Lancaster ironmonger, bought cheese, the most durable of dairy products often sold through the market, at Garstang and Preston fairs. He was also anxious to have his shop well stocked up in preparation for the local summer fair, for which he expected to have an inrush of people from the surrounding countryside into the town. [163]

Margaret Spufford shows how another group of retailing tradesmen, the chapmen, also relied on fairs, plotting the itineraries of some as they moved from fair to fair. She implies that they were looking for sale, but it seems just as probable that the fair served primarily as a means of stocking up.[164] There is evidence too of producers using the fair. The partners in what was to become the Coalbrookdale Company were assiduous in attending sales in order to drum up sales and to collect debts. This practice of theirs suggests that the fair was still acting as an interface between producers and those who sold well into the eighteenth century.[165]

The publication of *Owen's book of fairs* in the mid-eighteenth century and its frequent re-issue suggest that the fair was alive and well.[166] Owen listed the various specialisms of each fair. There is a substantial range covering much more than the livestock and the foodstuffs suggested by Mui and Mui. For example, in the 1756 edition Owen recorded that the August fair at Carlisle specialized in linen, the October one at Market Harborough in pewter, brass, hats and clothes, the one at Andover in May in leather and millinery goods, and the one at Portsmouth in July in the wares of shoemakers, hatters, milliners, mercers, cutlers, cabinet makers, linen and woollen drapers, along with silversmith goods, apparel ready made and bed furniture.[167] However, although the fair still had its place in the distributive network, Mui and Mui are probably right in supposing that it had ceased to be the main fulcrum of internal trade with many of its functions increasingly taken over by other systems.

---

[161] Turner (1984), *Diary*, 27 December 1760.

[162] Mui and Mui (1989), *Shops and shopkeeping*, p. 27.

[163] Stout (1967), *Autobiography*, p. 107 (1691), p. 90 (1688).

[164] Spufford (1984), *Great reclothing*, chapter 5, particularly p. 76.

[165] Raistrick (1976), *Dynasty of ironfounders*, for example, pp. 7-9, 99.

[166] Owen (1754), *Owen's book of fairs*. It was reissued in at least five times in the eighteenth century and several times in the nineteenth. The last edition came out in 1859.

[167] Owen (1756), *Owen's book of fairs*.

**Conclusion**

Retailing tradesmen operated within a network of relationships. Although there was obviously a linear, temporal progression from family to apprenticeship and from there, hopefully, into independent trade, the family remained crucial to the operation of a successful shop, as did the friendships, partnerships and associations acquired during apprenticeship. Once independent, the shop-keepers were at the end of the trading line, serving the final consumer, but many also had some wholesale trade or set up subsidiary outlets as a means of extending their customer base. Some even ventured into merchandizing.

Throughout the early modern period, changes in practice disturbed the pattern of operation, though they did not destroy it. Some tradesmen did not serve apprenticeships, some did not practise within the framework of an urban trading community and the networks of supply based on family connections, personal recommendation and trust were challenged by new methods of salemanship. Aspects of retailing regarded as characteristic of the so-called retailing revolution starting in the late nineteenth century can already be seen, while others often thought to have been swept away in the increasing pace of commercialization have proved resistant to change.

# Chapter 7

# 'I know not yet what that is, and am ashamed to ask':[1] accommodating innovation and novelty

People in their role of consumers are a potent force for innovation, being attracted by novelty, yet paradoxically innately conservative and resistant to change.[2] They also incidentally dislike being shown to be ignorant. In his study of innovation in the seventeenth and eighteenth centuries, Styles demonstrates how complex and delicate the relationship can be between these two aspects of human behaviour. He cites as example two products introduced in the second half of the seventeenth century. The first concerns the new or newly-adapted objects needed for the consumption of tea. Artefacts like tea pots and tea cups, sugar bowls and slop basins, tea tables and tea kettles, were all successfully marketed and readily accepted by a consuming public who had substantially to alter their eating habits and even the structure of their day and their social life, in order to accommodate the new beverage. By contrast another new commodity met a high level of resistance from consumers; imported cotton shirts had many advantages such as cheapness, comfort and ease of maintenance, but people against all reason continued to prefer linen. An ambitious marketing venture ended in costly failure.[3]

Such apparently irrational behaviour is disturbing for the historian who seeks to understand the dynamics of innovation and consumption in the early modern period. Nevertheless the problem must be addressed. From the middle of the sixteenth century, when the commercial implications of events like the opening up of the New World to trade and the fall of Constantinople were beginning to be felt, the producing, trading and consuming communities - and

---

[1]  Pepys (1987), *Diary*, 22 May 1662. Pepys was referring to a gift from a 'Captain Teddiman from the Streights' of 'some anchovies, olives and muscatt'. It was apparently the last that caused the problem.

[2]  Berg (1999), 'New commodities, luxuries and their consumers'.

[3]  Styles, J. (forthcoming), 'Product innovation in early modern London'.

that meant everybody - had to come to terms with a changed world. This chapter investigates some of the various means used in marketing innovation and novelty. For the most part it is not clear who was the chief instigator in the process of accommodation. As will become apparent, in some cases it was the importer or manufacturer, in others the retailing tradesman, but whoever started the process, it was the one at the end of the marketing chain who had to convince the customer that the product was worth buying. It is largely therefore from the perspective of the retailing tradesman that the challenge of the new is here addressed, even if it must always be born in mind that there were other participants in the process.

There is a further difficulty for the historian. Although the period under review extends from about 1550 to about 1820, the sources are much less accommodating, being largely associated with the latter half. It would be foolish axiomatically to equate this paucity of evidence in the early years with an absence of activity, although this may be the case to some degree, since the increased availability of cheap printing gave later operators opportunities their forebears did not have. Without the body of paper ephemera to illuminate sales techniques, the historian of the earlier period is left with wisps of evidence, invariably elusive, more often than not suggesting what might have happened rather than proving what did. It is a useful corrective to the frustrations of evidence to remember the introduction that probably had a more dramatic effect on the market and on consumption than any other occurred in the first few decades of the period. Very little is known about how tobacco was introduced, but the facts of its successful penetration of the market are well documented, indicating that the sixteenth-century merchant or tradesman was well able to exploit such facilities as were available in marketing. Tobacco is the marketer's dream come true and it happened some four centuries ago.

## Naming novelty

Modern producers and their advertising agencies expend much thought on names. An awareness of the importance of names is not a modern phenomenon. Thomas Fuller, writing in the 1650s of Norwich stuffs, explained how a new name could quicken flagging sales and how 'a pretty pleasing name, complying with the buyer's fancy, much befriendeth a stuff in the sale thereof'.[4] The labelling of many of the so-called New Draperies, no less than of other new fabrics of the early modern period, support Fuller's suggestion of a developed awareness of the importance of a name. Hardwearing woollens were given names like durance, perpetuano, semperternum, and (for those without the

---

[4]   Fuller (1662), *Worthies of England*, under Norfolk.

Latin) everlasting; while imitations with a hoped-for lustre from their more distinguished originals were called velveteen, satinet and camleteen; and the cheap and gaudy were associated with a supposed fashionability by designations like brilliant, none-so-pretty, pearl-of-beauty and alamode.[5] Josiah Wedgwood, the great potter, was equally conscious of the value of a name. 'They want a name - a name has a wonderful effect I assure you - Suppose you present the Duchess of Devonshire with a Set & beg leave to call them Devonshire flowerpots. You smile - Well call them Mecklenburg - or - or - what you please so you will let them have a name'.[6]

The merchants of the newly-founded East India Company (1600) demonstrated considerable skill and care in arranging for the manufacture and importation of cotton goods from India acceptable to British tastes,[7] but for the retailing tradesman the challenge had only just begun when the goods arrived in this country. Indian textiles were generally imported under native names. Many languages and dialects abounded on the sub-continent, and probably identical, or very similar, fabrics were thus traded under several different names, each importer being familiar only with those pertaining to the district in which he had an agent. The names were awkward and with little of the charm, fashion or romance of some foreign words. Only a few of the Indian terms ever became current in English, of which two, muslin and calico, spring to mind. For the rest they remained so unfamiliar that even the authors of *Hobson Jobson*, a nineteenth-century glossary of Anglo-Indian terms, could not define many of them. Words like Allejars, Bejutapants, Byrampauts, Cushtaes, Nicamees and Negampants never became current in English, though a few found their way into one booklet ostensibly intended for all 'Linnen Drapers, their Country Chapmen and for Semstresses, and in general for all persons whatsoever' published in 1696.[8] For the most part the precise meanings of these terms are now unknown.[9] The middlemen negotiating between the importer and the consumer, fixed on a few acceptable terms, either because they were known already through Arab and Spanish connections, like cotton itself, or because they were easily accommodated by English tongues, like calico, chintz, muslin,

---

[5] Coleman (1969), 'An innovation and its diffusion', p. 425, suggests the suspicion of inferior quality levelled at the New Draperies inspired names suggesting durability and other desirable characteristics.

[6] Wedgwood Museum MSS, E.18811-25, Wedgwood to Thomas Bentley, 9 February 1778, quoted in McKendrick (1982), 'Josiah Wedgwood', p. 112. The objects under discussion were mere flowerpots.

[7] Lemire (1991), *Fashion's favourite*, pp. 13-18.

[8] J.F. (1696), *Merchant's warehouse*, in the Dedication. J.F. gave information on several cotton textiles, such as bettilies, rafts, birompots and hummums. Virtually none of the ones he mentioned have been noted in English shops. None of these terms seems to have been anglicized, unlike European terms such as 'Honschoote says', modified to Anascotes in French and to Hounscots in English; see Coleman (1969), 'An innovation and its diffusion', p. 426.

[9] Yule and Burnell (1886), *Hobson Jobson*.

and romal. But while chintz, muslin and romal retained some distinguishing features, calico and cotton became generic terms covering a multitude of different fabrics, only having in common the raw material from which they were woven and, initially at least, their place of origin.

Instead a new vocabulary was developed in the shops, using well-known terms, which could differentiate the many fabrics for the discerning consumer. In the seventeenth century most of the terms used by the retailing tradesmen for the Indian textiles relied upon descriptors added to calico such as coloured, dyed, flowered, glazed, narrow, painted, stained, striped, supplementing various grades like fine or coarse. By the eighteenth century the word calico seems to have become rather less common, being replaced by a broader range of terms, many of them added as descriptors to cotton; hence printed and striped cottons, cotton checks, flowered cottons, striped and plain muslin, handkerchiefs printed and Indian bordered, and so on.[10]

The sixteenth-century Spanish physician, Nicolas Monardes in his work on Amerindian drugs faced similar problems to those involved in the trade of Indian textiles.[11] For each of the drugs he described and characterized, he tried above all to establish a generally accepted name, though he had only limited success. Amerindian nomenclature, like the oriental Indian, was by no means easy to European tongues, but it may have been less of a problem in medicine where the arcane merely added to the mystery and power of the physician. Drugs from the new world like Tacamahaca, Mechoacan and Guaiacan apparently experienced few of the problems faced by the new Indian cottons such as Bejutapants or Byranpants. They did become accepted, though they are to be found only in the stock of apothecaries and do not appear to have been sold by general tradesmen like mercers and grocers even though other drugs sometimes were. For other medicinal plants Monardes was unable to find any acceptable name, whether Amerindian or European. It may not be without significance that the otherwise unnamed purgative bean and the wood 'for the evilles of the raines and of the urine' did not find a place in the Materia Medica.[12]

Botanically the absence of a systematic method of characterization more sophisticated than the one Dioscorides had used for the corpus of Mediterranean plants in the first century, was to prove a handicap for another

---

[10] These examples are all taken from the collection of transcribed trade cards and billheads held by the Dictionary Project at the University of Wolverhampton.

[11] Monardes (1574), *Joyfull newes*. The 1574 Spanish edition entitled *Primera y segunda y tercera partes de la historia medicinal de las cosas que se traen de nuestras Indias Occidentales que siruen en Medicina*, was based upon two earlier works published in 1569 and 1571. It was the combined and extended edition of 1574, which was widely translated and which was 'Englished' as *Joyfull newes* by John Frampton, a former merchant with Spanish connections.

[12] Monardes (1574), *Joyfull newes*, pp. 52-3, 46-7.

century and a half.[13] Monardes solved the problem where he could by relating the new to the old by using the name of a recognized plant to label an Amerindian one. In some cases this was straightforward; anime, balsamo and china were reputable medicinal products of the old world and their labels were now attached to similar ones from across the Atlantic. Where the direct transfer of name was impossible Monardes exploited similarities; the Amerindian Ococoll was renamed Liquidamber because it was as 'precious as Amber' and with a similar smell and savour.[14]

It is unlikely that the plant called Tlilxochitl by the Amerindians, would ever have found acceptance in Europe with such an impossible name. With no medicinal uses it became known in England as the ideal flavouring for chocolate under the more attractive name of Vanilla.[15] The name of the sunflower was possibly equally impossible, but the names given to it in Europe were various and it took some while for a standard to establish itself. Gerard gave a list of no less than nine alternatives including in English Marigold of Peru and Golden flower of Peru, and in Latin Chrysanthemum Peruvianum, Flos solis and Corona solis.[16]

The makers of quack medicines were quick to appreciate the value of a name. An analysis of the many newspaper advertisements suggests that there was a vocabulary of terms deemed appropriate for such preparations, as well as a number of conventions applied in the construction of the name itself. Some terms were used with monotonous frequency like Balsam, Elixir and Cordial. Vegetable became common as the eighteenth century progressed, largely (one advertisement revealed) as an indication that the preparation did not contain any of the fashionable, but toxic, mercury.[17] A personal name, particularly prefixed with Doctor was common; some cachet was perceived if the name was obviously foreign as in Dr Boerhaave's Grand Balsam of Health and Dr Coetlogan's Balsamick ... Tincture. Tobacco and Snuff, Tea and Coffee, were each terms included in the names of medicinal preparations, presumably to provide alternatives to the real thing which would do good as well as give satisfaction; so Golden Snuff and the Incomparable Cephalic Snuff, Mayelston's famous Pectoral Balsamic Tobacco, Roes English Coffee and, Swedes Tea. Although exotic foreign parts had their attraction, hence Dr

---

13  See Gunther (1934), *The Greek herbal of Dioscorides*, pp. v-ix, for a brief account of Dioscorides work. It was two eighteenth-century works, Linnaeus (1753), *Species plantarum* and Linnaeus (1754), *Genera plantarum*, which finally established a generally recognized methodology for naming plants.

14  Monardes (1574), *Joyfull newes*, pp. 12-13, 22-3, 34-5, 20-22.

15  Houghton (1727), *Improvement of husbandry and trade*, vol. III, p. 120, quoting Hernandez, the Spanish botanist.

16  Gerard (1633), *Herbal*, under Sunflower.

17  Velno's Vegetable Syrup 'without a single particle of Mercury', *Aris's Birmingham Gazette*, 5 November 1770.

Hudson's Persian Restorative, British appears to have been more favoured, as in British Oil and British Powder for the Teeth.

Daffey's Elixir, one of the oldest and most successful of all quack medicines, with its combination of a maker's name with one of the 'buzz' words, appears to have provided the model for most subsequent competitors, though many were not content with such simplicity, instead stringing together a number of terms, as in the Oriental Vegetable Cordials, Godbold's Vegetable Balsam, Rowley's British Herb Snuff, and, one of the most popular, Dr Stoughton's Elixir Magnum Stomachum or the Great Cordial Elixir for the Stomach.[18]

What can not be assessed is the reaction of customers to curious names since no direct evidence of their opinions has come to light. Nevertheless, finding and establishing an attractive name can be seen as one of the core strategies for marketing a new product. It matters not whether the product was an exotic import, a quack medicine or mechanical toy, naming it does appear to have been the first step towards acceptability.

### Contextualizing novelty

If naming was important, it was only the first step and it will by no means explain in every case why one product found a place in the market and another did not. Marina Bianchi has formulated a theoretical model of one aspect of consumption which may throw light upon this difficult topic. She suggests that collecting can be viewed as a paradigm of consumption offering a useful explanation of the apparent irrationality of such consumer behaviour. If nothing else her model confronts the tension between desire for novelty and innate conservatism.[19] She suggests that the process of collecting requires firstly that the collected objects can be seen as a recognizably defined and understood set, and secondly that within that set each element should be new and different from all the others. 'Collecting, viewed this way', she argues, 'appears as a consumer strategy for managing and producing novelty.' Although Bianchi is looking at the theoretical relationship between collecting and consumption largely as it applies to the modern world, it is not difficult to extrapolate from

---

[18] The advertisements cited come from a number of newspapers published between 1740 and 1800, in particular *Aris's Birmingham Gazette*, the *Manchester Mercury* and the *Sussex Weekly Advertiser*. Most of the products referred to were advertised several times and in different newspapers. Any run of local newspapers will afford a string of identical and similar advertisements so it has not been felt necessary to give a reference for each example.

[19] Bianchi, M. (1996), 'Collecting as a paradigm of consumption', seminar paper at the Workshop on Consumption and culture in Europe, 1650-1850, Humanities Research Centre, University of Warwick. Bianchi has further developed her ideas on novelty in (1999), 'In the name of the tulip', particularly pp. 95-9.

her thesis a model of consumer response to innovation in the early modern period.

Viewed in this light the management of the Indian goods by the suppliers reveals what can only have been an intuitive understanding of consumer psychology. In some respects fashion is no more than a different facet of collectability, an alternative way of satisfying certain human aspirations to belong to a successful group. By embedding the new cotton fabrics into a set of descriptors already perceived as fashionable and desirable, the tradesman was able to balance novelty against security. Unlike the earlier New Draperies and cheap silks which were woven from known raw materials and were made attractive by fashionable names like alamode, none-so-pretty and the like, the cottons with a few exceptions were not so labelled. Instead the cottons and calicoes in all their variety were rendered exciting and fashionable, but nevertheless safe, through descriptors. During the eighteenth century terms like checks and stripes, which had once been descriptors, became the names of actual fabrics.[20] Once these terms achieved the status of substantives, they began to attract descriptors in their own right. For example Caspar Woolenhaupt of Luneburg in Nova Scotia (1809) stocked no less than six varieties of cotton checks of which one was further defined as 'furniture' and another as 'apron'.[21]

In a desperate attempt to stem the flow of imports and thus to save the threatened home woollen industry, Parliament attempted to ban first the use and then the sale of Indian textiles.[22] The attempt, though vain, probably stimulated the small domestic cotton manufacture of England to produce goods in the Indian style even if not to their quality. Thus the Indian goods, which a century earlier the merchants and tradesmen had been obliged to make acceptable to English customers, were now the models to which home manufacturers aspired. For some time these imitation goods were advertised to emphasize comparable quality with terms like 'as good as' or 'equal to'. P.I. Knight, shawl manufacturer of Norwich and London, advertised along these lines in 1785, offering shawls with 'a very near affinity ... to the real India

---

[20] *OED*'s first noted example of Stripes used as the name of a fabric is 1751, of Check the first maybe as early as 1614, though the next, which is indubitably a substantive and not an adjective, is 1885. However, probate inventories of retailing tradesmen and other similar documents in the eighteenth century, use both terms as substantives. The earliest noted that can clearly be identified as cotton or linen fabrics are the checks offered for sale by Henry Halford, Mercer of Evesham in 1705.

[21] Casper Wollenhaupt's inventory taken over four days (18-20 July 1809 and 5 January 1810) is given in Appendix 1 to Field (1992), 'Claiming rank', pp. 13-20. The reference cited for the Estate and will papers is RG 48, reel 841. Lemire (1991), *Fashion's favourite*, Appendix 1, lists at least 35 varieties of (cotton) checks and 27 stripes priced from under 12d. to over 24d. per yard. She culled these from various late eighteenth-century sources.

[22] 11 & 12 GUL3 c. 10 (1700) and 7 GEO1 stat. 1 c. 7 (1720/21).

shawls', though he implied that his were in fact better in that they had superior laundry properties over any other. Furthermore he played on the philanthropic sentiments of his potential customers in picture and in words by addressing his advertisement to 'the Promoters of Female Industry'. He suggested that 'the thousands of young females it [that is, his manufactory] gives constant employment will, he presumes, be a peculiar recommendation'. One of these young females, a child, is depicted working with her needle along with a man at a loom. Under is the pious aphorism, 'Train up a child the way it should go, And when old 'twill not depart from it'. Child labour was being dressed up as pious philanthropy and used to foster sales; how much better to 'Buy British' than to enrich the denizens of India![23]

Tea was another product of the Far East to the sale of which retailers had to accommodate themselves. In modern times, tea has become firmly associated with grocery, and even in the nineteenth century the seller who advertised himself as 'Grocer and Tea dealer' was a feature of many town directories. In the early eighteenth century, the appropriateness of the association was much less obvious. According to Bianchi's model, grocery might have been seen as a safe set from which to market the new commodity, since both need the same equipment and similar conditions of storage. However, there were real disadvantages to the association in the early eighteenth century. The term of grocer was generally applied either to one who sold in gross, that is, a wholesaler or to a small shopkeeper selling essentials to the lower strata of society. In neither sense were tradesmen calling themselves grocers likely to attract the sort of customer who wanted to buy tea. Instead it became attached to a wide variety of goods which had in common that they were already attractive to the right sort of customer. Most of these were essentially London goods and found largely in London shops, china dealers, haberdashers and milliners probably being the most common, such as the milliner, Mrs Johnson (1720), the haberdasher and pattern drawer, Francis Flower (1745), and the glass seller Robert Fleetwood (1721).[24]

It seems that many preferred to buy tea in London either through mail order or through visiting friends,[25] and the spread to the provinces was slow outside fashionable towns. Among those noted who sold tea were a book seller, Mr Rose of Norwich (1707), a draper, Francis Bennett of Bath (1744), an ironmonger, Walter Turner, of Newport, Shropshire (1745), and a toyman,

---

[23] Trade card of P.I. Knights, Banks Collection, 107.5.

[24] Johnson, *Post Boy*, 18 February 1720; Francis Flower, Attingham MSS, 112/6 Box 35/268; Robert Fleetwood, Orphans inventories 3161.

[25] For example, Blundell (1968-72), *Great diurnal*, 18 November 1725 and 8 January 1727, though it is not clear how the tea from London was ordered.

Cornelius Goldberg of Birmingham (1751).[26] These and other, to modern eyes, bizarre outlets continued throughout the century. However, tea dealers such as Henry Gough's Tea and Coffee Warehouse of Wolverhampton (1750) and Hayward's Tea Warehouse (from London) in Bath (1752) did appear in provincial towns, though it seems that some had to combine the sale of tea with other products, such as Jones's Druggist and Tea Dealer of Birmingham (1803) and Jo. Napier, Milliner and Tea Dealer of Thirsk, Yorkshire (1804), while others like Joseph Norgrave at the Tea Canister in Shrewsbury (1748) probably sold a much wider range of goods than their addresses suggest.[27]

As the century progressed, tea did find a place in the stock of the grocer, probably because of changing circumstances. Firstly, tea became a favoured drink of the poor so that it was stocked by the chandlers, shopkeepers - and the grocers - who served their needs, and secondly, the term 'grocer' broadened and was used by retailers in the town centre selling quality grocery with tea as part of their stock in trade. The presence of substantial and reputable grocers in provincial towns like Benjamin Boucher of Bridgnorth (1741) must in the long run have encouraged the gentry to buy their tea locally instead of from a London tradesman who stocked it as a profitable side line.[28]

If the successful marketing of Indian fabrics involved the use of appropriate nomenclature and of tea the appropriate outlets, introducing tobacco to its potential customers presented a different challenge and it may be more appropriate to consider a different model of consumption. Goodman suggests that the success with which a commodity crosses from one culture to another may depend on degree to which it can be accepted as having an appropriate cultural meaning.[29] Tobacco was widely used in different societies in central and southern America, being esteemed for its medicinal and hallucinatory properties and for its ability to allay the pangs of hunger. Each of these properties had a place in European culture. The Spanish invaders of central America payed much attention to plants of medicinal value and the acceptance of tobacco in this respect was made easier because it was believed erroneously to be related to henbane, which already had a place in the Pharmacopoeia. Tobacco's place in European medicine was firmly established in 1574 by

[26] Rose, *Norwich Gazette*, 18 May 1707; quoted in Kennedy (n.d.), *Between Bath and China*, p. 16; Walter Turner Lichfield Joint RO (1745); Cornelius Goldburg, *Aris's Birmingham Gazette*, 28 January 1751.

[27] Henry Gough, *Aris's Birmingham Gazette*, 10 December 1750; Haywards quoted in Kennedy (n.d.), *Between Bath and China*, p. 17; Jones and Jo. Napier, Banks Collection, 68.72 and 86.80 respectively; Henry Gough, Lichfield Joint RO, Wolverhampton Peculiar; Joseph Norgrave, Attingham MSS, 112/6 Box 36/179, 181, 192, 197, and Box 36a/92, 281. More is known about Norgrave's sales as the surviving documents are bills and not simply trade cards.

[28] Benjamin Boucher, Lichfield Joint RO, Bridgnorth Peculiar.

[29] Goodman (1993), *Tobacco in history*, chapter 3, on which much of this paragraph depends.

Monardes's history of medicinal plants in the New World. He not only set out its characteristics in the terminology of the day, but also listed a broad range of diseases tobacco could cure, including toothache and cancer.[30] It is not surprising then that some of the early provincial stockists were apothecaries or sellers of apothecary like John Staine of Derby (1615) and Kenrick Eyton of Chester (1624).[31] The hallucinatory properties of tobacco were hardly likely to receive official approval even if its capacity to relieve the pangs of hunger did, but both properties would have been attractive to sailors, who are known to have introduced the plant to the Old World. Here it may easily have found a place in the culture of the urban and the rural poor.

Unlike tea, tobacco made its appearance in provincial shops early. Although it is generally accepted that tobacco and the necessary smoking equipment only reached this country in the 1580s, it was in the provincial shops before the end of the century. For example, Thomas Fynis, mercer of Coventry, had only ¼ lb. of tobacco among his stock in 1598, but John Capel, mercer of Birmingham, along with many other tradesmen, had considerably more by 1629. By 1635 there was a specialist Tobaccoman in Atherstone, Warks., and in 1639 a shopkeeper in the village of Huyton, Lancs., had tobacco in three varieties, 'best', 'roll' and 'cut and dried'. Tobacco could be bought even in the apparently remote county of Cornwall; Robert Bennet, clothier of Tregony, had 25½ pounds of 'Puddinge & leafe tobacco' in 1606.[32] The sale of the necessary tobacco pipes was equally general; Thomas Cobbe, chapman of Sutton St James, Lincs., and Peter Harris, a general tradesman of Grandborough, Warks., each had tobacco pipes among his stock as early as 1613.[33] By the end of the seventeenth century it is rare to find any tradesman like a mercer, a grocer or a general shopkeeper who did not stock tobacco. Tobacco along with sugar, spices, soap and thread became one of the core commodities in the general shop, so that even the very smallest tradesman offered it among his wares. For example, George Bayley of Broseley died in 1717, with a personal estate valued at under £10. Of that £1 5s. 5d. consisted of 'Sope and Tobacco & Small things to sell'.[34] This widespread availability of tobacco in provincial shops supports Shammas's supposition that there was far too much for it all to have been consumed by an élite. In the 1620s annual consumption per capita

---

[30]  Monardes (1574), *Joyfull newes*, pp. 75-91.
[31]  John Staine, Lichfield Joint RO (1615); Kenrick Eyton, Chester RO WS 1634. Eyton was designated a mercer, but he sold only apothecarial goods.
[32]  Thomas Fynis Lichfield Joint RO (1598/99); John Capel, Lichfield Joint RO (1631); John Loveday, Lichfield Joint RO (1635); John Cross of Huyton, Lancashire RO, WCW 1639; Robert Bennet, Cornwall RO AP/B155/1-7.
[33]  Thomas Cobbe, Lincoln RO, INV 113/313; Peter Harris, Lichfield Joint RO, (1613/14).
[34]  Hereford RO.

may already have reached 0.01 lb., but by the 1690s it was over 2 lb. The rapid rise in imports of tobacco reflected the increased level of consumption.[35]

In one sense tobacco did fit Bianchi's model. It became incorporated into the body of European medicinal plants because it met the required criteria; medically it was possible to describe its properties in the Galenical terms in vogue at the time,[36] botanically it was believed to be related to a known European species, and its supposed curative powers corresponded to ones already understood in the Old World. Other medicinal plants were less fortunate, including most notably the Coca plant from which cocaine is derived, and Cinchona, the source of the two medicinally active alkaloids, quinine and cinchonine. Indeed, relatively few Amerindian medicines entered the European Pharmacopoeia. Francisco Hernandez, who was commissioned by Philip II of Spain in 1570 to study the Amerindian flora for its medicinal potential, achieved what has been acknowledged as a model of pioneering botanical investigation, but in its main purpose his research failed, probably because Amerindian medicine was too far removed from European orthodoxy and many of its plants too dissimilar to the European flora. During a seven year stay in the new world, Hernandez collected and described over 3,000 plants and ran clinical trials in a hospital in Mexico City, but largely in vain since few of the plants gained acceptance. His fellow countryman, the Spanish physician, Nicolas Monardes published in 1574 what was to be for many years the definitive work on the drugs from the New World, but he covered only a small fraction of those collected by Hermandez.[37]

An analysis of Monardes's work is instructive, demonstrating nicely the relationship between an adequate description and characterization of new materia medica and its successful adoption. Monardes attempted a threefold classification of each drug; firstly botanically, secondly along Galenical lines, and thirdly curatively. Botanically his work was already being done by the indefatigable Hernandez, but Monardes still had some difficulty in describing most of the Amerindian plants in terms intelligible to Europeans. His usual technique was to make safe by emphasizing similarities. So he described Mechoacan as 'the Ruibarbo [rhubarb] of the Indias', 'with little Grapes, of the greatnesse of a Coriander seede which is his fruite', while the Sassafras tree was 'the bignesse of a Pine Tree', with 'but one braunche of bowes, after the

---

[35] Shammas (1990), *Pre-industrial consumer*, p. 79.

[36] According to Galen, the second-century physician, human dysfunction was caused by an imbalance of the four humours, blood, phlegm, black bile and yellow bile. The art of the physician was to diagnose the imbalance and to correct it by the application of drugs possessed of opposite virtues. Thus ailments characterized by too much phlegm (cold and moist), could be alleviated by the application of medicines that were hot and dry.

[37] Goodman (1993), *Tobacco in history*, pp. 38-41; Monardes (1577), *Joyfull newes*.

maner of a Palme Tree', the smell like Fennel, the leaves 'which bee greene, after the maner of a Figge Tree', and the taste 'as the Sinamon is'.[38]

Monardes wrestled with Galen's humoral approach to medicine and his consequent method of classification although these were ill-adapted to incorporate Amerindian medical practice. With tacamahaca as with tobacco there was no difficulty. Each was readily characterized as hot and dry and each could be used to ameliorate conditions common to all humanity and recognized by Europeans as cold and moist. Some other drugs like Carauna were awkward. Monardes recognized that it was in many respects more effective than tacamahaca, but the Amerindians used it in ways that conflicted with European understanding. He apparently felt confident in characterizing it as hot, but unusually he did not express an opinion as to whether it was moist or dry. Perhaps it was because of this difficulty of characterization that Carauna rarely found a place in English shops, whereas tacamahaca did.[39]

Through the eyes of Bianchi's model, most Amerindian medicinal plants could not be characterized as new products fitting into an established and well understood set. As a result successful introductions were limited. Medicinally a few made the European pharmacopoeia, even fewer became widespread. Other plants that did cross the Atlantic came as food plants like the potato. This was very slow in establishing itself, although it was probably introduced into the British Isles in the 1560s. It was first grown extensively in Lancashire, possibly because it was more easily incorporated into a culture relying on pottage for sustenance rather than on bread, which was more common in the south.[40] The early pre-eminence of Lancashire as a supplier of potatoes seems to be supported by the diary of Nicholas Blundell, a gentleman with estates just north of Liverpool. In the 1710s he was fattening swine on boiled potatoes and selling small quantities at Liverpool market, by the 1720s his sales had doubled and he was setting substantial quantities of at least two varieties.[41] By mid-century the potato had reached the south. According to Gilbert White, it was only in the 1750s that the potato was first planted in Selbourne,[42] and it was in that decade that potatoes appeared regularly on the table of the Sussex shopkeeper, Thomas Turner, usually boiled as an accompaniment to meat. Even so, as food for the well-to-do the potato had barely a place in culinary literature before the nineteenth century. Hannah Glasse included a few ways for cooking potatoes (mostly with sugar) in her chapter on Fast-dinners (that is,

---

[38]  Monardes (1574), *Joyfull newes*, pp. 56, 59, 102-3.
[39]  Monardes (1574), *Joyfull newes*, pp. 16-17.
[40]  Stout (1967), *Autobiography*, p. 193 (1725); Holt (1795), *General view of the agriculture of... Lancaster*, footnote p. 63 and p. 57.
[41]  Blundell (1968-72), *Great diurnal*, for example, 20 October 1711, 2 May 1713, 5 March 1726, 26 March 1726, 21 January 1757. See also Holt (1795), *General view of the agriculture of... Lancaster*, pp. 57-63.
[42]  White (1982), *Journals of Gilbert White*, 3 October 1787 and footnote.

meatless), but none in the one on 'pretty little Dishes fit for a Supper, or Side-Dish...', while Mrs Raffald merely listed potatoes among the roots in season by month and used them not at all in her recipes. [43] In the last two decades of the eighteenth century, Parson Woodforde of Weston Longville, Norfolk, was regularly eating potatoes.[44] However, he does not appear to have served potatoes for the Tithe Audit day dinners to which the local farmers paying their dues were invited. The potato's potential as a cheap food was recognized in several recipes by the anonymous author of 'The way to save wealth shewing how a man may live plentifully for twopence a day'. His recommendations appear to have had little immediate effect, although later in the century its value as a food for the poor was recognized. In the 1750s a Dr James Stonehouse of Northampton published a recipe in the *Universal Magazine* for a 'cheap kind of soup' for the poor, including potatoes among the fillers along with ground rice and oatmeal.[45] By the 1790s potatoes were being used by the Overseers of the Poor in Birmingham to feed paupers on outdoor relief.[46] William Cobbett writing in the 1820s was vitriolic against the potato as a food for the poor, indicating that even at that date it had not gained general acceptance:

> To get this quantity of food, [in place of bread] fit to be eaten, in the shape of potatoes, *how many fires*! what a washing, what a boiling, what a peeling, what a slopping, and what a messing! The cottage everlastingly in a litter; the woman's hands everlastingly wet and dirty; the children grimed up to the eyes with dust fixed on by potato-starch; and ragged as colts, the poor mother's time all being devoted to the everlasting boilings of the pot! Can any man, who knows anything of the labourer's life, deny this? And will, then, anybody, except the old shuffle-breeches band of the Quarterly Review ... say that the people ought to be taught to use potatoes as a *substitute for bread*?[47]

Possibly one reason why the potato was slow to gain acceptance was the fact that it was hardly ever sold through the shops except by the seed merchants. Grown on a small scale in gardens by the curious, and experimented with tentatively in the kitchen, no one was in the business of seriously marketing it. Only when it was well-established as satisfactory for animal feed did it become incorporated in the diet the poor. It was at this stage that it had a small presence

---

[43] Glasse (1747), *Art of cookery made plain and easy*, p. 105; Raffald (1769), *Experienced English housekeeper*.

[44] For example, Woodforde (1924), *Diary*, 30 June 1784, 8 April 1796.

[45] Noted by Thomas Turner, who copied the recipe into his Diary, Turner (1984), *Diary*, 27 January 1758.

[46] *Aris's Birmingham Gazette*, 11 January 1790.

[47] Cobbett (1821), *Cottage economy*, p. 77-8.

in the back street shops.[48] The reasons for its ultimate acceptance by the poor remain obscure. One may have been that early potato matures during the so-called 'hungry gap' before the start of the grain harvest, another that its incorporation into conventional rotations resulted in plentiful, and therefore cheap, supplies.

Maize was even slower in becoming acceptable than the potato. Even in the eighteenth century it barely found its way into the market place and thence into the kitchen. Although on the Bianchi model, it should have been easily incorporated into the set of imported grains and other farinaceous material, this does not seem to have happened. Not easily grown in this country, it had no advantages over European grains as a bread or pottage corn and it was apparently not acceptable as a pudding grain in the way rice or sago were. Some must have been used since, as Indian corn it was occasionally stocked in the shops and Zachariah Parkes, a manufacturer of mills in Birmingham, thought it worthwhile to make and to advertise steel mills for grinding it.[49] Such was the prejudice against it that as late as 1856 it was condemned even for feeding poultry.[50] Other American food products were more successful or were seen as food spices and not medicinal, like Pimento. This was sold in England by those who dealt in grocery and was further made acceptable by its common names of Allspice and Jamaican Pepper.

## Displaying novelty

Display is and always has been an essential tool of the salesman. In the most primitive market the wares are still laid out as they always were in such a way that they attract the eye of potential customers. It was one of the underlying tenets of regulating trade in the middle ages that it should take place in the open market where the wares could be seen and the transaction witnessed.[51] When trade was conducted in a fixed shop, display was no less important, though it may have taken different forms. It is no less display when the shopkeeper holds out in his hands an item he wishes to sell even if alternatives are not on view. With novelty there is a different priority involving a period of familiarization preceding direct persuasion to buy. A particular form of this technique was used by eighteenth-century tradesmen, but it remains conjectural as to how common it was or whether it had been used in earlier times as the sources are not helpful. However, Josiah Wedgwood's skill in displaying his

---

[48] For example the shop of William Wood of Didsbury, 1785-89, see Mui and Mui (1989), *Shops and shopkeeping*, p. 214.

[49] Banks collection, 58.33.

[50] *Cottage gardener*, 2 December 1856, 140/2, quoted in *OED* under Indian corn.

[51] See chapter 3, section entitled 'The concept of an open market'.

wares is thoroughly documented,[52] and one aspect of his skill is particularly relevant to Bianchi's model. In Wedgwood's showrooms he had a model dining room with a complete dinner set laid out, changed regularly. Not only was each pattern introduced into a known set of patterns, but individual items must also have been introduced into an accepted set of table ware. Potential customers, seeing a dinner set consisting of plates and dishes in various sizes, gravy jugs and sauce boats, were indoctrinated in the most pleasant way possible into what a proper dinner set should contain, even if their own dinner ware fell far short of this ideal. Their horizons were stretched to accommodate a range of equipment beyond their own, but one that was safely within an accepted set. The device of the displayed acceptable set was also used by other tradesmen. In an advertisement addressed to 'FAMILIES FURNISHING KITCHENS' Stone & Co. offered 'a complete Set' of Kitchen ware including such esoteric items as a Turbot Kettle (as well as a 'Carp or fish-kettle') and 'Two scollops' all for the price of £8 8s. Even if Stone sold very few complete sets, he was planting in the public's mind an idea of what a proper kitchen should contain, thus creating a safe set into which novelty could be introduced.[53] The approach was slightly different in the construction and furnishing trades, where the use of architectural drawings and pattern books were widely used to familiarize potential customers with what was fashionable and hence what was new. Most of the seventeenth-century products of this type were architectural, but during the eighteenth furniture makers became skilled in this type of selling. The most notable exponent was Thomas Chippendale, who published in 1754 *The gentleman and cabinet maker's director*; the safe set of Bianchi transferred to print. Not only was the full range of furniture laid out on paper but items were contextualized in perspective drawings. In addition to his *Director*, Chippendale opened a show room where his designs were displayed in a manner not dissimilar to that used by Wedgwood.[54]

The anxieties of provincial customers looking to furnish their more public rooms were also addressed by similar techniques, though probably rather later. The upholsterer, cabinet maker and internal designer, Joseph Howe of Birmingham, took display of fashionable goods out of the show room and into the home. Howe offered 'Perspective and Geometrical Designs displaying the entire Furniture of Suits of Rooms in the highest style of fashionable and tasty elegance'.[55] With such devices as these the concept of the set became

---

[52] McKendrick (1982), 'Josiah Wedgwood'.

[53] Advertisement in *The Times*, 25 January 1788. I thank Karin Dannehl for allowing me to use her material in advance of publication.

[54] This paragraph draws heavily on Saumarez-Smith (1993), *Eighteenth-century decoration and design*, and in particular pp. 11-13, 132-3.

[55] Joseph Howe, LSH, 09/618. Joseph Howe of Ellis Street, Birmingham, was in Pigot's *Directory* for 1830 and in Whites for 1849. The card may be beyond the end of our period.

personalized to fit particular aspirations, discreetly modified to introduce new ideas and new commodities under the guise of fashion.

Francis Place had mixed fortunes in his experiments of using display to introduce novelty. When searching for a suitable shop he was anxious to see not only that it was in a respectable neighbourhood, but also that it had a good window in which to display his wares. He took a lease on a shop in Charing Cross and immediately began negotiations with 'Mercers and Woollen Drapers and Trimming Sellers' from whom he obtained sufficient to make 'a handsome display in the windows'. However, his experiments with display were only partially successful. He opened the shop 'with a handsome shew of choice mercery goods' followed in a few days with 'some very fashionable waistcoats'. This was profitable and he sold a considerable number, although at the time 'there was no shop at the West end of the Town which exposed first rate fashionable articles for dress in the window'. As he pointed out waistcoats were fashionable, and any novelty lay in new designs or patterns. However, a more daring display of 'Pantaloons ornamented with silk braid' was initially a failure probably because, as he observed, they had not then become common and 'were worn by very few persons excepting Cavalry Officers'. [56] Displaying novelty within the context of current fashion was successful, but going outside that frame was not. Place's experiments illustrate well Style's conclusion that 'the process of product innovation involved an extended negotiation between supplier and consumer, in which success for the supplier was far from guaranteed'.[57]

## Servicing novelty

If tradesmen selling tobacco did feel the need to offer instruction on how to use tobacco when it was first introduced, no evidence has survived. Directions for use and other informational material became an important weapon in promoting the introduction of new commodities and innovation in the old. Probably the producers of unorthodox medicines led the way with this technique. Quack cures must have a history going back well before the first use of the term, but it is likely that any promotional or instructional material was verbal. The introduction of printing, the establishment of simple printing presses in many towns in England and the arrival of the local newspaper were a gift to the quack. Most branded medicines were advertised heavily in the local newspapers, and nearly all at the very least set out the disorders for which a patient could hope to be cured. For example, an advertisement for Friars

---

[56] *Autobiography of Francis Place*, vol. II, pp. 83-5, 98.

[57] Styles, J. (forthcoming), 'Product innovation in early modern London'.

Balsam in 1743 claimed it 'cures all Manner of Strains and Bruises ... heals any Cut or Green Wound (if not Mortal) ... 'Tis a good Medicine for Coughs, Colds, Consumptions, Asthma's, Dropsies, Gout and Rheumatism, Cholick, Flux, Piles, Pain in the Bowels or Stomach, and Tooth-Ach'. It could also, as the promoters advised, be used by horses and dogs no less than Man.[58] Some advertisements also gave directions for use as well as setting out supposed curative powers. For example, the one for Daffey's Elixir appearing in almost the first issue of *Aris's Birmingham Gazette*, promised printed directions with every bottle, also that 'a Number of great Cures performed by this Elixir is given to any Person, Gratis, who pleases to ask for them'.[59]

The use of directions, either sold with the preparation or printed in the advertisement, was particularly appropriate for those sexual disorders for which the sufferer might have been reluctant to seek professional help. Quack remedies of this type abounded. 'Desault's Grand Specific Antivenereal Pills and Lineament' were offered with precise instructions on how to eat the one and to rub on the other. When cured his 'Balsamic Strengthening Electuary' offered, also with instructions, some hope of cure for 'those Infirmities of the Seminal Vessels which hinder Procreation'.[60] Perhaps the apex of the genre was attained by the advertisement for the 'Grand Transcendent Restrictive Electuary for ... Veneral Disease' which promised a Book of Directions on how to use the preparation.[61]

The technique was used for other goods that were new in some way. The introduction of Sago and Tapioca, though easily fitting into the genre of grocery, nevertheless presented the vendor with the problem of unfamiliarity. Sago had been known since the sixteenth century and it had established itself as invalid food by the seventeenth. It remained so classified by some for another century,[62] although things were changing. During the 1740s it was stocked by several London grocers who chose to list it in their advertisements along with other esoteric commodities like tea, coffee and chocolate, and Batavia Arrack.[63] A trade card of another London company Stringer and Leach (*c.* 1767) promoted 'Bowens Patent Sago Powder' with a recipe to make it up into Sago Jelly.[64] This was intended for medicinal use, but the recipe given by Hannah Glasse in 1747 clearly was not since it included two quarts of milk, half a

---

[58] *Aris's Birmingham Gazette*, 24 January 1743.

[59] *Aris's Birmingham Gazette*, 28 December 1741.

[60] *Aris's Birmingham Gazette*, 3 January 1743.

[61] *Aris's Birmingham Gazette*, 29 September 1760.

[62] It was advertised by Henry Wright, Chemist, Druggist and Colourman in 1760 and by Daniel Lynch Chymist and Druggist in 1790, both of Manchester and both in the *Manchester Mercury*, respectively 2 September 1760 and 24 August 1790.

[63] The earliest noted is in the trade card of Wilson and Thornhill, Attingham MSS, 112/6/Box 35c/1.

[64] Stringer & Leach of London, Heal collection, 102*.1.

pound of fresh butter, nine eggs, with currants and sweet wine to taste all baked under a puff pastry lid.[65] By the 1790s Sago was a product sufficiently popular to attract brand names and no longer in need of promotion *per se*.[66] In like manner tapioca was difficult to market having had a bad press since its discovery, so that at least one seller promoted it with a recipe.[67]

'Portable Soup', a terrifying concoction of strong broth reduced to a jelly and dried in the sun, was probably invented in the 1750s and was sold for the use of travellers. Elizabeth Raffald gave a recipe for making it at home, but the proprietors of an Italian and Oil Warehouse, Burgess and Son, sold it ready made and gave instructions on how to use it in their promotional hand bill.[68] Burgess was one of two major sellers of preserved food in London who were particularly skilful in their use of promotional recipes with new products. In the same hand bill he offered printed directions and/or a recipe with every bottle of his 'NEW INVENTED SAUCE a l'ESPANGNOLE' and of his 'BENGAL CURRIE POWDER', as well as helpful tips and recipes in the hand bill itself for other products. The catalogue of Skill, Purveyor General and Oilman (1800), is even more impressive. He gave as his address 'the OLD Italian and French Warehouses And FISH SAUCE and PORTABLE SOUP Manufactories' and, like his address, his catalogue was long, running to four pages. With every item there was a piece of skilful puffery but advice and directions on use, recipes and appropriate accompaniments abounded.[69] Such tradesmen both invented and promoted a huge range of preserved foodstuffs for the luxury market.

Other innovations presented the same problems of presentation, one particular group being products for house decoration. Although the nature of the development is not understood, it seems that in the mid-eighteenth century improvements in grinding, and/or the production of suitable oils made it possible to sell paint ready mixed rather than as separate ingredients. One of the first noted to market this innovation was James Ward of Stockport (1760) who offered his varnishes and paints ready made up with 'particular Directions how to prime, finish and perform the different Sorts of Painting about New Buildings'.[70] Joseph Emerton, Colourman of London offered printed Directions about using his colours for house painting so that 'any Gentlemen, Builders, &c. may set their servants or Labourers to paint their Houses' with, for the

---

[65] Glasse (1747), *Art of cookery*, p. 106. Raffald (1769), *Experienced English housekeeper*, pp. 84-5 had similar recipes, one with the addition of cream.

[66] *Aris's Birmingham Gazette*, 7 June 1790, 'Morgan's genuine Sago Powder'.

[67] Trade card of M. Crew, 'Tapioca Importer & Seller', London (n.d.), Heal Collection, 102*.2.

[68] Raffald (1769), *Experienced English housekeeper*, pp. 5-6; Burgess & Co.'s hand bill, Banks collection, 89.4 .

[69] Banks Collection, 89.36* [*sic*] .

[70] *Manchester Mercury*, 15 July 1760.

Ladies, instructions and necessary varnish etc., for Japanning. In like manner Mr Pope of London encouraged his customers to buy the new fangled and fashionable paper hangings by offering them 'made according to the plan given, & every breadth match'd & numbered, so that they are put up with the greatest ease by any country upholsterer'. The eighteenth century saw the introduction of several branded inks, presumably with hoped-for improved characteristics, so Raper's Toyshop offered theirs with Directions for use.[71]

Tradesmen found themselves obliged to offer services no less than directions for use. Although the élite had probably always relied to some extent on specialists to service their furnishings and dress, provincial tradesman of the seventeenth century and the eighteenth were also pressured to service new products and innovations by customers who did not necessarily have access to London specialists. These continued to flourish, some with extraordinarily specific specialisms, like N. & M. Tenniel of London who styled themselves 'Silk Stocking Cleaners' (before 1797) claimed royal patronage and the ability to restore 'Silk Stockings to their Original Colour without using Hot Press or Mangle'.[72] Their advertisement suggests that they were among the élite in the trade, and that there were many silk stocking cleaners who did use the hot press and the mangle. However, most services were offered either by the producers or by retailing tradesmen. For example, Mary Wilks, a milliner of Shrewsbury, (1742) offered the highly skilled work of starching,[73] the 'real Hatmaker' Redman of Stratford, Essex, (1791) not only made hats, but also 'Dyed clean'd & Cock'd [them] in the most fashion'ble Tast', and Morris's Tunbridge Ware Manufactory of Brighton (1815) offered repairing and revarnishing.[74] William Bignall, a 'working Silversmith from London' offered to mend 'any sort of Curiosities in any Metal whatsoever' and to repair and polish any Gentleman's plate 'so as to look like new', while a fellow Birmingham tradesman, Andrew Inys offered to clean 'Foul Leather Breeches' and to stretch them if required with his 'new invented Machine'.[75] This emphasis on restoring objects to a condition 'as new' was an important element in the services offered. Not only was the appearance and function restored, but also the objects themselves were rendered respectable, and therefore safe, again.

One of the most common, and one of the earliest, services offered was furnishing funerals. This was frequently combined with the sale of drapery and mercery by tradesmen such as William Sissons of Sheffield (17--) who offered

---

71 Emerton, *Evening Advertiser*, 3 January 1740; Mr Pope, *Public Advertiser*, 15 May 1755; Raper's, *General Advertiser*, 8 January 1750.

72 Banks Collection, 72.223.

73 Attingham MSS, 112/6, Box 356/33.

74 Banks Collection, 72.185 and 122.13.

75 *Aris's Birmingham Gazette*, 2 April 1750 and 27 August 1750.

'Mourning on the shortest notice and Fashionably made'.[76] Husband and wife teams were not uncommon, the one keeping the shop and the other supplying a service. J. Callow, a silk mercer and haberdasher, moved from London and set up shop in Birmingham while his wife, presumably using the fabrics he sold, did 'Dress making in the first style of Fashion' and executed 'Wedding Orders & Fancy Balls Dresses'. Funerals were also arranged with 'every Article in Fashionable Family Mourning'.[77] The subtleties of the Callows's advertisement are considerable. The information of the move from London assured Birmingham provincials of an up to date modality. Any uncertainty they may have felt about how to use the new fabrics and trimmings were allayed as Mrs Callow would do the making-up for them in the first style of fashion. It is probable that the willingness of tradesmen like Sissons and the Callows to furnish funerals, weddings and fancy dress balls did much to elaborate and crystallize perceptions of what was proper for these occasions. It is perhaps significant that two of the new modish fabrics of this period, crape and á-la-mode, became particularly associated with funerals, the one of the dead and the other of the living, thus becoming incorporated into the set of appropriate adornment for these occasions.

Another set of tradesmen who frequently offered to furnish funerals were those involved in the furniture trades. Since many of them also sold textiles, their motives may have similar to the drapers and mercers, but there was probably an alternative motive as well. Selling furniture and furnishings, whether or not these were made on the premises, was frequently combined with carrying out appraisals and/or with buying household furniture second-hand. It was a clever nexus giving the tradesman control over the furniture trade at several levels. Peter Burcham, 'carver, chair & cabinet maker' whose Cabinet Warehouse was situated near Holburn Bridge in London in the 1750s and 1760s, advertised his wares both wholesale and retail in a florid trade card replete with coats of arms, gothic scrolls and elaborate candlesticks. In small print at the foot he offered 'Funerals decently performed, Goods Appraised and the most Money given for Household Furniture'. He is typical of many other apparently grand London tradesmen, each of whom must have had a back entrance and a back room for the less fashionable items of furniture bought in household sales.[78] The easy disposal of unwanted goods had a twofold influence on the market. Firstly, it made space for the new and fashionable in

[76] Birmingham Central Reference, LSH, 08/494.

[77] Birmingham Central Reference, LSH, 09/619. Jackson's Habit-Warehouse in London (1770) also offered ready made dresses for sale as well as 'a book of several hundred prints coloured, which contain the dress of every nation', Heal (1925), *London tradesmen's cards*, vol. XXII. If Jackson had access to a copy of Randle Holme (1688), *Academy of Armory*, this would have supplied him plentifully with ideas on so-called national dress.

[78] Peter Burcham's card is reproduced in Heal (1988), *London furniture makers*, pp. 17 and 29.

the homes of those who could afford it and, secondly, for those who could not, it gave access to a vision of what they could only aspire towards and the opportunity to participate on the fringe.

## Adapting the business to accommodate novelty

Marketing novelty did not come cheap; on the contrary a considerable investment was required. The new products and novelties of the early modern period, introduced as they were at a time when the customer base was changing, presented a threefold challenge in processing, packaging and presentation. Each of these required in varying proportions equipment, extra personnel, space and money.

Of the new products tobacco made the most demands on the retail tradesman. Although some was processed at the port of entry, much arrived at the shop as imported. In consequence, as we have seen, many tradesmen selling tobacco and/or tobacco products had the wherewithal to process them by the end of the seventeenth century. The equipment, including the troughs, the press and the cutting engine, was quite valuable, being usually valued for probate at £2 or more, roughly equivalent to the value of a cow in milk. Such equipment had to have its own space, usually called a tobacco room, as soaking, fermentation, pressing and cutting were hardly operations that could be conducted in the shop itself. In addition, extra staff may well have been needed; William Stout, for example, employed one skilled in rolling and cutting his tobacco.[79] Other new products were less demanding, although snuff needed vessels for steeping and a mortar and pestle, sugar, if bought in the loaf, needed sugar nippers or other means to break it up, and coffee needed a roaster and a grinder.

Packaging became more pressing with the new products and with the arrival of customers who had only small sums to spend. As the consumption of tobacco and of sugar in the seventeenth century, and of tea in the eighteenth, spread down the social scale, their success in this new market depended upon the tradesmen's willingness to make up small packets to be sold for cash through the shop window, or over the counter to the credit worthy. The ever informative William Stout reveals the scale of the problem. Most of his own sales, and that of other Lancaster tradesmen, seems to have been made on market days. As an apprentice he spent much of the week packaging up new goods like sugar and tobacco, as well as prunes and nails in packets of appropriate sizes ready for the rush.[80] He is less informative about his own

---

[79] Stout (1967), *Autobiography*, p. 162 (1710).
[80] Stout (1967), *Autobiography*, p. 79 (1682).

practices, but presumably his apprentices, his sister or he himself had to do the same in his shop.

An advertisement of 1741 suggests that by the mid-eighteenth century some producers were aware of the problem of packaging in small lots and boosted their own sales by assisting their retailing customers in theirs. For example, the proprietor of the Virginia Factory offered gratis 'Penny Papers to make up the Tobacco ... [bought] at the said Factory with a Print of Admiral Vernon, and a Spaniard on his knee'. The offer included tobacco at a discount and a mould to facilitate the packing.[81] This particular offer was directed at inns and coffee houses, hence the papers designed to carry only one pennyworth of tobacco, but shopkeepers had the same problem though on a slightly larger scale. Wills was one of the other eighteenth-century tobacco companies that packaged their own tobacco and/or provided retailers with the papers.[82] Thomas Turner, the mid-eighteenth-century Sussex shopkeeper, spent many an evening with his wife, packaging up tobacco in four ounce lots.[83] His diary does not record the packing of tea likewise, possibly because that was not yet in demand by his less affluent customers. Three decades later William Wood's customers were buying tea an ounce or half an ounce at a time usually with half a pound of sugar.[84] Since the only surviving records of Wood's trading activity lies in his Customers' Book, there is no information on how, or if, he packaged goods prior to sale. Clues elsewhere suggest that packaging became increasingly burdensome as the eighteenth century progressed and the costs and trouble of packaging in small parcels are reflected in newspaper advertisements. For example, John Hodgson in 1785 offered tea 'fully 25 per cent cheaper than any warehouse in London' in packages of 'not less than one pound'; rather more generously but still beyond the pockets of most of Wood's customers, Edward Eagleton was offering tea, as he claimed, 'for the benefit of the poor ... at reduced prices in small quantities not less than 2 ounces'.[85]

Novelties and new goods needed to be presented to the potential customer before they could be sold profitably. It is no accident that large windows, display boards and counters noted in chapter 3 were introduced first by tradesmen specializing in novelty, such as haberdashers, milliners, goldsmiths, and the sellers of ceramics and glass. It would have been fruitless to offer for sale new style and fashionable buttons or ribbons, gold and silver ware, china or glass, if the potential customer were not given the opportunity to see such goods and to lust after them. Two foreign travellers noted the skill with which

[81] *London Morning Advertiser*, 4 September 1741.
[82] Alford (1973), *W.H & H.O. Wills*, frontispiece.
[83] For example, Turner (1984), *Diary*, 12 April 1754, 17 February 1757.
[84] Mui and Mui (1989), *Shops and shopkeeping*, p. 213.
[85] *Morning Post*, 27 January 1785 and 3 February 1785, both quoted in Mui and Mui (1989), *Shops and shopkeeping*, p. 257.

retailers used their windows for display. Rouquet wrote of the mercers who make their shops:

> ... as deep as possibly they can: the further end is generally lighted from above a kind of illumination which joined to the glasses, the sconces and the rest of the furniture, is in regard to those who are passing by, frequently productive of a theatrical effect, of a most agreeable vista.[86]

A few years later Carl Phil Moritz was making much the same point even more forcibly about the presentation of novelty in London:

> ... care is taken to show, as far as practicable, all works of art and industry to the public. Paintings, machines, precious objects - all can be seen advantageously displayed behind great clear-glass windows. There is no lack of onlookers standing stock-still in the middle of the street here and there to admire some ingenious novelty. Such a street often resembles a well-arranged show cabinet.[87]

With new groceries, drugs and tobacco, presentation in this fashion was hardly an option, although the German traveller Johanna Schopenhauer described a practice by at least one London apothecary intended to entice the curious inside. 'The apothecaries', she wrote, 'decorate their windows with large glass vases filled with brilliantly coloured spirit or water and place between them bunches of artificial flowers. At night, when the lamps burn behind these coloured glasses, each shop gleams like Aladdin's cave'.[88] Whereas this sort of display must have had its place, for most purposes promotional and informational advertisement was probably more important for these goods. Although shopkeepers apparently had some dislike of advertising in provincial and national newspapers, this was an alternative mode of display that familiarized potential customers with novelties and new products. Many advertisements were designed almost as items of news. For example, the Birmingham milliners, Mary and Sarah Holmes, produced a cleverly sustained programme in the 1750s, ostensibly to inform the public of their business activities, but in fact also displaying the goods they had on offer. They first advertised in *Aris's Birmingham Gazette* in 1750 to announce their removal to new premises. Their notice was repeated several times with long lists of goods on offer. The following year they were announcing their retirement from the business of selling, along with yet another list of goods, but in their final advertisement it emerged that their retirement was only partial as they

---

86 Rouquet (1755), *The present state of the arts*, p. 121, quoted in Saumarez-Smith (1993), *Eighteenth-century decoration and design*, p. 134.

87 Moritz (1965), *Journeys of a German in England in 1782*, pp. 100-101.

88 Schopenhauer (1988), *A lady's travel*, 18 January 1790, p. 138.

continued to make up millinery which again was listed though in less detail.[89] Similar advertisements announcing the setting up of new businesses, take overs, temporary closures through fire, removals, the arrival of new seasons goods and the like can be found in almost any edition of any provincial or national newspaper. Many of them are accompanied by lists of goods on offer. The advertisement focusing on a particular tradesman is less common, though the device was used by some, particularly by grocers, colourmen and druggists, who may have felt more than most that their customers needed to be familiarized with new products.

For the petty shopkeepers like those whose purchases were recorded in the Day Book of the early nineteenth-century tea dealer and grocer, Andrew Melrose, advertisement was probably not an option and an alternative method of promotion had to be found. Two of Melrose's retailing customers, Mrs Taylor and Alexander Grieve, each regularly purchased a good strong quality of black tea in two grades. Presumably they promoted it to their own customers through personal recommendation, the cheapest form of marketing and one that continued so long as the small shop survived.[90]

## Novelty becomes safe

It is all too easy to find examples of attitudes suspicious to change in the early modern period, though one must wonder how often they were fuelled by fears for existing commercial interests. For example, the colour derived from logwood, an excellent new dyestuff from America, was declared 'false and deceitful to the queen's subjects at home, and discreditable beyond seas to our merchants and dyers'. The use of logwood as a dyestuff was prohibited by an act of 1581 which remained in force for 60 years.[91]

Although such attitudes seem to have been more common in the sixteenth century and the early seventeenth than later, eighteenth-century diatribes against novelty were still not unusual. With this in mind, it might reasonably be supposed that terms denoting newness or novelty would have been used with caution, except in the sense of fresh or of this season as opposed to old or of last year. This is not so. The paucity of trade cards, bill heads and newspaper advertisements for the seventeenth century renders it impossible to be certain that the readiness of tradesmen to use such terms during the eighteenth denoted a change of attitude, but it seems likely. Tudor governmental activity had been directed towards encouraging industry and thereby reducing imports. Patent

---

[89] *Aris's Birmingham Gazette*, particularly 19 March and 16 July 1750, 23 September 1751 and 3 February 1752.

[90] Mui and Mui (1989), *Shops and shopkeeping*, pp. 206-7, 209.

[91] *Vegetable substances* (1833), p. 338.

law until 1776 discouraged mere improvement,[92] and many so-called patents of invention seem to have been used by entrepreneurs to pre-empt the opposition rather than genuinely to forward progress. It is only during the second half of the seventeenth century and into the eighteenth that newness seems to have become respectable. Entrepreneurs took out genuine patents of invention and diarists and other writers recorded the new with wonder and delight. Even economists, including Adam Smith, wrote approvingly of novelty. Societies like the Royal Society founded in 1662 and the Society for the Diffusion of Knowledge (1827) encouraged and sometimes rewarded innovation and invention as did Parliament, not always felicitously. For example, a Dr Williams was awarded £2000 in 1773 by Parliament for the discovery of new fast dyes of green and of yellow using weld and an unspecified mordant. It was only after he had been paid, that his claims were discovered to be fraudulent. In 1804 the Society for the Encouragement of the Arts awarded a Gold Medal to Sir H.C. Englefield for a new pigment prepared from madder, and in the same year another to Mr Coston for his experiments to imitate the Leghorn plait used in making straw hats, as a result of which others found several English grasses could be used for the purpose.[93]

The search for a replacement for Leghorn plait reflects an approach to innovation which has only recently received attention from historians. Imitation is not only the sincerest form of flattery, it is also a driving force towards innovation. From the sixteenth century onwards many manufacturers, not just those makers of imitation Leghorn plait directed their thoughts towards making products as good as or identical to those from abroad, while others were using imitation to produce genuine novelty.[94] Wedgwood made vases in the shape and form of Etruscan funerary urns but in ceramics instead of metal, the Dutch developed Delft Ware in imitation of Chinese porcelain, and Oriental lacquered goods were the inspiration behind the decorative finishes given to British papier mâché and tinware. In each case a new and original art form arose out of imitation.

In these cases, and countless others, real innovation and invention was rendered safe by its association with goods already perceived as fashionable and desirable. It is in contexts like these that the term new became acceptable to consumers and therefore profitable to use by advertisers. Just as common was newest, though this had the added connotation that it was even better than merely new. Products advertised as new or newest cover the whole range;

---

92 In Morris v. Branson, Lord Justice Mansfield rejected objections based on mere improvement stating that if valid they 'would go to repeal almost every patent that was ever granted'; quoted in MacLeod (1988), *Inventing the industrial revolution*, p. 13.

93 *Vegetable substances* (1833), pp. 381, 356 and pp. 159-66.

94 The ideas developed in this section owe much to a Seminar given by Maxine Berg, 'Imitation and innovation', on 17 May 1999 at the University of Wolverhampton.

beaver and Leghorn hats, millinery, watches, cabinet work, chintzes, handkerchiefs, buckles, dance tunes - the list is endless. Even an apothecary shop and its equipment offered for sale in 1743 were declared to be 'new and after the modern fashion'.[95]

Not surprisingly Fashion and Taste were two terms most often combined with new, but advertisers were clearly desirous of associating newness with some of the attributes most esteemed by the respectable. So millinery, black gauzes, Ladies 'Cushions, Braids and Curls' were all 'in the newest taste', while other goods were 'new ... and very fashionable and genteel', 'new and elegant' or 'in the newest and neatest taste'. Even in the advertisements for auctions of second-hand household furniture where new was obviously inappropriate, terms such as 'genuine', 'modern' and 'elegant' were used in juxtaposition. Invention and improvement likewise became acceptable, turnery wares were 'after the newest inventions', a rectifying still and worm of the 'newest construction', watches of the 'newest improved make'. Toys were 'new fashioned' and shaving-cases 'new-invented.[96]

## Conclusion

Thus were innovation and novelty made acceptable. For some products it was a matter of finding the right name, for others of containing them in recognizable and safe sets. In all cases it was necessary for there to be an appropriate cultural meaning. The incorporation of the new into the established corpus of traded goods became easier when terms such as new and modern became desirable in themselves. The advertisement of the 'Silk manufacturers and mercers', R. Goolden & Co., epitomises the way that new permeated the language of the successful salesmen when they offered a 'very fashionable and genteel Assortment ... entirely new, and the Produce of the best Manufacturers in England and for elegance of Fancy and Taste none can excel'.[97]

---

[95] *Aris's Birmingham Gazette*, 23 May 1743.

[96] These are taken from *Aris's Birmingham Gazette*, *Piercy's Coventry Gazette*, *Sussex Weekly Advertiser*, the *Daily London Post*, the *Public Advertiser*, the *Evening Advertiser* and the *London Chronicle*, but examples can be found in the advertisements of almost any eighteenth-century newspaper.

[97] *Aris's Birmingham Gazette*, 9 April 1770.

# Conclusion

There is a vigorous debate among scholars between those who see continuity as the most significant feature of history and those who look for discontinuity and change. The history of retailing has until recently largely been written by those of the latter school. Historians viewing retailing from the perspective of the mid-twentieth century look for the beginnings of what they see as the significant features of the modern system: the mass market, shopping (as distinct from buying), the department store, multiple outlets, advertising, to name but a few, and on the whole they fail to find them as part of the retailing scene in the early modern period. They conclude therefore that the retailing sector was slow to adapt to a changing world and remained much as it had always been until after 1850. Thereafter change is seen to have been rapid and dramatic.

Studies by Jefferys and Davis are the classic expositions of this approach. They present the wholesale and retail sectors of mid-nineteenth-century Britain as 'examples of those trades that still bore the marks of the old system rather than the new', with methods of buying and selling 'very much as they had been a hundred years before'.[1] Davis concludes that 'a dull calling attracted dull recruits'.[2] These classic expositions of early modern trading, while they describe recognizable practices current at some times in the period and in some sections of the trade, hardly do justice to the complexity and dynamism of retailing as set out in the preceding chapters. But these images of a traditional and unresponsive and, worst of all, a dull sector, have created a historiographical myth that has been hard to dispel despite vigorous refutations by Willan, Mui and Mui, and others. It is with this myth in mind that Benson and Shaw have recently suggested that 'It is probably with some relief that students of retailing turn from the early modern period to the nineteenth and twentieth centuries'.[3]

Recent historians have challenged this negative attitude to early modern retailing. But they have tended to concentrate on looking for the development of what might be seen as modern aspects of retailing, such as shop design,

---

[1] Jefferys (1954), *Retail trading*, chapter 1; Davis (1966) *History of shopping*, chapter 12.

[2] Davis (1966) *History of shopping*, p. 252.

[3] Benson and Shaw (1999), *Retailing industry*, vol. II, p. 1, opening sentence.

display, advertisement, and shopping as a leisure activity, rather than to study the early modern period in its own right and to ask questions about how well the retail sector responded to the challenges of the day.[4]

The aim of this study has been twofold: first to investigate continuity and change between retail systems of the early modern period and those coming both before and after; and secondly to assess how far the retail sector met the challenges confronting it at a time of economic, social and political change.

In attempting to do this, the historian is confronted with a serious challenge in the matter of sources. Of those sources already familiar to historians, most are weighted towards innovative tradesmen, with far fewer about the ordinary petty shopkeeper, apart from the diatribes of writers who saw such operators as the underworld of retailing. For the period before the Restoration there is an apparent dearth of sources, with the obvious danger that this could lead to overmuch reliance on the few there are.[5] This apparently gloomy prognosis about sources proved to be unfounded. There are sources in variety which, if used imaginatively and constructively, give a coherent picture of retailing in the early modern period, although conclusions about retailing in the sixteenth century are more tentative than those for the eighteenth. Furthermore it is possible to delineate both continuities and discontinuities with medieval no less than with modern retailing

One of the most dramatic changes for the retailing sector during the early modern period occurred in an area outside its direct control. Political and economic theory in the early sixteenth century was hostile to retailers in a number of ways. The Church, no less than the government, had long cherished views on a fair price and an open market. The two were intertwined and so long as they were accepted, and to some extent enforced by custom and by law, there were severe restrictions on many aspects of retailing practice including shop design and fixed pricing. Remnants of these ideas continued to surface at times into the seventeenth century (for example, in the planning legislation after the Great Fire of London in 1666 and in the attacks on Quaker retailers), but had virtually disappeared by the eighteenth. Shopkeepers were thus left free to explore innovative ways of practising their craft at the interface between themselves and their customers, and some were quick to avail themselves of the opportunity. The most marked change was the increased preference for the fixed shop with trading taking place inside its doors. Effective use of space to accommodate different modes of selling, the exploitation of new technological

---

[4] For example, McKendrick (1982), 'George Packwood'; Walsh (1995), 'Shop design'.

[5] Chartres (1977), *Internal trade*, p. 9, warned then against the dangers of 'attributing to the survival of data an undue weight'. It is a danger that has not reduced with time.

possibilities in the use of glass and lighting, and tentative experiments with rapid turnover and sales for cash, resulted in some businesses that would have been quite alien to their medieval predecessors but quite recognizable to their late nineteenth-century successors. Amongst all this innovation some shopkeepers retained traditional layouts and practices, perhaps because they felt these were more appropriate to the needs of their community, perhaps because they were slow to recognize opportunity. Both in change and in refusal to change there was risk, and the level of business failure appears to have been high.

Further shifts in economic and political thinking also made life easier for the retailing tradesman, though perhaps less dramatically. Political arguments against luxury were effectively demolished in the late seventeenth century and the early eighteenth, while the laws regulating dress had disappeared some hundred years before. Economic anxieties about the importation of luxuries were slower to disappear, but became less important as home produced goods replaced imports in many spheres of trade. As a result retailers were better able to supply the market at all levels with the luxuries and conveniences so much in demand.

Last but not least, economists came to recognize the importance of the retail sector to the national economy. Whereas in the sixteenth century retailers were seen as serving little useful purpose and were castigated for encouraging luxury and dangerous imports; by the eighteenth their contribution was acknowledged and even welcomed. Coincidentally or not, retailers as a pressure group became a force to be reckoned with. Although it was primarily the London shopkeepers who organized the campaign against the Shop Tax in the 1780s, provincial tradesmen proved themselves quite capable of acting collectively as well.

The guild system and the concomitant town organization are generally regarded as outdated relics from medieval times and in an advanced state of decay by the seventeenth century. This widely held belief needs to be questioned. Apprenticeship, the bedrock of the whole guild system, continued to be the usual mode of entry into the respectable end of the trade. Although open to abuse, as it always had been, it remained for many the foundation on which the essential networks of trade beyond the family were built at a time when poor communications made such networks essential. In those sections of the trade where networking was less important, particularly in the world of the ephemeral petty shopkeeper, apprenticeship was of no importance. In other respects the trade companies may have continued to serve some purpose in encouraging the maintenance of standards and in acting against adulteration and other fraudulent practices, even if their capacity to enforce was trickling away.

Another survival from the middle ages, the combination of market and fixed shops on the same site, proved remarkably resilient in the face of change.

Its strength lay partly in the symbiotic relationship between two types of trading, a link that has only begun to be broken in small country towns during the last few decades. In the early modern period people like the Lathams and the Blundells came to the market to do business and then stayed to shop. The format of market place with shops surrounding it remained an active feature of many nineteenth-century towns, central to the life-styles of many people. As late as the 1960s and 1970s, when fewer country people came to market to sell, many still came on the one bus of the week to buy at the market, combining this with buying from shops. The relationship between market and fixed shop is invariably noticed by historians, but equally invariably dismissed as outdated. It has unfortunately been the subject of little study, but it would seem that this arrangement of shops clustered round an active market place was an appropriate one for certain conditions and therefore remained successful so long as those conditions survived. It became part of the 'modern' economy of retailing only marginally changed from a system that had its roots in the middle ages.

The retailing community did not remain wedded to the market place when circumstances indicated opportunities in relocation. The movement towards town improvement encouraged the development of élite residential areas in many towns, and the shopkeepers were quick to follow their customers. Fashionable shopping streets, long a feature of London, spread to the provinces, not just in the resorts of the élite, like Tunbridge Wells, Bath and Brighton, but to many towns of medium size, and some industrial towns like Manchester or Birmingham. The shopping arcade, often regarded as a twentieth-century or even a post-war development is recognizable in the London New Exchange and in the Pantiles of Tunbridge Wells even if the details are different.

At the bottom end of the market a new type of fixed shop seems to have emerged in the seventeenth century, termed by contemporaries the petty shop. Petty shopkeepers gave ready access to many who might have found it difficult to get to market as towns increased in size and more workers were tied to waged employment. Such shops caused a good deal of alarm at the time, but solid evidence concerning numbers and distribution is slim. The few probate inventories that have emerged show that some were very small and many were probably ephemeral. But as a genre, they were survivors. The petty shop was a feature of early modern trading and it remained in much the same form and character into modern times. New methods of retailing do not seem to have been instrumental in causing its demise until well into this century.[6]

---

[6] For the petty shop in the nineteenth century, see Benson (1983), *Penny capitalists*, chapter 10.

The complexity of many early modern retailing enterprises has received less recognition than it deserves. All but the most inferior tradesman, who probably depended on one supplier, exploited a large network of wholesalers, producers and even importers to stock their shops. Some sales were negotiated personally in time-consuming visits to a supplier, for others the negotiation was more remote using samples or patterns cards and correspondence or agents. Some goods were bought at annual fairs, a venue also used to settle accounts. The range of suppliers, some personal or familial acquaintances, others mere business associates, required careful accounting and a proper appreciation of alternative methods of payment; long or short-term credit, cash or a combination. Sometimes the specific choice was imposed by the supplier, but the autobiographical account of Francis Place makes it clear that retailers could and did at times exploit the alternatives to their own advantage.

It was not only in the matter of managing the supply side of the business that retailers showed enterprise and adaptability. Two methods of expansion generally regarded as characteristic of the modern age were not uncommon in the provinces in the early modern period. Some shops were of such a size that their owners found it necessary to arrange their stock in structured ways. The division between the grocery side of the business and the textiles was commonplace, often with the two departments clearly in different areas, or even different rooms. More complex divisions into half a dozen or more sections, are not unknown. The inevitable use of skilled counter staff in these departmentally structured shops is shown in the sources for the eighteenth century; for the early period it is the lack of evidence that precludes definite conclusions, although common sense dictates that a shop divided into several sections required such staff. Expansion could alternatively be arranged by opening secondary outlets. Sources of several sorts indicate this solution to surplus resources was adopted in both the seventeenth century and the eighteenth. Multiple outlets were a flexible way of expanding, and could not have occurred if there had not been a pool of possible managers, in the form either of apprentices approaching the end of their term, or of indigent widows, or of journeymen without the resources to strike out on their own. The use of secondary outlets, though common, was on a small scale with few shopkeepers investing in more than one at any time, but the seeds of a modern phenomenon were clearly sown.

From the start of the early modern period, consumer goods were available in many, but not all, market towns. By the second half of the seventeenth century it is likely that every market town had at least one shop selling a wide range of goods, and in some parts of the country shops were established in large villages as well. This made consumer goods available to all who attended market and some who did not, that is to a large proportion of the population. The evidence used by many historians to indicate a substantial rise in the use of consumer goods throughout all strata of society is proof of the success of retailers in distributing them.[7] For a sector dismissed as traditional, unresponsive and dull, its achievements in marketing new goods like tobacco, sugar, tea, coffee and chocolate, new textiles of cotton, silk and worsted, and novelties like Birmingham and London wares is truly remarkable. Although Defoe liked to use hyperbole to make a point, perhaps he was not so far off the mark when he wrote prophetically, 'The inland trade of England ... is the foundation of all our wealth and greatness; it is the support of all our foreign trade, and of our manufacturing ... This inland trade is in itself at this time the wonder of all the world of trade, nor is there anything like it now in the world, much less that exceeds it, or perhaps ever will be, except only what itself may grow up to in the ages to come; for ... it is still growing and increasing'.[8] In the creation of this expanding and dynamic 'wonder of the world of trade', the 'Complete tradesman' played an important part.

---

[7] For example, Weatherill (1988), *Consumer behaviour*; Shammas (1990), *Pre-industrial consumer*.

[8] Defoe (1987), *Complete English tradesman*, pp. 222, 223.

# Appendix

# List of tradesmen

All tradesmen referred to in the text are listed here with such details as are known about their occupation, place of operation and dates. They are also indexed under 'tradesmen'.

Ackerman, Henry, China dealer of London, *ob.* 1722
Addison, Robert, (saddlery) of Carlisle, Cumberland, *ob.* 1665
Aldridge, Mrs Ann, (occupation unknown) of London, *fl.* 1710s and 1720s
Allen, Thomas, mercer of Midhurst, Sussex, *ob.* 1716
Allen, William, mercer of Tamworth, Staffs., *ob.* 1604
Armson, John, grocer and hosier of Leicester, *fl.* 1760
Ashley, Richard, mercer of Worcester, *ob.* 1688
Backshell, Thomas, (mercery) of Broadwater, Sussex, *ob.* 1748
Baker, Ann, widow (wine) of Ipswich, Suffolk, *ob.* 1626
Ballard, John, mercer of Bewdley, Worcs., *ob.* 1667
Barlow, Obidiah, (iron) of Sheffield, *fl.* 1692
Barnett, Margaret, goldsmith and jeweller of Shrewsbury, *fl.* 1770
Barney, Mrs, milliner of Wolverhampton, Staffs., *fl.* 1780
Bayley, George, shopkeeper of Broseley, Shrops., *ob.* 1717
Beald, John, (mercery) of Portsmouth, Sussex, *ob.* 1587
Beard, George, shopkeeper of Chailey, Sussex, *fl.* 1750s
Beare, John, (mercery) of Ludham, Norfolk, *ob.* 1589
Bedford, Sarah & Co., cut glass maker of London, *fl.* late eighteenth century
Beeley, Robert, shopkeeper of Eyam, Derby., *ob.* 1752
Bennet, Robert, clothier of Tregony, Cornwall, *ob.* 1606
Bennett, Francis, draper of Bath, Somerset, *fl.* 1744
Bettisons, (perfumery, trinkets and toys) of Margate, Kent, and London, *fl.* 1794-1804
Bignell, William, working silversmith of Birmingham (from London) *fl.* 1750
Blair and Sutherland, gunsmiths of Birmingham and London, *fl.* 1802
Boucher, Benjamin, grocer of Bridgnorth, Shrops., *ob.* 1741
Boulton, Matthew, (brassware, toys, etc.) of Soho, Birmingham, 1728-1809
Bourne, Joan, (hats) of Bridgnorth, Shrops., *ob.* 1674
Boxall, William, mercer of Kirdford, Sussex, *ob.* 1754

Boyle, Thomas, pin maker of London, *ob.* 1720

Browne, G., chemist, druggist and oilman of Manchester, *fl.* 1782

Browne, Thomas, mercer of Northwich, Cheshire, *ob.* 1748

Brownhill, Mr, (confectionery) of Liverpool, *fl.* 1710s

Brownrigge, Roger, saddler of Coventry and Rugby, Warks., *ob.* 1604

Brunskill, Gualter, grocer and ironmonger of Lancaster, *fl.* 1735

Bryer, John, grocer of Lancaster, *fl.* 1680s-1729/30

Burbage, George, book seller of Leicester and Loughbrough, Leics., *fl.* 1760

Burcham, Peter, carver and chair and cabinet maker of London, *fl.* 1750s and 1760s

Burgess, J. and Son, Italian and oil warehouse of London, *fl.* 1790s

Butler, Richard, woollen draper of Basingstoke, Hants., *ob.* 1671

Bysshe, Thomas, mercer of Petworth, Sussex., *ob.* 1711

Callow, J., haberdasher and silk mercer of Birmingham (from London), probably early nineteenth century

Capel, John, mercer of Birmingham, *ob.* 1629

Castleton, Humphrey, saddler of Shifnal and Wellington, Shrops., *ob.* 1665

Chaddock, John, (shop), Lancashire, *fl.* 1663-66

Chippendale, Thomas, cabinet maker of London, 1718-79

Chorley, Mr, haberdasher of Liverpool, *fl.* 1700s

Close, V. & Son, (earthenware) of Hanley, Staffs. and Boston, Lincs., *fl.* 1810

Cobbe, Thomas, chapman of Sutton St James, Lincs., *ob.* 1613

Cokke, haberdasher of London, *fl.* 1584

Cole, Benjamin, (linens and lace) of London, *fl.* 1710s

Cole, S., silk mercer of London, *fl.* 1760

Collis, Edward, linen draper of Northampton, *ob.* 1625

Cotton, Mr, mercer of Liverpool, *fl.* 1710s

Couldham, John, linen draper of Great Yarmouth, Norfolk, *ob.* 1613

Coward, Henry, ironmonger of Lancaster, *fl.* 1673-98

Cowin, George, shopkeeper of Candlesby, Lincs., *ob.* 1725

Coyney, William, linen draper of Manchester, Lancs., *ob.* 1713

Crew, M., tapioca importer and seller of London, n.d.

Cross, John, shopkeeper of Huyton, Lancs., *ob.* 1639

Crychlow, Thomas, draper of Derby and Ashbourne, Derbyshire, *ob.* 1601

Cullen, Mr, mercer of ?Devon, *fl.* 1644-46

Dore, Elizabeth, (mercery) of Newport, Isle of Wight, *ob.* 1685

Dore, Richard, (mercery) of Newport, Isle of Wight, *ob.* 1654

Doughty, William, mercer of Wellington, Shrops., *fl.* 1691-1716

Durrant, Samuel, mercer of Lewes, Sussex, *ob.* 1782

Edwards, John, toyman of Birmingham, *ob.* 1733

Ellis Robert, mercer of Oxford, *ob.* 1597

Elmhirst, William, apothecary and surgeon of Ouslethwaite, Lancs., 1721-73

Emerton, Joseph, colourman of London, *fl*. 1740s

Eyton, Kenrick, mercer of Chester, *ob*. 1624

Farror, J. , china ware, of ?Birmingham, *fl*. 1790

Faux, William, (mercery) of Lincoln, *ob*. 1708

Fisher, James, (fish) of London, *fl*. 1737

Fitzherbert, Richard, haberdasher of Coventry, Warks., *ob*.1580

Fleetwood, Robert, glass seller of London, *fl*. 1721

Flint and Palmer, (drapery) of London, *fl*. 1780s

Flower, Francis, haberdasher and pattern drawer of London, *fl*. 1745

Fynis, Thomas, mercer of Coventry, Warks., *ob*. 1598

George, Edward, mercer of Shrewsbury, *fl*. 1662

George, Owen, mercer of Shrewsbury, *fl*. 1662

Gibson, Edward, (mercery) of London, *fl*. 1751-52

Gill's Hat Warehouse of London, *fl*. 1798

Gilly, William, (pewter) of Bury St Edmunds, Suffolk, *ob*. 1716

Goad, John, ironmonger of Lancaster, *fl*. 1721

Godsalve, Elin (general shop) of Lancaster, *fl*. 1711-15

Goldberg, Cornelius, toyman of Birmingham, *fl*. 1751

Goolden, R. and Co., silk manufacturers and mercers of Birmingham, *fl*. 1770

Gorsuch, Mrs Mary, (toys) of ?Liverpool, *fl*. 1700s

Gough, Henry, tea and coffee warehouse of Wolverhampton, Staffs., *fl*. 1750s

Gray, Robert, (drapery) of London, *fl*. 1606-18

Greatorex, Mr Ralph, mathematical instrument maker of London, *c*. 1625-1712

Green, John, druggist and grocer of Birmingham, *fl*. 1780

Green, Richard of Lancaster, *fl*. 1690s to 1700s

Green, Robert, chapman of Shrewsbury, *ob*. 1667

Green, Thomas, (grocery) of Lancaster, *fl*. 1680s-1700s

Greenwood, Augustin, merchant of Lancaster, 1656-1701

Grieve, Alexander, (grocery) of Edinburgh, *fl*. 1818-19

Hall, Anne, (mercery) of Warwick Bridge, Cumberland, *ob*. 1670

Hamar, James, mercer of Rochdale, Lancs., *fl*. 1655-59

Hand, Richard, chelsea bun maker of London, *fl*. 1718

Hanson, Edward, mercer of Manchester and Bolton, Lancs., *ob*. 1584

Harding, Howell & Co. of London, *fl*. 1809

Hardman, Thomas, mercer of Manchester and Warrington, Lancs., *ob*. 1583

Harris, Peter, (general shop) of Grandborough, Warks., *ob*. 1613

Harrison, Thomas, girdler of Southampton, Hants., *ob*. 1554

Hartley, Richard, mercer of Tadmarton and Swalcliffe, Oxon., *ob*. 1729

Hayward, Roger, blacksmith of Watford, Herts., *ob*. 1592

Hayward, tea warehouse of Bath, Somerset (from London), *fl*. 1752

Heely, Thomas, button and toy maker of Birmingham, *ob*. 1764

Hickman, Jonathan, mercer of Wolverhampton, Staffs., *ob*. 1701

Hill, Samuel, (linen drapery, *fl.* 1730s

Hockenhall, William, grocer of Newcastle under Lyme, Staffs., *ob.* 1733

Hodgson, John, merchant of Lancaster, *fl.* 1684-1711

Holbey, Henry, haberdasher of Norwich, *ob.* 1671

Holmes, Mary and Sarah, milliners of Birmingham, *fl.* 1750s

Holt, Mrs, Italian warehouse of London, *fl.* late eighteenth century

Horne, Susan, grocer's widow of Arundel, Sussex, *fl.* 1719-35

Horne, Thomas, grocer of Arundel, Sussex, *ob.* 1719

Horsley, Ann, (general shop) of Bedwardine, Worcs., *ob.* 1692

Howe, Joseph, upholsterer, cabinet maker and internal designer of Birmingham, *fl.* 1830s 1840s

Hurst, Mr, mercer of Liverpool, *fl.* 1710s

Hurt, Elizabeth, mercer's widow of Coventry, Warks., *ob.* 1578

Hyde, Joseph, (mercery) of Wednesbury, Staffs., *ob.* 1743

Inys, Andrew, (cleaning leather breeches) of Birmingham, *fl.* 1750

Ireland, John, book seller of Nottingham, *fl.* 1760

James, John, mercer of St Ives, Cornwall, *ob.* 1645

James, Mary (grocery, chandlery and soap boiling) of ?Birmingham, *fl.* 1770

Jefferson, Lancelot, (general shop), of Westward, Cumberland, *ob.* 1685

Jones, Hugh, mercer of Shrewsbury, *fl.* 1719

Johnson, Alexander, mercer of Woodstock, Oxon., *ob.* 1681

Johnson, Edmund, mercer of Woodstock, Oxon., *ob.* 1689

Johnson, Joshua, mercer of Wellington, Shrops., *fl. c.* 1660-95

Johnson, Mrs, milliner of London, *fl.* 1720s

Jones, druggist and tea dealer of Birmingham, *fl.* 1803

Jones, Richard, (general shop) of Baschurch, Shrops., *ob.* 1739

Justice, Margaret, (millinery) of Wellington, Shrops., *ob.* 1687/88

Keary, G., (tea) of Liverpool, *fl.* 1760

Keelings, confectioners of London and Tunbridge Wells, Kent, n.d.

Kervin family of Coventry, Warks., *fl.* sixteenth and seventeenth centuries

Kilbee family of Coventry, Warks., *fl.* sixteenth and seventeenth centuries

Kirton, Joshua, book seller of London, *ob.* 1667

Knight, P.I., shawl manufacturer of Norwich and London, *fl.* 1785

Lancaster, Mrs, (grocery) of Liverpool, *fl.* 1700s

Lintott, William, mercer of Harting, Sussex, *ob.* 1710

Loveday, John, tobaccoman of Atherstone, Warks., *ob.* 1635

Lowe, Roger, (general shop) of Makerfield, Lancs., *ob.* 1679

Luck, Samuel, mercer of Steyning and Newhaven, Sussex, *ob.* 1706

Lutwych, Richard, (linen drapery, haberdashery and grocery) of Birmingham, *ob.* 1750

Lynch, David, 'chymist' and druggist of Manchester, *fl.* 1790

Madgwick, John, linen draper of Lewes, Sussex, *fl.* 1754-64

Mall, William, mercer of Bishops Castle, Shrops., *ob.* 1648

Malpas, Richard, glover of Bridgnorth, Shrops., *ob.* 1754

Margesson and Collison, haberdashers of Southwark, London, *fl.* 1762-65

Maries, Richard, felt maker of Norwich, *ob.* 1590

Marshall, Benjamin, mercer of Lincoln, *ob.* 1665

Masie, Mrs, (grocery) of ?Devon, *fl.* 1640s

Mason, Simon, apothecary of London, *fl.* 1715

Mayes, Edward, gent (mercery), of Manchester, Lancs., *ob.* 1621

McGuffog, draper of Stamford, Lincs., *fl.* 1780s

McLeod, James, book seller and stationer, Birmingham, *fl.* 1760

Melrose, Andrew, tea dealer and grocer of Edinburgh, *fl.* 1812-34

Mercier, Dorothy, print seller and stationer of London, *fl.* 1750s

Millward, Robert, mercer of Newport, Shrops., *ob.* 1700

Milward, Joseph, nailer of Belper, Derby., *fl.* 1760

Monsford, William, draper of London, *ob.* 1721

Morgan & Sanders of London, *fl.* 1809

Morris, Tunbridge ware manufactory of Brighton, Sussex, *fl.* 1815

Motley, Richard, (mercery) of Newport, Shrops., *ob.* 1709

Moulson, Mr, (wines and spirits) of London, *fl.* 1740-53

Moyseley, John, mercer of Coventry, *ob.* 1545

Napier, Jo., milliner and tea dealer of Thirsk, Yorks., *fl.* 1804

Needham, Locke & Bushell, linen drapers, mercers and haberdashers of London and Manchester, *fl.* 1782

Newall, Lawrence, mercer of Rochdale, Lancs., *ob.* 1649

Nodes, goldsmith, jeweller, sword cutler and toyman of London and Brighton, Sussex, *fl.* 1789

Norgrave, Joseph at the Tea canister, Shrewsbury, *fl.* 1748

Norman, Henry, (mercery) of Midhurst, Sussex, *ob.* 1769

Oakley, John, grocer and tea dealer of Shrewsbury, *fl.* 1794

Oldfield, James, mercer of Macclesfield. Cheshire, *ob.* 1634

Packwood, George, (shaving equipment) of London, *fl.* 1794-96

Paget, Charles, hat maker of London, probably eighteenth century

Palmer, Roger, (upholstery) of Coventry, Warks., *ob.* 1544

Pares, John, mercery, of Rochdale, Lancs., *ob.* 1623

Parkes, Zachariah, manufacturer of steel mills, Birmingham, probably nineteenth century

Peake, Thomas of Warrington, Lancs., *fl.* 1667

Peirce, Henry, mercer of Harting, Sussex, *ob.* 1754

Phillips family, mercers of Wellington, Shrops., *fl. c.* 1500-*c.* 1710

Place, Francis, tailor of London, 1771-1854

Plant, William, (general shop) of Ingoldmells, Lincs., *ob.* 1747

Pope, Mr, (paper hangings) of London, *fl.* 1755

Pym, Mr William, tailor of London, *ob. c.* 1672

Raper, (toy shop) of London, *fl.* 1750s

Redman, real hat maker of Stratford, Essex, *fl.* 1791

Revett, Thomas, fruiterer of Manchester, *fl.* 1790

Richmond, William, grocer of Penrith, Cumberland, *ob.* 1670

Ridings, Samuel and John, haberdashers of Manchester, *fl.* 1756-64

Robert le Espycer of Shrewsbury, *fl.* 1309

Roberts, (general shop) of Penmorfa, Caernarvon., *fl.* 1788-98

Rogerson, R., washing-machine maker of Warrington, Lancs., and London, *fl.* 1789

Rose, Mr, book seller of Norwich, *fl.* 1707

Rothwell, William, chapman of Bolton, Lancs., *ob.* 1623

Ruffe, Thomas, of Oswestry, Shrops., *ob.* 1720

Rumney, John, pewterer of Penrith, Cumberland, *ob.* 1671

Salked & Wilson, linen drapers, haberdashers and hosiers, of London and Shrewsbury, *fl.* 1770

Salters & Co., hat makers of London, *fl.* 1794-1804

Scoles, John, tea warehouse of Manchester, *fl.* 1790

Scrase, Thomas, victualler of Lewes, Sussex, *fl.* 1754-64

Seldon, George, mercer of Liskeard, Cornwall, *ob.* 1634

Seymour, Timothy, mercer of Shrewsbury, *fl.* 1695

Sharples, William, mercer of Warwick, *ob.* 1583

Shearman, John, (linens) of London, *ob.* 1723

Shepperd, haberdasher of London, *fl.* 1585

Sherwyn, Elizabeth, pewterer and brazier of Shrewsbury, *ob.* 1686/87

Sherwyn, Humphrey, pewterer and brazier of Shrewsbury, *ob.* 1686

Silverlock, William, mercer of Westbourne, Sussex, *ob.* 1678

Sissons, William, (drapery and funeral services) of Sheffield, Yorks., eighteenth century

Skill, purveyor general and oilman of London, *fl.* 1800

Slanne, Charles, (mercery) of Newbury, Berks., *ob.* 1667

Smith and Co, (drapery) of ?London, *fl.* 1790

Smith, Messrs of Bridgnorth, Shrops., *fl.* 1790

Smith, Thomas, (haberdashery) of Shrewsbury, *ob.* 1670

Socket, Andrew, mercer of Wellington, Shrops., *fl.* 1660s-1720s

Staine, John, apothecary of Derby, *ob.* 1615

Staker, Henry, mercer of Chichester, Sussex, *ob.* 1719

Steell, Nathaniel, (hard wares) of Falmouth, Cornwall, *ob.* 1764

Stephens, Susan, (general shop) of Leighton, Shrops., *ob.* 1680

Stone & Co., manufacturers of double block tin and iron kitchen ware of London, *fl.* 1788

Stores, Samuel, (mercery) of Warbleton, Sussex, *ob.* 1711

Stout, John, woollen draper of Lancaster, 1714-76

Stout, William the younger, mercer of Lancaster, 1706-69

Stout, William, wholesale and retail grocer and ironmonger of Lancaster, 1665-1752

Stretch, Isaac, watchmaker of Birmingham, *ob.* 1716

Stringer and Leach, (grocery) of London, *fl.* 1760s

Tatum, Hannah, saleswoman of London, *fl.* 1740s

Taylor, Mrs, (grocery) of Edinburgh, *fl.* 1818-19

Taylor, Jasper, oilman of London, eighteenth century

Taylor, Richard, mercer of Shrewsbury, *fl.* 1613

Tench, Mr., ?mercer of ?Cheshire, *fl. c.* 1600

Tenniel, N. and M., silk stocking cleaners of London, *fl.* 1790

Thickpenny, Barnard of Nottingham, *ob. c.* 1760

Thomas, Betty, ('forraine goods') of Liverpool, *fl.* 1710s

Thomas, John, mercer of Shrewsbury, *fl.* 1662

Thomas, Richard, mercator of Southampton, Hants., *ob.* 1447

Thomas, Samuel, mercer of Shrewsbury, *fl.* 1662

Towsey, Elizabeth and Susannah, (millinery and haberdashery) of Chester, *fl.* late eighteenth century

Troughtwood, John, ironmonger of Lancaster, *fl.* 1690s-1700s

Truelock, gunsmith of London, *fl.* 1660s

Turlington, John, spectacles maker of London, *ob.* 1669

Turner, Moses, mercer of Framfield, Sussex, 1733-1812

Turner, Richard, shop servant of Lewes, Sussex, 1742-74

Turner, Thomas, shopkeeper of East Hoathly, Sussex, 1729-93

Turner, Walter, ironmonger of Newport, Shrops., *ob.* 1746

Tyler, Elias, (general shop) of Leighton, Shrops., *ob.* 1686

Unthank, John, merchant of Orton and Kirby, Cumberland, *ob.* 1735

Vallor, Thomas, mercer of Harting, Sussex, *ob.* 1678

Walker, James, dry salter of Leeds, Yorks., *ob.* 1781

Ward, James of Stockport, Cheshire, *fl.* 1760

Warre, Edward, mercer of Tenbury, Worcs., *ob.* 1677

Waterhouse, Talbot, confectioner of London, *fl.* 1743

Webb, William, mercer of Brailsford, Derby., *ob.* 1674

Wedgwood, Josiah, potter of Etruria, Staffs., 1750-95

West's millinery warehouse of London, probably eighteenth century

Whitaker, John, saddler of Stourbridge, Worcs., and Bridgnorth, Shrops., *fl.* 1770

Whitfield Yates, J., (linens, drapery and haberdashery) *fl.* 1757

Widmere, Sylvester, mercer of Marlow, Bucks., *ob.* 1668

Wilks, Mary, milliner of Shrewsbury, *fl.* 1742

Wilson and Thornhill, (grocery) of London, *fl.* 1742

Wilson, Robert, glover of Carlisle, Cumberland, *ob*. 1648

Willsons, (grocery) of London, *fl*. 1741-53

Wood, Ralph, (oil) of Nottingham, *fl*. 1760

Wood, William, (provisions) of Didsbury, Lancs., 1720-90

Wollenhaupt, Caspar, (general shop) of Luneburg, Canada, *ob*. 1809

Wootton, Thomas, grocer of Bewdley, Worcs. *ob*. 1667

Wray, William, mercer of Ripon, Yorkshire, *fl*. 1580-1600

Wright and Ormandy, stationers of Liverpool, n.d.

Wright, Benjamin, mercer of Wellington, Shrops., *ob*. 1700

Wright, George, chandler of Lincoln, *ob*. 1702

Wright, Henry, chemist, druggist and colourman of Manchester, *fl*. 1760

Wright, Stephen, mercer of Wellington, Shrops., *fl*. 1660s

Yates, Mr, grocer of Brackley, *fl*. 1737-48

Yeong, George, pewterer of Norwich, *ob*. 1623

# Bibliography

Quotations from primary sources quoted in other secondary sources have been acknowledged in a footnote but not listed here unless used further in this study.

**Primary sources**

*Berkshire Record Office (Reading)*
Probate records.

*Birmingham Central Reference, Local Studies & History Department*
Trading ephemera.

*Borthwick Institute (York)*
Probate records.

*British Library*
Anon. (1786), *Policy of the tax upon retailing considered.*
*Autobiography of Francis Place*, MS ADD 35 142-4.
'Way to save wealth, shewing how a man may live plentifully for twopence a day, London, printed and sold by G. Conyers', 1506/520 [formerly 7074.b.42 (1-4), A collection of tracts].

*British Museum, Prints and Drawings*
Banks collection of trade cards and bill heads.
Heal collection of trade cards and bill heads.

*Cumbria Record Office (Carlisle)*
Probate records.

*Cheshire Record Office (Chester)*
Mercer's account book DDX 326.
Probate records.

*Cornwall Record Office (Truro)*
Probate records.

*Corporation of London Record Office (London)*
Orphans inventories.

*Coventry Record Office (Coventry)*
Parish registers.

*Guildhall Library (London)*
Prints.

*Hampshire Record Office (Winchester)*
Probate records.

*Hertford County Record Office (Hertford)*
Probate records.

*Lancashire Record Office (Preston)*
Probate records.

*Lichfield Joint Record Office (Lichfield)*
Probate records, regular series.
Probate records, peculiars of Bridgnorth, Ellesmere, Shrewsbury St Mary's, Wolverhampton.

*Lincolnshire Archives Office (Lincoln)*
Probate records.

*Manchester Public Library (Manchester)*
Wood's Customers Ledger 1786-91, MS F942.

*Norfolk Record Office (Norwich)*
Probate records.

*Northamptonshire Record Office (Northampton)*
Probate records.

*Oxfordshire Archives (Oxford)*
Probate records.

*Public Record Office (London)*
P.C.C. Wills and inventories.

*Shropshire Records and Research (Shrewsbury)*
Attingham MSS (112/).
Bridgnorth Horse Toll books, 1644-1720, Bridgnorth Corporation Records 4001/Mar.1/268-7.
Bridgewater collection (212/).
Eyton collection (665/).
Forrester MSS (296/).
Orleton Trustees MSS (999/).
*Shrewsbury Mercers Company, Book 1, Admission of Brothers*, MSS 4257.
*Shrewsbury Mercers Company, Book 6, Admission of Freemen*, MSS 4262.

*University of North Wales Library (Bangor)*
Penmorfa shop ledger, Bangor MS82.

*West Sussex Record Office (Chichester)*
Probate records.

*Worcestershire and Herefordshire Record Office (Hereford)*
Probate records.

*Worcestershire and Herefordshire Record Office (Worcester)*
Probate records.


**Official and Parliamentary Papers**

*Acts and Ordinances of the Interregnum 1642-1660*, collected and edited by C.H.
     Firth and R.S. Tait for the Statute Law Committee, three volumes, Stationery
     Office, London.
*House of Commons Journal.*
*Statutes at large of England and of Great Britain from Magna Carta to the Union of*
     *the kingdoms of Great Britain and Ireland*, ed. John Raith, printed by George
     Eyre and Andrew Strahan, 10 volumes (1811).


**Edited primary sources and books published before 1850**

Ablett, W.H. (ed.) (1876), *Reminiscences of an old draper*, London.
Adams, D.P. and Cannock Grammar School (n.d., *c.* 1975), *Probate inventories of*
     *Cannock 1562-1791*, privately printed.
Adams, S. (1995), *Household accounts and disbursements books of Robert Dudley,*
     *Earl of Leicester, 1558-61, 1584-86*, Camden, fifth series, vol. 6, Cambridge
     U.P. for the Royal Hist. Soc., Cambridge.
Anon. (1677), 'Englands great happiness; or a dialogue between Content and
     Complaint wherein is demonstrated that a great part of our Complaints are
     causeless', printed by J.M. for Edward Croft, London, reproduced in
     McCulloch, J.R. (ed.) (1856), *A select collection of early English tracts on*
     *commerce*, Political Economy Club, London, pp. 251-74.
Anon. (1680), 'Britannia Languens, or a discourse of trade ...', printed for Tho. Dring,
     London, reproduced in McCulloch, J.R. (ed.) (1856), *A select collection of*
     *early English tracts on commerce*, Political Economy Club, London, pp. 275-
     504.
Anon. (1681), 'The trade of England revived: and the abuses thereof rectified in
     relation to ... hawkers ... shopkeepers ... companies, markets, London',
     reproduced in Thirsk, J. and J.P. Cooper, (eds) (1972), *Seventeenth-century*
     *economic documents*, Clarendon Press, Oxford, pp. 389-403.
Anon. (1778), *Instructions for Officers who take account of coffee, tea, cocoa-nuts,*
     *and survey chocolate-makers in the country*, printed in London.
Barbon, Nicholas (1690), *A discourse of trade*, London, edited by J. Hollander
     (1905), Johns Hopkins Press, Baltimore
Best, H. (1857), *Rural economy in Yorkshire: being the farming and account books of*
     *H. Best*, edited by Charles Best Robinson, Surtees Society, 33.

Blackstone, W. (1765-69), *Commentaries on the laws of England*, four volumes, Clarendon Press, Oxford.

Blome, Richard (1673), *Britannia, or a geographical description of the kingdoms of England, Scotland and Ireland ... illustrated with a map of each county ...* , Thomas Roycroft for R. Blome, London.

Blundell, Nicholas (1968-72), *The great diurnal of Nicholas Blundell of Little Crosby, Lancashire*, edited by Frank Tyrer, Record Society of Lancashire and Cheshire, Liverpool, three volumes.

Burney, F. (1778), *Evelina: the history of a young lady's introduction to the world*, new edition 1821, Edward Mason, London.

Campbell, R. (1747), *The London tradesman*, reprinted (1969), David and Charles, Newton Abbott.

Carpenter, John Gent (1632), *A most excellent instruction for the exact and perfect keeping merchants books of accounts, by way of debitor and creditor after the Italian method ...* , I.B., London.

Clare, Martin (1758), *Youth's introduction to trade and business ... revised by ... Benjamin Webb*, J. Fuller, London.

Cobbett, William (1821), *Cottage economy*, new edition (n.d.) published by Harris Edwards Publications, Shrewsbury.

Collyer, Joseph (1761), *Parent's and guardian's directory and youth guide, in the choice of a profession or trade*, R. Griffiths, London.

Cromarty, D. and R. (1993), *The wealth of Shrewsbury in the early fourteenth century: six local Subsidy Rolls 1297-1323; text and commentary*, published for the Shropshire Arch. and Hist. Soc., by Alan Sutton, Stroud.

Defoe, D. (1722), *The fortunes and misfortunes of the famous Moll Flanders*, paperback edition (1978), Penguin English Library, Penguin Books, Harmondsworth.

Defoe, D. (1724-27), *Tour through the whole island of Great Britain*, Folio Society edition of 1983, based on the editions (1928 and 1962), published by J.M. Dent.

Defoe, D. (1726), *The complete English tradesman*, paperback edition (1987), based on the 1839 edition, Alan Sutton, Gloucester.

Defoe, D. (1728), *A plan of the English commerce*, new edition (1967), Augustus M. Kelley, New York.

Dives Pragmaticus (1563), *A booke in Englysh metre, of the great marchaunt man called Dives Pragmaticus*, reproduced in facsimile ... (1910), with an introduction by Percy E. Newbery, Manchester U.P., Manchester, and Bernard Quaritch, and Sharratt and Hughes, London.

Dryden, J. (1682), *The Medal of John Bayes; a Satyr against folly and Knavery* (1712 edn), London.

Eland, G. (ed.) (1931), *Purefoy letters, 1735-1753*, Sidgwick & Jackson, London.

Elmhirst, William (n.d.), *Ledger of William Elmhirst, surgeon and apothecary, 1769-1773*, edited by Sigsworth, Eric and Valerie Brady, privately printed Humberside Polytechnic.

Exwood, Maurice and H.L. Lehmann (trans. and eds) (1993), *The Journal of William Schellinks' travels in England, 1661-1663*, Camden fifth series, volume 1, Royal Historical Society, London.

Field, Richard Henning (1992), 'Claiming rank: the display of wealth and status by eighteenth-century Luneburg, Nova Scotia, merchants', *Material History Review*, pp. 1-20.

Fiennes, Celia (1984), *The illustrated journeys of Celia Fiennes, c. 1682-c. 1712*, edited by Christopher Morris, Macdonald & Co., London (taken from the 1982 edition published by Webb & Blower, Exeter).

Fuller, Thomas (1662), *The history of the worthies of England endeavoured by Th. Fuller*, edited by J. Fuller, I.G.W.L. and W.G., London.

Gerard, J. (1633), *The Herbal, or a General Historie of Plants, the Complete 1633 edition as revised by Thomas Johnson*, facsimile edition (1985), Dover and Constable, New York and London.

Glasse, Hannah (1769), *The art of cookery made plain and easy by a lady*, facsimile edition (1983), Prospect Books, London.

Gray, Todd (1995), 'Devon household accounts, 1627-59', *Devon and Cornwall Record Society*, new series, 38, Exeter.

Gunther, Robert T. (1934), *The Greek herbal of Dioscorides illustrated by a Byzantine A.D. 512, Englished by John Goodyer A.D. 1655, edited and first printed A.D. 1933*, Hafner, London and New York.

*History and general directory of the borough of Birmingham* (1849), Francis White & Co., Sheffield.

H.N. Merchant in the City of London (1684), *The compleat tradesman or the exact dealers daily companion*, London.

Holme, Randle (1688), *Academy of armory, or a storehouse of armory and blazon*, vol. I, for the author, Chester.

Holme, Randle (1905), *Academy of armory, or a storehouse of Armory and blazon*, vol. II, edited by I.H. Jeayes, Roxburghe Club, London.

Holt, John (1795), *General view of the agriculture of the county of Lancaster*, printed for G. Nicol, London.

Houghton, John (1727), *Husbandry and trade improv'd: being a collection of many valuable materials relating to corn, cattle, coals, hops, wool, &c.*, revised by *Richard Bradley*, three volumes, printed for Woodman and Lyon, London.

Houghton, John (1728), *Husbandry and trade improv'd: being a collection of many valuable materials relating to corn, cattle, coals, hops, wool, &c.*, revised by *Richard Bradley*, volume 4, printed for Woodman and Lyon, London.

Hyde, Ralph (1994), *A prospect of Britain: the town panoramas of Samuel and Nathaniel Buck*, Pavilion Books, London.

J.F. (1695), *Merchant's warehouse laid open, or the plain dealing linen-draper, showing how to buy all sorts of linens and Indian goods*, London.

J.G., Gent. (1720), *Great Britain's vade mecum containing a concise geographical description of the world ... the several counties of England ... a short view of trade*, D. Browne, London.

Johnston, J.A. (ed.) (1991), 'Probate inventories of Lincoln citizens 1661-1714', *Lincoln Record Society*, 80.

Kenyon, R.L. (n.d.), 'Quarter Session orders', *Shropshire County Records*, 14.

Langland, William (1362), *The vision of William concerning Piers Ploughman*, ed. Skeat, E.E.T.S, 1867-85; 1886.

Leach, A.F. (ed.) (1900), 'Beverley town documents', *Selden Society*, 14.

Lichtenberg, G. (1938), *Lichtenberg's visits to England as described in his letters and diaries*, edited by M. and W.H. Quarrell, Clarendon Press, Oxford.

Linnaeus, Carl (1737), *Genera planatarum eorumque characteres naturales secundum namorum*, Luguni Batavorum.

Linnaeus, Carl (1753), *Species planatarum exhibentes plantas rite cognitas ... ,* Holmiae.

Lowe, Roger (1938), *The diary of Roger Lowe of Ashton in Makerfield, Lancashire, 1663-74,* edited by W.L. Sachse, Longmans, Green & Co., London, New York and Toronto.

Mackenzie, Eneas (1827), *Descriptive and historical account of ... Newcastle upon Tyne,* two volumes, Newcastle upon Tyne.

Macky, John (1722), *A journey through England in familiar letters from a gentleman to his friend abroad,* two volumes, J. Pemberton, London.

Malcolm, Alexander, teacher of mathematics (1632), *A treatise on book-keeping in the Italian method of debtor and creditor,* London.

Mandeville, Bernard (1714), *The fable of the bees, or private vices, public benefits,* printed for J. Roberts, London, edited by Philip Harth (1970), Penguin Books, Harmondsworth.

Mason, Simon (1754), *A narrative of the life and distresses of S. Mason, etc.,* printed for the author, Birmingham.

McCulloch, J.R. (ed.) (1856), *A select collection of early English tracts on commerce,* Political Economy Club, London.

Mitchell, L.G. (1973), *The Purefoy Letters, 1735-1753,* Sidgwick & Jackson, London.

Monardes, N. (1571), *Joyfull newes out of the Newe Founde Worlde,* translated by John Frampton, reprinted (1925), Constable, London.

Moritz, C.P. (1965), *Journeys of a German in England in 1782,* translated and edited by Reginald Nettel, Jonathan Cape, London.

Mun, Thomas (1664), 'England's treasure by forraign trade, or the balance of our forraign trade is the rule of our treasure', in McCulloch, J.R. (ed.) (1856), *A select collection of early English tracts on commerce,* Political Economy Club, London.

Owen, R. (1857), *The life of Robert Owen written by himself,* 1st edn, Effingham Wilson, London, new edition (1967), Frank Cass & Co., London.

Owen, William (1754), *Owen's book of fairs in England and Wales ... to which is added an abstract of all the acts of parliament relating to fairs,* London, new edition (1756).

Pepys, Samuel (1985), *Diary of Samuel Pepys,* transcribed and edited by Robert Latham and William Matthews, Bell and Hyman, London.

Pigot and Company (1830), *Commercial Directories of Birmingham, Worcester and their environs,* London.

Postlethwayt, Malachy (1757), *Britain's commercial interest explained and improved in a series of dissertations on several important branches of her trade and police,* two volumes, printed for D. Browne, London, reprinted in facsimile (1968), Augustus M. Kelly, New York.

Raffald, Elizabeth (1769), *The experienced English housekeeper,* new unabridged edition (1997), with an introduction by Roy Shipperbottom, Southover Press, Lewes, Sussex.

Reed, Michael (ed.) (1988), 'Buckinghamshire probate inventories 1661-1714', *Buckinghamshire Record Society,* 24, Cambridge.

Rees, Abraham (1819-20), Rees's *Manufacturing industry,* edited by Neil Cosson (1972), David and Charles reprints, Newton Abbot.

Roberts, E. and K. Parker (eds) (1992), 'Southampton probate inventories 1447-1575', *Southampton Records Series,* XXXIV, Southampton U.P., Southampton.

Roberts, Stephen K. (ed.) (1994), 'Evesham Borough records of the seventeenth century 1605-1687', *Worcestershire Historical Society*, new series, 14, Worcester.

Roche, Sophie Van la (1933), *Sophie in London*, translated by Clare William, Jonathan Cape, London.

Rothstein, N. (ed.) (1987), *A lady of fashion; Barbara Johnson's album of styles and fabrics*, Thames and Hudson, London and New York.

Rouquet, A. (1755), *The present state of the arts in England*, edited (1970), R.W. Lightbourn, London.

Saussure, Cesar de (1902), *A foreign view of England in the reign of George I and George II*, translated and edited by Madame van Leyden, John Murray, London.

Schopenhauer, Johanna (1988), *A lady's travels: journeys in England and Scotland from the diaries of Johanna Schopenhauer*, translated and edited by R. Michaelis-Jena and W. Merson, Routledge, London.

Smith, Adam (1776), *The wealth of Nations*, new edition (1910), two volumes, J.M. Dent & Sons, London.

Speed, J. (1611/12), *The counties of Britain; a Tudor atlas by John Speed*, new edition (1988), with an introduction by Nigel Nicolson, Pavilion Books Ltd in association with the British Library, London.

Stout, William (1967), *Autobiography of William Stout of Lancaster, 1665-1752*, edited by J.D. Marshall, Barnes & Noble, New York.

Stow, John (1598, revised 1603), A s*urvey of London written in the year 1598*, edited by Henry Marley (1912), Routledge, London, paperback edition (1959), Alan Sutton, Stroud.

Stubbs, P. (1581), *The anatomie of abuses, contayning a discoverie or briefe summarie of such notable vices and imperfections, as now raigne in many Christian countreyes* ... , new edition (1877) by F.J. Furnivall, New Shakespere Society, series VI, no. 4.

T.M. (1621), 'A Discourse of Trade, from England unto the East-Indies', the second impression corrected and amended by T.M. London, printed by Nicholas Okes for John Pyper', reprinted in McCulloch, J.R. (ed.) (1856), *A select collection of early English Tracts on commerce*, London, Political Economy Club, pp. 1-48.

Trinder, B. and J. Cox (eds) (1980), *Yeomen and Colliers in Telford; probate inventories for Dawley, Lilleshall, Wellington and Wrockwardine*, Phillimore & Co., Chichester.

Turner, Thomas (1984), *The diary of Thomas Turner, 1754-1765*, edited by David Vaisey, Oxford U.P., Oxford and New York.

*Vegetable substances: materials for manufacture*, (1833), Library of entertaining knowledge, Society for the Diffusion of Useful Knowledge.

Weatherill, Lorna (1990), 'The account book of Richard Latham', *Records of Social and economic history*, new series, XV, O.U.P. for the British Academy.

Webster, William, writing master (1721), *An essay on book keeping by double entry ... An attempt towards rendering the education of youth more easy and effectual*, London.

White, Gilbert (1931), *The journals of Gilbert White*, edited by Walter Johnson, Routledge & Kegan Paul, London, paperback edition (1982), Futura, Macdonald & Co., London.

Whiteman, Anne (1986), *The Compton census of 1676: a critical edition*, printed for the British Academy by O.U.P., London.

Willan, T.S. (1962), *A Tudor Book of Rates*, Manchester U.P., Manchester.

Wilson, Thomas (1572), *A discourse upon usury by way of dialogue and oration*, edited by R.H. Tawney (1925), B. Bells & Son, London, reprinted (1962), Cass & Co., London.

Woodcroft, Bennet (1854), *Alphabetic index of patentees of inventions*, with an Introduction and Appendix of additions and corrections compiled in the Patent Office Library, new edition (1969), Evelyn Adams and Mackay Ltd, published by Augustus M. Kelly, New York.

Woodforde, James (1924), *The diary of a country parson 1758-1802*, five volumes, O.U.P., Oxford, paperback edition of selected passages (1978), edited by John Beresford, O.U.P., Oxford.

W.S. (1581), *A compendious and brief examination of certayne complaynts*, new edition (1929), entitled *Discourse of the common wheal of this realm of England*, edited by Elizabeth Lamond and W. Cunningham, Cambridge U.P., Cambridge.

Zeal, Zachary (pseudonym) (1764), *Seasonable alarm to the city of London on the present important crisis: showing ... that the new method of paving the streets ... and pulling down of the signs, must be ... pernicious to the health and morals of the people of England*, W. Nicoll, London.

## Newspapers

*National Publications*

*Cottage Gardener*
*Evening Advertiser*
*General Advertiser*
*The Guardian*
*London Morning Advertiser*
*Morning Post*
*New General Advertiser*
*Post Boy*
*Public Advertiser*
*The Times*

*Local Publications*

*Aris's Birmingham Gazette*
*Leicester Journal*
*Leicester and Nottingham Journal*
*Liverpool Chronicle*
*Manchester Mercury*
*Norwich Advertiser*
*Norwich Gazette*
*Piercy's Coventry Gazette*
*Salopian Journal*

*Sussex Weekly Advertiser*
*Universal Magazine*
*Williamson's Liverpool Advertiser*


**Secondary sources**

Adburgham, A. (1964), *Shops and shopping 1800-1914*, new edition (1981), George Allen & Unwin, London.

Alexander, D. (1970), *Retailing in England during the Industrial Revolution*, Athlone Press, London.

Alford, B.W.E. (1973), *W.D. & H.O. Wills and the development of the U.K. tobacco industry 1786-1965*, Methuen, London.

Arnold, James (1977), *Farm waggons and carts*, David and Charles, Newton Abbot.

Barker-Benfield, G.J. (1992), *The culture of sensibility, sex and society in eighteenth-century Britain*, University of Chicago Press, London.

Barley, L.B. and M.W. (1962), 'Lincolnshire shopkeepers in the sixteenth and seventeenth century', *Lincolnshire Historian*, 2, pp. 7-21.

Basing, P. (1990), *Trades and crafts in medieval manuscripts*, British Library, London.

Beier, A.L. (1974), 'Vagrants and the social order in Elizabethan England', *Past and Present*, 64, pp. 3-29.

Ben-Amos, Ilana Krausman (1991), 'Failure to become freemen: urban opportunities in early modern England', *Social History*, 16/2, pp. 155-72.

Benson, J. (1983), *The penny capitalist: a study of nineteenth-century working-class entrepreneurs*, Gill and Macmillan, London.

Benson, John (1999), *The rise of consumer society, 1880-1980*, Longman, London.

Benson, J. and G. Shaw (1992), *The evolution of retail systems, c. 1800-1914*, Leicester U.P., Leicester, London and New York.

Benson, John and Gareth Shaw (eds) (1999), *The retailing industry*, three volumes, I.B. Tauris, London and New York.

Benson, John, Andrew Alexander, Deborah Hodson, John Jones and Gareth Shaw (1999), 'Sources for the study of urban retailing 1800-1950, with particular reference to Wolverhampton', *The Local Historian*, 29/3, pp. 167-82.

Berg, Maxine (1985), *The age of manufactures 1700-1820*, Barnes & Noble, Tolowa, New Jersey.

Berg, Maxine (1999), 'New commodities, luxuries and their consumers', in Berg, Maxine and Helen Clifford (eds), *Consumers and luxury: consumer culture in Europe 1650-1850*, Manchester U.P., Manchester, pp. 63-82.

Berg, Maxine and Helen Clifford (eds) (1999), *Consumers and luxury: consumer culture in Europe 1650-1850*, Manchester U.P., Manchester.

Berger, Ronald M. (1980), 'The development of retail trade in provincial England, ca. 1550-1700', *Journal Ec. Hist.*, 1, pp. 123-28.

Berger, Ronald M. (1993), *The most necessary luxuries; the Mercers' Company of Coventry, 1550-1680*, Pennsylvania State University Press, Pennsylvania.

Bermingham, Ann (1995), 'Introduction: The consumption of culture: image, object, text', in Bermingham, Ann and John Brewer, *The consumption of culture 1600-1800: image object and text*, Routledge, London and New York, paperback edition (1997).

Berry, Christopher (1994), *The idea of luxury: a conceptual and historical investigation*, Cambridge U.P., Cambridge.

Bianchi, Marina (1999), 'In the name of the tulip. Why speculation?', in Berg, Maxine and Helen Clifford (eds), *Consumers and luxury: consumer culture in Europe 1650-1850*, Manchester U.P., Manchester, pp. 88-102.

Blackman, J. (1963), 'The food supply of an industrial town: a study of Sheffield's public market 1780-1900', *Business History*, 5/1 and 2, pp. 83-97.

Blackman, J. (1967), 'The development of the retail grocery trade in the nineteenth century', *Business History*, 9/1 and 2, pp. 110-17.

Borsay, P. (1989), *The English urban renaissance: culture and society in the English provincial town, 1660-1770*, Clarendon Press, Oxford.

Braudel, F. (Paris, 1979), *The structures of every day life: the limits of the possible*, being volume I of *Civilization and capitalism, 15th-18th century*, translated and edited by S. Reynolds, Perennial Library (1985), Harper & Row, New York.

Braudel, F. (Paris, 1979), *The wheels of commerce*, being volume II of *Civilization and capitalism, 15th-18th century*, translated and edited by S. Reynolds, Perennial Library (1986), Harper & Row, New York.

Breen, T.H. (1986), 'An empire of goods: the anglicization of colonial America 1690-1776', *J. British Studies*, XXV, pp. 467-99.

Breen, T.H. (1988), 'Baubles of Britain; the American and consumer revolution of the eighteenth century', *Past and Present*, 119, pp. 73-104.

Breen, T.H. (1993), 'The meaning of things: interpreting the consumer economy in the eighteenth century', in Brewer, John and Roy Porter (eds), *Consumption and the world of goods*, Routledge, London and New York, pp. 249-73.

Brown, E.H. Phelps and Sheila Hopkins (1956), 'Seven centuries of the prices of consumables compared with builders' wage rates', *Economica*, XXIII, pp. 296-313.

Brown, J. and S. Ward (1990), *The village shop*, Rural Development Commission in association with Cameron & Hollis, Moffat, and David & Charles, Newton Abbot.

Brundage, J.A. (1995) *Medieval canon. law*, Longman, London and New York.

Burnby, Juanita G.L. (1983), *A study of the English apothecary from 1660 to 1760; Medical History*, Supplement no. 3, Wellcome Institute for the History of Medicine, London.

Burnett, John (1979), *Plenty and want: a social history of diet in England from 1815 to the present day*, revised edition, Scolar Press, University paperback edition (1983), Methuen, London.

Campbell, C. (1987), *The romantic ethic and the spirit of modern consumerism*, Basil Blackwell, Oxford.

Chambers, R. (1888), *The book of days: a miscellany of popular antiquities in connection with the calendar*, two volumes, J. & R. Chambers, London and Edinburgh.

*Chambers's concise gazetteer of the world, topographical, statistical, historical*, W. & R. Chambers Ltd, London and Edinburgh (n.d. but pre-1914).

Chartres, J.A. (1977), *Internal trade in England, 1500-1700*, Studies in economic and social history, Macmillan, London and Basingstoke.

Chartres, J. (1990), *Agricultural markets and trade, 1500-1750: chapters from the agrarian history of England and Wales 1500-1750*, volume 4, Cambridge U.P., Cambridge.

Clark, Peter and Jean Hosking (1993), *Population estimates of English small towns, 1550-1851*, Working paper No. 5, Centre for Urban History, University of Leicester.

Coleman, D.C. (1969), 'An innovation and its diffusion: the New Draperies', *Ec. Hist. Rev.*, 2nd series, 22, pp. 417-29.

Collins, Diane (Summer 1993), 'Primitive or not? fixed shop retailing before the Industrial Revolution', *Journal of Regional and Local Studies*, 13/1, pp. 4-22.

Connor, R.D. (1987), *The weights and measures of England*, H.M.O., London.

Corfield, P. (1976), 'Urban development in England and Wales in the sixteenth and seventeenth centuries', in Coleman, D.C. and A.H. John (eds), *Trade, government and economy in pre-industrial England*, Weidenfeld & Nicolson, London, pp. 214-47.

Cox, Nancy (Summer 1993), 'The distribution of retailing tradesmen in north Shropshire, 1660-1750', *Journal of Regional & Local Studies*, 13/1, pp. 4-22.

Cox, Nancy (1994), 'Objects of worth, objects of desire: towards a dictionary of traded goods and commodities 1550-1800', *Material History Review*, 39, pp. 24-40.

Cox, Nancy and Jeff Cox (1984), 'Probate inventories: the legal background', Part I, *The Local Historian*, 16/2, pp. 133-45; Part II, *The Local Historian*, 16/2, pp. 217-28.

Cressy, David (1993), 'Literacy in context: meaning and measurement in early modern England', in Brewer, John and Roy Porter (eds), *Consumption and the world of goods*, Routledge, London and New York, pp. 305-19.

Crossick, Geoffrey and Serge Jaumain (1999), *Cathedrals of consumption: the European department store, 1850-1939*, Ashgate, Aldershot.

Davis, D. (1966), *A history of shopping*, Routledge & Kegan Paul Ltd, London and Toronto.

Deane, Phyllis (1979), *The first industrial revolution*, Cambridge U.P., Cambridge.

De Marchi, Neil (1999), 'Adam Smith's accommodation of "altogether endless" desires', in Berg, Maxine and Helen Clifford (eds), *Consumers and luxury: consumer culture in Europe 1650-1850*, Manchester U.P., Manchester, pp. 18-36.

De Vries, Jan (1993), 'Between purchasing power and the world of goods: understanding the household economy in early modern Europe', in Brewer, John and Roy Porter (eds), *Consumption and the world of goods*, Routledge, London and New York, pp. 85-132.

Dyer, Alan David (1973), *The city of Worcester in the sixteenth century*, Leicester U.P., Leicester.

Dyer, C. (1989), *Standards of living in the later Middle Ages; social change in England c. 1200-1520*, Cambridge Medieval Textbooks, Cambridge U.P., Cambridge.

Dyer, C. (1994), *Everyday life in Medieval England*, Hambledon Press, London and Rio Grande.

Earle, Peter (1989), *The making of the English middle class: business society and family life in London 1660-1730*, Methuen, London, paperback edition (1991).

Edwards, Peter (1988), *The horse trade of Tudor and Stuart England*, Cambridge U.P., Cambridge.

Elliot, Douglas J. (1975), *Buckingham: the loyal and ancient borough*, Phillimore, London and Chichester.

Emerson, F.G. (1991), *Elizabethan life: home, work and land*, Essex R.O., Chelmsford.

Fisher, F.J. (1934-35), 'The development of the London food market 1540-1640', *Ec. H. R.*, 1st series, V, pp. 46-64.

Fraser, W.H. (1981), *Coming of the mass market, 1850-1914*, Macmillan, London.

French, H.R. (2000), '"Ingenious and learned gentlemen": social perceptions and self-fashioning among parish élites in Essex, 1680-1740', *Social History*, vol. 25/1, pp. 44-66.

Gerhold, Dorian (1993), *Road transport before the railways: Russell's London Flying waggons*, Cambridge U.P., Cambridge.

Gilchrist, John (1969), *The church and economic activity in the Middle Ages*, Macmillan, London.

Goodman, Jordan (1993), *Tobacco in history: the culture of dependence*, Routledge, London and New York.

Harte, N.B. (1976), 'State control of dress and social change in pre-industrial England', in D.C. Coleman and A.H. John (eds), *Trade, government and economy in pre-industrial England*, Weidenfeld & Nicolson, London, pp. 132-65.

Hatcher, John and C. Barker (1974), *A history of British pewter*, Longman, London and New York.

Hay, Douglas (1999), 'The state and the market: Lord Kenyon and Mr Waddington', *Past and Present*, 162, pp. 101-62.

Heal, Ambrose (1925), *London tradesmen's cards of the XVIII century: an account of their origin and use*, B.T. Batsford, London (replicated 1968 by Dover Publications, New York).

Heal, Sir Ambrose (1953), *London furniture makers, from the Restoration to the Victorian era 1660-1840*, new edition (1988), with an additional chapter by R.W. Symonds, Portman Books, London.

Hennell, Thomas (1934), *Change in the farm*, Cambridge U.P., new edition (1984), entitled *The old farm*, Robinson Publishing, London.

Hey, David (1980), *Packmen, carriers and packhorse roads: trade and communication in north Derbyshire and south Yorkshire*, Leicester U.P., Leicester.

Holderness, B.A. (1972), 'Rural tradesmen, 1660-1850: a regional study in Lindsey', *Lincolnshire Hist. & Arch. Journal*, 7, pp. 77-83.

Hunt, Margaret R. (1996), *The middling sort: commerce, gender and the family in England 1680-1780*, University of California Press, Berkeley, Los Angeles and London.

Jefferys, J.B. (1954), *Retail Trading in Britain, 1850-1950*, Cambridge U.P., Cambridge.

Keene, D. (1990), 'Shops and shopping in medieval London', in Grant, L. (ed.), *Mediaeval Art, Architecture and archaeology in London*, British Archaeological Association Conference Transactions 1984, British Archaeological Association, pp. 29-46.

Kennedy, Rachel (n.d. but *c.* 1999), *Between Bath and China: trade and culture in the West Country 1680-1840*, Museum of Eastern Art, Bath.

Kowalski-Wallace, Elizabeth (1997), *Consuming subjects: women, shopping and business in the eighteenth century*, Columbia U.P., New York and Chichester.

Lancaster, G. and Massingham, L. (1993), *Essentials of marketing*, McGraw-Hill, 2nd edn, London.

Langford, Paul (1989), *A polite and commercial people; England 1727-1783*, O.U.P., Oxford, paperback edition (1992).

Larwood, Jacob and John Camden Hotton (1866), *A history of signboards from the earliest time to the present day*, John Camden Hotton, London.

Laughton, J. and C. Dyer (1999), 'Small towns in the east and west Midlands in the later Middle Ages: a comparison', *Midland History*, vol. XXIV, pp. 24-52.

Lemire, B. (1988), 'Consumerism in pre-industrial and early industrial England: the trade in secondhand clothes', *J. British Studies*, 27, pp. 1-24.

Lemire, B. (1991), *Fashion's favourite: the cotton trade and the consumer in Britain, 1660-1800*, Pasold Research Fund in association with O.U.P., Oxford.

MacLeod, Christine (1988), *Inventing the Industrial Revolution: The English patent system 1660-1800*, Cambridge U.P., Cambridge.

Martin, J.M. (1984), 'Village traders and the emergence of a proletariat in South Warwickshire, 1750-1851', *Ag. Hist. Rev.*, 32, pp. 179-88.

Mass Observation (1947), *Browns and Chester: a portrait of a shop, 1780-1946*, ed. H.D. Willcock, Lindsay Drummond, London.

Mathias, P. (1967), *Retailing revolution: a history of multiple retailing in the food trades based upon the Allied suppliers group of companies*, Longman, London.

McKendrick, N. (1982), 'George Packwood and the commercialization of shaving: the art of eighteenth-century advertising or "The Way to Get Money and be Happy"', in McKendrick, N., J. Brewer and J.H. Plumb, *The birth of a consumer society: the commercialisation of eighteenth-century England*, Europa Publications Ltd, London, pp. 146-96.

McKendrick, N. (1982), 'Josiah Wedgwood and the commercialization of the potteries', in McKendrick, N., J. Brewer and J.H. Plumb, *The birth of a consumer society: the commercialisation of eighteenth-century England*, Europa Publications Ltd, London, pp. 100-145.

Mendenhall, T.C. (1953), *The Shrewsbury Drapers and the Welsh wool trade in the XVI and XVII centuries*, Oxford U.P., Oxford and Geoffrey Cumberlege, London.

Miller, M. (1981), *The Bon Marché bourgeois culture and the department store, 1869-1920*, George & Unwin, London.

Mitchell, S.I. (1981), 'Retailing in eighteenth and early nineteenth-century Cheshire', *Historical Soc. of Lancs. & Cheshire*, 130, pp. 37-60.

Money, John (1993), 'Teaching in the market place, or "Caesar adsum jam forte Pompey aderat": the retailing of knowledge in provincial England during the eighteenth century', in Brewer, John and Roy Porter (eds), *Consumption and the world of goods*, Routledge, London and New York, pp. 335-80.

Mui, Hoh-Cheung and L.H. Mui (1989), *Shops and shopkeeping in eighteenth-century England*, Routledge, London.

Patten, John (1972), 'Village and town: an occupational study', *Ag. Hist. Rev.*, 20, pp. 1-16.

Ponsford, Clive N. (1978), *Time in Exeter*, Headwell Vale, Exeter.

Porter, Roy (1989), *Health for sale; quackery in England 1660-1850*, Manchester U.P., Manchester and New York.

Purvis, Martin (1992), 'Co-operative retailing in Britain', in Benson, J. and G. Shaw (eds), *The evolution of retail systems, c. 1800-1914*, Leicester U.P., Leicester, London and New York, pp. 107-34.

Raistrick, Arthur (1953), *Dynasty of iron founders: the Darbys and Coalbrookdale*, Longman, Green & Co., London, new impression (1970), David and Charles, Newton Abbot.

Ripley, Peter (1984), 'Village and town: occupations and wealth in the hinterland of Gloucester, 1660-1700', *Ag. Hist. Rev.*, 32, pp. 170-78.

Rowlands, M (1967-68), 'Industry and social change in Staffordshire 1660-1760: a study of probate and other records of tradesmen', *Lichfield & S. Staffs Arch. & Hist. Soc.*, IX, pp. 37-58.

Sanderson, Elizabeth C. (1996), *Women and work in eighteenth-century Edinburgh*, Macmillan, Basingstoke and London.

Satchell, J.E., J.M. Glover, M.L. Ryder, G.W. Taylor and H.E. Garland (1990), 'The Kendal pattern book', *Textile History*, 21/2, pp. 223-43.

Saumarez-Smith, Charles (1993), *Eighteenth-century decoration and design in domestic interiors in England*, Weidenfeld and Nicolson, London.

Scola, Roger (1992), *Feeding the Victorian city: the food supply of Manchester 1770-1870*, edited by W.A. Armstrong and Pauline Scola, Manchester U.P., Manchester and New York.

Shammas, Carrole (1990), The *Pre-industrial consumer in England and America*, Clarendon Press, Oxford.

Shammas, Carole (1993), 'Changes in English and Anglo-American consumption from 1550 to 1800', in Brewer, John and Roy Porter (eds), *Consumption and the world of goods*, Routledge, London and New York, pp. 177-205.

Shaw, Gareth (1992), 'The evolution and impact of large-scale retailing in Britain', in Benson, John, and Gareth Shaw (eds), *The evolution of retail systems c. 1800-1914*, Leicester U.P., Leicester, London and New York, pp. 135-65.

Shaw, G. and M.T. Wild (1974), 'Retail patterns in the Victorian city', *Trans. Inst. Br. Geog.*, pp. 278-91.

Spufford, Margaret (1974), *Contrasting communities: English villages in the sixteenth and seventeenth centuries*, paperback edition (1979), Cambridge U.P., Cambridge.

Spufford, Margaret (1981), *Small books and pleasant histories: popular fiction and its readership in seventeenth-century England*, Past and Present Publications, Cambridge U.P., Cambridge, paperback edition (1985).

Spufford, M. (1984), *The great re-clothing of rural England: petty chapmen and their wares in the seventeenth century*, Hambledon, London.

Sterne, W.M. (1976), 'Fish marketing in London in the first half of the eighteenth century', in Coleman, D.C. and A.H. John (eds), *Trade, government and economy in pre-industrial England*, Weidenfeld & Nicolson, London, pp. 68-77.

Strasser, Susan, Charles McGovern and Matthias Judt (eds) (1998), *Getting and spending: European and American consumer societies in the twentieth century*, Cambridge U.P., Cambridge.

Styles, John (1993), 'Manufacturing, consumption and design in eighteenth-century England', in Brewer, John and Roy Porter (eds), *Consumption and the world of goods*, Routledge, London and New York, pp. 527-54.

Styles, John, (1994), 'Clothing the north: the supply of non-élite clothing in the eighteenth- century north of England', *Textile History*, 25/2, pp. 139-66.

Styles, J. (forthcoming), 'Product innovation in early modern London', *Past and Present*.

Swetz, Frank J. (1987), *Capitalism and arithmetic; the new math of the 15th century*, Open Court, La Salle, Illinois.

Tawney, A.J. and R.H. (1934-35), 'An occupational census of the seventeenth century', *Ec. Hist. Rev.*, 5, pp. 25-64.

Tawney, R.H. and Eileen Power (1924), *Tudor economic documents*, three volumes, Longmans, Green & Co. Ltd, London.

Thackeray, William Makepeace (1848), *Vanity fair: a novel without a hero*, new edition (n.d.), Odham Press, London.

Thirsk, J. (1978), *Economic policy and projects; the development of a consumer society in early modern England*, Clarendon Press, Oxford.

Thirsk, J. and J.P. Cooper (1972), *Seventeenth-century economic documents*, Clarendon Press, Oxford.

Thomas, Keith (1983), *Man and the natural world; changing attitudes in England 1500-1800*, Allen Lane, London.

Thurlow Leeds, E. (1923), 'Oxford tradesmen's tokens', in H.E. Salter (ed.), *Surveys and tokens*, Oxford Historical Society, lxxv, pp. 355-453.

Trinder, Barrie (1992), *Blackwell encyclopedia of industrial archaeology*, Blackwell, Oxford.

Veblen, T. (1925), *The theory of the leisure class: an economic study of institutions*, George Allen & Unwin, London.

Vickery, Amanda, (1993), 'Women and the world of goods: a Lancashire consumer and her possessions, 1751-81', in Brewer, J. and R. Porter (eds), *Consumption and the world of goods*, Routledge, London and New York, pp. 274-301.

Vickery, Amanda (1998), *The gentleman's daughter: women's lives in Georgian England*, Yale U.P., New Haven and London.

Walsh, C. (1995), 'Shop design and the display of goods in eighteenth-century London', *J. of Design History*, 8/3, pp. 157-76.

Walsh, Claire (1999), 'The newness of the department store: a view from the eighteenth century', in Crossick, Geoffrey and Serge Jaumain (eds), *Cathedrals of consumption: the European department store, 1850-1939*, Ashgate, Aldershot, pp. 46-71.

Weatherill, L.M. (1986), 'Consumer behaviour and social status in England, 1660-1750', *Continuity and Change*, 1, pp. 191-216.

Weatherill, L. (1988), *Consumer behaviour and material culture in Britain, 1660-1760*, Routledge, London.

Weatherill, L. (1993), 'The meaning of consumer behaviour in late seventeenth and early eighteenth-century England', in Brewer, J. and R. Porter (eds), *Consumption and the world of goods*, Routledge, London and New York, pp. 206-28.

Westerfield, R.B. (1915), *Middlemen in English business, particularly between 1669 and 1760*, Yale U.P., reprinted (1968), Augustus Kelley, New York.

Willan, T.S. (1970), *An eighteenth-century shopkeeper: Abraham Dent of Kirkby Stephen*, Augustus M. Kelley, New York.

Willan, T.S. (1976), *The inland trade: studies in English internal trade in the sixteenth and seventeenth centuries*, Manchester U.P., Manchester.

Williamson, G.C. (1967), *Trade tokens issued in the Seventeenth Century, (a new and revised edition of William Boyne's work)*, 3 volumes, B.A. Seaby Ltd, London.

Wilson, C. (1965), *England's apprenticeship 1603-1763*, Longmans, Green & Co., London.

Winstanley, Michael J. (1983), *The shopkeeper's world, 1830-1914*, Manchester U.P., Manchester.

Yule, Col. H. and A.C. Burnell (1886), *Hobson Jobson; a glossary of Anglo-Indian words and phrases* (new edition, 1968, W. Crookes, ed.), Routledge & Kegan Paul, London.

**Unpublished dissertations**

Walsh, Claire (1993), 'Shop design and the display of goods in the eighteenth century',
V & A/RCA M.A. dissertation.

Watts, S. (1995), 'The small market town in the large multi-township parish: Shifnal, Wellington, Wem and Whitchurch, *c.* 1535-*c.* 1660', unpublished Ph.D. thesis, University of Wolverhampton.

# Index

DH

381.
109
41
COX